PENGUIN BOOKS

THE FIRST SEX

Elizabeth Gould Davis was born in Kansas, but her family moved so often that she was well traveled by the age of ten. The schools she attended are as far apart as Winthrop, Massachusetts, and Balboa in the Canal Zone. Miss Davis received her A.B. at Randolph-Macon College and, after a brief marriage, went on to earn her master's degree from the University of Kentucky in 1951. She is currently a librarian in Sarasota, Florida. Because she realized that there was no definitive work proving the historical dominance of women, she began *The First Sex*, a book she felt compelled to write.

ELIZABETH GOULD DAVIS

THE
FIRST SEX

Penguin Books Inc
Baltimore, Maryland

Penguin Books Inc
7110 Ambassador Road
Baltimore, Maryland 21207, U.S.A.

First published by G.P. Putnam's Sons 1971
Published in Penguin Books 1972

Printed in the United States of America

*Dedicated to the memory of
my sister Barbara*

*whose tragic death in 1968 impelled
this work, for "to put away my grief
I purposed to commence a booke."*
                              (Marie of France)

Contents

THE FIRST SEX

In a word, life begins as female. The female is not only the primary and original sex but continues throughout as the main trunk. . . . The further development of life serves to strengthen this gynaecocentric [female-centered] point of view. Yet statements of the androcentric [male-centered] theory are met with everywhere. Not only do philosophers and popular writers never tire of repeating its main propositions, but anthropologists and biologists will go out of their way to defend it while at the same time heaping up facts that really contradict it and strongly support the gynaecocentric theory. . . . The androcentric theory . . . is deeply stamped upon the popular mind, and the history of human thought has demonstrated many times that scarcely any number of facts opposed to such a world view can shake it.

—LESTER FRANK WARD

Introduction

⋙ This work is the result of the convergence of two streams of thought: the first, that the earliest civilization we know was but a renewal of a then dimly remembered and now utterly forgotten older one; and the second, that the impelling and revivifying agent in what we know as civilization was woman. These two originally separate streams, each springing independently from its own well of evidence, flowed finally into a broad river of conviction that could no longer be denied expression.

The first conviction, now shared by a growing number of the "cognitive minority," [1] was that something must have preceded the earliest historical societies to account for the many incongruities, as the Soviet ethnologist M. M. Agrest called them, that occur throughout the world. These unaccountable anomalies, like the flash of a gold tooth in an infant's mouth, startled one's complacency about the intellectual superiority of modern man and jolted the old belief in the technical ignorance of our remote ancestors.

The thought kept intruding itself that modern man was a *repeater*—that every discovery he made and every invention he conceived had been discovered and invented before, in a forgotten past civilization of tens or even hundreds of thousands of years ago.

The second stream of thought was that in ancient times, indeed well into the historical era, woman had played a dominant role. The tradition shared by all early peoples, but glossed over by later historians and myth-interpreters, that it was woman who had preserved the germ of the lost civilization and had brought it into its second flowering was too insistent to be ignored. The primacy of goddesses over gods, of queens over kings, of great matriarchs who

15

had first tamed and then reeducated man, all pointed to the fact of a once gynocratic world. The further back one traced man's history, the larger loomed the figure of woman. If the gods and goddesses of today are but the heroes and heroines of yesterday, then unquestionably the goddesses of historical times were but the reflected memory of the ruling hierarchy of a former civilization.

The existence of such a civilization would account, as no other theory could, for the universality of certain customs, rites, and taboos that could not have been disseminated in historical times. It would explain the similarity of creation myths throughout the world and would account for the apparent kinship of the mythical gods and heroes of all peoples. It would explain the worldwide tradition of the wonderful strangers, the existence of the ancient maps, the otherwise incomprehensible origin of language, the anomalous gold mines of Thrace and Kransnoyarsk, the incongruous optical lens of ancient Nineveh, and the "worked gold thread" found embedded in a rock deposit that was formed millennia ago. It would explain the Sumerian seals depicting the true structure of the universe, the accuracy of ancient calendars and sundials, the ancient megalithic buildings and monuments scattered over the face of the earth, the Seven Sages of ancient Greece and their evident knowledge of scientific truths later discredited and forgotten, and the legends of Hermes Trismegistus, Thoth, and other wizards of antiquity. And it would account for the universal tradition of a great cataclysm that once engulfed the world in a holocaust of flame and flood.

"Chance," wrote Sylvain Bailly, "could not account for such wonderful coincidences. They must all have been derived from one common source." [2]

When recorded history begins we behold the finale of the long pageant of prehistory, the pageant of the great lost civilization that constituted the source of all these "wonderful coincidences." The curtain of written history rises on what seems to be the tragic last act of a protracted drama. On the stage, firmly entrenched on her ancient throne, appears woman, the heroine of the play. About her, her industrious subjects perform their age-old roles. Peace, Justice, Progress, Equality play their parts with a practiced perfection.

Off in the wings, however, we hear a faint rumbling—the rumbling of the discontented, the jealous complaints of the new men who are no longer satisfied with their secondary role in society. Led perhaps by the queen's consort, the rebellious males burst onstage, overturn the queen's throne, and take her captive. Her consort moves to center stage. He lifts his bloody sword over the heads of the courtiers. The queen's subjects—Democracy, Peace, Justice, and the rest—flee the scene in disarray. And man, for the first time in history, stands triumphant, dominating the stage as the curtain falls.

The deterioration in the status of women went hand in hand with the Dark Ages that followed this patriarchal revolution as it moved slowly westward from the Near East, reaching Western Europe only in the fifth century of our era. In Europe and the British Isles the last remnant of the great world civilization, the Celts, maintained the tradition of female supremacy until the fall of Rome, when waves of Germanic barbarians sweeping down from the northeastern forests met the surge of Oriental Christianity as it spread upward from the Mediterranean. Between these two millstones of "masculism," the Celts were finally crushed. Yet even in defeat they managed to preserve the guttering flame of civilization, for "right while they were being annihilated by the barbarians, the Celts were civilizing them. . . . The Celts held out against the invading savages until they had almost ceased to be savages." [3]

Yet, despite the Celts, Teutonic-Semitic patriarchy finally prevailed in Europe. Celtic culture was forgotten, the Celtic goddess religion went underground, Celtic customs and beliefs degenerated into "pagan" superstitions, and Celtic feminism was condemned as sinful by the patriarchal conquerors. The implacability with which Western man has since retaliated against woman serves only to confirm the truth of her former dominance—a dominance that man felt compelled to stamp out and forget. What was "this dark necessity, this envenomed misogyny," that "compelled man to tear down the hated sex," [4] if not a form of retaliation—of compensation for his own former condition of servitude, combined with a fear of woman's eventual resurgence to her former power. "Is it not remarkable," asks Karen Horney, "that so little attention is paid to man's underlying fear and dread of women . . ." and that his hatred should be overlooked even by its victims, the women themselves.[5]

Yet it is man's fear and dread of the hated sex that has made woman's lot such a cruel one in the brave new masculine world. In the frenzied insecurity of his fear of women, man has remade society after his own pattern of confusion and strife[6] and has created a world in which woman is the outsider. He has rewritten history with the conscious purpose of ignoring, belittling, and ridiculing the great women of the past, just as modern historians and journalists seek to ignore, belittle, and ridicule the achievements of modern women. He has devalued woman to an object of his basest physical desires[7] and has remade God in his own image—"a God that does not love women."[8] Worst of all, he has attempted to transform woman herself into a brainless simulacrum, a robot who has come to acquiesce meekly in the belief in her own inferiority.

So long has the myth of feminine inferiority prevailed that women themselves find it hard to believe that their own sex was once and for a very long time the superior and dominant sex. In order to restore women to their ancient dignity and pride, they must be taught their own history, as the American blacks are being taught theirs.

We must repudiate two thousand years of propaganda concerning the inferiority of woman. The pope recently removed the age-old stigma of the Jews as "Christ murderers," and the United States has sought by law to destigmatize the American black. But who has spoken for woman? Who has stepped forward to remove "God's curse" from Eve?

It seems evident that the time has come to put woman back into the history books, and, as Mary Wollstonecraft suggested two hundred years ago, to readmit her to the human race. Her contribution to civilization has been greater than man's, and man has overlooked her long enough.

Recorded history starts with a patriarchal revolution. Let it continue with the matriarchal counterrevolution that is the only hope for the survival of the human race.

Prologue:
The Lost Civilization

*Nowhere in history do we find a
beginning, but always a continuation.
. . . How then shall we understand the end,
if the beginning remains a mystery?*
—J. J. BACHOFEN

 Only a hundred years ago the history of the world seemed very simple. If the creation of man had not, after all, taken place one sunny Friday morning in October of the year 4004 B.C., as had been pronounced by Bishop James Ussher and widely believed before Charles Darwin, at least this new thing, evolution, had only recently produced man. It was firmly believed that the world was young and the human race far younger, that civilization had progressed predictably and smoothly from savagery to its nineteenth-century state of near perfection, and that man—the male of the human species, that is—was indeed the focal point of the universe and the lord of all creation.

If man had evolved from savagery by a slow but steady ascent, as Darwin and Thomas Huxley said he had, so too had society. There had been and could be no turning back. "Onward and upward" was the cry. Civilization was believed to have started in the Nile Valley around 2500 B.C., before which date men had lived in caves as semibrutes. Historians merely smiled at Manetho's claim that the history of Egypt extended back 17,000 years before his own time, or nearly 20,000 years before Darwin. This, of course, said the Victorians, was impossible, since man had not even appeared on earth at so early a date!

Now we know that man has been on earth for more than a million years, that the history of Egypt actually did reach back as far as Manetho said, that a great civilization, the Sumerian, preceded the civilization of Egypt, and that it is more than likely that an even greater civilization preceded that of Sumer.[1] The deeper the archeologists dig, the further back go the origins of man and society—and the less sure we are that civilization has followed the steady upward course so thoroughly believed in by the Victorians. It is more likely that the greatest civilizations of the past have yet to be discovered.

A study of the rise and fall of known civilization hints strongly at a great worldwide civilization preceding the Dark Ages which we call prehistory—a term that is rapidly losing its meaning through the testimony of the spade. We know that a dark age in Europe followed the destruction of the great Greco-Celto-Roman civilization in the fifth century A.D., that a dark age in the Aegean followed the destruction of the great Minoan-Mycenaean civilization of Greece around 1000 B.C., and that a dark age in the Near East followed the destruction by the pastoral Semites of the great matriarchal city states of Sumer around 2500 B.C.[2] So we have the tail end of what seems to be a rhythm running through history, with a great universal civilization rising and falling about every 1,500 years. What then of the so-called dark age that preceded the civilization of Sumer? Could it have been preceded by an even greater civilization that ended before the dawn of written history?

Evidence of this earlier civilization is piling up rapidly. Where it originated is a moot question. But that it was worldwide can hardly be doubted in light of recent evidence.

The Evidence of Language

If man has grown steadily more civilized, more intelligent, and more complex through evolution, why has his language undergone an evolution in reverse? It is obvious that the languages of today are far less complex than the classical languages; and philologists tell us that Latin, Greek, and Sanskrit are less complex than the common Indo-European language from which they all evolved. If these dead languages are a maze of case endings, declensions, and conjugations that make the learning of them so difficult for modern students, the original language was an even more difficult maze.

Yet few laymen seem to be worried by the discrepancy in the fact of this highly sophisticated original language, on the one hand, and the widespread belief, on the other hand, that early man communicated by grunts! How can we reconcile the fact that the complex Latin language, for example, is a simplification of an earlier prehistoric language, with the prevalent belief that language evolved through onomatopoeia—a sort of baby talk composed of imitative sounds? The two are utterly irreconcilable.

Where, then, did the original common language come from, and who invented it? Certainly not the familiar caveman, complete with club and bearskin, of popular imagery. Jean Jacques Rousseau, two hundred and fifty years ago, wrote: "I am so convinced of the impossibility that languages should owe their original institution to merely human means that I leave the problem to anyone who will undertake [to solve] it." [3] Rousseau, of course, pictured our ancestors very much as we picture them; in fact, the popular image of the caveman owes its origin in part to Rousseau himself and his "noble savage" concept. And, of course, he could not conceive of this savage as the inventor of language. The problem stumped him. And it would stump us too if we did not know that mankind is far, far older than Rousseau thought.

Georg Wilhelm Hegel, in *Reason in History,* writes: "It is a fact of philological evidence that the language man spoke in his early *rude* condition was highly elaborate; and a comprehensive, consistent grammar is the work of thought." [4] How could *"rude"* (rough, ignorant, uncouth, uneducated, uncivilized) ancestors have worked out a comprehensive, consistent, and highly elaborate grammar? If they could do that, they could not have been so terribly rude. And if they were rude, who worked out their grammar for them?

Theodor Mommsen writes that "language is the true image and organ of the degree of civilization attained" and acknowledges that the rude Indo-Europeans, before they had divided into the classical and modern nations of Europe and Asia, had a very extensive vocabulary.[5]

The conclusion to be drawn is that either our rude ancestors did not invent their own language or that they were not so rude and uncouth as we are today, when simple English grammar is beyond the grasp of the majority of Americans.

An interesting fact about this original language is that it seems to have been born in a subarctic locale, since the oldest root words common to all its descendants refer to northern latitudes—reindeer, spruce, snow, fir, etc. This curious fact seems to contradict the evidence that our present civilization itself originated in the mountain plains of southeastern Europe and Anatolia. These two contradictory assumptions could be reconciled if one adopted the cataclysmic theory or the theory of the shifting of the poles as advanced by Immanuel Velikovsky, Hugh Brown, and others. Then the plains of Anatolia could once have been subarctic, and the subtropical fauna excavated in recent years beneath the arctic ice could have been grazing in a tropical jungle at the time of some world cataclysm.

Pythagoras, in the sixth century B.C., taught the theory of the shifting of the poles, attributing the belief to the Egyptians and the ancient people of India. These people also spoke of an ancient race of red men (red-haired?) who had ruled the world from a now submerged continent[6] prior to the last-but-one cataclysmic shifting of the poles, which they placed in the tenth millennium B.C., and of a later cataclysm five millennia later, about the time of the submergence of the Antarctic continent and of the floods of myth and legend.

The philological fact of one original language is borne out in myth. The Bible (Genesis 2) says that "the whole earth was of one language and one speech." Flavius Josephus says that "all creatures had one language at that time,"[7] implying that the beasts also spoke. Louis Ginzberg says that language came down from above, complete with an alphabet for writing.[8] The Sumerians believed that language and all the arts of civilization were bestowed upon them by a mysterious creature, half human and half fish, who emerged from the sea and later returned to it. Looking at this legend, the distinguished exobiologist and space physicist Carl Sagan suggests that this sea creature may have been a visitor from space.[9]

But that is another story. What interests us here is the worldwide tradition of a once common language, a tradition found not only in the Mediterranean region and in Europe, but in Asia, Africa, and the Western Hemisphere. It is accompanied by indications of a common source not only for language but for all the arts and practices of civilization. That this common source antedates the Egyptian and even the Sumerian civilization is now accepted. Historians, before the discovery of Sumer, marveled that the Egyp-

tian civilization seemed to have sprung full blown, without benefit
of a barbaric prehistory. Now it seems equally remarkable that the
Sumerian civilization seems to have done the same. Obviously then,
there is something behind Sumer, too, to account for its apparently
sudden achievement of civilization at the very dawn of recorded
history. Indeed it may well be, as S. R. K. Glanville said, that "the
science we see at the dawn of history was not science at its dawn but
represents the remnants of the science of some great and as yet un-
traced civilization of the past." [10]

Evidence of the Maps

Civilization, according to H. J. Massingham, "was consciously
planted" around the world by a people called "the ancient mariners," tentatively identified with the seafaring people of Crete.[11]
Writing in the early years of this century, Massingham was daring
enough in his attribution of world travel to a people of the third
millennium B.C., but now we know that the "ancient mariners" belonged to an even more remote period in history than Massingham
assumed. For, incredible as it may seem, these ancient mariners
drew an accurate map of a continent, Antarctica, that disappeared
under three miles of solid ice at least 6,000 years ago and whose
very existence was unknown to modern man until A.D. 1820! [12]

Modern scientific instruments have affirmed that the continent
of Antarctica became glacierized no later than 4000 B.C. and that it
has lain under an impenetrable mountain of ice ever since. This
fact, plus the probability that Antarctica lay in temperate latitudes
prior to 4000 B.C. combined with the further fact that tremendous
coal deposits have been detected there indicating forest growth,
leads to the incredible thought that Antarctica must have been
mapped by an *Antarctican—prior* to its glacierization 6,000 years
ago. Was this Antarctic cartographer an Atlantean? And was the
vast continent of Antarctica once the vast continent of Atlantis?

A map, drawn by one Orontius Fineus in A.D. 1532 from an ancient map now lost, delineates the coastline and rivers of the lost
continent of Antarctica with such accuracy as to coincide almost
exactly with modern maps drawn with the assistance of highly sophisticated instruments through the masses of ice that now obscure
these coastlines and rivers. The Orontius Fineus map is presumed

to be based upon the same map on which the now famous Piri Reis map is based. When the latter map, dated 1513, was discovered in 1929, modern cartographers could not believe that it was the work of either medieval or ancient map makers. It was far too accurate to have been made without certain instruments that were not even invented until centuries later.

In the 1930's and 1940's, other maps of the thirteenth to sixteenth centuries continued to turn up, confounding modern science by their precision. The odd thing about these maps was that on them the unexplored regions of the medieval world were more accurately drawn than the parts which had actually been explored in ancient or medieval times! For example, Mercator's later maps, in which had been incorporated parts of the world mapped by Ptolemy and later geographers, were *less* accurate than his earlier map based entirely on the now lost map of remotest antiquity. In one of these medieval world maps, the Pacific coastline of the Americas looks exactly as it does in modern atlases. Yet no part of this coast had been even so much as dreamed of in the Middle Ages. Even Columbus was unaware of the Pacific Ocean.

The mystery of the maps was eventually explained. The original ancient map of unknown origin had been rescued by the Christians when they burned the great library at Alexandria in Egypt in the fifth century and had been taken to Constantinople. There it had lain until the crusade of the thirteenth century, during which the Venetian fleet attacked Constantinople and carried off the map with other loot to Venice, where contemporary cartographers saw and used it. Where it ultimately disappeared is unknown.

Thus we know the source of the amazing medieval maps. But we do not know who, or what race of people, drew the original map on which they were based.

When Gibbon, in the eighteenth century, said of Byzantium and the great Byzantine civilization that it saved "not a single work of history or philosophy or literature from oblivion," he did not of course know of this one piece of parchment so fortuitously saved—the ancient map which had been copied and recopied through countless millennia until it ended in Byzantium. And yet this one map has thrown more light on prehistory and revealed more of the ancient civilization that produced it than have all the archeologists, historians, and theorists of all the ages since.

Who were these ancient mariners who sailed the seven seas 10,000 years before the Christian era? Who were they who mapped the world with an accuracy never again achieved until the twentieth century of the present era? Whoever they were, there can be no doubt that their scientific knowledge was equal to our own. And certainly they had oceangoing, far-ranging ships that were capable of sailing around the globe. They traveled not only up and down our own Pacific Coast, which they mapped quite thoroughly and accurately, but they also visited the Arctic Circle, the Antarctic, Africa, Australia, and the islands of Oceania, as we shall see.[13]

The Ancient Mariners

Whoever these ancient mariners may have been, they probably account for the "wonderful stranger" tradition among so many of the world's primitive peoples. Massingham points out that people in the most unlikely places—from the Arctic to Australia to the Ocean Islands—have, or once had, customs and traditions that they themselves can no longer account for and which seem to serve no purpose in their lives. Among such traces of the passage of the wonderful stranger were the wearing of a shell imitation of overlapping plate armor by the peaceful Eskimos; the mummification of the dead by the natives of the Torres Strait in Australia, a custom which could not have been borrowed from Egypt, as the Egyptians were notoriously timid of the sea and of sea travel;[14] the widespread custom of polishing flint instruments, a process that served no useful purpose and must have been done only to imitate the high polish of the metal instruments used by the wonderful strangers; and, above all, the great megalithic monuments scattered over the face of the globe, the "Kilroy was here" of the ancient mariners. Other remnants of a forgotten influence among savage peoples that surprised and mystified the explorers of a much later age were the apparently meaningless moral taboos such as incest and blood taboos observed by otherwise amoral primitives and the prevalence of penis mutilation, the origins of which customs will be discussed later.

Among all these primitive peoples, from Yucatan to Tasmania, the wonderful stranger tradition involved a blue-eyed, golden- or red-haired race of people. This in itself would seem to eliminate the ancient Cretans, for they, like all the "Mediterranean race" who founded the civilization that we know, were a smallish, slim, neatly built people, with dark hair and white skin, small, straight noses, and longish heads, as we can see from their ancient carvings and portraits from Sumer, Egypt, and Crete. They were non-Semitic and non-Aryan, and nobody knows where they came from or into what modern race they disappeared.

It is interesting to note that the Egyptians, members of this dark-haired Mediterranean race, in historical times scoured Europe and Asia for redheads to serve their goddess temples. Could this demand for red-haired people have been prompted by the Egyptians' dimming memory of the long-lost superrace who had once taught them the arts of civilization? And could the connection with the goddess temples have been a reflection of the religion of the lost civilization, which had bequeathed goddess worship to the Egyptians, as it had to all the Mediterranean and early Indo-European peoples and to the Semites as well?

And, if so, who were these golden strangers? Among known races, red hair appears *only* among the Celts of Europe. Terence Powell says that "the Celts were remarkable to Mediterranean eyes for their height, their fair skin, blue eyes, and blond hair." [15] Could the Celts we know of, the "golden strangers" of prehistoric Britain, and the "tall, fair race, red-blond of hair" of Ireland[16] have been the last survivors of that ancient unknown civilization, which even to them was but a faint half-memory kept alive by a tradition they no longer understood?

For Herodotus tells us that their sacred relics were a plow, a yoke, an ax, and a *drinking cup* all of purest gold. "They guard these sacred relics with most special care," says Herodotus, "and offer annual sacrifices in their honor. They say that these relics fell from the sky a thousand years before Darius." [17] All of these relics are symbols of matriarchy: the plow and the yoke symbolize respectively the invention of agriculture and the domestication of animals, both traditionally attributed to the women of the matriarchal age; the ax is the primordial symbol of the matriarchal civilization which culminated in Crete, where the double-ax had a very special significance; and the drinking cup was a sacred emblem in the ancient goddess rites that survived in Argos and

Aegina even in Herodotus' day, and in Ireland as late as the second century A.D.[18]

The sacred yoke of Herodotus' report may have evolved into the golden torque of the later Celts, a Celtic adornment that has been identified by R. E. M. Wheeler with other sacred emblems of the ancient Aegean. All these relics were "of purest gold." Gold was a precious metal in Herodotus' day, and a thousand years before Darius (and here a thousand years only means a very long time) gold, like all metals, was scarce. However, the ancient mariners were metal workers, and that they mined the world for gold is attested by the remains of their worked mines from England to Thrace, and from Siberia to Rhodesia. Among the enigmas of the classical Greek world were the worked gold mines of Thrace discovered in the fifth century B.C.[19] Moreover, "gold" was a word of the original Indo-European language.[20]

Another story states that the ancestors of the Celts came from "an island near Gades [Cadiz on the Atlantic Coast of Spain], beyond the Pillars of Hercules [Gibraltar] upon the Ocean [the Atlantic]." [21] Could this island have been Atlantis? And could Atlantis have been the home of the ancient mariners? Herodotus goes on to say that according to this account, the mother of the Scythians was "queen and sole mistress of the land." A strange thing about this story is that the description of this mermaidlike queen fits the description of the strange sea creature who brought the arts of civilization to the Sumerians!

Before leaving the ancient mariners, it is interesting to note a few casually collected evidences of an ancient seafaring civilization of several millennia ago. These are from actual newspaper reports collected by that indefatigable clipper of newspapers, Charles Fort:

> London *Times,* June 22, 1884—A worked *gold* thread was found embedded *in stone,* eight feet deep, in a stone quarry below Rutherford Mills on the River Tweed.
>
> A perfectly formed cut-iron nail with a perfect head found embedded in a piece of auriferous quartz in California, no date given.
>
> A nail found in a nine-inch-thick block of stone from Kingoodie Quarry, North Britain, 1845.
>
> Another nail in quartz crystal in Carson, *Nevada,* in 1884.

A crystal lens ("not an ornament but a true optical lens apparently ground by modern methods," said the British Scientific Association *Journal*) found buried in a house at Nineveh during excavations in 1871. "British Scientific Association finds it impossible to accept that crystal lenses had ever been made by the ancients," adds Fort.[22]

Where then *did* these evidences of a technological civilization come from, found as they all were in places where they could not have been deposited within the past 10,000 years?

We are a long way from knowing who the ancient mariners were. But it is only through conjecture, analysis, and synthesis that we are ever likely to find out. And the analysis and synthesis of myth, primitive customs, archeological evidence, and language lead to the conjecture that the lost civilization of the ancient mariners was a woman's civilization.

"The elder world was full of memories and myths of such a lost civilization—a civilization prior to those of Egypt and Sumer, not a merely barbaric precursor of them, but an ancient culture of superior status, from which they derived" and from which their civilizations had, in many respects, degenerated.[23]

Plato's ideal republic was more a looking back at this former glory than a looking forward. In *Critias* he had spoken of the former primacy of the goddess and of the equality of men and women in ancient times.[24] In the *Republic* he envisions a similar ideal world where only excellence of intellect will be the criterion for leadership and where women will have all the advantages of education and all the opportunities for advancement available to men. "Public offices are to be held by women as well as men," as was the way of the ancients.[25]

In the chronicles of all peoples tales of an elder race "universally point to a fixed belief in the prior existence of a culture of undoubted antiquity and excellence. . . . This regime of the elder world was regarded as ending in cataclysm . . . and it is invariably spoken of as having existed at a period so remote that only the broad outlines of its history [have survived in tradition]." [26]

For when cataclysm strikes, as Plato says in the *Timaeus*, "it leaves only those who are deficient in letters and education. And then we have to begin all over again as children, and know nothing of what happened in ancient times." [27] "The survivors of each destruction," he continues in *Critias*, "were ignorant of the art of writing and remembered only the names of their former chiefs and a little about their deeds. For many generations the survivors directed their attention to the supplying of their needs, to the neglect of events that had happened in times long past. For inquiry into antiquity is introduced only with leisure, and when the necessaries of life are beginning to be provided, but not before." [28]

When a modicum of security had finally been achieved and the people were at last free to explore their own past, little was left for them to base their history upon save the dim memories, handed down from generation to generation by word of mouth, of the names and deeds of long-dead heroes and heroines. These former leaders became the deities and demi-deities, heroes and heras, of the new world, and their deeds embodied the mythical record of their descendants. For, as Peter Buck has said, "the mythology of today is but the history of yesterday." [29] And "myths are the memory of real events experienced by the human race," as Bachofen so presciently observed a hundred years ago.[30]

"What, after all, do we know of the ancient world so far, to permit us to adopt an attitude of negation to the deep-rooted tradition so oft-repeated in the most venerable chronicles that at a period almost transcending the imagination a civilization of a high order, from which all the cultures of this planet proceeded, shone, flickered, and like a shattered sun, cast its broken light upon the dark places of our star?" [31]

Two hundred years ago, the great French academician, astronomer, philosopher, and man of letters Sylvain Bailly wrote in his *History of Ancient and Modern Astronomy:* "The only rational supposition remains that there must have been a great original nation, now utterly extinct, and of whose history no document remains, who had advanced to a very high degree of perfection in the sciences and the arts; who sent colonies to the other parts of the world; who, in fine, were the instructors, and communicated their knowledge to peoples more barbarous than they." [32]

Part I

The Gynocratic World

I can't make out why a belief in a
Father-God's authorship of the universe, and
its laws, should be considered any more scientific
than a belief in the inspiration of this
artificial system by a Mother-Goddess.
                                        —ROBERT GRAVES

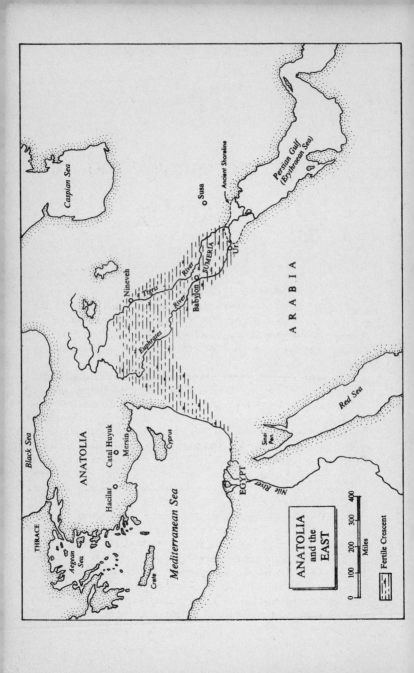

1

Woman and the Second Sex

Without a knowledge of the
origins, the science of history
can come to no conclusion.
—J. J. Bachofen

The Origins

"When above the heavens had not been formed, when the earth beneath had no name, Tiamat brought forth them both. . . . Tiamat, the Mother of the Gods, Creator of All." So runs the earliest recorded account of the creation of the universe and of man.[1]

In *all* myth throughout the world, from the sun's rising beyond the farthest shores of Asia to its setting west of the farthest islands of the vast Pacific, the first creator of all is a goddess. Her names are as many and as varied as the peoples whom she created and who worshiped her as the first principle. In later myth she is replaced by a god—sometimes deliberately, as in the case of 'Anat and Jehovah; sometimes by an arbitrary change in sex but not in name, as in the cases of Ea in Syria, Siva in India, and Atea in Polynesia; and sometimes by a gradual metamorphosis from female to male, as in the case of Metis-Phanes.

In earliest Greek mythology the creative principle is Metis—female intelligence. She is the creator of all who, like Phoenician-Carthaginian Tanit, like Tiamat, like Gaia, like 'Anat, creates the world without a male partner. Originally she was all female. By the time of Orpheus, however, she had become bisexual—a hermaphrodite, Metis-Phanes, creator and begetter in one body. Her final transformation by classical times into all male Phanes illustrates the ancient concept of the evolution of the human race;

33

for the original femaleness of all human beings is reflected in the belief among the ancients, and voiced by Plato in the *Symposium*, that the human race was once unisexed—male and female combined in one self-perpetuating female body.[2]

In the Orphic religion, contrary to St. Paul's error, "man was of woman, and not woman of man." [3] Thus the modern concept that woman was made for man is of very recent origin. Yet from Saint Paul to Rousseau, who says in *Emile* that the "body of woman is made expressly to please Man," the canard has been widely repeated. (In the nineteenth century a prominent Anglican divine told his congregation that the lines on the cantaloupe were made expressly for man's convenience in slicing it!)

But on what is the assumption that woman's body was made for man's convenience based? Who is to say that the reverse is not the truth and that man's body was not made expressly to please woman? On the biological evidence, the latter assumption seems more logical than the contrary assumption and its endorsement by those arch antifeminists, Paul and Rousseau.

Woman's reproductive organs are far older than man's and far more highly evolved. Even in the lowest mammals, as well as in woman, the ovaries, uterus, vagina, etc., are similar, indicating that the female reproductive system was one of the first things perfected by nature. On the other hand, the male reproductive organs, the testicles and the penis, vary as much among species and through the course of evolution as does the shape of the foot—from hoof to paw. Apparently, then, the male penis evolved to suit the vagina, not the vagina to suit the penis.

Proof that the penis is a much later development than the female vulva is found in the evidence that the male himself was a late mutation from an original female creature. For man is but an imperfect female. Geneticists and physiologists tell us that the Y chromosome that produces males is a deformed and broken X chromosome—the female chromosome. All women have two X chromosomes, while the male has one X derived from his mother and one Y from his father. It seems very logical that this small and twisted Y chromosome is a genetic error—an accident of nature, and that originally there was only one sex—the female.

Asexual reproduction by females, parthenogenesis, is not only possible but it still occurs here and there in the modern world, perhaps as an atavistic survival of the once *only* means of reproduction in an all female world. Since the discovery of the proof of parthenogenesis by Jacques Loeb in 1911, "it has been known that the male is not necessary for reproduction, and that a simple physicochemical agent in the female is enough to bring it about." [4]

Susan Michelmore describes a bird the *female* of which possesses one ovary and one testis, either of which organ may become active under various circumstances.[5] This phenomenon hints at the original constitution of the human—male and female in one female body. When half of this being broke away, the two sexes appeared. The catastrophe that caused the male mutation and the breaking off, or crippling, of the X chromosome to form the deformed Y is perhaps symbolized in Plato's race memory of the separation of the sexes.

The first males were mutants, freaks produced by some damage to the genes caused perhaps by disease or a radiation bombardment from the sun. Maleness remains a recessive genetic trait like color-blindness and hemophilia with which it is linked. The suspicion that maleness is abnormal and that the Y chromosome is an accidental mutation boding no good for the race is strongly supported by the recent discovery by geneticists that congenital killers and criminals are possessed of not one but *two* Y chromosomes, bearing a double dose, as it were, of genetically undesirable maleness. If the Y chromosome is a degeneration and a deformity of the female X chromosome, then the male sex represents a degeneration and deformity of the female.

Not only does the Y chromosome have a negative effect in the heredity of males, but now it has been found, in studies by Curt Stern and Arthur Jensen, that the extra X chromosome in females accounts not only for the greater freedom of girls from birth defects and congenital diseases, a fact which has been long known, but also for the superior physiological makeup and the superior *intelligence* of women over men.

"Women are the race itself . . . the strong primary sex, and man the biological afterthought," as a nineteenth-century scientist and forerunner of Ashley Montagu wrote.[6]

In prehistoric times "man was the despised sex," as Robert Graves wrote with typical Gravesian prescience in 1955.[7] For subsequent archeological research has revealed the extent of "man's subservience to women," [8] and the secondary role played by men in the period immediately preceding the present historical era.

"Man was the weaker sex. . . . Men could be trusted to hunt, fish, guard the herds, mind the flocks and gather certain crops, as long as they did not transgress matriarchal law" or interfere with government.[9] "Woman was the dominant sex, and man her frightened victim." [10]

"The men occupy a position which could not but enhance the natural superiority of women. . . . Woman towers above man, and the physical beauty which distinguishes the women of matriarchal states reflects the prestige of her position," writes Bachofen. "The very names of the men reflect the contempt inspired by their marauding ways. The ignominy implied in all their names marks the contrast between the dominant woman and the servile man." [11]

Typical names given to early men, as cited by Bachofen, reflect the contempt in which the male sex was held: Sintian, meaning *thief;* Ozolae, meaning *bad smell;* Psoloeis, meaning *dirty.* What names! Sintian, Ozolae, Psoloeis—Thief, Stinker, Dirt! The Tom, Dick, and Harry of old.

"Men were but the servers of women," wrote Charles Seltman of the pre-Mycenaean Greeks.[12] And the same was true throughout the ancient world. The myth of Hercules and Omphale portrays the relationship between Bronze Age woman and man. Omphale, the great queen of Lydia, chooses Hercules, the muscular wild man, as her slave and sex object. He is enslaved by her, not to serve as her bodyguard or warrior but merely to serve as her lover. Between sexual bouts she sends him on dangerous or degrading missions— the "labors of Hercules"—some of which typify the work demanded of men by ancient women: degrading, dirty work such as cleaning out the Augean stables or picking up piece by piece the excrement of the giant Stymphalian birds. All of her commands, these demeaning ones as well as the merely whimsical ones, such as stealing the Amazon queen's girdle, Hercules obeys without demur.

With typical male ratiocination, as Graves says, men have interpreted this myth as a horrible example of the power a licentious and wicked woman can exert over even the noblest of men. But that is not its meaning at all. In fact, this myth, like most, contains a kernel of historical truth. No doubt there was a queen of Lydia named Omphale, and there were certainly many men in early times named Hercules, or Heracles. (The very name means "son of a glorified ancestress," Hera,[13] the heroic concept having been originally feminine.) And with equal lack of doubt, one of these was a slave owned by Queen Omphale, whose exploits, carried out at her bidding, were transformed by later patriarchal writers into the wondrous deeds of Hercules.

"Heracles was bought [for three silver talents] by Omphale, Queen of Lydia, a woman with a good eye for a bargain; and he served her faithfully," writes Graves, quoting Apollodorus.[14]

The strange initiatory rites and sex customs among primitive peoples that so amazed the European explorers of the sixteenth to nineteenth centuries bear out the worldwide tradition of the original and natural inferiority of men. In all male initiatory rites of puberty, past and present, the rituals consist entirely in men's pretending to be women, "as if men can become men only by . . . taking over the functions that women perform naturally," as Margaret Mead writes.[15]

These rites, including penis mutilation, castration, mock childbirth, and menstruation, and the custom of carving up the male pudendum to resemble the female vulva, are well-nigh universal and date back to remotest antiquity. That the slitting of the male penis is an overt attempt to emulate women is attested to by the fact that in Australia the name for the slit penis derives from the word vulva, and those who have undergone the operation are known as "possessors of a vulva."[16]

In the *Journals of Expedition and Discovery into Central America,* a missionary describes the *mica,* the 'slitting of the penis, in the following words: "There is a cleft of the urethra from the apex of the penis down to the scrotum, done with a piece of sharpened quartz. I have not been able to learn the reason for this strange mutilation. When questioned they reply, *'That is the way our ancestors did,* and so we have to do the same.'"[17]

In the same journal, a Monsieur Gason describes the same operation as performed in a tribe of Australia: "It is performed by placing the young man's penis upon a piece of tree bark, after which the penis is cloven with a bit of flint stone, and there is then applied to the wound another piece of bark to keep it from closing."[18]

A later traveler in Australia reports that "an incision is made

from the glans to the scrotum by means of a piece of sharpened
flint stone, and there is then applied a piece of bark to prevent the
cut edges from closing over. Men who have undergone this operation must urinate sitting down. Lifting the penis, they make water
as our women do." [19] The operation apparently has no effect on
the man's potency or fertility, for "in erection the member which
has been so operated becomes very wide and flat. This is something
which many missionaries have seen, having prevailed upon native
men and women to have intercourse in front of them." [20] Could
this be one reason for the original operation in the remote past—
that women found sexual intercourse with such a deformed penis
more piquant than otherwise, just as, much later, the Moslem
women found intercourse with the uncircumcised Christians more
rewarding than that with their own docked men? [21]

Theodor Reik reports that the initiation of young boys at puberty was to signify their rebirth as children of the father and
not of the mother. The men imitate the women, and "the entire
initiation ceremony gives the impression that the father really
gives birth to the child. . . . They carry the boys . . . as women
carry babies; and even perform the same purifying rites as women
do after childbirth." [22] The male mother dons a skirt and squats
on the birth stool. While he grunts and groans and grimaces in
mock labor, the young man, naked and glistening with red paint,
crawls under the skirts and is suddenly expelled between the older
man's legs, while everyone shouts for joy—everyone, that is, except
the "mother," who promptly faints from her labors. The Greeks
had a similar custom, for in *The Bacchae*, Euripides has the god
Zeus say to the infant Dionysus: "Enter now life's secret portal,
motherless mystery; Lo, I break mine own body for thy sake. . . .
Come, enter this, my male womb." [23]

The couvade, the custom in which the father takes to his bed
during his wife's delivery and is attended and administered to by
the medicine man, is a modification of the older rite in which the
father goes through the actual motions of childbirth. "Whole societies," writes Margaret Mead, "have built their ceremonial upon
an envy of woman's role and a desire to imitate it." [24] Some cultures go so far as to introduce synthetic male menstruation, and
even in the menopause "we find an attempt to emphasize the male
analogue."

Margaret Mead goes on: "To the Occidental, bred in a society that has exalted . . . men and depreciated the role of women, this all seems far-fetched." [25] But farfetched or not, so it is, and was, and has always been—the subconscious desire of man to perform as women do. This primordial sexual envy has been the basis of man's latter-day compulsion to "depreciate the role of women" and to belittle all things feminine, particularly the feminine functions that he so greatly wishes to emulate.

That this ritual mimicry of women by men is very ancient is suggested by the remark quoted above by the primitive—"that is the way our ancestors did. . . ." It is possible that the ancestors learned the custom, as well as so much else, from the ancient mariners. Yet it is unlikely that a people so advanced as the ancient mariners obviously were could have inaugurated such rites in the form in which they came to be practiced. It must be that these customs are a degeneration of something quite different, something that the savages misinterpreted. Could it be that the "natives" were not imitating a male imitation of women but were emulating the actual natural functions of the ancient mariners themselves, the leaders of the great fleets which visited them—the women? The femininity of the ancient mariners, particularly of their captains and admirals, would explain a number of other abstruse customs and legends found around the world. It must be remembered that in myth it was the Great Goddess who invented the ship, and in all myth the goddess is synonymous with gynocracy: where the goddess reigned, woman ruled.

If the leaders of the ancient mariners were indeed women not only would primitive initiatory rites be explained but also the universality of the belief in woman as civilizer and educator of man.

Woman the Civilizer

Contrary to the pusillanimity of early man in the memory of the ancients was the exalted position—the divinity, even—of women. Throughout the ancient world the tradition prevailed that women held the secrets of nature and were the only channels through which flowed the wisdom and knowledge of the ages. This belief is reflected in the priority of female oracles, prophets, priests, Sybils, pythonesses, maenads, Erinyes, shamanesses, and so on.

"Women were the originators and repositories of all culture . . .
and the source of the first civilization." [26] In fact, women dragged
man, kicking and screaming, out of savagery into the New Stone
Age, as anthropology and archeology have learned and as myth and
tradition have always asserted.

"Women organized the home crew to pound the corn, thresh
the grain, comb the wool, dry the skins, etc. They invented pottery
and weaving, discovered how to keep foods by cold storage or by
cooking. Women, in fact, invented industrialization," writes Buckminster Fuller.[27]

These nurturing chores, now looked down upon by men as
"women's work," were indeed women's work—the first important
work of human society. "Men could be trusted to hunt and fish,"
as Graves says,[28] so long as they did not interfere with the important work of the community. Men acquiesced in this discrimination, not from masculine pride but because they believed
that women were better able to perform these tasks which they,
the women, had invented and inaugurated.

The achievements that distinguish the New Stone Age from
the Old are "the making of pots, the weaving of textiles, the planting and harvesting of crops and the domestication of animals." [29]
"And woman . . . did the weaving and she invented pottery
making. More than this, she must be credited with the planting and
harvesting of grain, for while her lord and master enjoyed himself,
she gathered fruits and nuts and edible seeds, and sooner or later
observed that the seeds dropped on the midden pile produced
newer and bigger plants." [30] Thus she invented agriculture, and
with it civilization, for "out of agriculture rose a settled community and a surplus of provender which allowed the few . . . to
think and plan and build civilization." [31]

"She was the only true begetter of the New Stone Age," writes
MacGowan, "for she invented milling stones to grind seeds, while
her man was still a paleolithic," a savage of the Old Stone Age.[32]
"Perhaps she watched the wearing away of mortar and pestle and
milling stone as she ground her seeds into flour between them,
and the idea occurred to her . . . that it was possible to grind
stones into axes and other implements"; and thus she invented
manufacture.[33]

So let us revise the old stereotype, planted in our minds by the textbooks, of shaggy caveman discovering that salting the fish and cooking the food would preserve them from spoiling; that clay shaped into pots and baked on the hearth would hold liquids; that reeds woven together would make baskets, shelters, clothing, containers; that stones chipped and rubbed into shape would make tools and implements. Let us correct the old impression that it was shaggy man who first saw the usefulness of fire and thought of ways to preserve and utilize and create it; that shaggy man first found that a log placed under his burden would roll it, and invented the wheel; that shaggy man discovered that a floating log would bear his weight and carry him across the river, and invented boats. Above all, let us dismiss the incongruous picture of shaggy caveman decorating his pottery and basketry with dainty designs and painting his cave-home walls with exquisite delineations of nature.

For it was not man but woman who made all these discoveries and invented all these crafts—woman, eternally struggling to make the best of things, to provide food and shelter for her children, to make "home" comfortable for them, to soften and brighten their lives, and to make the world a safer and more pleasant place for them to grow in. While man pursued his hobbies of hunting and fishing and holding his "lodge" meetings, woman initiated and carried on the real work of the world. "Woman invented work, for primitive man was only an idler," MacGowan writes.[34]

"It was woman the gatherer, not man the hunter, who fed the primitive family," writes Irven DeVore of Harvard. "As still happens, man's activity got the publicity and made the biggest outward impression, but it was woman's quiet work which kept things going. . . . Woman was the real provider for the household. . . ."[35]

Even the Jesuit scholar Joseph Goetz affirms the ancient supremacy of woman: "Everything points to the growing of plants for food having originated with the woman. . . It is here that individual property ownership originated. . : . It is the woman who owns the fields and dwellings. . . . Marriages are matrilocal. The man lives with his wife in *her* village, or else remains with his mother. Economy and law revolve around the woman. The universe thus centered on her is the vegetal aspect of nature with which through *technical domination* she has became associated," as she has with the meteorological and astronomical phenomena which affect plant growth and the well-being of the society.[36]

When woman with her industry and inventiveness, says Briffault, had finally enabled man to live in security in a woman-dominated civilization, he established the custom of taking over her ideas and commercializing them. (*Plus ça change, plus c'est la même chose.*) The land itself, however, continued to belong to the women, and in Europe, even in comparatively late historical times, "the man must come as a suitor to the woman, through whom alone he could enter into possession of the land." [37]

The oldest words in the languages of all the Indo-European peoples, words dating back to the gynarchic age before the separation of the nations, are the words that apply to women's work: the words for spinning and sewing; for grinding and milling grain; for grain itself, and agriculture, field, and plow; for the taming and breaking-in of animals; for the use of fire in cooking and of salt in preserving foods; for the art of counting in numbers; for axle, cart, wagon, ship, and oar; for the building of walls and houses and boats; and for the wearing of clothes for adornment.[38] Furthermore, myth and tradition credit women with *all* the inventions and discoveries these words connote. And mythology, we repeat, is the memory of real events experienced by the human race.

"Who will continue to ask why . . . all the qualities that embellish man's life are known by feminine names?" [39] Why justice, peace, intelligence, wisdom, rectitude, devotion, liberty, mercy, intellect, nobility, concord, gentleness, clemency, generosity, kindliness, dignity, spirit, soul, freedom—all, all are feminine? "This choice is no free invention or accident, but is an expression of historical truth. . . . The accord between historical facts and the linguistic phenomenon is evident." [40]

The Logos

"Both in agriculture, which was invented by women, and in the erection of walls, which the ancients identified with the matriarchal era, women achieved a perfection which astonished later generations." [41] "From the banks of the Nile to the shores of the Black

Sea, from central Asia to Italy, women's names and deeds are interwoven with the history of the founding of cities which became famous." [42]

The worldwide tradition that women first built towns and walls reflects not only the fact that women were the first civilizers but that the mysterious megaliths, whose engineering secret was already lost in early patriarchal-historical times, were the work of the matriarchal period.

The Greek legend of Amphion, the notes of whose lyre caused large stones to rise into walls,[43] bears out the universal belief among primitive peoples that these huge stone structures, from Gizeh to Avebury, from India to Yucatan and Peru, were built by means of some power long lost to mankind. The Spaniards in the sixteenth century were told by the Incas that the ancient megalithic ruins of Peru and Colombia were built by a remote people who merely struck a note of music and the mammoth stones rose and slid into place. And Herodotus reports that among the Lydians the tradition was preserved in his time that the megalithic monuments of Lydia had been built by the women of old. Even the remarkable engineering works of historical Babylon, numbered among the seven wonders of the world, were credited by the ancients to the genius of two queens, Semiramis and Nitocris.[44]

The Old Testament ascribes the invention of civilized arts to Tubal-Cain. But who is Tubal-Cain? Cain himself, as we shall see in a later chapter, is but a symbol of the old matriarchal city states that were overthrown by the pastoral nomads—the Abels.[45] Tubal-Cain postdates him, yet he is oddly credited with inventing civilized arts that had *predated* Cain. The mystery's solution lies in the name itself—Tubal.

The Interpreter's Dictionary of the Bible, under "Tubal," says that Tubal (in Hebrew Tub-Hal) means "one who brings forth" —a female—thus giving the name Tubal-Cain a doubly feminine connotation.[46] *The Mythology of All Races* tells us that the original of Tubal was Tibir; and in the same volume we find that Tibir, or Tibirra, was another name of the Sumerian Great Goddess, Tiamat.[47]

The Sumerian epic of Tagtug [Tibir] and Dilmun speaks of an early time "when Tibir had not yet *laid a foundation*," a reference that corroborates the belief that women laid the first foundations, that is, of walls and cities, and were thus the first fashioners of civilized society—the Tubal-Cains of actuality.

Just as the story of Noah and the Ark is borrowed from the Sumerian epic of Gilgamesh, and the creation story from the Babylonian epic of Enuma Elish, so the entire Cain-Tubal-Cain cycle in Genesis is borrowed from the epic of Tagtug and Dilmun—and Tagtug, or Tibir, is Tubal-Cain.[48]

Here we have a link, if a somewhat tenuous one, of Sumer and the lost civilization with the Celts. For Herodotus writes that the Great Goddess of the Celts in his time was known as Tabiti,[49] which could have been a Celtic corruption of the older name, Tibirra, as Tubal was a Hebraic corruption of Tibir.

Athene, a later aspect of the Great Goddess, was credited by the Greeks with having invented the "flute, the trumpet, the earthenware pot, the plough, the rake, the ox-yoke, the horse-bridle, the chariot, the wheel, the ship, the art of numbers, fire, cooking, weaving and spinning."[50] In other words, woman invented or discovered or first practiced music, ceramics, agriculture, animal domestication, land transportation, water transportation, commerce, mathematics, handicrafts, domestic economy and industry. What else of any use has been invented in the centuries since the end of the matriarchal era?

Woman the Divine

"Woman by her very nature was considered to participate in that of the divinity."[51] "Men looked upon her as divine."[52] "Women were held sacred."[53] "Women, by means of their intuition, gave the first mighty impulse to the civilization of the human race."[54] But what is this "intuition" that women are supposed to have in place of brains? Let the incomparable H. L. Mencken answer the question:

All this intuition is no more and no less than intelligence—intelligence so keen that it can penetrate to the hidden truth through the most formidable wrappings of false semblance and demeanor. . . . Women decide the larger questions of life correctly and quickly, not because of intuition, but simply and solely because they have sense. They see at a glance what most men could not see with search-lights and telescopes; they are at grips with the essentials of a problem before men have finished debating its mere externals. . . . It is a rare, rare, man who is as steadily intelligent, as constantly sound in judgment, as little put off by appearance, as the average woman.[55]

This superiority of intellect exerted a strong influence on primitive man. Men could not help but believe that woman was closer to the deity than was man and that she had a superior understanding of the laws of nature—laws that baffled his dimmer perceptions and rendered him dependent on woman as the interpreter between man and man and man and deity.

"Woman manifests justice unconsciously but with full certainty; she is naturally in herself just, wise. That is why the battle lines parted at her bidding, why she was the arbiter who could compose quarrels among tribes and among nations. . . ." [56]

"Woman dominated man. She was a fascinating magician before whom his soul trembled. . . . From her sprang poetry, music and all the arts." [57]

When the cave paintings at Altamira in Spain were first discovered less than a hundred years ago, the world was astounded at their beauty and artistic perfection. Certainly no chinless, prognathous, skin-clad savage could have conceived or executed them! They were attributed to Cro-Magnon man, the ancestor of modern Europeans, and were described by earlier archeologists, androcentric "antiquarians," as magic symbols drawn by men to induce the animals depicted to yield quietly to their human hunters.

But there were many holes in this hypothesis: their location in low-ceilinged sleeping quarters which were difficult of access and rarely used by man; their feminine delicacy of line; their feeling of compassion for the hunted beasts; the caricaturish depictions of the hunters—certainly not flattering to the male of the human species; and the presence of imprints of women's and children's hands on the walls around the paintings.

"The paintings must have been art for art's sake" and not magic symbols as originally assumed. "They were painted on walls of rock shelters used as living quarters" [58] to brighten it up—like new slipcovers and draperies. And what man ever bothered to brighten up rooms in which he spent little or no time?

"Cave art is genuinely a woman's art," writes the artist Violeta

Miqueli;[59] and far from being a merely utilitarian medium, it "is animated by a single motive, namely, the appreciation of the beauty of form," as Henry Fairfield Osborn observes.[60]

The wild animals painted on the cave walls are idealistically beautiful. Their grace of movement and delicacy of line go far beyond the requirements of any utilitarian depiction for magic purposes. The wounded animals are shown with expressions of human grief and shock on their faces, and the dying ones are the embodiment of despair.

In contrast to the animals, the human male hunters are shown as mere sticks—figures such as a child might draw of the human form (and perhaps the children did draw them). They wear animal masks that are far more ferocious and bestial than are the faces of the hunted animals. (These unflattering depictions of men remind one of the "shambling, cretinous-looking warriors" shown on the famous Warrior vase found at Mycenae.[61] Could this, too, have been the work of women artists?)

The most convincing evidence of all that these cave paintings are the work of women are the prints of women's and children's hands upon the walls around the paintings. It was as if some prehistoric woman, alone on a rainy day with her children, had set out to amuse them by showing them where the men were—hunting the wild animals. She had made her paint and drawn her compassionate likenesses of the poor hunted animals and had then allowed the children to draw in the image of what served as "daddy" in those matriarchal days when "men served women only as hunters and warriors," as Seltman says.[62] Having still a little paint left, and the rain still preventing the children from going out to play, this Cro-Magnon mother absently dipped her hand into the paint and pressed it against the wall. The children imitated her action. And twenty thousand years later, Señor Don Marcelino de Sautuola, exploring the cave at Altamira with his little daughter, discovered them—the hand prints, the animals, and the little sticks of men.

And the world wondered.

Myth, legend, and tradition all attribute the invention of decorative arts to women, and archeology and anthropology bear out the tradition. Similarly music, song, poetry, and dance are traced to the women of primordial ages by mythology.

2

Mythology Speaks

But where are those origins to be found? The answer is not in doubt. In myth, the faithful picture of the oldest era.

—J. J. BACHOFEN

Renewal and Diffusion

European explorers of the great Age of Discovery, the fifteenth through the eighteenth centuries A.D., were struck by the similarities they found among primitive tribes who were so cut off from the world that they were unaware even of the people on the next island. The Europeans were amazed to find that certain beliefs and legends, myths and traditions, customs and taboos, were worldwide and varied only in nonessentials from Siberia to the South Seas.

It was the discovery of these unaccountable similarities that led anthropologists of the nineteenth century, primarily the Germans Georg Waitz and Adolf Bastian, to formulate the "autochthonous" theory of local evolution—that is, the theory that all peoples progress through certain stages of development without benefit of contact or example. By the twentieth century this theory "had lapsed into the oblivion from which it should never have emerged," as A. C. Haddon says,[1] and its place had been taken by the "diffusionist" theory. This theory, now accepted by more perceptive scholars, claims "that development took place in one centre only and thence spread over the face of the earth."[2]

Where this original center might have been is undecided. Recent archeological research seems to point to a source in Anatolia, but Anatolia may have been only a last outpost of the original civilization. The big question is whether "diffusion" was effected by migration of peoples from a central origin or whether civilization

47

"was consciously planted around the world" in a lost age when world travel was a commonplace.

If migration from a central origin were the answer, it would seem that there would not have been the retrogression that has obviously taken place among the world's peoples. "Conscious planting" by a superior race would account for the fact that with the demise of the central civilization, the whole world not only ceased to advance but actually receded into savagery. Our explorers found that the "savage" peoples around the globe, "by their folklore, their customs, and their hazy ideas of metaphysics, betrayed their status," not as genuine primitives fresh from the creator's hands, but for what it was—"the status of *a civilization degraded into savagery.*" [3]

The further back we go in the investigation of peoples, as of language, the more sophisticated we find them to have been. In Ireland, the very first settlers, the Firbolgs, the "little people" of Irish myth, retained an ancient knowledge that even their conquerors, the brilliant and gifted Tuatha De Danann, found not wholly comprehensible. And the Milesians who conquered the Tuatha, like all the later Celts, "had lost the complex astronomical system, and retained the old ideas about the immortality of the soul only in the vaguest way." [4]

"The common religion of the archaic civilization," writes John Rhys, "from the Baltic to Gibraltar, was Druidism." [5] And Druidism was the religion of the Celts. Druidism can be traced back into the most remote antiquity, continues Rhys, beyond Celtic Europe and into the Aegean area. The Druids were once all women—Druidesses; and even in Roman times, as Caesar comments, these lady Druids were consulted by the Celtic chiefs of Gaul. In the first century of the present era, according to Tacitus, the object of Druid worship was a Great Goddess whose shrine was in a grove of oaks upon an island in the sea.[6]

Sumer and the Celtic Cross

"The science of the Druids of historical times, their knowledge of astronomy and physics, and their ideas of the immortality of the soul, were far too elaborate to have been invented by barbarians." [7] Where, then, did they acquire this ancient wisdom—a wisdom evidenced by the mariners, and later, much later, by the Thracian Orpheus?

Dare we hypothesize that the center of the great lost civilization, wherever it may have been located, was destroyed by the general world cataclysm of the tenth millennium, when the North Pole shifted to the Sudan Basin, and that the scant remnant of its leaders found refuge in the mountain fastnesses of Aegean Thrace? For in Thrace the ancient knowledge of science was handed down to Orpheus' time; in Thrace the classical Greeks found evidence of an ancient technology far beyond their own capacities.[8] Thrace, according to Apuleius, was the original home of witchcraft (woman-wisdom), and in the vicinity of Thrace dwelt the nation of Amazons, that blue-eyed race of women who lived entirely without men, murdering any man who dared approach their boundaries. (Celtic mythology includes a land of women similar to the nation of Amazons of Aegean legend. "The tradition of the land of women," writes John A. McCulloch, "still exists in Irish folklore." [9])

Perhaps it was *only* the wisewomen who escaped the great catastrophe, and in order to maintain the race, reproduction by parthenogenesis became commonplace. This would account for the myth of the ancients, preserved by Plato, that *all* their ancestors were female and for the method of reproduction practiced by the Amazons. For, according to legend, although they were manless, the Amazons reared their girl babies and destroyed the boys born among them. Thrace, we may add, was also the site of the birth and the murder of Orpheus, the "mystery man of antiquity."

Above all, in Thrace the Druids had their origin. Druidism may well have been the ancient and original religion, and it would be interesting to trace this primary religion from its origin through Sumer, into historical Celtic Europe, and on into modern times.

In Sumerian myth the creator goddess Tiamat appeared out of the waves of the Erythraean Sea (the Persian Gulf of today), as a "fish-woman" and taught men the arts of life: "to construct *cities*, to found temples, to compile laws, and, in short, instructed them in all things that tend to soften manners and humanize their lives," as Berosus of Babylon reported in the fourth century B.C. "From that time, so universal were [her] instructions, that nothing material has been added," says Polyhistor.[10] This event was believed to have taken place about 16,000 B.C., but a later date seems more rea-

sonable. Tiamat may have been a matriarchal queen of the Thra-
cian-Anatolian remnant of the lost civilization, who some time in
the ninth or tenth millennium journeyed to her colony on the Persian Gulf and reinstructed her people in the lost arts of civilization.
The Euphrates River ran then, as it does today, from central Anatolia down to its outlet on the Persian Gulf, and geological evidence
is that it was far wider and deeper even in Biblical times than it is
now.

Tiamat may have sailed down this broad river from Anatolia or
nearby Thrace in a ship whose figurehead was the mermaidlike
creature of the ancient legend, half fish, half human. In later Babylonian myth the mer*maid* had become a mer*man*—Oannes. But
mer*men* are an anomaly in mythical zoology, and Oannes is obviously a late patriarchal attempt to masculinize the bringer of civilization.

It is pertinent to our hypothesis of the close connection vertically
of the matriarchal Celts and the lost civilization that mermaids in
later mythology were almost exclusively Celtic. "The prevalence of
tales of mermaids among Celtic populations," writes Sabine Baring-
Gould, "indicates these nymphs as having been originally *deities*
of these peoples." [11] It also indicates that the Celts, who in historical times had no navy, must at one time have had a close connection with the sea, the habitat of mermaids. Morgan le Fay of Arthurian romance, Morrigan of Irish folklore, and Morgana of the
Danish and Italian Celtic remnant are all one and the same fairy
queen, whose name means "Child of the sea," *mor* being the Celtic
word for sea.

The connection of the cross with the Celtic mermaid or water
goddess as displayed on ancient pre-Christian Celtic coins offers
a fascinating field for study. These coins have been found at Marseilles, Loiret, Quimper, and other parts of Gallic France, as well
as in Spain and Brittany, and they indicate that the cross was the
symbol or insignium of the ancient Celtic goddess, who may have
been one with Tiamat herself.

Significantly, the cross was a Druid emblem also; and the Druid
cross, like those on the Celtic coins, had rounded arms of equal
length—the shape of a shamrock or a four-leaf clover. It is for this
reason, and not for any Christian analogy, that the shamrock is

revered in Celtic Ireland and the four-leaf clover is considered lucky throughout the modern Celtic world.

It is intriguing to find that this same equiarmed cross was an emblem of Poseidon, the Greek god of the sea, the "water god" who, according to Plato, had been a deity of the Atlanteans, whose chief city was named for him. In Cretan-Greek mythology, Poseidon was the son-consort of the Great Goddess of Mycenae and Crete, the goddess Potnia. In the natural evolution of myth, goddesses almost inevitably turn into gods, especially when they are very important creator goddesses. W. R. Smith writes that he was astonished to find that the goddesses of the ancient Semites "changed their sex and became gods" actually in historical times.[12] And Buck points out that as recently as five hundred years ago, Atea, the great god of Polynesia, was a goddess.[13] And so it may have been with Poseidon. He may originally have been a goddess—*the* goddess, in fact, Tia-mat-Potnia, the creator Great Goddess of Sumer, Crete, Atlantis, and of the Celts. His emblem, the cross, would therefore have been originally the emblem of the Great Goddess, as it seems to have continued to be in the Celtic religion.

The equiarmed cross has been found on funerary urns of the gynarchic Etruscans and, most significantly, on an ancient Phoenician coin bearing on its obverse an image of the sacred bull, symbol of gynocracy. At the site of ancient Byblos a coin has been found that depicts the goddess Astarte (Ishtar-Tiamat) holding an identical cross and resting her foot on the prow of a ship!

This Celtic cross, as distinguished from crosses of other kinds of which there are very many, traveled far and wide in prehistoric times, for it has turned up in far-off Oceania marked on the sacred stones of New Guinea and of Easter Island. In Australia was found a pendant amulet of greenstone, carved in the shape of the Celtic cross, an exact duplicate of an amulet found in Egypt at Tel el Amarna, the site of the ancient city where Nefertiti and the Pharaoh Akhnaton held court thirty-five hundred years ago.

The Algonquin and Sioux Indians of North America, as well as the Arctic Athabascan and the tribes of Central America, associated the equiarmed cross with the moon goddess (the water goddess), and the Araucanian moon priestesses employed it in their sacred rituals. In China and Tibet the Celtic cross "figured prominently in the shrines of the Great Goddess, and was widespread as a religious symbol throughout western Asia." [14] In the ruins of the Acropolis at Susa, ancient capital of the Persian Empire which was situated on the site of an even more ancient Sumerian city, this cross has been found on shards of vases from the temple.

And finally, in Spain ancient Celtic coins have been found on which the Celtic cross is associated with the bull and the crescent—both of which are ancient symbols of the goddess and of female supremacy.

The Christian cross, with its long upright and short cross arms, has a different history, as we shall see in Chapter 6 ("Sexual Symbolism").

The Celtic-Druidic influence is far greater in our modern lives than is generally realized. It is from the Druids that most Christians derive their belief in the survival of the soul and in the guardian angels as spirits of the beloved dead. Hesiod, "the poet of the matriarchates," in the eighth century B.C. wrote of the belief in angels as the guardian spirits of the dead,[15] a concept which was no longer entertained by the Greeks of the classical age. The idea of the survival of the soul in angel form was no doubt common to the original religion and was preserved *only* among the Celts. What Gerard Murphy calls the "strange loveliness of Celtic mythology" may have its foundation in the fact that Celtic myth is the last echo of the primal universal religion of the matriarchal age—a religion that remains buried deep in the subconscious of modern man as part of his very psyche.

These ideas are denied and discouraged by Christianity, as they were by Judaism. Saint Paul insists that our only hope for survival lies in the resurrection of the body at the last judgment; and the Old Testament, like Egyptian Atonism, teaches that there is no immortality of any kind. In Christian and Judaic angel-lore, both derived from Persian cosmogony, the angels represent a completely separate creation—never human, and only half divine. Moreover, in Christian belief the angels are masculine, whereas in the early Greek and Celtic religions the angels, the spirits or *animae* of the dead, are *always* feminine.

It is an ironic sidelight on Christian symbolism that the male angels depicted in church art are representations of none other than the Great Goddess herself. For when her cult was mercilessly wiped out in Rome and her temples were converted to Christian use, her winged image continued to be engraved on Roman coins, in defiance of the new Christian hierarchy in Constantinople. What could the beleaguered church then do but adopt her as the "angel of the Lord," the Archangel Michael? [16]

But back to Thrace. From Thrace a later generation crossed over the narrow Hellespont into Anatolia and established there the "prehistoric" towns of Catal Huyuk, Mersin, Hacilar, and Alalakh, among others which have been excavated recently by archeologists. The knowledge remembered by these matriarchal peoples accounts for the blossoming, as we have conjectured, of the great Sumerian civilization, "which never seems to have had a beginning," as historians complain. "Overnight, as it were," writes Thorkild Jacobsen, Harvard Sumerologist, "[Sumerian] civilization . . . flashes into being, complete in all its main features." [17] Their knowledge of astronomy exceeded that of modern man until A.D., 1930 for it was not until 1930 that Clyde Tombaugh discovered the ninth planet, Pluto, and only in 1781 and 1846 respectively had William Herschel discovered Uranus, the seventh planet, and Urbain Leverrier, Neptune, the eighth. Yet on seals dug up at ancient sites in what was Sumer, our sun is shown with all *nine* planets revolving around it. Not only that, but these same seals show other suns than ours, with other yet undiscovered worlds in orbit around them. [18]

The sun-centered universe and the plurality of worlds, a belief that was branded as heresy by the Christian Church as recently as four hundred years ago, was known to the ancient Sumerians seven thousand years ago. Whence had they gleaned this knowledge?

Evidence is piling up that Anatolia, which earlier archeologists had dismissed as a place arid of any traces of an early civilization, may have been the germinating point of all historical civilizations. Not only did the seeds of the ancient lost civilization lie dormant there, finally to burst forth into the great civilizations of Sumer, Crete, and Egypt, but when these had been destroyed by the patriarchs, the original seed found fallow ground again in Anatolian Ionia. Thence it blossomed in late historical times into the glory that was Athens and into the great Celto-Ionian civilization that ended only fifteen hundred years ago with the coming of official Christianity and the resultant fall of Rome, the two related events which ushered in the Dark Ages of medieval Europe.

Orpheus and Druidism

Thrace was the source of the Anatolian miracle, the link between
the great lost civilization and all the civilizations of historical times,
including our own. "The Thracians," wrote Herodotus, "dwell
amid lofty mountains clothed with forests and capped by snow.
. . . Their oracle is situated upon their highest mountain top, and
their prophet is a woman." [19] From Thrace came the nine Muses,
"mountain goddesses," and Thrace was the home of the mysterious
maenads, of whom we shall have more to say presently.

In Thrace the goddess Diana was worshiped, and her worship
took a form similar to that practiced by the ancient Celts of the
British Isles: both the Thracians and the Celts, according to Herodotus, invariably accompanied their offerings to the goddess, *as no
other peoples did,* with "wheaten straw": From remotest antiquity,
writes Herodotus, "the Hyperboreans" (the people of the far north,
i.e., the British Isles) had sent offerings to the Temple of Diana at
Delos. These gifts, wrapped in *wheaten straw,* were sent overland
across Europe to the Adriatic Sea, down to the Sea of Corinth to
Euboea, and then to Tenos, "whence the Tenians, without stop-
ping at Andros, brought them finally to Delos" in the Aegean Sea.
"The women of Thrace," he goes on, "in their sacrifices to the
queenly Diana bring *wheaten straw* always with their offerings. Of
my own knowledge I can testify that this is so." [20] But the usually
ingenious Herodotus had no explanation for the similarity in the
customs of these two widely separated peoples.

It was the Delian Diana herself, according to Geoffrey of Monmouth, who directed the first Britons to England. When Brutus, the
mythical founder of Britain, sought her out on Delos, she promised
him that he would be the sire of a great race: "Beyond the setting
of the sun, past the realms of Gaul, there lies an island in the sea.
Down the years this island will prove an abode suited to your people. There a race of kings will be born from your stock, and the
whole circle of the world will be subject to them." [21]

Significantly, this Brutus, father of the British Celts, was an
Anatolian. Expelled from Italy, where he had gone with the defeated Trojans under Aeneas, he sought refuge in Greece, whence
he was also expelled. On Delos he learned his true destiny, and by

way of thanks to the goddess he promised that she would become the goddess of his people forever. "My people shall worship thee down the ages, and shall dedicate temples to you." [22] And history proves him true to his word, for the Christians found the Celts of Gaul, Britain, and Ireland devoutly worshiping the goddess Dana, "the Goddess of the forest glades and the wild woodlands," and sending yearly tributes to her ancient shrine on Aegean Delos.

Diana was a very ancient Aegean goddess, far older than the Hellenic Greek myth of her twin birth with Apollo on Delos would make her. It must be remembered that the Greek myths as they have come down to us were late Hellenic interpretations of far more ancient legends. In many cases the goddess had been split up and renamed in accordance with her various appellations in different parts of the world. Just as in late myth the thunder god became Zeus, Thor, Jupiter, Jove, Jehovah, Yahweh, etc., in earlier myth the Great Goddess had become known as Potnia, Ceres, Cybele, Athene, Diana, Artemis, 'Anat, Isis, Ishtar, Astarte, Minerva, Dana, etc.

Dana (Diana) was the goddess of the Celts of Europe and the British Isles. Her name has been immortalized in many place names from the River Don in Eastern Europe to London itself,[23] and to Ireland, where the Tuatha De Danann, the "people of the goddess Dana," were early Celtic settlers. The oak tree, sacred to the ancient Thracians and to the Celtic Druids, was connected with this goddess. Even in Italy the Grove of Diana at Ariccia, whence Aeneas plucked the mistletoe (the "golden bough"), was a grove of *oaks*. And the mistletoe was a Druidic sacred fetish.

The Celtic Dana and the Delian Diana of classical Greece must both have originated in Thrace, where her temple, as Herodotus said, "was on their highest mountain top" and whose "prophet was a woman." The maenads were the priestesses of this Thracian goddess and were therefore like the later Celtic priests of Dana, *Druids,* custodians of the ancient wisdom.

Thracian Orpheus is said by both Plato and Plutarch to have had access to ancient knowledge lost in Hellenic times. He knew, for example, that the sun and not the earth was the center of our universe, that other universes with other suns existed in the vastness of space, and that other worlds besides our own revolved around our sun. "The Egyptians," writes Richard Knight, "certainly could not have taught Orpheus the plurality of worlds and true solar system which appear to have been the fundamental principles of his philosophy. Nor could he have gained his knowledge from any people of whom history has preserved any memorials, for we know none among whom science had made such a progress that a truth as remote from common observation and so contradictory to the evidence of unimproved sense, would not have been rejected, as it was by all sects of Greek philosophy save that of Pythagoras." [24]

Pythagoras, after Orpheus, taught not only the plurality of worlds, the sun-centered universe, the theory of cataclysmic evolution, the periodic shifting of the poles, and the spherical shape of the earth, but also the theory of reincarnation and the immortality of the soul. Could he have learned all this from Orpheus? And where had Orpheus learned it if not in Thrace, his homeland, that land of craggy mountain fastnesses where the scientific knowledge of the ancient mariners had been preserved when long forgotten elsewhere.

"Thrace was certainly inhabited by a highly civilized people at some remote period," writes Knight, "for when Philip of Macedon in the fifth century B.C. opened the gold mines in that country he found that they had been worked before with great expense and ingenuity by a people well versed in mechanics, to whom no memorials whatever were then extant in any part of the known world." [25]

Here we have again the gold mines, the mines of the ancient mariners who scoured the world for gold and who knew more about our universe than modern science has yet been able to learn. Orpheus, the Thracian, passed on his knowledge of the cosmos to Pythagoras. Could it have been Orpheus too who let Epicurus into the secret of the atomic theory? Both Pythagoras and Epicurus were among the ancient philosophers whose works were deliberately destroyed during the Dark Ages of Europe when, as Gibbon charges, the light of learning was deliberately quenched by the Christian Church.[26] Thus over two millennia were to pass before Kepler, Galileo and Copernicus rediscovered that which Orpheus, Aristarchus, and Pythagoras had proclaimed to the ancients and before Albert Einstein stumbled upon the ancient atomic theory of Epicurus. Sir William Harvey, in his discovery of the circulation of the blood, was only finding anew what the ancients had been aware of, as Philostratus states.[27] The theory of evolution too, twenty-four hundred years before Darwin, had been known to Anaximander but was later discredited by Aristotle.[28] Aristotle, "the wisest of the pagans," was revered by the early Christians, who therefore preserved his works while criminally destroying the works of his betters. He was a herald of medieval ignorance, an unwitting ally of the church fathers. It was because of Aristotle's denial of the ancient truth, known to the Sumerians, the Chaldeans, and the early Greeks, that the earth was a sphere revolving around the sun, that the Christian Church was able for so long to defend its dogma that the earth was a platform supported by the columns of hell and roofed by the vault of heaven, over which the sun obligingly rose and set.

But all these things were known to the sages of the pre-Aristotelian world of the seventh and sixth centuries B.C.—the time of the Seven Sages so revered by the classical Greeks for their possession of ancient truths, truths discarded or discredited by the time of Plato and forgotten by the time of Plutarch. Could Orpheus have been the transmitter of the "ancient wisdom" to the sages? And could it be that he died for revealing it? According to myth, Orpheus was murdered by the maenads for various worldly reasons. But if the maenads were Druidesses, as I have surmised, they were in reality the custodians of the ancient wisdom and Orpheus was killed by them because he, himself a Druid, had revealed their secrets.

According to later Hellenic mythology, Orpheus was slain by Zeus "for divulging divine secrets." [29] Zeus is obviously an anachronism here, for the new god could not have been privy to the divine secrets, or the "ancient wisdom," as the Greeks called it. The reason given in the later myth for Orpheus' execution may be the true one, but his executioners were the maenads, the Druidesses, not Zeus.

The Druids, like Orpheus and Pythagoras, taught the immortality of the soul and the theory of reincarnation, a fact which led the classical writers of Rome to conclude that the Druids of Gaul and Britain "had been influenced by Pythagoras." [30] The shoe, however, is on the other foot. Orpheus and Pythagoras had been influenced by the Druids—the maenads of Thrace. It was from them that Orpheus had learned the ancient wisdom which had been passed on to the Seven Sages, of whom Anaximander, the tutor of Pythagoras, was one.

According to Porphyry, Pythagoras was born on the Aegean island of Samos of an Etruscan father and a Cretan mother. At an early age he was sent to Miletus in Caria to be instructed by Anaximander. Later he studied under Aristoclea at the great college at Delphi in Phocis, where later another woman, Theoclea, a pupil of Pythagoras, was to become high priestess. Porphyry relates an esoteric tale of one Zalmoxis, a *Thracian* lad whom Pythagoras loved, "who was also called Thales." [31] Now Thales was one of the Seven Sages of Greece, a possessor of the "ancient wisdom," and is supposed to have come from Caria. But was he actually a Thracian, like Orpheus before him? And was Zalmoxis, also like Orpheus, a Druid?

Porphyry has very little to say about the mysterious Zalmoxis; yet he emphasizes the seemingly irrelevant fact that "he wore a bandage about his forehead." [32] This may be a reference to an ancient pre-Druidic aspect of the original goddess religion, for it is reminiscent of the band worn by the maenads in some Greek bas-reliefs and of the headbands worn by later Druids and Druidesses of Europe. Geoffrey of Monmouth writes that when the Celtic Brutus and his followers sought out the goddess Diana on her island, "they wrapped fillets round their brows *according to the age-old rite*." [33] (Author's italics.) Celtic warrior queens too are shown wearing this band about their temples. Celtic queens were considered incarnations of the goddess, and "ancient king and Druid owed allegiance to the Goddess incarnate in the Queen." [34]

"I conclude," writes E. R. Dodds, "that Orpheus is a Thracian figure of much the same character as Zalmoxis—that is, a shaman [priest], or prototype of shamans. . . . He, Orpheus, combines the professions of poet, magician, religious teacher, and oracle-giver. . . . Like shamans everywhere he pays a visit to the underworld. Finally his self lives on as a singing head. . . . Such mantic heads appear in northern mythology and in Irish tradition." [35]

In "northern mythology and Irish tradition," shamans are Druids. The Druids of Celtic societies, like Orpheus, combined the professions of poet, magician, religious teacher, and oracle-giver. In Irish Celtic legend Cuchulain, like Orpheus, pays a visit to the underworld. In Welsh Celtic myth the hero Bran, again like Orpheus, continues to speak after his head has been severed from his body.

In the Greek myth of Orpheus and Eurydice, Orpheus repairs

to the underworld to retrieve Eurydice, who has gone there unwillingly. But Eurydice is a typical Celtic underworld queen, a fairy queen, sister to the Celtic Lorelei (mermaid) who lures men into danger. The list of Celtic heroes enchanted by fairy women is endless—and it begins with Orpheus.

Orpheus is said to have been able to charm the very stones and trees with charismatic eloquence; and eloquence was ever a trait of the Celts. Moreover, the Celtic Gauls, according to Lucian in the second century A.D., worshiped Orpheus in the form of Ogmios, their god of eloquence; and the Irish Celtic god Ogma was also a god of poetry and speech.

The oak tree was sacred to the Druids of Gaul and Britain; and at Zonë in Thrace in classical times there was a grove of oaks sacred to *Orpheus.*[87]

It seems obvious then that Orpheus was an early Druid and, therefore, an early Celt. He was a *renegade* Druid, however, and he met his death at the hands of the Druidesses—the holy wisewomen of Thrace. Thus just as Thrace is the missing link between the lost civilization and the historical civilizations, so Orpheus, the mystery man of antiquity, is the link between the ancient religion and the historical Druidism that has left so deep a mark on modern Western religious belief.

For Druidism was a *goddess* religion; and the Christians of Europe long remained true to their ancient goddess. The Romans had sought to abolish Druidism in their provinces—even going so far as to cut down the sacred oaks of Mona (Anglesea) in the Irish Channel—but only because of its necromantic aspects. They had no objection to goddess worship—they practiced it themselves. The Irish Celts, credited with having been the most easily "converted" of the pagans, were not converted at all. They merely changed the name of their goddess to Mary and went on worshiping her as before. And ritual Druidism went underground with the faerie folk.

The Sacred Bull

Perhaps the most widespread cult of the ancient world was the cult of the bull, the beast sacred to the Great Goddess. Even in the most remote reaches of myth and antiquity, wherever the goddess reigned supreme we find the sacred bull beside her. The ancient

Cretan god Poseidon, son of Potnia (the Powerful One), was a bull-god as well as a fish-god. Plato tells us that Poseidon was the god of Atlantis and that on Atlantis the bull was worshiped. The first ruler of Atlantis, mentioned by Diodorus Siculus in the first century B.C. but not by Plato, was Queen Basilea, who *predated* Poseidon. She it was, writes Diodorus in his mammoth *Library of History,* who brought order and law and justice to the world, after a bloody war against the forces of evil and chaos. She was a *warrior* queen, after the Celtic fashion, a prototype of Cartismandua, Veleda, Boadicea, and Tomyris.

Queen Basilea became the Great Goddess "of a hundred names yet only one personality," who was subsequently revered throughout the ancient world.[38] The unimaginable antiquity of this great queen is illustrated by the fact that she was said to be the daughter of Gaia, the primeval goddess who in later Hellenic myth created the world from Chaos, and was thus antecedent to Cronos, old "father time" himself, who was Gaia's son.

Wherever goddess worship spread, the sacred bull accompanied it. In India, where the bull is worshiped to this day, the bull cult was part of the goddess cult that prevailed there until Rama's time. Apis, the bull-god of Egypt, sacred to Isis, has long been known, as has the bull-god, the "golden calf," of ancient Palestine and Syria. This was Moloch, sacred to the Syrian goddess Ea (Tiamat), who was known and worshiped as 'Anat or Neith among the Jews.

Excavations at Nineveh, Babylon, and Ur, as well as at lesser cities of the Tigris-Euphrates valley, reveal that the bull accompanied the worship of the great fish-goddess, Tiamat, who is often depicted as a mermaid as on a seal dug up at Nineveh.[39] Poseidon has been identified as a later aspect of this same fish-goddess.[40]

The bull cult of ancient Crete has been well publicized through the story of the Minotaur, who represented generations of sacred bulls kept in luxury in the Labyrinth, and to whom, possibly, captive youths and maidens were occasionally sacrificed. He was sacred to the ancient goddess Potnia, prime deity of Crete and later of Mycenae. The bull and the labyris, the double ax of Crete, were the symbols of goddess worship and matriarchal rule throughout the ancient world, and they have been found carved or painted on the walls of caves of Paleolithic Europe, of temples of Neolithic Anatolia, and at Stonehenge in England, as well as in Bronze Age

Crete, Ionia, Pylos, Mycenae, Tiryns and in Italian Umbria and Rome.

In pre-Hellenic Athens the sacred bull took part in the cult of the Great Goddess Athene,[41] as Aristophanes recalls in both *The Frogs* and *The Clouds*. The bull cult in Greece, however, went out with the advent of Zeus in the eighth century. For, contrary to popular belief, Zeus did not achieve any stature in Greek religion, according to W. K. C. Guthrie, until the time of Hesiod and Homer.[42] Homer's elevation of Zeus in the *Iliad* was an anachronism, as Leonard Cottrell points out.[43] Zeus was a very minor god at the time of the Trojan War. That Homer knew this himself is shown by the fact that in the *Iliad* he gives Athene priority over Zeus, the king of the gods.

It was not until the sixth century B.C. that the Greek religious "reformers," as Guthrie calls them,[44] promoted Zeus to first place in the Greek pantheon. Orpheus must have lived just prior to the time of Greek religious reform. Some myths place him among the Argonauts of the generation before Troy, about 1300 B.C., but more reliable evidence dates him after the Dorian invasion and more or less contemporary with Thales, Anaximander, and Pythagoras of the sixth century, or, at the earliest, with Thamyris and Sappho of the seventh. (Sappho is said to have rescued his singing head from the beach at Lesbos.)

In Orpheus' homeland, Thrace, the bull had long been sacred to the goddess, yet in Orphic religion, which preached the supremacy of Zeus over Hera, the bull continued to hold its ancient place. This fact constitutes further proof that Orpheus was a renegade Druid, a heretic to the old religion. For the Druids of Thrace had always worshiped the bull, and bull worship persisted among the later Celts as late as the fourth century A.D.[45]

"The bull was worshiped by the Celts and its immolation was part of the Druidic ceremony,"[46] as it had been in the Orphic and Athenian religions. In India, Egypt, Crete, and Anatolia, the bull was not immolated, *i.e.*, sacrificed. The Celtic Picts of Scotland worshiped the bull and the goddess down to the seventeenth century when the Scottish church found it necessary to denounce bull sacrifice among the peasantry as sacrilegious.[47]

We can follow the bull cult from its point of origin in the locale of the lost civilization (call it Atlantis, or what you will) to prehistoric Sumer, and to historic Babylon, Crete, Egypt, Syria, and Greece. It thrived in Thrace and in Celtic Europe and Britain until modern times. And it always followed the goddess cult. Its last manifestation in organized religion was in Druidism.

In the past decade in archeological work at the site of the "oldest town in history," [48] Catal Huyuk in Anatolia, the link between the mythical and the historical has been found. For there, where the Great Goddess was undeniably supreme, the only creature who shares her shrines and temples is her sacred bull. "She was *the* Divinity, and with her went the sacred bull of Plato's lost continent." [49]

3

The Golden Age
and the Blessed Lady

The tradition of the Golden Age
arose from the natural regrets expressed by
the first colonists of the ancient people
when they recalled to remembrance the happy
territory of their nativity, and painted it
in glowing colors to their children.
                        —Sylvain Bailly

The Ages of Man

⋙ According to the Hellenic Greeks there had been five ages of man, of which all but the last, the Hellenic-Doric Iron Age, had been matriarchal. The Iron Age was characterized by Hesiod, who lived in it, as "the unworthy successor of the earlier ages." Degenerate, cruel, unjust, libidinous, unfilial, treacherous, were some of the adjectives applied to his own time by Hesiod, the poet. He has been called "the first nostalgic reactionary in Western civilization," for he bewailed the new ethic of male supremacy and denounced the triumph of patriarchy as a triumph of shameless robbery, force, and strife,[1] much as Gibbon and others were to bewail the triumph of Christianity over the gracious gods and goddesses of Greece.

The first age, the Golden Age, had been the time of paradise on earth, when "there were no gods" or kings, and "men lived without labor, never growing old, laughing much, and to whom death was no more terrible than sleep."[2] This was the time of the great lost civilization, which had become in the memory of man only an idealized, remote, and unrecapturable dream of childhood—man's "first fine careless rapture"—when the immortals walked this earth as human men and women.

The second age, the Silver Age, was the time of the powerful gynocracies that distinguished the revived civilization after the passing of the lost civilization. This age lasted many thousands of years, ending only in historical times. It was the time of the flourishing of the great civilizations of Sumer, Egypt, and Crete and is the stage of civilization to which poets refer as the Golden Age.

In the Silver Age, "men were utterly subject to their mothers, and dared not disobey them even though they lived to be a hundred years old." [3] They never made sacrifices, never made war, and never learned to hunt and kill.[4] Erich Fromm attributes the sense of bliss that pervaded this age to the belief in the Great Goddess, the mother goddess, who loved all her children equally, in contrast to the later father god whose love was conditioned upon blind obedience, conformity, and strict compliance with the paternal dicta.[5]

"The myth of the Golden Age," writes Graves, "derives from a tradition of tribal subservience to the . . . goddess; . . . the myth of the Silver Age also records matriarchal conditions, such as those surviving into recent times among the Picts [of Scotland]." [6] (And according to Terence Powell, the Celt authority, the Picts were pure Celts.[7])

The third age, following the Silver Age, was the early Bronze Age—a time when Crete still reigned supreme in the Aegean and throughout the known world. It was the time also when the first Greeks wandered across the sea into the Peloponnese from Anatolia, around 3000 B.C.,[8] and adopted the Cretan cult of the Great Goddess Potnia, whom they obviously identified with their own ancient Anatolian deity. These were the Achaeans, who about fifteen hundred years after their arrival in Greece absorbed the Cretan culture and established the great Minoan-Mycenaean civilization on the Mainland. It was during this age that men first learned to eat the flesh of animals.[9]

The later Bronze Age, the fourth age of man, was the heroic age of the Greeks. Its people were Homer's Achaeans, the Mycenaean heroes of Troy. Its last great king was Agamemnon, and its great city was Mycenae. The fifth and last race were the Dorians of the Iron Age, who swept down from Europe through Thrace around 1000 B.C., two hundred years after the Trojan War, destroyed the

Minoan-Mycenaean civilization, and brought the Dark Ages to Greece. They, like the Achaeans and Mycenaeans, were Indo-Europeans but, unlike these earlier Greeks, they brought with them their own new god—a male god, Zeus. It was they who abolished goddess worship and set up shrines to Zeus and his family throughout Greece. It was in Thrace, that land of mystery, that Zeus and the Dorians fought their first battles against the goddess, a fact which is memorialized in myth.[10]

During and after the invasion of the Dorians and the descent of Greece into temporary barbarism, the Silver Age was looked back upon with deep nostalgia as a time of peace and progress. To the non-Greeks this era became the Golden Age, and even Hesiod was to designate it as such. For this age had been one of worldwide advancement, and its passing was mourned for centuries to come by poets of many nations.

The Golden Age

Contrary to the popular impression that our early ancestors lived on warfare and violence, all the evidence, historical as well as archeological, points to the fact that man was pacific and warfare unknown before the patriarchal revolution. The classical age was aware of this truth, even though the Greeks and Romans knew less about their own past than we do today. Their gynocratic past "had been buried and forgotten," writes Jane Harrison about the Athenians;[11] and in Cato's time the Romans had forgotten that their mothers not long before had sat in the Roman Senate.[12]

Yet the Roman poets, like the poets of Greece, knew intuitively that there had been a time in the not too distant past, before the birth of the gods, when earth had been a semiparadise of peace and tranquillity, presided over by an omnipotent goddess. In the *Eclogues* Virgil prays for the return of the golden age, when "Justice [Themis] will reign *again* "and free the earth from never-ceasing fear." [13] And Lucretius recalls the vanished time when "terror and darkness were dispelled" by the goddess, "mother of the gods, sole mistress of all things, without whom nothing can be glad or lovely." [14]

That these atavistic dreams of the poets were not myths is proven by the research of modern scholarship. Anthropologists, historians, and archeologists now acknowledge the fact that the "first stages of mankind were peaceful and constructive" and ask why "barbarism succeeded the absolute peace of primitive mankind." [15] James Breasted emphasizes the pacific habits of the early Egyptians. They were "totally unwarlike," he writes, until they were taught violence by the invading nomadic Hyksos in the seventeenth century B.C.[16] And Sir Arthur Evans vouches equally for the peaceableness of the ancient Cretans. "The Minoans lived a comfortable life in peaceful conditions," he writes. "We have found nothing that suggests war, nothing to imply civil strife, or even defence against foreign raids." [17] And this condition lasted until the destruction of Knossos by the great earthquake and fire of the fifteenth century.

Sir Leonard Woolley, in excavating the predeluge city of Ur, found evidence of a "civilization of an astonishingly high order." And Cottrell adds, "We know from other excavations from Persia to the shores of the Mediterranean that these antediluvian peoples were considerably advanced," [18] and considerably unwarlike. "Curiously enough there were never any weapons," writes Woolley of early Alalakh,[19] and no evidence of human strife or violence has been found in any of the ancient cities of the Near East until late in the third millennium, when the patriarchal nomads first invaded the "sown lands of the Fertile Crescent." [20]

The prehistoric occupants of Britain, says Massingham, had no frontiers, no fortresses, no weapons, and no warrior class, for they needed none.[21] And August Thebaud, who firmly believed that nothing good could come from "paganism," reluctantly admits that the prehistoric, pre-Christian Irish had reached a "very high degree of civilization" in which peace and tranquillity seemed to prevail.[22]

"Of old, throughout all countries, religion possessed certain things in common, which belonged to the creeds of all nations, and were evidently derived from the primitive tradition of mankind. Such were the belief in a golden age, and in the fall from a happy beginning," wrote Thebaud in 1878.[23] And G. Eliot Smith, the anthropologist, wrote in 1924, before the more recent archeological revelations: "The careful analysis of all the available evidence seems to point clearly to the conclusion that the world once really enjoyed some such Golden Age as Hesiod describes." [24]

More and more, archeology is proving that there was indeed a golden age—a gynocratic age that endured for untold millennia, up past the dawn of written history. The recent excavations at Mersin and Çatal Huyuk in Anatolia would be sufficient to confirm the fact of its feministic character if there were no other evidence. Man was pacific, deity was feminine, and woman was supreme. Peace and justice prevailed under an all-merciful goddess, and the long robes of her priestesses remain to this day the habit of the male priests who followed after.

Monotheism, once thought to have been the invention of Moses or of Akhnaton, was worldwide in the prehistoric and early historical world. As E. O. James writes, "It seems that Evans was correct when he affirmed that it was 'a monotheism in which the female form of divinity was supreme.' " [25] Even almighty Yahweh, the god of Moses and the later Hebrews, was originally a goddess—Iahu-'Anat, whose very name was stolen from that of the Sumerian goddess. Theodor Reik asks whatever happened to the original goddess of the Jews. Then he answers his own question: "The Torah forms the base upon which Judaism rests. *She* is considered older than the world and *is assigned a cosmic role* [*in creation*]. . . . Even in this diluted form we recognize the primal female goddess." [26] (Author's italics.) And Robert Aron worries about the pre-Mosaic Jews. Whom did they worship before Jehovah? he asks. And then he comes to the Reikian conclusion: The Torah, older than God. [27]

As any perceptive reader of the Old Testament can realize, the Hebrew nation had a hard time suppressing goddess worship, representing as it did a deep nostalgia for the old days of peace and plenty. Raphael Patai points out forty places in the Old Testament where goddess worship among the Hebrews is mentioned, [28] even after all the patriarchal editing of later times. In the time of Jeroboam, the goddess shared the temple with Jehovah; and the reason Jezebel has such a bad reputation among Christians and Jews is that she was pro-goddess and anti-Jehovah and had converted King Ahab to her belief in the goddess.

"So deeply ingrained was . . . the goddess cult in Palestine," writes E. O. James, "that it survived all attempts at drastic reformation by the . . . Yahwists until the end of the monarchy." [29]

Even after the exile, as Jeremiah laments, the people persisted in worshiping the queen of heaven, whom "our fathers, our kings, and our princes" have always adored; "for then we had plenty, and were well, and saw no evil," [30] whereas Jehovah had brought evil times "and nothing but misfortune." [31]

The Hebrews, like peoples throughout the world, long remembered the golden age and its Great Goddess; for in the Age of Discovery the tradition was found to have survived among the primitives who had been cut off from the mainstream of civilization for thousands of years. Among the remnants of a forgotten influence retained among savage tribes that surprised and mystified our European explorers were the universal belief in a lost paradise similar to the Garden of Eden of Judeo-Christian myth and the belief in the primacy of a Great Goddess who was creator of the world and mother of all the gods.

The Blessed Lady

In original myth, as we have said, including the Judaic (and, therefore, that of Judaism's elder child, Christianity), there is an original Great Goddess who creates the universe, the earth, and the heavens, and finally creates the gods and mankind. Eventually she bears, parthenogenetically, a son who later becomes her lover, then her consort, next her surrogate and finally, in patriarchal ages, the usurper of her power.[32] In the measureless eons of her exclusive reign, however, she inaugurates civilization in all its aspects. Under her rule the earth enjoys a long period of peaceful progress during which time cities are built, law and justice are instituted, crops are planted and harvested, cattle are domesticated for their milk and wool, fire is discovered and utilized, the wheel is invented, ships are first constructed, and the arts, from ceramics and weaving to painting and sculpture, are begun.

Then suddenly all is ended. Paradise is lost. A dark age overtakes the world—a dark age brought on by cataclysm accompanied by a patriarchal revolution. Nomads, barbaric and uncivilized, roving bands of ejected, womanless men, destroy the civilized city states, depose the queens, and attempt to rule in their stead. The result is chaos. War and violence make their appearance, justice and law fly out the window, might replaces right, the Great Goddess is replaced by a stern and vengeful God, man becomes carnivorous, property rights become paramount over human rights, woman is degraded and exploited, and civilization starts on the downward path it still pursues.

Such is the theme of all myth—from the Golden Age of the Greeks and Romans to the Garden of Eden of Jew and Christian, the Happy Hunting Ground of the American Indian, and the Avaiki of the Polynesians—all ending in a fall from paradise and in utter failure.

Oswald Spengler attributes the failure of modern civilization to a "Faustian" quality in modern man, as opposed to what he terms an "Apollonian" quality in ancient man.[33] His definition of "Faustian" man is analogous to our definition of patriarchal man, to whom "conflict is the essence of existence"; while his definition of "Apollonian" man accords with our view of ancient Gynarchic man, to whom "all conflict was evil."

"The civilization of the classical world," writes Ruth Benedict, "was built upon [Spengler's] Apollonian view of life; and the modern world has been working out in all its institutions the implications of the Faustian view." [34] Hence, the patriarchal, or masculist, disorder of society.

Edward Carpenter drew this distinction between ancient matriarchal Apollonian man and modern patriarchal Faustian man when he wrote: "Her [woman's] powers are more co-ordinated, more in harmony with each other, where his [man's] are disjointed and in conflict. . . . The point is that man, with his uncoordinated nature, has during these latter centuries dominated the other sex and made himself the ruler of society. . . . So naturally we have a society made after his pattern—advanced in mechanical invention, but all involved in a whirling confusion and strife, which on its human side is an *utter failure*." [35]

Spengler, Carpenter, and all the philosophers and poets since Hesiod who have mourned the decline of Western civilization, are, like Gibbon, mourning the passing of the matriarchal age and deploring the "force and strife" that characterize our modern patriarchal society. What all these men really want is a return to the golden age of matriarchy and the restoration of the great goddess. "Her cult [meets] certain vital needs of mankind at all times," writes James.[36] And Graves adds: "There can be no escape from the present more than usually miserable state of the world . . . until the repressed desire of the Western races, which is for some form of Goddess worship, . . . finds satisfaction at last." [87]

In recent months, a French artist[88] and an American clergyman[89] have written books in which they explain world history as the working out of a master plan by some space hierarchy to create a perfect race in our galaxy, using earth as a laboratory. According to this hypothesis, several experimental races have been planted here only to be destroyed eventually as failures. Among such failures were the preadamic peoples who were wiped out before Eden and the race of Adam (earthman) destroyed in the Flood. The re-created postdiluvian race was scheduled for destruction around the beginning of our era, and Jesus, a spaceman, was sent to warn the worthy of their impending doom. All evidence, writes Paul Misraki, points to the intended destruction of the human race around the middle of the first century A.D. But then something happened to change the ordained plan. Earthman was reprieved at the last minute and given a second chance. What happened? According to Misraki, the "death" of Mary happened. About the year 50 C.E., Mary was returned bodily to the superrace from whom she had come and at once began to plead for man's reprieve. At her request the "end" was postponed and is still being postponed through Mary's continuing intercession—wherefore the appearances at Lourdes, Fatima, etc.

This hypothesis accords well with that of many distinguished scientists—Agrest, Shklovskii, Sagan, Freeman J. Dyson, Thomas Gold, to name a few—that the main line of humanity was *planted* here at different intervals in the past by a colonizing race from some distant star. According to this theory, the planted race has been held back and degraded by interbreeding with the indigenous types, the products of evolution via the apes, of whom Neanderthal man was one result.

Neanderthal man, the brutish caveman of popular fancy, did not die out but was absorbed by the unevolved races, the planted colonists, of whom Cro-Magnon man was an exponent. If one examines the remains of Neanderthal man and compares them with the remains of Cro-Magnon man, one finds it hard to believe that they could both have evolved along the same lines and from the same ancestor. Neanderthal man was short, squat, shaggy, small-brained, uncreative—more animal than man. Cro-Magnon man, and woman, who appeared "suddenly" out of the nowhere in southwestern Europe about twenty thousand years ago, was tall, erect, creative, and intelligent—more intelligent, judging by his brain pan, than modern man. While Neanderthal man was chinless, browless, prognathous, and hairy, Cro-Magnon man had a well-defined chin, a high forehead, a small jaw, and was almost devoid of body hair.

Where did he come from? How did he arrive so suddenly in south*western* Europe—Spain and France—without apparently having traversed middle Europe, if he came from the east, or Italy, if he came from Africa? The crossing from Africa by way of Gibraltar into Spain would have been impossible, as it remained for thousands of years, owing to the fatal whirlpools and hidden shoals—the Scylla and Charybdis of the ancients. Some have guessed that he came from the west, from the Atlantic ocean, and some have guessed that he came from the sky.

Misraki's hypothesis, therefore, is merely a Christianized version of the colonization theory as opposed to the evolutionary theory of man's origin on earth. Omitting Adam, Jesus, and Mary from Misraki's account, we have left the lost civilization, the revival of civilization at Sumer, and the Great Goddess as guide and supervisor of the whole affair. Is Mary, then, merely a new manifestation of the goddess who, according to the *Enuma Elish,* was "Creator of all and Mother of mankind"?

For it is a fact that the most frequent visitor to earth, according to mystics and visionaries both great and small, is a "lady." Christians have always assumed her to be Mary, but non-Christians have given her different identities. Lucius called her the Queen of Heaven, and she called herself, when she appeared to him: "The Mother of all things, master and governor of the universe, chief of the powers divine, queen of all that dwell in heaven and in hell; at my will the planets of the sky and the winds of the seas are disposed. My divinity is adored throughout the world, by many names. For the Phrygians call me Mother of the Gods; the Athenians, Athene; the Cyprians, Venus; the Cretans, Diana; the Sicilians, Proserpine; the Eleusinians, their ancient Goddess Ceres; some Juno, some Minerva, some Hera, others Bellona, others Hecate, others Rhamnusia. But the Egyptians, which are excellent in all kinds of ancient knowledge, do call me by my true name, Queen Isis." [40]

And to further correlate this blessed lady with the blessed Mary of Misraki, she adds, as an indication of her Mary-like intercessionary powers: "I alone may prolong thy days beyond the time the Fates have ordained." [41]

The identity of the virgin goddess Isis with the Christian virgin goddess Mary is pointed out by Carpenter: "The Virgin Mary with the holy child in her arms can be traced by linear descent back to Egyptian Isis with the infant Horus, and thence to the constellation Virgo shining in the sky. In the representations of the zodiac in the Temple of Denderah in Egypt, the figure of Virgo is annotated by a smaller figure of Isis with Horus in her arms; and so the Roman church fixed the celebration of Mary's assumption into glory at the very date of the said constellation's disappearance from sight in August, and her birth on the date of the same constellation's reappearance in September." [42]

The frequent appearances throughout history of a lovely lady in "white and shining vestments, her fair hair garlanded with a crown of flowers," [43] as Apuleius described her two thousand years ago and as the children of Fatima described her only fifty years ago, is most significant. Why is the blessed one always a lady? Why never a gentleman? The explanation may lie, as Graves says, in Western man's repressed desire for a goddess. But it also may lie in the fact that the blessed one, the ruler of the universe, *is* a woman—the Great Goddess of man's first million or more years.

4

Archeology Speaks

*Tested by historically established
truths, the mythical tradition is seen
to be an authentic, independent record
of the primordial age, a record in which
invention plays no part.*

—J. J. BACHOFEN

The Great Goddess

The universal desire of mankind "to depict Her and worship
Her image heralded the birth of art." "Between 9000 and 7000
B.C.," says James Mellaart, "art makes its appearance in the Near
East in the form of statuettes of the supreme deity, the Great Goddess." [1] Her image, carved on a bird's beak no larger than a man's
fingernail, or struck out of a megalith weighing hundreds of tons,
abounded throughout the world. Archeologists dig them up nearly
every day, these effigies of the original deity of man.

They are the earliest works of art ever discovered, one, the Venus
of the Wildenmannlisloch Cave, dating back *seventy thousand
years*.[2] The area of their finds stretches from Ireland to Siberia,
through the Mediterranean area, the Near East, and Northern
Africa. Earlier archeologists, or "antiquarians" as they were called
in the nineteenth century, brushed them off as fertility charms.
But this explanation has been abandoned in the light of growing
evidence that they represent man's first fumbling attempts to
depict the godhead. An analogy may be drawn between the assumption that these figures were fertility charms and the possible assumption of some future civilization that our crucifixes were merely
good-luck charms. "No one looking at these dainty little figures
would form the impression that they were intended to induce fertility by magical means," writes Ivar Lissner.[3]

73

"That the worship of the Goddess was an integral element in the megalithic culture of Europe," writes E. O. James, "is shown by the recurrence of its symbolism in the form of statue-menhirs and other designs in Brittany, the Channel Isles, and in Britain itself. . . ." The goddess was the dominant influence "from India to the Mediterranean," and archeological evidence "has revealed the unique position occupied by the Goddess" *throughout the ancient* world. "Moreover it is now becoming increasingly evident that she had a wide-spread influence and played a very significant rôle in the subsequent development of the ancient religions from India to Palestine, from Neolithic times to the Christian era. . . . *Her cult was the most effective rival to Christianity."* [4] (Author's italics.)

Since James wrote in 1957, revolutionary new evidence has been uncovered in Anatolia of the accuracy of his assumptions. The evidence for the gynarchic origins of our civilization and for the primary worship of a female deity is astonishing, as we shall see in the following section. Also, however, other evidence has accumulated that not all the archeological finds of female effigies were meant to represent the goddess. Among the goddess figures there are portraits of living women. There is no appearance of stereotype, even in digs at the same location dating from the same period. The images vary from slim-hipped, small-boned lovelies to gross caricatures of pregnancy—all breast, buttock, and belly. The faces vary as greatly—from featureless blobs to expressions of delicate winsomeness and mystic wisdom. In Egypt there is no question of their humanness, found as they were among male effigies. "The statuettes of the Nagadah I culture [fourth millennium B.C.] molded in clay or carved in bone, include the first *human* portraits in the round. What is remarkable is the predominance of female figures," writes Wolfhart Westendorf.[5]

"Remarkable" is the word invariably employed by archeologists when they come upon evidence of the former dominance of women. "Remarkable" will be the reaction of archeologists of the eightieth century, digging in the ruins of the lost civilization of the twentieth; for any evidence that women even existed in the last few centuries of the Christian era will be utterly lacking. Future archeologists will find that all our statues are of men, all our coins bear male likenesses, the cornerstones and capstones of all our public buildings are carved with the names of men only, and all our archives preserved by chance in subterranean caves will deal solely with the deeds of men. Records of women's former existence will be as scarce in the archeological finds of the future as are the records of men in the prehistoric archeology of today. Eventually one of our future archeologists will come up with the astounding theory that Christian era man was able to reproduce himself partheno- or anthropogenetically and, like the Amazons of old in reverse, murdered his female offspring and reared only the males.

The Matriarchal Theory

It is "remarkable" that the many varied and highly expert author-archeologists in the excellent series *Ancient Peoples and Places*⁶ express their wonder at the evidence they have found that women were once preeminent in each of their areas of research, from the Near East to Ireland. Each writes as if this ancient dominance of women were unique and peculiar to his archeological province. Yet taken all together these archeological finds prove that feminine preeminence was a universal, and not a localized, phenomenon.

Bachofen recognized the truth of our gynocratic origins without benefit of the archeological discoveries of modern times. He wrote in the nineteenth century, basing his conclusions only on the study of "ancient authors, myth, surviving customs, place names, and language," that: "All [the evidence] joins to form a single picture and leads to the conclusion that matriarchy is not confined to any particular people, but marks a [universal] cultural stage" preceding that of the patriarchal system.⁷ It was "a cultural stage that was overlaid or totally destroyed by the later development of the ancient world." ⁸

Max Muller, before Bachofen, had sensed in the ancient myths a universality suggestive of a common origin in historical fact but concluded that the key to their interpretation had been irrevocably lost. Myths were interpreted by the majority of nineteenth-century scholars, from Grimm to Bulfinch, as "manifestations of

natural phenomena, and the individuals of the stories as imper-
sonifications [sic] of natural forces," as Sabine Baring-Gould
remarks.[9] This was the anthropomorphic theory of mythology in
which, as Baring-Gould says, "all heroes represent the sun, all
villains the demons of night and winter, all spears and arrows the
lightning, and all cows and sheep and dragons and swans the
clouds." [10] Bachofen insisted, and rightly as it turns out, that myths
represent not fictions but historical realities: "All the myths relating
to [matriarchy] embody a memory of real events experienced by
the human race." [11]

Early Greek history was shrugged off as mythological fancy born
in the fertile imaginations of Hesiod, Homer, and Herodotus.
We know now that Homer, whom Alexander Pope called "the
most inventive of poets," [12] invented nothing. Archeology has
shown that Homer in the *Iliad* was a reporter purely and simply,
that Herodotus was amazingly accurate in his accounts of ancient
peoples and their histories and cultures, and that Hesiod was
more historian than mythologist: "What he [Hesiod] has to say
of the first idyllic condition of mankind," writes Erwin Rohde,
"and its gradual deterioration is given not as an abstract exposi-
tion . . . but as a traditional account of what actually happened—
in fact, as *history*." [13]

The accumulating archeological evidence of the matriarchal
origins of human society calls for a drastic rewriting of the history
of mankind on earth. "The original matriarchy is obvious," writes
Graves, "despite the patriarchal interpretation of the Old and
New Testaments." And James Hastings' *Encyclopedia of Religion
and Ethics* states that "it is certain that by far the most frequent
process throughout the world has been the transition from mother-
right, [matriarchy], to father-right, [patriarchy]." [14]

"The violence of the antagonism against the theory of matriarchy
arouses the suspicion that it is . . . based on an emotional prejudice against an assumption so foreign to the thinking and feeling
of our patriarchal culture," writes Erich Fromm.[15]

Yet the theory "has been irrefutably confirmed," says Campbell,
by such archeological breakthroughs as the decipherment of the
Cretan Linear B tablets—"a preHellenic treasure trove" [16]—and
by the recent excavations in Anatolia.

Catal Huyuk

In the few years since Campbell wrote those words in 1964, far more astonishing proof of Bachofen's theory has come to light in Anatolia, particularly at Catal Huyuk, "the oldest town known in the history of civilization." [17] Since 1950 archeology has been busily at work in modern Turkey uncovering incontrovertible facts that have caused historians to revise their entire concepts of the remote past of human history.

Among these new facts is the unsuspected (by some) antiquity of civilized human society. The society of the ninth millennium B.C.—more than ten thousand years ago—has now been found to have been more civilized than many subsequent societies of historical times. Contrary to the recently held belief that Anatolia had been bypassed by man until the Hittite emergence there in the second millennium, archeology now reveals that the great Hittite civilization of historical times *"was not a beginning but the end* [author's italics] of a long period of development. It was not brought" there, but evolved there, as Jean Marcadé writes.[18]

The recent "discovery of the Anatolian Neolithic has revolutionized the prehistory of the Near East" [19]—and of the world. It has knocked into a cocked hat the popular theory, still accepted by laymen and still disseminated in the textbooks, that our present civilization originated in the Tigris-Euphrates valley of Iraq, among a Semitic people. For, contrary to previous belief, Anatolia was not "colonized" by Semitic or Oriental peoples from Mesopotamia and Palestine but was itself the source of these and other civilizations and was "an important centre in the diffusion of culture" in the Near East and the Aegean.[20] Its people have been found to have been primarily of Indo-European stock, and pottery found in northern Anatolia can be traced to European Thrace and the Danube region.[21]

Since 1966 detailed reports have been made on three prehistoric towns in Anatolia: Mersin, Hacilar, and Catal Huyuk. And in all of them the message is clear and unequivocal: ancient society was gynocratic and its deity was feminine. At all three sites "the cult of the goddess was predominant," says Alkim,[22] and her predominance continued throughout the Neolithic and well into the

Bronze ages, for "in the Bronze age levels the main theme is [still] the great goddess." [26]

James Mellaart, the archeologist in charge of the first digs at Catal Huyuk, was overwhelmed by the implications of the earliest revelations there. That the civilization expressed at Catal Huyuk was woman-dominated, he writes, "is . . . obvious." Mellaart commenced his excavations at Catal Huyuk late in 1961, and the work still goes on. For the ancient city covers more than thirty-two acres of land and consists of at least twelve levels—city piled upon city dating back perhaps to the year 10,000 B.C. The earliest radiocarbon dating available gives a reading of 7000 B.C.—nine thousand years ago—but internal evidence suggests that the city may have been over a thousand years old even then; and the lowest levels had not then been reached.

Mellaart's report, written in 1966 before the completion of the excavations, shows that Catal Huyuk, whatever its name may have been ten thousand years ago, was not only a matriarchal but a utopian society. There had been no wars for a thousand years. There was an ordered pattern of society. There were no human or animal sacrifices; pets were kept and cherished. Vegetarianism prevailed, for domestic animals were kept for milk and wool—not for meat. There is no evidence of violent deaths. Women were the heads of households, and they were reverently buried, while men's bones were thrown into a charnel house. Above all, the supreme deity in all the temples was a goddess.[24]

Each of these findings corroborates Bachofen's' idea of what early matriarchal societies were like. In his *Mutterrecht,* published in 1861, over a hundred years before the discovery of Catal Huyuk, he wrote: "An air of tender humanity permeated the culture of the matriarchal world, that primordial race of women with whom all peace vanished from the earth. . . . Matriarchal states were famed for their freedom from strife and conflict. . . . Matriarchal peoples assigned special culpability to the physical injury of any living creature, even of animals." [25] Yet Alkim wonders at the absence of defensive walls in the earlier levels of Hacilar and marvels at the apparent lack of violence toward wild animals depicted in the wall paintings of Catal Huyuk.

Bachofen's belief in the "historicity of myth" thus finds surprising confirmation, for in Catal Huyuk we have the confirma-

tion of the myth of the golden and silver ages, when men lived
on the fruits of the ground, drinking the milk of goats, and were
"utterly subject to their mothers."

In the golden age of Judeo-Christian myth, paradise was a land
"flowing with milk and honey." And it may surprise the patriarchal
Jews and Christians of today to learn that milk and honey both
symbolize feminine rule. In masculine paradises, like that of
Islam, *wine* is served. Milk symbolizes gynarchy for obvious reasons, and honey because the honeybee "represents the feminine
principle in nature. The life of the bee shows matriarchy in its
clearest and purest form," and Aristotle considered bee society
more advanced than that of man.[26]

"The Greek historians," contrary to the historians of the Christian era, "realized the important truth that tradition and myth
were based on facts," as A. M. Hocart writes.[27] And so in Greek
thought the myths of the golden and silver ages were accepted
as reflections of an actual stage in human history. And now archeology indicates that the Greeks were right.

Probably of primary interest to the prehistorian, "the tracer of
lost peoples," is the physical proof—"touch-and-handle proof,"
to borrow Jane Harrison's phrase—at Catal Huyuk of the close
connection between the Anatolians and the Cretans. We have long
known that the bull was a gynarchic symbol and that the bulls'
horns were phallic symbols sacred to the goddess. In the excavations of Crete some years ago the sacredness of the bull was made
plain, as was also the popularity of the national Cretan sport of
"bull-leaping," a game in which the players might be injured but
never the bull. Plato wrote, in *Critias*, that bull-leaping was a
sport popular in Atlantis, and since ancient Crete had been forgotten in classical Greece and her ruins were unknown, modern
scholars have wondered where Plato derived the idea. We still do
not know that, but we do know now where the Cretans derived
the idea of bull-leaping—from no other people than the Anatolians
of Catal Huyuk.

"We can recognize," writes U. Bahadir Alkim of the University
of Istanbul, "the sport of bull-leaping—one of the favorite themes
of Cretan painting—in wall paintings at Catal Huyuk," nine thousand years ago.[28]

An important revelation at Catal Huyuk was the abundance

of bulls' horns found in the goddess shrines and their resemblance to the "horns of consecration" of Crete and the later Aegean.[29] Of equally great significance is the fact that the labyris, the sacred double ax of Crete, symbol of the goddess and of matriarchal rule, is found painted on the temple walls of Catal Huyuk.[30] The double ax, "the sign of Imperial might," was the symbol of gynocratic power in Crete as it was among the Lycians, the Lydians, the Amazons, the Etruscans, and even the Romans.[31] It has been found in the graves of Paleolithic women of Europe, buried 50,000 years ago.[32] And it appears carved in the sacred stones of pre-Celtic Stonehenge in England, facts which bespeak the close connection between early Stone-Age Europe, the mysterious build- ers of Stonehenge, and the ax-cultists of the prehistoric Aegean world, and Anatolia.[33] For, as Bachofen could not have known but as we now know, it was also the symbol of matriarchal power in Anatolian Catal Huyuk ten thousand years ago.

"The cult of the goddess and the worship of the bull," con- cludes Alkim, "are features common to Catal Huyuk and Hacilar in Anatolia on the one hand, and to the Minoan religion on the other, which prove the existence of a bond between Anatolia and Crete" in prehistoric times.[34]

Another revelation in Anatolian archeology is the proof offered of the "subservience of man" to women, as Mellaart expresses it.[35] The inferior position of the male sex in ancient societies had long been postulated by scholars from Lewis Henry Morgan and Bachofen to Briffault and Graves. But proof, except in the later modified matriarchates of Crete and Etruria, had been lacking. Now we can see that in civilized societies of four to ten thousand years ago, man was indeed the "second sex" and woman was su- preme.

Of interest in the discoveries at Catal Huyuk is the evidence for vegetarianism, evidence which will force us to revise the old picture of the hunting caveman dragging his kill home to his wife and children. For as we shall see, carnivorousness was a late develop- ment in human history, and hunting man came *after* agricultural man.[36]

But of primary interest is the evidence disclosed at Catal Huyuk that funerary honors and reverent burial were reserved primarily for women. This phenomenon had been discovered earlier in

Italian Umbria and had been thought a custom peculiar to the Etruscans of the millennium immediately preceding the Christian era. But Catal Huyuk reveals that the custom was by no means peculiar to any one people, any one place, or any one time. We will find that it prevailed throughout Europe and the Near East from as early as 50,000 B.C. up into the early centuries of the present age.

Even Tombs Have Tongues

A myth that patriarchal historians have delighted to perpetuate is that in ancient times wives were oft interred with their husbands' bones, as were dogs and horses. But this equation of women with animals is an exclusively Judeo-Christian concept and did not exist in the pre-Semitic Near East or in pre-Christian Europe. The wishful belief in the expendability of women was voiced as late as 1943 by an archeologist who, in describing a tomb discovered at Mycenaean Dendra, reconstructs the burial as follows: "Then the king's servant, his dog, and *possibly his wife* [author's italics] are laid in their places, covered with earth, and large stone slabs are placed over the filled pits." [37]

The author of this unwise deduction very wisely uses the precautionary "possibly" in connection with the martyred wife; for subsequent archeological research has shown the utter impossibility of any such wife sacrifice in Mycenaean or any other ancient Western civilization or pre-Semitic Eastern civilization. The situation was far more likely to have been reversed—men buried in women's tombs, as in the case of the unknown Egyptian pharaoh buried at Sakkara as well as of the Sumerian queen Shubad.

Like the tombs discovered at Catal Huyuk where the buried skeletons were far more apt to be women's than men's,[38] these fourth-millennium tombs at Ur and Sakkara speak in loud accents of the ancient priority of women. And, like the above-mentioned tomb at Dendra, their significance was at first misinterpreted by the male-oriented archeologists who discovered them.

When the magnificent tomb of Shubad was discovered at Ur in the early 1920's, speculation was rife as to her identity. It was naturally assumed that she was the wife of some great king. But of what king? There was no king buried anywhere nearby. It was then conjectured that she was the "sacred" bride of a king or god, sacrificed in some prehistoric agricultural ceremony. In 1939 F. Bohl offered the opinion that "in a sacred marriage rite the bride of the god may be killed, but the man who impersonates the god is not likely to be similarly treated," [39] an error that more recent scholarship has rendered ridiculous: for in ancient religions it was the young husband of the goddess-queen who was ritually sacrificed, not the bride of the god-king, since god-kings were unheard of. The only male deity so far discovered in ancient times has been the small child occasionally depicted with the goddess, as in the wall paintings at Catal Huyuk.

Moreover, Shubad was obviously no virginal bride. Her remains indicated that she was a woman of forty, mature and regal. She was obviously a queen in her own right; and the fact that her name does not appear on the predeluge Sumerian king lists indicates only that she, like so many other ancient queens, fell a victim to later editing by masculist historians.

The unknown pharaoh buried at Sakkara about the same time that Shubad was interred at Ur, too, is omitted from history. Yet the splendor of her tomb leaves no doubt that she was once a mighty monarch. With her were found the bones of uncountable men, together with the tools of their trade, who were sacrificed and buried with her—"craftsmen who would serve the dead woman in the afterlife." [40] If the Christian soul winces at this evidence of human sacrifice, let it not be forgotten that the early Christians, and even Jesus himself, sacrificed living animals; and the difference is one of degree, not of kind.

When the tombs of Italian Tuscany were unearthed in the nineteenth century, their implications were astonishing. For in every tomb the place of honor was reserved for the *materfamilias,* the woman head of the family. So invariable was this rule that Raniero Mengarelli, nineteenth-century archeologist, "formulated a new law: that in Etruscan tombs the body of the man, on the left, was disposed on a kliné (a platform); that of the woman, always on the right, in a sarcophagus. . . . It seems," writes Jacques Heurgeon, "that the purpose of this difference was to make sure that a certain category of the dead—the women—would have a more sacred character. . . . The sarcophagus functioned as a kind of reliquary protecting *particularly precious* [author's italics] remains." [41]

This evident reverence for women in Etruria is echoed in the tombs found so recently at Catal Huyuk in far-off Anatolia, where "the privileged dead found in the shrines . . . were most, *if not all* [author's italics], . . . of the female sex." [42] And another echo is heard even in farther off Wessex in fifth-millennium England, where, as J. F. S. Stone writes: "It would seem that the rite of disc-barrow burial was reserved very largely for women-folk;" [43] and again in Paleolithic Europe of fifty thousand years ago. For Frederic-Marie Bergounioux says that most of the graves of that remote period "contain only a single, richly ornamented, *female* [author's italics] skeleton." [44] Reverence for women was indeed an ancient and long-enduring custom of the human race.

Since 1943 archeological evidence of this philogyny has popped up all over Europe. In Mycenaean Greece the majority of the tombs unearthed in recent years have been found to be empty, devastated by grave robbers in antiquity. Predictably it was assumed that the most magnificent of these rifled tombs were those of kings. Yet one of the few unmolested tombs so far revealed, one of great wealth and munificence, has proved to be that of a young girl, "a small girl who was laid to rest in this deep grave with a good assortment of precious ornaments," reports G. E. Mylonas. "Around her skull was a diadem made of gold, with beads of crystal and of amethyst suspended from it." [45]

Patriarchal myth has handed down the stirring tradition of prehistoric European burials in which the big chief is laid to rest with his faithful steed, his faithful retainers, and his numerous wives—all the latter buried alive, as "reconstructed" by Axel Persson above. In the first place, our European ancestors—Celtic, Greek, or Roman—were all monogamous. In the second place, the great "chief" found in the typical Celtic grave is far more apt to be a woman than a man.

In 1954 at Reinheim, near Saarbrücken, Germany, the grave of a fourth-century B.C. Celtic woman was unearthed. It was proclaimed the richest Celtic grave yet discovered—until a similar grave was found in France at Vix near Châtillon-sur-Seine. This too was the grave of a woman. In both graves gold abounded, in excess of any treasure yet found in Celtic warrior graves. Golden bracelets, flagons, *cups* and *torques* had been buried with the body in each grave, and both graves had been lined with heavy oak, so thick that remnants of the planks still survive after twenty-three centuries under the ground. The oak lining is a feature that has not yet been found in any Celtic *men's* graves in Europe or in Britain. "It was as if they had considered women to be of a superior essence," as Heurgeon says of the Etruscans, and the oaken lining served as "a kind of reliquary protecting particularly precious remains." [46]

The most mystifying aspect of these and other Celtic women's graves is the presence in all of them of golden torques. The torque was a peculiarly Celtic ornament, a yokelike circular band, opened at the front, that was worn about the neck by Celtic *men*. It is present in paintings and sculptures of Gallic and British warriors that survive from Roman times, outstandingly in the well-known statue of the dying Gaul. And it is never seen on women. Yet, to quote T. G. F. Powell, the great Celt authority, "it is interesting that the most splendid gold torcs come from *women's* [author's italics] tombs. There are examples from very few warrior graves," and these latter are of bronze, not gold. "*Bronze* torcs are known from some few warrior graves; and yet for the living, as opposed to the dead, the torc was essentially a male ornament." [47] Why, then, do they appear most frequently in women's graves? And why gold in women's graves and bronze in men's?

Powell worries about this inconsistency too and with typical male ratiocination offers an untenable hypothesis: "This is only put forward as a possible explanation for the absence of gold torcs from men's graves," he hedges; "but, a man's torc might well have been inheritable as a symbol of the headship of the family or tribe" [48] and thus, presumably, have been handed down from father to son. Brave try as this is, it does not come close to explaining the prevalence of gold torques in women's graves, the occasional presence of bronze torques in men's graves, or what happened to the gold torques that were handed down from father to son. Gold torques do not simply evaporate, and they would be somewhere now if they had ever existed.

A far more plausible explanation is that the gold torque was a symbol of supreme authority and that the bronze torques were something like brands worn by the warriors to signify their debt of service and fidelity to the owners of the gold torques—the women. It is significant that the gold torques average six to six and a half inches in diameter, while the bronze torques measure eight to eight and a half inches. Since the large Celtic male would have been choked by a six-inch torque, and since the women did not wear torques, it seems more than probable that the small gold torque was merely a symbol—a symbol of authority that was buried with its owner to indicate *her* status as "head of the family or tribe."

Powell's alternative hypothesis is that the torques in women's graves "could have been head ornaments." But this idea is bashed by the finding with the gold torques of diadems—definitely head ornaments—as worn by the little Mycenaean girl and by the Celtic lady buried at Vix.[49] No. The golden torques must have been a survival of the sacred objects connected with the ancient matriarchal civilization, like the lunar ax and the golden cup of Aegina, Argos, and of Celtic Britain,[50] all of which, Herodotus noted, were sacred relics among the Celts—"golden relics which had fallen from the sky."

"From the Tigris in Asia to Portugal," writes Bergounioux of Paleolithic Europe and Asia Minor, "the ritual representation of the goddess is to be found. . . . In Champagne, in France, she is shown carrying an *ax*"—fifty thousand years ago![51]

And in nearly all these ancient figures of the great goddess of fifty millennia ago, she "who was the source of everything both good and harmful," as Bergounioux describes her, is shown wearing "a *cylindrical necklace* [author's italics]."[52] And what is a "cylindrical necklace" if not a *torque?*

The bulls' horns found in the goddess shrines at Catal Huyuk are, as Alkim says, "prototypes of the 'horns of consecration' shown in the Cretan palaces of a much later period."[53] And these Aegean "horns of consecration," writes R. E. M. Wheeler, were no other than the golden torques of the later Celts of Europe.[54]

The golden yoke of Herodotus' account, the "cylindrical necklace" of Paleolithic Europe, the bulls' horns of Neolithic Anatolia, the horns of consecration of highly civilized Bronze Age Crete and the Aegean, and the golden torque of Celtic Europe were all one and the same thing—the symbol of goddess worship, of matriarchal rule, and of female supremacy throughout the ancient world.

5

Anthropology Speaks

We discern in primitive customs the
remains of an ancient and pure system,
derived from wise instructors, which
has been corrupted by superstitious
and degraded peoples.

— Sylvain Bailly

The First Family and the Origin of Taboos

Of supreme importance in the archeological revelations of Anatolia has been the confirmation of the myth of female authority in the golden and silver ages of man—the proof that woman domination was a fact not only of Paleolithic and Neolithic life but that it endured into the highly civilized Bronze Age of historical times.

The popular concept of the primitive family group, complete with domineering father, cowed and submissive mother, and tumbling human cubs littering the cave-home floor, has been completely discredited; yet it remains the image of "caveman" life as portrayed in the widely disseminated media of comic strip and television serial today.

The fact is that the earliest human family consisted of a woman and her children. "The patriarchal family was entirely unknown," writes Lewis Henry Morgan. "It was not until after *recorded* civilization commenced that it became established." [1] Fatherhood and the idea of permanent mating were very late comers in human history. So late, as a matter of fact, is the idea of paternity that the word for father does not even exist in the original Indo-European language, as the philologist Roland Kent points out.[2]

The *Encyclopaedia Britannica* (1964 edition) says that where no *word* existed in the ancient Indo-European language for any concept or object, it may be accepted as a truism that that concept or object was unknown to the Indo-Europeans. And since this original language did not break up into the classical and modern languages that have descended from it, according to Kent, until about 3000 B.C.,[8] it seems obvious that fatherhood was unknown even as recently as five thousand years ago.

Even today there are peoples who believe that sex and pregnancy are completely unrelated. Bronislaw Malinowski describes tribes which believe that it helps to have the virgin's vagina opened by a man for the easier entrance into the womb of the future child's spirit, but the idea that the man has anything whatever to do with the making of the baby is beyond the comprehension of the natives.

In various islands of Oceania where many traces of the original worldwide gynocracy survive, a man looks upon his own children as the children of his wife. "Whatever he does for the child is a payment (*mapula*) for what their mother, his wife, has done for him."[4] Thus in the native mind the gratitude the husband feels for his wife, "and not any idea, however slight or remote, of physical fatherhood," is the reason for a man's interest in his offspring. "It must be clearly understood that physiological *fatherhood* does not exist in the mind of the natives."[5]

Our earliest ancestors were no wiser. Man felt no obligation for the protection or support of his offspring, for the simple reason that he was unaware that he had any offspring. Children belonged to women, who alone were their creators and begetters. Thus the full responsibility for the children fell to the mother, as it still does among the higher mammals as well as among some human groups, such as the American blacks, the Melanesians, and the Micronesians.

The male of the species was "a marauding beast" and "woman was his sexual prey," as Briffault has expressed it.[6] Women, in order to protect themselves and their children from these marauding beasts, soon banded together and formed the first communities—manless except for the young boys of the group. "When the gens appeared, it united several sisters with their children and descendants in the female line, in perpetuity, in a tribe which became the unit of organization in the social system."[7] The extended period of this stage of society, lasting thousands upon thousands of years, may be realized from the multiplicity of taboos that arose from it

and from the persistence with which these taboos have lasted—
many into modern life in America by way of Christian codes of
conduct. The most persistent of these taboos is that of incest—a
prohibition decreed by the earliest matriarch to protect herself
and her daughters from the sexual abuse of her growing sons.

The Crime of Incest

Incest is so unspeakable a crime among certain modern primitives that ridiculous extremes are adopted to prevent it. In the
Pacific islands brothers and sisters are separated from infancy on,
and "death will mysteriously fall on a boy who *eats* with his sisters
or his mother." [8] That this was a matriarchically ordained custom
is proven by the fact that in Hawaii it was abolished in the nineteenth century by a *queen*—Kaahumanu—when she "openly ate
with her son in public," as Peter H. Buck, the Maori authority on
the Polynesians, relates.[9]

In Melanesia "there is a remarkable avoidance between a boy
and his sisters and his mother, beginning when he is first clothed." [10]
In New Caledonia brothers and sisters must avoid each other
throughout life, even to the extreme of going out of their way to
avoid an accidental meeting.[11] And in Polynesian Tonga, a man
owes his first respect and allegiance to his *sister*, yet he may never
enter her house.[12]

"In Samoa and Tonga two social customs prevail," writes Buck.
"One is the brother-sister taboo, which includes cousins bearing
the same relationship as brother and sister"—*i.e.*, maternal, or cognatic, cousins. "After ten years of age, brothers and sisters were
brought up in different houses and they ceased to play together.
If one was in a house the other may not enter. . . . The other
custom was the great respect paid by men to their sisters. In Tonga
the sister was regarded as superior in rank to the brother, and this
superiority was shared by her children. In Samoa, the *sister's children* were sacred." [13] (Author's italics.)

Compare this twentieth-century report on the Pacific islanders
to a first-century report on the Celts of Europe: "Sister's children
are held in great esteem by their uncles as well as by their fathers;
indeed, they regard the relation as *even more sacred* and bind-

ing." [14] (Author's italics.) That this sister worship is a survival of the original universal civilization can hardly be doubted. It prevailed not only in the unspoiled Pacific in modern times but among the Celts of Europe two thousand years ago. The Celts, whom Tacitus miscalled Germans, seem to have retained the customs and traditions of the old civilization longer than any other civilized peoples of historical times.

"In Ceylon a father is forbidden to see his daughter at all after she has arrived at puberty" or a nubile son his mother.[15] Among the Todas of India a girl considers herself polluted if her clothing brushes that of a male relative; and "a case is mentioned of a girl expressing horror when inadvertantly touched by her father." [16] In Korea boys were taught that it was "unmanly" to enter the rooms set apart for their sisters and their mother.[17] And in prewar Japan the males and females of the family lived completely segregated lives, any chance of physical contact being considered dangerous in the extreme.[18]

These customs imply an aversion to incest that cannot be explained on biological grounds. Incest is quite common among animals, and there are no genetic arguments against it. "Brother-sister matings and those between parents and offspring are common throughout the animal world, without any apparent detriment to the species," writes the zoologist Susan Michelmore.[19] Thus the church's ban on cousin marriages has no basis in genetics, as is claimed, but stems, like the savage's fear of incest, from the maternal discipline of males. The *materfamilias* once found it necessary to take stern measures to control the lust of her sons for the protection of her daughters and herself and so bred into her offspring an ineradicable horror of incestual sexual relations.

As the boys of the maternal family group became older, numbers of them left home to join the marauding bands of adult males. But gradually more and more of the boys remained at home and became civilized. From these home-staying males of the maternal clans descended the people of the great gynocratic city states that were the glory of the earliest historical societies. From the males who left the influence of the mother to become nomads and hunters, womanless except through seizure and rape, descended the barbaric hordes who upset civilization in the Near East when they overthrew the city states in the third millennium B.C., as the nomadic Dorians were to destroy the Aegean civilization some fifteen hundred years later.

Archeology corroborates the evidence of anthropology here, for as G. Ernest Wright says: "Semitic groups living as nomads around the fringes of the Fertile Crescent, moved into the sown lands [of the matriarchal city states] as early as 2500 B.C., and by 2300 B.C. a Dark Age had descended upon the country, following the destruction of every major city-state center as far as these have been investigated." [20] The Sumerian city of Ur was one of these great city states, and the Bible records the invasion of one such nomadic horde into its sown lands when the tribe of Terah descended upon it. Shechem in Canaan, another of the great city states, was later the victim of the Semitic tribe of the barbaric nomad Abraham, when "he went forth to go into the land of Canaan . . . unto the place of Sichem."

The taboo of incest, initiated to protect the women of the family group, was eventually extended to include all women of the tribe; and the custom of "marrying out" was adopted. "In the primitive world today," writes E. B. Tylor, "there prevails widely the rule called 'exogamy', or marrying-out, which forbids a man to marry a woman of his own matriarchal clan—an act which is considered criminal and may be punished with death." [21] Among certain Indian tribes of North America, "the children take the clan name or totem of the mother; so if she were of the Bear clan, her son would be a Bear and he might not marry a Bear girl. . . . In India a Brahman is not to marry a wife whose clan name is the same as his, nor may a Chinese take a wife of his own surname." [22] The same restrictions were applied in the great and sophisticated Roman civilization, which allowed marriage between agnatic kin, those related on the father's side, but outlawed marriage between cognates, relatives on the mother's side. The custom survives among young people today in the play-superstition that it is unlucky to marry a person whose surname is the same as one's own.

The Sanctity of Woman's Blood

Next to the incestual taboo, the most potent and lasting of gynarchic taboos is that connected with woman's blood. This taboo, which remained in effect down through medieval times and accounts for the church's habit of *burning* women alive while merely beheading or quartering men, was imposed in the gynocratic age also to protect menstruating girls and to protect all women from the brutal rages of their male relatives.

Remnants of the belief in the powerful sanctity of woman's blood are found today not only in the Christian rite of "churching" women after childbirth to destroy the dangerous power inherent in the placental blood but also in the customs and taboos of less "civilized" peoples. It is almost universally believed among primitives, as among the early Hebrews, that for a man to touch a woman who is menstruating, who is pregnant, or who is recently delivered of a child is dangerous for the *man*. "If a woman have an issue of blood . . . whosoever toucheth her shall be unclean," wrote the author of Leviticus three thousand years ago.

"Nature would appear to have taught the savages of Australia," writes Paolo Mantegazza, "that which Moses, the inspired of God, imparted to the Hebrews for the conserving of their health." [23] Mantegazza fell into the common error of interpreting these ancient taboos as safeguards for men, an explanation difficult to comprehend; for certainly intercourse during menstruation or pregnancy is fraught with more danger to the female than to the male. Yet the fallacy persists that feminine taboos were designed to protect men from the baneful influence of women.

In South Africa, for example, if a man touches his wife during her menstrual period "his bones will become soft and he will lose his strength." [24] Even to occupy the same room with a menstruating woman is considered enervating, while the actual sight of a woman's blood may cause death. A Fan of West Africa "so weak that he could hardly move was suspected to have become so by seeing the blood of a woman." [25] And among the Damaras of southern Africa "men may not see a lying-in woman else they will become weak and will be killed in battle." [26]

"One would never have done," writes Mantegazza, "if he were to undertake to mention all the peoples among whom the menstruating woman is looked upon as impure, or if he were to undertake to give the lengthy list of all the superstitions which still surround to our own day the act of menstruation, the menstrual blood, and everything that has to do with the mysterious genital function of woman." [27]

These universally believed fairy tales about the danger to men of menstruating women and pregnant women and women in child-bed have the ring of tales told by old country nurses—tales of ogres and hobgoblins—to instill obedience through fear in their charges. And that is precisely what they were originally intended to do. They were tales told by primordial matriarchs to scare little boys into obedience and respect for women. That so many anthropologists, like Mantegazza, concluded that these blood taboos were designed to protect the male is naïve. Like the fear of incest, these taboos are the end result of ancient teaching designed to protect women and girls. If later their meaning was distorted to imply a protection of men from women, it was because man's ego made a virtue of a necessity forced upon him by his mother, in an age when he "dared not disobey her."

Later, when women had organized society into true civilization, these two taboos (and, of course, *taboo* means *sacred*)—the sacredness or taboo of female relations and of all women's blood—became the tenets and very basis of the law. Matricide, the murder of the mother, involving a combination of these two most potent of taboos, was the most unspeakable of crimes, a crime for which there could be no expiation, no forgiveness, here or in the here-after. Even in Oedipus' time, patricide was no crime. Oedipus' crime consisted not in killing his father but in committing incest with his mother—a crime that not even his self-inflicted blindness and exile could wipe out. This myth is a purely matriarchal myth; and Erich Fromm goes so far in his matriarchal interpretation of it as to postulate that Jocasta, not Oedipus, was the object of the divine wrath—the wrath of the Great Goddess. It was Jo-casta's sin, according to Fromm, the sin of allowing her child to be abandoned and exposed for the benefit of her husband—a justi-fiable expedient to the patriarchal mind but the crime of crimes in the matriarchal view[28]—that caused all the woes of the house of Laius. It is significant that in the Oedipus myth it is Oedipus' daughters, Antigone and Ismene, who are the strong and courageous characters, while the sons are depicted as weak and vacillating, dis-loyal and self-seeking.

The later legend of Orestes, who was pursued by the matriarchal Achaean Furies for killing his mother and was later forgiven by the patriarchal Dorian gods because he had done it to avenge his father, symbolizes the very late transition from mother worship to father honor which took place after the Dorian invasion of Greece and the accompanying patriarchal revolution there.

Strength and Sexual Selection

Mystical power and superior intelligence might account to some extent for the awe and fear in which women were held by ancient men; but there must also have been some physical fear on the part of the men to have held them in such abysmal subjection for so many ages. All evidence of myth, tradition, and physiology, as well as that of anthropology, points to an original equality of the sexes in size and strength.

Biologically speaking, as Michelmore says, "It is logical that the male should be the smaller partner. His only function is to provide spermatozoa; and though the human egg is only just visible to the human eye, the sperm is far, far smaller." The male, in the view of nature, is only a "glorified gonad," in which size is irrelevant.[29]

The probability that women were once the physical equals of men is indicated by such myths as that of the Lemnian women, who easily vanquished their menfolk in a civil war in which all the males were slain, and in the similar legend of the women of Amathonte who steadfastly refused to have intercourse with the men, and in the legends, probably historical, of the Amazons who lived manless all but one night of the year and destroyed even their own male babies, rearing only their daughters.

The myths of such women as Atalanta who wrestled or raced all male challengers and the worldwide myths of maidens who chose as suitors only those rare males who could best them in physical combat also more than hint at an original physical equality of the sexes.

As late as the year A.D. 1908, the Atalanta myth survived in Siberia, where it was reported of the Koryak that the suitor who could not overtake his beloved in a foot race was rejected by her.[30] In Malacca, Malaysia, in the nineteenth century, a similar test was in fashion. The bride would run away into the forest with the groom after her. If the latter was outrun and returned alone, "he was met with the jeers of the wedding party and the match was declared off." [31]

Aelian wrote of the ancient Sacae that the bridegroom had to do battle with his intended and subdue her before she would consent to be his wife.[32] And modern writers have reported the custom as surviving in localities as far apart as the Arctic Circle and South Africa. In the Cape Colony "a Makuana suitor has to throw the girl in a wrestling match in order to secure her hand," and she will not consent to be his wife until he has thus proved himself.[33] Among the Samoyedes of northern Russia, as in Kamchatka and the Tungus, marriage is not agreed to by the girl until the suitor "has got the best of her by force." [34]

Thus the popular myth illustrated in modern comics of the caveman clubbing his chosen bride over the head and dragging her off by her hair is a very distorted depiction of a once universal custom: that of sexual selection by the woman of a "superior sire," a custom which prevailed when men and women were equal in size and strength.

These customs, says Crawley, contrary to modern masculist theory, "have nothing to do with marriage by capture" or with the subjugation of women.[35] They are manifestations of the right of the woman to select her mate by combat, so to speak—the very form of sexual selection that led eventually to the muscular disparity between the sexes. For, as Lester Frank Ward says, "if the male appears to excel in size and strength it's because female preference has weeded out the little weak males in favor of superior sires. She has sacrificed her original advantage for the good of the race." [36] Karen Horney understands that masculine muscularity was "an acquired sex difference," fostered by sexual selection on the part of the females,[37] and the fact that modern men on the whole continue to be larger and stronger than women is an indication of the recency of this method of selection. Among the Celts of Europe young men and women were still equal in size and strength as late as the first century A.D., as Tacitus says: "The young men marry late; nor are the maidens hurried into marriage; the same age and a *similar stature* is required; *well matched* and vigorous they are wed." [38] (Author's italics.) Edward Carpenter sees a deterioration in the human race since the transference of selection privileges from the female to the male:

Among most of the higher animals, and indeed among the earlier races of mankind, the males have been selected by the females on account of their prowess, superior strength, or beauty, and this led to the evolution of the race at large of a type which was the ideal of the female. But when in the later history of mankind, property-love set in, this action ceased. Woman then became "property," and man began to select women for the characteristics that were pleasing to *him*, and consequently the quality of the whole race began to be affected. With the return of women to freedom, the ideal of the female might again resume its sway and give to sexual selection a nobler influence than when exercised by males. The feminine influence might thus lead to the evolution of a more manly and dignified race than has been disclosed in these last days of patriarchal civilization.[39]

Mary Wollstonecraft observed two hundred years ago that men were wont to marry the poorest specimens of womanhood and make them the mothers of the race.[40] And quite recently Horney wrote: "Women presenting the specified traits [that man's ideology has attributed to them—dependence, weakness, limited intelligence] are more frequently chosen by men." [41] At the same time, "women," says Carpenter, "have been forced [by social mores and by pecuniary necessity] to accept many . . . types of men that women really free would not countenance for their mates or for the fathers of their children." [42] For the female sex, as Edmond Perrier writes, "is the sex of physiological foresight." [43] "The female is the guardian of hereditary qualities. . . . While the voice of Nature, speaking to the male sex, says to him: Fecundate! it gives to the female a different command and says to her: Discriminate!" [44]

The modern trend in which later twentieth-century "Aquarian" boys are tending to select as mates strong, capable, and intelligent girls who can support them is probably a good omen for the future of the race. Also it portends an eventual reversal of latter-day sexual roles and a return to the original state of affairs, when man was secondary and woman the backbone of home, family, and society. How she lost this position is a question that will concern us as we proceed.

She may, as the expression goes, have "asked for it." For when the bands of marauding males, eaters of roots and berries, rejects from the civilized communities, defied their apish heritage and became hunters, a new dimension was added to sexuality. While the men who had chosen to remain at home with the women continued as plant growers and agriculturists under the supervision of their mothers, the wild men, out of the desperation of hunger, became killers of flesh, which they devoured raw.[45]

The wild habits and raw meat diet of the undomesticated males no doubt led to their gradual sexual development—and eventually to their conquest of the matriarchs. For Louis Berman points out that meat-eaters have larger sexual organs than vegetarians,[46] and this development may have proved irresistible to the women. It is thus possible that the women of the old gynocracies brought on their own downfall by selecting the phallic wild men over the more civilized men of their own pacific and gentle world.

6

Fetishes and Their Origins

Nothing pleasant or unpleasant
exists by Nature, but all things
become so by habit.
—EPICTETUS

Phallus Worship

The original worshipers of the phallus were women. As archeology in recent years has shown, the early peoples in what we have heretofore called prehistoric times considered the male to have been ancillary to the female, sexually as well as in all other respects. There is even evidence that it was woman's sexual preference that determined the ultimate size of the male phallus.

The recently excavated goddess shrines in the Near East reveal phalluses of all shapes and sizes. The fact that these, and such phallic symbols as the bulls' horns, are the only masculine touch found in the ancient shrines indicates that the original worshipers of the phallus were the women themselves. Phalluses abound, but no other male element is so much as suggested among the myriads of representations of women uncovered by archeology, as though to the women, who were all that counted, the only thing about a man that was to be valued was his sex organ, made for her pleasure and fulfillment. "These masculine symbols were seen in relation to the Goddess, and it was to please her that they abound in her shrines." [1]

Significantly, in Egyptian mythology it was Isis herself, the primary deity, who established phallus worship. When Typhon murdered her consort, Osiris, and cut him up into little bits, Isis went about gathering up the pieces. But nowhere could she find the missing penis. She therefore ordered a wooden lingam to be made, and this she set up in her chief temple at Thebes. It was for this reason that all the goddess temples in Upper and Lower Egypt were

97

adorned with wood or stone phalluses. The myth memorializes the fact that phallus worship was decreed by women as part of the goddess cult throughout the world.

It was not until the patriarchal revolution that phallus worship became the purely masculine preoccupation that it remains to this day. When men appropriated phallus worship to themselves, they went overboard and carried it to the ridiculous extremes men usually resort to when they take over feminine occupations and institutions.[2]

The ancient Jews swore oaths, not on their own Bible as the Christians do but on their genitals, the word "thigh," as in "place thy hand upon (or beneath) my thigh and swear," being but a euphemism for the penis and/or the testicles. Among the Jews, also, for a woman to touch with her hand the sacred genitals of her husband was a crime calling for severe punishment—the amputation of the offending hand, no less.[3]

In India, after the patriarchal revolution there, phallus worship by men went beyond reason. At a certain time each day the priest was wont to go about the streets naked, ringing a little bell. The bell was to summon all pious women to the duty of kissing and embracing the exposed genitals of the priest. It was in India too that triumphant male phallicism reached its very height—in the story of "the biggest lingam in the world." This allegory was no doubt a form of propaganda designed to win women back to a custom of which they had grown tired, perhaps from overexposure to it. At any rate, the story is that when the god Siva, who in earlier myth had been a goddess, by some mischance lost his penis, it was found sticking in the ground. It soon penetrated the lower worlds, and its length increased until its top towered above the heavens. This strange sight attracted the attention of Vishnu and Brahma, and these two gods decided to investigate the situation.

"Brahma ascended to heaven to ascertain the upper limits of the lingam, and Vishnu betook himself to the nether regions to discover its depth. Both returned with the news that the lingam was infinite. . . . So they both fell down and worshipped it, and bade all men and women do likewise." [4] And thus mankind was taught that the lingam was infinite in its influence and that all women, as well as men, must worship it.

Phallus worship did not completely die out among women, as

witness the historical fact of the conquest of the town of Embrun in France in 1585. When the Reformation Protestants took the town they found that the sacred statue of Saint Foutin had been embellished with a magnificent stone phallus, which had been dyed red by the libations of wine poured upon it by the local ladies.[5]

Saint Foutin was worshiped throughout the south of France. His name is said to have been a corruption of "Photinus" the first bishop of Lyons, "to whom the people had transferred the distinguishing feature of Priapus." [6] His image, always adorned with the Priapic magnificence, was displayed in Provençal churches as late as the seventeenth century. Bishop Photinus must have been quite a man, for even a colossal natural rock formation in Auvergne was nicknamed Saint Foutin because of its resemblance in shape to a penis. The saint's penis was most often made of wood, which the women scraped, boiling the sawdust scrapings in water and drinking the resultant brew as an aid to fertility.

In most churches the saintly penis became so worn down as to need periodic replacing, until some unknown priest thought up an "inexhaustible" penis that was restored by a miracle. "This miracle, however, was a very clumsy one, for the phallus consisted of a long staff of wood passed through a hole in the image of the saint, and as the phallic end in front became shortened, a blow of a mallet from behind thrust it forward so that it was restored to its orginal length." [7]

It is possible that the saint's penis, whether made of wood or stone, was put to a more intimate use by his devotees. There is evidence that in Catholic churches as late as the seventeenth century women were occasionally practicing the old pagan Roman custom of actual intercourse with the saint, as Roman matrons often did, when they sat upon the erect penis of Priapus in order to become fruitful.

Castration and the Priesthood

Feminine phallus worship led in archaic times to penis sacrifice —castration of the male—as a religious rite. In the matriarchal ages, after men were finally admitted to the priestly class, it was evidently these *castrati* who were chosen to share the custodianship of the temples with the long-robed priestesses of the goddess.

As late as 1902, the anthropologist Crawley wrote, referring to his own times: "One of the most complex problems is that of the adoption of feminine dress by priests, shamans, and medicine men." [8] For it is a strange phenomenon that even long after the demise of the goddess and her priestesses, the priests of her successor, the god, continued to be effeminate.

Graves points out that even in historical times the male priests of Zeus, Apollo, and others of the new male pantheon were required to wear false breasts, long hair, clean-shaven faces, and flowing robes. These two latter requirements were carried over into the Christian Church, and the clean-shaven face and flowing robes distinguish the monks and priests of certain Christian sects to this day—survivals of the time when only women were deemed worthy to tend the Great Goddess.

But the Christian priestly robe is not the only such survival in the modern world. The bardashes, the medicine-men priests of the North American Indian tribes, are so called because of their feminine accomplishments. The word is French for hermaphrodite, or homosexual. The shamans of Siberia and the Arctic, as well as the medicine men of American Indian tribes such as the Crow, the Sioux, the Iroquois, and the Chukchi, habitually wear women's clothes and live as women. [9]

In Borneo the "highest grade of Shaman among the Dyaks is one who has changed his sex, assumed feminine dress, and occupies himself with feminine pursuits." [10] In India priests of the goddess Huligamma wear female dress, as do the priestly sect of Vallabhachars who attend the shrines of Krishna, the god. In Bengal the custom is repeated, as also in the Congo where the *nganga*, the medicine men of the Bangala, dress as women. Even in far off Tahiti the sect of male priests called *arreoi* were required to dress and live as women. [11]

Like Herodotus, who reported in the fifth century B.C. that the priests of the northern barbarian tribes had "the feminine sickness," [12] modern observers have ascribed this universal effeminacy of holy men to sexual abnormality. Crawley attributes it to "a congenital tendency towards inversion," [13] and Lowie writes, "In some primitive communities what we should regard as pathological phenomena in the sexual sphere are intimately related with religious activity." [14] Edward Westermarck says: "There is no doubt that these phenomena are cases of sexual inversion, congenital or acquired. . . . The *significant fact* is that *throughout history* [author's italics] the priesthood has had a tendency towards effemination.'' [15]

This is, indeed, the significant fact. But its significance lies not in the presumed effeminacy of holy men but in the fact of the original femininity of the religious idea. The custom of female dress and manners among priests is attributable not to an endemic homosexuality among them, as Westermarck, Lowie, and others assume, but to an extremely ancient habit among mankind, a habit so thoroughly embedded in the human subconscious as to be ineradicable even after four millennia of masculism—the habit of regarding deity as female.

Nineteenth-century and early twentieth-century scholars, who as a body refused to accept the overwhelming evidence for the original gynocratic basis of human society, nonetheless collected valuable data which have been helpful to modern scholars in their reconstructions of early social organization. Sir James Fraser cites stunningly convincing evidence of the survival of gynarchic customs and taboos throughout the world, yet he misinterprets this evidence and considers it of so little significance that he omits it in his own one-volume abridgement of his mammoth twelve-volume work. In volume six of the original he cites case after case of male priests being required to dress as women, from the priests of Hercules at Cos in the fifth century B.C. to the shamans of North America in the nineteenth century A.D. Yet in the abridgement[16] every reference to this facet of religion is omitted. It is possible, of course, that the omission was intentional—that by the time of the abridgement of 1922 Fraser had finally realized the vastly important implications of this phenomenon and had decided for the sake of male supremacy to suppress it.

Male Circumcision

The fact that even in imperial Rome the devotees of the goddess Cybele were still cutting off their penises and testicles and offering them at the shrines of the goddess indicates that in early times it was customary for men to observe this practice in honor of the Great Goddess. Probably to clean up the shrines, as well as to halt the wholesale and woman-bilking castration of the men, women initiated the custom of offering the foreskin in place of the whole, and circumcision was adopted as an amelioration of castration.

There can be no doubt that circumcision is a survival of the goddess cult. Abraham, in declaring circumcision a covenant between man and God, was attempting to rationalize a matriarchal custom that could not be abolished, as in Christian times the church adopted and rationalized many goddess rites that could not be eliminated. The fact is, however, that Abraham never practiced or advocated circumcision. The Egyptian Moses was the instigator of the custom among the Hebrews, and the authors of Genesis attributed it, as they did so many later rites, to the early patriarch Abraham in order to lend an aura of antiquity to their comparatively new Jehovah religion.

Circumcision is a great deal older than either Moses or Abraham. Herodotus writes that "the Syrians of Palestine [the Jews] themselves confess that they learnt the custom of the Egyptians." [17] The Egyptians had practiced it in honor of Isis since time beyond memory; and the Nubians, who Strabo, writing in 7 B.C., avers were strongly woman dominated even in his own day, had "always" practiced it. The Colchians on the shores of the Black Sea, who were an ancient colony of the Egyptians placed there by Sesostris before 3000 B.C., had also "always practiced circumcision." [18] And that was at least a thousand years before Abraham.

That circumcision is a survival of the offering of the penis to the goddess is borne out by the fact that in olden times the rite was always performed in early manhood, not in infancy as is the modern way. Among the Arabs and in some African tribes today circumcision takes place at puberty. And there is evidence that the bar mitzvah, the rite of manhood among the Jews, was once the time of circumcision.

The ancient Romans were dumbfounded at this Jewish and Arab rite, and it aroused all sorts of speculation among the classical writers. A scholiast on Horace's Satires offered one of the most ingenious explanations of it: "The Jews were deprived of their foreskins; the reason for which was that Moses their king and legislator, having from want of cleanliness a diseased prepuce, was compelled to cut it off, and fearing the deprivation might expose him to ridicule, ordered them all to undergo a like operation." [19]

The foreskin of Jesus Christ was one of the most precious relics of the Middle Ages. So popular was it that there existed no fewer than twelve of them at one time in Europe! The Holy Prepuce at Chartres, however, was the most potent, merely to look upon it being sufficient to render the most sterile woman fruitful.[20] This was carrying things to ridiculous extremes; but a French philosopher of the nineteenth century carried another foreskin, that of Adam, to even more ridiculous extremes. This great thinker somehow arrived at the conclusion that when God put Adam to sleep he intended only to circumcise him. But when he stood there with the severed prepuce in his hand, he had a better idea of what to do with the leftovers. And he made woman, Eve, out of Adam's foreskin! [21]

Circumcision of boys is practiced today for hygienic reasons accruing to the welfare of the boy. Physicians of the nineteenth century pooh-poohed the cleanliness motive, maintaining that circumcision served no healthful purpose and was merely a barbaric and useless form of torture.

But recent news items announce that cancer of the cervix in women may very well be caused by a virus transmitted by uncircumcised men.[22] Perhaps, then, the Jews, the Arabs, and Saint Peter have been right all along. For it was Saint Peter who wanted Christian converts to undergo circumcision and Saint Paul who did not. Paul wanted converts at any price, and the prospect of circumcision had already in Paul's experience cooled the ardor of not a few prospective Christians. Paul won out, and Christians were not circumcised.

Except, that is, the Christians of Abyssinia and the Christian Copts of Egypt, with whom the tradition was too ancient to be abandoned. So abhorrent to Coptic women was an uncircumcised male that they burned his bedding and shattered his eating utensils if by any chance they had entertained one unaware, as Voltaire reports in his *Philosophie de l'histoire*.[23]

On the other hand, non-Christian women of Turkey "prefer cohabiting with those who retain the foreskin (the Christians) than with the Jews and Turks, as the pleasure of sexual union is greatly increased by the friction of the prepuce." [24]

Philo reports that the Egyptians knew a disease they called carbo, of a "very dangerous character, and very difficult to cure, to which all those who retained the prepuce were peculiarly liable." [25] What this disease was is unknown, but it may have been syphilis. Syphilis did not invade modern Europe until late in the fifteenth century, when Columbus' sailors brought it back from the New World. But in former days, could not the ancient mariners have brought it back from that same New World to ancient Egypt, where the doctors were more successful in containing it than were the doctors of the "enlightened" sixteenth century A.D.?

In the Muhammadan religion, circumcision is a must; and it was originally decreed not by Muhammad but by Ishmael, son of Hagar, who was circumcised by Sarah, wife of Abraham, according to Islamic belief.

Many and varied are the reasons given by earlier travelers for the strange Eastern custom of circumcision: to prevent masturbation; to prevent libertinism; to render washing more facile, since Muhammadans are permitted to use only one hand in washing their genitals; to protect against a worm that likes to breed in the fold of the foreskin; because the prepuce, if left uncropped, would grow too long and would interefere with sexual intercourse; and, finally, because the "prepuce may oppose the free egress of the seminal fluid in the conjugal embrace, and it is to circumcision that the great fecundity of the Jews and Arabs is to be attributed." [26]

All of these so-called explanations bear the mark of patristic, masculist logic. The real reason for male circumcision lies buried in the great mysterious mind of the primordial queen who decreed it back in the springtime of the world for the sole benefit of the chosen sex, the women.

The Breast Fetish

Among the revelations at Catal Huyuk that startled its excavators in the early 1960's were the many pairs of female breasts that adorned the walls of the goddess shrines. These disembodied mammaries protruded from the flat surface of the walls as if they had an existence of their own. This phenomenon of ninth-millennium Anatolia had not been repeated in Crete or elsewhere in the later Aegean, as so many other Anatolian wall decorations had been.

But, *mirabile dictu,* nearly a thousand miles away in southern Italy, identical breasts *were* found in a goddess temple that was dated six or seven thousand years *after* Catal Huyuk to a period prior to Rome or the Hellenic colonization of Italy. Among these numerous pairs of "female busts" were a large number of "strange female flowers, faces of women crowned with a calyx of flower petals." [27] This is all very strange and exciting, but even more strange and exciting is the later identification of the temple where these busts and flower faces were found and its connection with Jason and the Argonauts.

Strabo, in the first century B.C., had written of a temple in Lucania in southern Italy which had been founded by Jason during the Argo voyage twelve or thirteen centuries earlier and dedicated to the goddess Hera. Strabo called this the Heraion of Silaris, the Hera Temple of Silaris, Silaris being the Roman name for the River Sele. In Jason's time Hera was still the Great Goddess of northern Greece, and Thessaly, Jason's homeland, was in northern Greece. The objective of the Argonauts, of whom Jason was the captain, was Colchis on the eastern shore of the Black Sea, in northern Anatolia. The shortest route from Thessaly to Colchis would have been across the Aegean Sea, through the Hellespont to the Sea of Marmara, through the Bosporus into the Black Sea, and so on eastward to Colchis. Italy would have been very much out of the way.

Obviously then, Jason's visit to Italy must have been made on the return journey from Colchis, when he was fleeing with Medea. For the fact that a temple to Hera, the Greek goddess, *was* dedicated in Italy before the Greek colonization of the peninsula, cannot be denied. Not only Strabo but Plutarch, two hundred years later, testifies to the fact and that the Heraion was the work of Jason. The temple still stood in Plutarch's time. However, when post-Renaissance antiquarians, intrigued by the newly discovered accounts of Strabo and Plutarch, started looking for the Heraion along the banks of the Sele, no vestige of the temple could be found. The search was finally rewarded, however, in 1935—thirty years before Catal Huyuk—by the finding of the female busts and the flower faces in a field three miles from the river. Further excavations eventually revealed the remains of the temple itself, and votive offerings inscribed with the name Hera made it "quite certain that the temple was indeed [Strabo's] Heraion of Silaris." [28]

So everyone was satisfied. But—what of the breasts? They excited little interest at the time, as of course the breasts of Catal Huyuk were still unknown in 1935. What connection was there between the two? How did Anatolian breasts of the eightieth century reach Italy of the twelfth? If the detached breasts had been universal symbols of the Great Goddess, why did they not appear elsewhere with others of her numerous symbols? If the breasts were a fad only of the Anatolian ninth millennium, why do they suddenly reappear beyond the seas seven thousand years later? And why are the lovely little flower faces not found anywhere at all except at the Heraion of Silaris?

Where and what is the connecting link? Colchis, where reposed the Golden Fleece the Argonauts were after, was in Anatolia. Medea, the enchantress, although in the Hellenic myth she is called the daughter of the king, was in actuality the queen of Colchis. This is proven by the story of her tearing her brother Absyrtus limb from limb and scattering his parts over the countryside, as Osiris' limbs were scattered by Typhon. This is the way that many mythical gods and heroes met their deaths, from Tammuz in Syria to Dionysus in Thrace. In all of the myths the dismembered party represents the consort of the queen—he who is sacrificed, ritually dissected, and scattered to the winds to insure the crops. The "green man" or the "corn man" festival of modern Europe is a Celtic survival of this ancient Mediterranean fertility rite.

In the Argonaut myth, Medea left Colchis with the Argonauts, having fallen in love with Jason. The Argo is pursued by the Colchians, who want both their queen and their Golden Fleece back. And it is then that the visit to Italy may have been made. Eventually Medea and Jason return to Thessaly where Medea, to oblige Jason, murders his uncle, the king of Thessaly. Again they are forced to flee, and here again may have been the time of the stop in Italy. Later they come to Corinth, where Jason falls in love with Glaucë, the daughter of Creon, the king, and Medea in revenge kills both Glaucë and Creon. She then murders her own two sons by Jason and flees to Athens, where Aegeus, the father of Theseus, gives her asylum from Jason's wrath. In Athens she attempts to destroy Theseus, and for this she is banished by Aegeus. But she lives to avenge herself again by magically arranging the deaths of Theseus' wife Phaedra, the Cretan princess Theseus had abducted after slaying the Minotaur in the Labyrinth at Crete, and of Hippolytus, Theseus' son by the queen of the Amazons. Aesclepius restores Hippolytus to life, and the goddess Diana bears him away to her sacred grove at Ariccia in Italian Latium—the Grove of Diana Nemorensis whence Aeneas was later to pluck the golden bough. In Ariccia, Hippolytus has a son, Virbius, who is one of the Etruscans who resist the settlement of Aeneas and the Trojans in Latium after the fall of Troy.

And what has all this to do with the breasts at the Heraion of Silaris?

Very importantly it brings together in one continuing myth ancient Catal Huyuk, Egypt, Colchis, Jason, Medea, Thessaly, Athens, Aegeus, Theseus, Phaedra, Crete, the Minotaur, Aeneas, Troy, Corinth, Creon, the Argonauts, Aesclepius, Hera, Diana, the Grove of Nemi, Virbius, Hippolytus, the Amazons, the Etruscans, the Trojan War, Latium, Lucania, and the Heraion of Silaris. And this one continuing myth all takes place in the lifetime of one individual—Medea. And Medea is the queen of Anatolian Colchis who presumably visited Italy with her husband Jason when he founded the temple of Hera in Lucania.

Which all leads up to the question: were the breasts and flower faces Medea's contribution to the Heraion? And are they *Colchian* symbols of the Great Goddess—symbols once common in the Anatolian cradle of civilization, handed down to Egypt where they were later obliterated during patriarchal ages, and preserved only in Egypt's Anatolian colony at Colchis? Perhaps excavations at the site of Colchis will some day reveal the originals of the flower faces and will provide the missing link between the breasts of Catal Huyuk and those of ancient Italy.

We shall then have proof that Medea did exist, that she did visit Italy with Jason, that together they did found the temple of Hera in Lucania, that the ancient myths are indeed to be read as history, and that the ancient world was a far more closely knit community than has been realized heretofore.

The phenomena of Catal Huyuk and Silaris bear witness to the fact that the female breasts, like the phallus, were orginally objects of woman worship. At Catal Huyuk they are rivaled in number only by the bulls' horns interspersed among them. The horns, of course, symbolize the male phallus, the generating cause of childbirth, while the breasts symbolize the nurturing aspect of child care. Women revered both breast and penis as instruments of motherhood. It was only after the patriarchal revolution, when men had appropriated to themselves both phallus worship and the breast fetish, that these organs acquired the erotic significance with which they are now endowed.

Ever since modern history began, men have been bemused by the mammary glands. Juvenal, two thousand years ago, waxed rapturous over the oversized bust of a lady acquaintance, and Strabo praised the "majorem papillam" of the women of Meroë. Breasts have been favorite subjects of poets, sculptors, and artists of all stripes ever since masculine art was born.

Great size, however, has not always been required or even desired. It can be seen from Greek sculpture of the classical age that the beauty-loving Greeks preferred smaller breasts, slimmer hips, and broader shoulders than are allowed by modern judges of feminine beauty. The very ideal of female physical perfection, nonetheless, remains the Venus of Praxiteles. Phryne, the famous Greek courtesan who posed for Praxiteles' Venus, as well as for the Venus of Apelles, is described as having had "the most admirable of mammae," which, without being large, "occupy the bosom, rise from it with nearly equal curves on every side, and equally terminate in their apices." [29]

It was the incomparable perfection of Phryne's *mammae* that saved her life when she was falsely accused of treason by a jealous lover. She was defended by the great orator Hyperides, who, wasting no words, called her as a witness and, throwing aside her veil to reveal her breasts, "at once disarmed the most inveterate of her critics and won her acquittal." [30]

It was this Phryne who magnanimously restored the razed walls of Thebes after Alexander's attack. For centuries thereafter the restored walls bore the proud inscription: "These walls, demolished by Alexander the Great, were restored by Phryne the whore."

In the Middle Ages breasts had shrunk even from the parsimonious (by modern standards) Greek ideal. A fourteenth century work on feminine beauty defines pulchritude as consisting of narrow shoulders, small breasts, large belly, broad hips, fat thighs, short legs, and a small head—which probably explains the unattractiveness of the ladies portrayed by medieval artists.

By the late eighteenth and early nineteenth centuries this ideal had changed remarkably little. T. Bell, in 1821, recommended that in profile the *mons Veneris* should be more prominent than the bosom! This protruding pubis was to be balanced behind by equally protruding buttocks, the whole balanced on large muscular thighs and short legs.[31]

Today, we allow nothing to protrude except the breasts—and with these there is absolutely no limit as to size or prominence. Desmond Morris, in *The Naked Ape,* observes that women's breasts have become so much of a sex symbol through selective breeding for size and roundness that they are no longer efficient as nursing implements. This bodes ill for the future of the race, because at no time in history has the large bosom been an object of so much reverence as it is in the United States today.

Thus we find that, just as the male of the human species owes his penile development to early sexual selection on the part of women, so the female of the species owes her modern mammary magnificence to male sexual preference.

It is questionable, however, whether male preference for large breasts is really based on sexuality. Men like to think that big breasts are "sexy" and that their own weakness for them implies a tigerish sexiness in themselves. The truth is that the overblown breast is admired by modern men not as a daring sex symbol, as they like to think, but as a mother symbol. The first impression a child receives is that of his mother's breast, and he spends the rest of his life trying to recapture the sensations of cherished warmth and comfort that are connected in his subconscious mind with the female breast.

Sexual Symbolism

Pyramids, breast-shaped, "rising equally on all their sides and equally terminating in their apices," are sex symbols representing the feminine principle in creation—unalterable, immovable, indestructible. "Egypt is the land of stereotyped matriarchy," writes Bachofen, "and its whole culture is built on the woman cult." [32]

Breast symbolism in general is rarer than lingam (phallic) or yoni (vulva) symbolism. Of phallic symbols there are many—the obelisks of Egypt and the Washington Monument in the District of Columbia are said to fall in this category. But yoni symbols, the representation of the female pudendum, are more numerous and offer far more variety.

The hot cross bun and the pocketbook roll were originally symbolic of the lingam and the yoni respectively. These goodies had always been baked for the festival of the goddess Oestre, the goddess of fertility, from whose name we get both the word "oestrus" signifying animal sexual heat and the word "Easter," and whose movable feast day became our Easter—the day of the risen Lord. The church permitted the baking of these pagan symbols, requiring only that for Easter they be adorned with a holy cross; and thus to this day we bake and eat hot cross buns at Eastertide in honor of the risen lingam.

The cowrie shell is universally regarded as a yoni symbol, as is the humble horseshoe when nailed for luck over a doorway. The most basic and by far the oldest sex symbol is the tau, or the short-armed cross, the letter T, in which ancient symbol the upright represents the phallus and the crosspiece the yoni, or vulva. This symbol, representing sexual intercourse, is as old as man, and it was thus an easy matter for the church to endow it with sanctity as an object of reverence. Men and women had been worshiping it since time began.

The tau-rus, the bull, symbol of gynocracy, was a strong sex symbol, representing the male principle in the feminine world. His horns were sex symbols *par excellence,* and they adorn many a goddess shrine unearthed in recent years. The bull became the sacred symbol of Crete, and the Minotaur, half man and half bull, was an object of reverence and not the monster that modern fairy tales have made of him. His mother, Pasiphaë, was indulging in an ancient woman cult when she bade Daedalus construct a heifer image in which she could conceal herself and be impregnated by the sacred bull.

The ancient sacredness of the bull in gynocratic societies is perpetuated today in the term "papal bull"—the pope's edict. It derives from the ancient queen's having pronounced her laws from the center of a crescent formed by her priestesses, the crescent being in the shape of a bull's horns as well as of the new moon.

The crescent moon was sacred to the goddess, and Mommsen writes of the vast antiquity of the custom of dispensing justice at the time of the new moon.[38]

The curved double ax of Crete, the unmistakable symbol of queenly justice, was reminiscent of both the bull's horns and the new moon, both sacred to the goddess.

Time was measured by the moon's phases, and "in all languages the moon received its name from the fact that men measured time (mensis) by her." [34] The words "menses" and "menstruation" derive from this fact, as does "mensuration," measurement. The lunar year of the matriarchal calendar consisted of thirteen months —hence the bad luck of the number thirteen, all survivals of the ancient gynocracies of Europe having been branded as evil and ill-omened by the Christian Church.

The thirteen lunar months are still called in England "common-law months," each consisting of twenty-eight days. "Twenty-eight was a sacred number, in the sense that the moon was worshipped as a woman whose menstrual cycle is twenty-eight days and that this also is the true period of the moon's revolution in terms of the sun. . . . The system was probably evolved in matriarchal Sumeria." [35] In earlier times, the mysterious red rains that still are reported periodically in the world's press as "rains of blood" were believed to have been the very menstrual blood of the moon goddess. And the modern medico-genetic symbol for the female, the small plus sign under a circle, is actually the ancient pictograph of the Great Goddess—her equiarmed cross topped by the full moon.

As late as the reign of Edward II a May Day song went: "How many months be in the year? There are thirteen, I say." In Tudor times the last line was amended to read "there are but twelve, I say," to conform to the solar year adopted by the patriarchs.

If the number thirteen became unlucky because of its association with the gynocracies, other symbols of feminine power continued as *good*-luck charms. It is still a lucky omen to see the new moon over the left shoulder—the left side being the feminine side It was for this reason, however, that the left became the dark side and the word for left—Latin *sinister*—acquired an evil connotation.

All crescent-shaped objects represent the goddess and the feminine principle, including the crescent of the old Russian and the Turkish and Libyan flags, the crescent flag having originally been a Roman legionary ensign carried by those legions dedicated to the goddess. The curved crescent-shaped lines cut into the stones of

medieval cathedrals, which so mystified the "antiquarians" of the
nineteenth century, were actually surreptitious invocations to the
goddess. The symbol of the vulva consists of two crescents joined
at the tips, a symbol that abounds in Christian Ireland.[36] The
pointed oblong formed by thus joining the crescents and enclosed
within a delta has been found carved in rocks dating from prehistoric times to the Middle Ages. Its closest parallel today is the four-
letter word found carved or scribbled on the walls of men's rooms
and comfort stations.

This was no doubt the symbol engraved on the many famous
pillars of Sesostris that dotted the countries that this ancient
Egyptian had conquered. Herodotus, who saw some of the surviving pillars in his travels more than two thousand years after Sesostris, wrote that "they were carved with emblems to mark that
they were a nation of women" [37]—in other words, with the
female sex symbol. Herodotus, fifth-century Greek patriarch that
he was, interpreted them as insults to the manhood of the conquered peoples. But Thomas Wright, another great traveler more
than two thousand years after Herodotus (1778), thought otherwise:
"The belief in the *salutary* power of this image [the female sex
symbol] appears to be a superstition of great antiquity. The universality of the superstition leads us to think that Herodotus erred in
the explanation he has given of them. The truth is that Sesostris
left this symbol as a *protection* for the people of the district in
which they stood." [38] (Author's italics.)

And knowing what we now know of the ancient Egyptians, we
agree with Wright's interpretation. Even in Herodotus' time, as
he himself reports,[39] Egypt was a woman's country, the female sex
was sacred, and her symbol could have had none but a beneficent
and "salutary" meaning.

The yoni itself is crescent-shaped, like the new moon, and in
India the word means "altar"—a sacred place.[40]

"The Ark is a female symbol," writes Goldberg.[41] Like the Torah of the Jews, it represents the female principle—the original
deity of the Jews and creator of God and man.[42] The ark was
brought to the Hebrews by Moses from Egyptian temples of the
goddess Isis, to whom the ark had been sacred for millennia before
Moses. To the Jews it represented the womb, the cradle of all life.
The ark of the Jews became the Tabernacle of the Christians, and

it is revealing that in the Roman Church the Virgin Mary is called the "Tabernacle of God." Noah's Ark symbolized the womb of the goddess who salvages and protects all her creatures. The Noah myth is not a Hebrew but a Sumerian myth, based on overtly gynarchic ideas, as embodied in the epic of Gilgamish from which it was stolen.

The Egyptian sphinx—a beast with a woman's head—represents woman's headship over man, the beast, and is symbolic of "the primacy of Isis over Osiris." [43] Yet its great age suggests that it pre-dates Osiris by many eons and is a product of the time when "there were no gods."

"In the face of this mystery," wrote George Rawlinson about the Sphinx in 1887, "all questions are vain." [44] But conjecture is not vain, and it would be interesting to conjecture a bit about this mystery.

The Sphinx is rivaled only by the great Pyramid itself in its gigantic proportions and its massive grandeur, as well as in its un-fathomable age. Could it be a monument to Basilea, Diodorus' antique queen who more than fifty thousand years ago brought order to the world and created civilized society out of chaos? Diodorus says that Basilea was a native of Atlas, which in early times was a nation of northern Africa, not too far from the site of the Sphinx at Egyptian Gizeh.

Basilea was a warrior queen who used force and violence to quell the anarchic conditions of early society—an anarchy caused by the refusal of the males to behave themselves. Men, in the early stages of their emergence into the human state, remained bestial and un-controlled sexually. Woman, however, who was the advance guard in the march toward humanhood as she was to be the advance guard in the climb toward civilization, very early rebelled against the rough and ready sexuality of the males.

"Exhausted by man's lusts," writes Bachofen, "woman was first to feel the need for regulated conditions and a purer ethic." [45] "Degraded by man's sexual abuse, her sense of outrage and the fury of her despair spurred her to armed resistance, exalting her to that warlike grandeur which was rooted in her need for a higher life. . . . Everywhere the assault on her rights provoked her resistance, and she resorted to bloody vengeance." [46]

The entire female sex, led perhaps by Basilea, declared war on the men—and Amazonism was born. "Amazonian phenomena are interwoven with the origins of all peoples. They may be found from Central Asia to the Occident, from the Scythian north to West Africa, and beyond the ocean. . . . Everywhere Amazonism is accompanied by violent acts of bloody vengeance against the male sex." [47]

Yet Amazonism, despite its savagery, was a necessary step toward civilized society, and "it signifies an appreciable rise in human culture. . . . In it lies the first germ of the matriarchy which founded the civilization of all peoples. And this is thoroughly confirmed by history." [48] For without it, and the power it gave the women over the men, there would have been no advancement and the human animal would have remained forever in the twilight zone between beast and man, from which stage only the fear of women eventually raised him.

Thus, the feminine dominance we see so firmly established at the beginning of history was the result of the first great revolution —a revolution that was fought in the name of decency, purity, and social progress, a revolution, moreover, that was led and won by a woman, Basilea. Whether Basilea ever existed or not is irrelevant. Even if she represents only the individualization of a stage in human culture, the important fact in the Basilea story is that it was woman who first brought law and order into a chaotic world by curbing and taming the beast in man and thus making civilization possible.

And the great Sphinx, with its serene and majestic woman's head towering over its crouching beast's body, could well be her monument. Who is to deny it?

Yet, incredibly, nineteenth-century antiquarians referred to the Sphinx as "he"! [49]

7

Mother-Right

*Myth demonstrates the authenticity
of Mother-Right. The contrast between
mythical conceptions and those of subsequent
days is so marked that where more
recent ideas prevailed, it would not have
been possible to invent the phenomena of
Matriarchy.*

—J. J. BACHOFEN

The Mothers

Jane Ellen Harrison's remark about the incongruity of the male adopting the role of mother can be expanded to include the "inherent futility and ugly dissonance" of the father-god taking over the role and functions of the mother-goddess. Yet so far have we come in historical times from the original concept of the deity as female that, as Mary Daly writes, it would seem less blasphemous to refer to God as "it" than as "she." [1]

Perhaps the greatest trouble with the world today is that for some two or three thousand years, and particularly in the past fifteen hundred years, mankind has been worshiping the wrong deity and pursuing the wrong ideals. When man substituted God for the Great Goddess he at the same time substituted authoritarian for humanistic values. Man's relation to God became that of a child to its father, whose love and goodwill can be won only by blind obedience and conformity, as Fromm points out, whereas in the elder world the man-god relationship had been that of the child to its mother—a mother whose love is unconditional and whose goodwill can be taken for granted.[2]

When the goddess of justice gave way to the god of vengeance, man became harsh and inhuman and authoritarianism replaced compassion as the law of life. The dehumanization of modern

society, so resented by modern youth, is the natural and pre-
dictable outgrowth of advanced patriarchalism. In our effort to
conform with blind obedience to the demands of the vengeful
God and his stern preceptors on earth, we have lost the arts of
gentleness and concern. The indictments of "whitey" by American
blacks are indictments not of white, or Caucasian, racial characteristics but of patriarchal traits: arrogance, self-interest, indifference
to the suffering of others, authoritarianism, and the violent enforcement of man-made laws.

Patriarchal peoples place more importance in property rights
than in human rights and more emphasis on rigid moral conformity than on concepts of justice and mercy. Matriarchal societies, as studied by scholars from Morgan and Bachofen to Malinowski and Mead, are characterized by a real democracy in which
the happiness and fulfillment of the individual supersede all other
objectives of society. There is a philosophy of live-and-let-live in
which the dignity and self-hood of each individual is respected
and nurtured. Sexual morals are a matter of personal conscience,
not of law; and "illegitimate" children are unknown for the same
reason that the Spartans denied the possibility of bastardy in ancient
Sparta: that every child born of woman is a legitimate child.

The same conflict between matriarchal and patriarchal values
occurs in the questions of abortion and capital punishment. In
a matriarchal society a woman's body is her own, and to her is
left the decision whether to retain or expel the fetus within her.
In classical Greece and Rome, which were matrilinear but not
matriarchal or gynarchic societies, this privilege was retained by
the women until the fourth century A.D. It was Constantine,
the first *Christian* emperor of Rome, who made induced abortion
a crime;[3] and so it has remained in the majority of Christian
countries to the present time. Capital punishment also is a patriarchal institution—the inexorable law of an eye for an eye. Matriarchates are satisfied with the penitence of the murderer and
the full compensation by him to the victim's dependents. But the
patriarchs must have bloody vengeance, even if the execution of
the culprit wreaks more havoc than benefit on the survivors of the
victim.[4]

In the matriarchal view, the very right of society to establish
arbitrary mores is questioned; and the right of law to enforce conformity to these mores is absolutely denied.

One of the most shocking lapses of morality, in the patriarchal view, is manifested in the birth of fatherless babies. Throughout the patriarchal age women have suffered outrageously for this breach of male property rights, and their unfortunate babies have suffered even worse. Yet the only thing wrong with fatherless families, so deplored by present-day sociologists, is not that they are fatherless but that the mothers do not have the support and approval of society. In a normal, well-regulated, woman-centered society, this would not be the case. The father is not at all necessary to a child's happiness and development, the voluminous writings on the subject by government and related social agencies notwithstanding. For many millennia, in many parts of the world women did, and still do, bring up very fine children without the help of men.

But in our patriarchal society a manless woman is an object of scorn and her children are either pitied or frowned upon. Thus it is our patriarchal mores alone that demand a father in the home—not nature or the well-being of the child.

Contrary to modern sociological tenets, it is not the father-dominated but the mother-centered home that is the happiest. If one asks a group of children who is "boss" at home, those who answer "mother" do so with a bouncy self-assurance, while those who answer "dad" betray a telltale resentment bordering on hate, bespeaking the child's intuitive knowledge that this is a perversion of the natural order of things: that in the home the mother should be boss. When man ceases to be obedient to the lady of the house, the house is turned upside down.[5]

"Mom" has taken a terrific beating in the past few years, being blamed for everything from crime in the streets to slumps on Wall Street. But the truth remains that mom is still by far the greatest influence for good in the life of every child, especially of her sons. One can hardly think of a great man in all of history who was not either fatherless entirely or was so cut off from his father for one reason or another as to have had no contact with him in his formative years. Even in the few cases where there was a father present, it was the son who was the mother's favorite and who was most strongly influenced by her who became great. "Almost without exception . . . the presidents of the United States have been Mama's boys,"[6] and so have the great statesmen, from Pericles and the Gracchi to Winston Churchill and Franklin D. Roosevelt.

"The main contribution made by the fathers of great men is that they gave their wives and sons an unacceptable example which had to be surpassed." [7] In classical myth the heroes and gods are reared exclusively by their mothers. The semihistorical Theseus was reared at Troezen by his mother and did not see his father, Aegeus, until he was grown. It will be remembered that the great Achilles grew up among the women, dressed in girl's clothes. And in the Homeric "Hymn to Hermes," Apollo relates that he was reared by the women and his father "took no heed." [8]

The idea of feminine authority is so deeply embedded in the human subconscious that even after all these centuries of father-right the young child instinctively regards the mother as the supreme authority. He looks upon the father as equal with himself, equally subject to the woman's rule. Children have to be taught to love, honor, and respect the father, a task usually assumed by the mother. Generations of young mothers have been shocked and dismayed on discovering that their children have no instinctive regard for "father."

In nearly every child's experience it is the mother, not the father, who loves all the children equally, stands by them without regard to their worth or lack of it, and forgives without reservation. These are attributes which in the New Testament are given to "God the Father"—but they are exclusively *maternal* qualities, not paternal.

"When nowadays we speak of God as Father we strongly delimit the sources of life," as Harrison says.[9] "The idea of motherhood produces a sense of universal fraternity among all men, which dies with the development of patriarchy," writes Bachofen.[10] The only nation in the world that calls its homeland the fatherland, as opposed to the mother country, is Germany, a land which demonstrated all the excesses latent in extreme patriarchy in the Nazi bloodbath of a few years past. "The family based on father-right is a closed organism, whereas the matriarchal family bears the typically universal character that stands at the beginning of all development." [11]

"The optimistic conception of the next world characteristic of the earlier matriarchal peoples," writes Sybille von Cles-Redin, "in which they believed in resurrection in the all-renewing bosom of the Great Goddess, seems subsequently to have given way to a gloomy pessimistic view of the hereafter. With the retreat of the maternal world and the appearance of the new male gods, the world grew uglier, the idea of destruction more dominant, and the hope of salvation dimmed." [12]

"The relationship which stands at the origin of all culture, of every virtue, of every nobler aspect of existence, is that between mother and child. It operates in a world of violence as the divine principle of love, of peace, of union. Paternal love appears much later. Woman is the source of all benevolence, all culture, all devotion, and of all concern for the living and grief for the dead." [13]

Maternal love was not only the first kind of love. For many millennia it was the only kind. When woman, after she had tamed man, extended her love for her children to include their father, then perhaps man began to learn for the first time what love was. At least he learned to appreciate and be grateful for woman's love, even though he was not emotionally equipped to return it in kind. Eventually he came to depend on woman's love as one of the basic necessities of life. Yet she is still trying to teach him what love really is. For, as Reik points out, when men speak of "love" they are really talking about "scrotal frenzy." [14]

Our modern society, writes Eisler, "is the result of the subjugation of an original frugivorous and agricultural population by hunters who thereafter mainly held the upper-hand. . . . The hunters, the robbers, the pirates, are the conquerors, the wild men, who subdued the fruitgrowers all over the world." [15] But the statesmen, the heroes, the saints, are the fruit growers whose maternal genes prevailed in the inevitable commingling of the tribes.

Thus "the masculine character of our civilization has its origin not in any innate difference in the sexes, but in a preponderance of *force* in the male, which is not at all bound up with the question of civilization." [16] But it was this force, the acquired muscularity of the inferior sex, that led to the patriarchal revolution that is still being waged in the Western world and to the continuing decline of civilization. For "so long as force is supreme—physical force of the individual—society is impossible." [17]

The Natural Superiority of Queens

John Stuart Mill took note of the fact of the superiority of queens over kings and asked why female monarchs, although they had been a minority in historical times, had invariably proved better rulers than kings.[18] Even that eighteenth-century misogynist Montesquieu conceded that women made the best rulers: "Their very weaknesses [sic] generally give them more lenity and moderation, qualifications fitter for good administration than severity and roughness." [19]

This strikes one as somewhat odd reasoning, but it shows that in the eighteenth century, just as today, women's virtues, "lenity and moderation," are characterized as "weaknesses" rather than as the strong and desirable qualities they really are, while men's "severity and roughness" are made virtues—which they are not. As Ashley Montagu says, unless men forego aggressive severity and roughness and adopt some of woman's "weaknesses," civilization is doomed.[20]

As an example of woman's natural talent for rulership and administration in modern times we need go no further than Mill's own land, England. In the history of that great country the greatest eras bear women's names: The Elizabethan Age of Discovery and Expansion, both geographical and intellectual; the age of Queen Anne, when "reason" triumphed in the rapid advancement of the sciences, arts, and letters; and the Victorian Age of the Pax Britannica.

Russia's greatest period prior to the Revolution of 1917 coincided with the reign of a queen, Catherine the Great. And Spain under Isabella achieved the position of world leadership it held in the fifteenth and sixteenth centuries. It was during the long regency of Queen Catherine de Medici in the sixteenth century that France rose to her status as the cultural and intellectual center of the world—a status maintained down to our own time. "Women rulers," writes Montesquieu, "succeed alike in moderate and despotic governments, as the example of England and Russia show; and in Africa and the Indies they are very easy under female administration." [21]

Many writers have begrudgingly noted this phenomenon and have attributed it to the fact that queens have better advisers than kings!—which at least merits them a high rating as adviser-pickers, if nothing else. The more likely answer, however, as Graves, Briffault, Bachofen, James, Fuller, and others have observed, is that men respond better to women's rule—that the very idea of queendoms fulfills an ancient need in man and answers an atavistic longing for the old days of feminine authority, the golden age of queendoms, when peace and justice prevailed on earth and the gods of war had not been born.

Matriliny

"Men feared, adored, and obeyed the matriarch." [22] She took lovers, but for her pleasure, not to provide her children with a father, a commodity early woman saw no need for. Once the relevance of coition to childbirth was recognized by men as well as by women, the status of men gradually improved. The tribal queen, or matriarch, then chose a consort, who "acquired executive power only when permitted to deputize for the queen." [23]

When the king was thus deputized for the queen he wore her robes, padded himself with false breasts and, as a symbol of power and authority, borrowed the queen's lunar ax, the Cretan royal symbol as well as the emblem of gynocracy throughout the ancient world. The king continued to hold his position only by right of marriage to the hereditary queen, and the throne remained matrilinear even in late historical times, long after the triumph of patriarchy. "The King remained under the Queen's tutelage," writes Graves, "long after the matriarchal phase had passed";[24] and long, long after queens had been replaced by kings, "the king derived his right" not from his father but from his mother or wife. "He takes a wife not to beget heirs, for his sons will not succeed him; he takes a wife in order to gain power," and to legalize his right to the throne.[25]

The king was always chosen from outside the royal family, the succession going from queen to daughter, and "the king's coronation consisting entirely in his marriage ceremony with the queen." [26] Kings by marriage eventually sought ways to retain the throne and devised numerous schemes to this end. Incest within the royal family became one method, the king on decease of his wife marrying his own daughter, the heir, or arranging for his son to marry her, which accounts for the widespread custom of sister-brother marriages among royal families of historical times.[27] The Romans established the vestal college to contain the heiresses and to discourage outsiders from attempts on the matrilinear throne through marriage with the royal ladies. That this ploy did not always succeed is attested to by the case of the vestal virgin Rhea

Silvia, who in spite of all precautions became the mother of King Romulus. In Palestine King David established the royal harem for the same purpose—to isolate the woman of the rightful royal house of Saul and to preserve the monarchy in his own family.

"The wide-spread law of female descent lies deep in the history of society," writes Tylor.[28] It was only natural that in a world where paternity was unknown, inheritance should have been confined to the female line. But this maternal priority does not explain why a woman's *sons,* certainly as certifiably her own children as her daughters, were excluded from the inheritance. Nor does it explain why this matrilinear inheritance, or matriliny, should have continued, as it did, long after the establishment of patriarchy and well into historical times. "A gens," says Morgan, "consisted of a female ancestor and her children, together with the children of her daughters and of her female descendants through females in perpetuity. The children of her sons, and of her male descendants through males, were excluded." [29]

"Descent in the female line," wrote Ernst Curtius, "occurs to this day in India; it existed among the ancient Egyptians; and beyond the confines of the East it appears among the Etruscans, the Cretans, the Lycians, and among the Athenians. It would be an error," warns this patristic nineteenth-century Teuton, "to mistake the custom as an *homage* offered to the female sex! It is rather rooted in primitive custom and primordial society." [30]

Herodotus' account of matriliny among the Lycians of his day is well known. But three centuries after Herodotus, Polybius reports that in Locris, near neighbor to Attican Athens, matriliny prevailed even at that late date: "The Locrians themselves have assured me that all nobility of ancestry among them is derived from women and not from men." [31]

The universality of matriliny among all peoples is indicated by the fact that it still survives in the twentieth century A.D. in Oceania —that vast area of the world where matriarchal customs have survived into our own time. "According to the legal principles of the Melanesians . . . only people descendant in the female line from the original ancestress are entitled to the rights of citizenship, hereditary rights to territory, etc.," reports Malinowski.[32] And Mantegazza writes: "Before the advent of the Christian missionaries, the Polynesians were a typically matriarchal people. Women were legally in a position a great deal superior to that of the men . . . and descent and inheritance were in the female line." [33] According to Buck, these conditions still prevail in Polynesian Samoa and Tonga;[34] and Benedict reports similar customs among the Zuni Indian tribes of North America.[35]

The many myths and fairy tales of fair maidens who, like the Sleeping Beauty, are locked up in towers or dungeons or guarded by fierce dragons have their basis in the universal institution of matriliny. The fair maiden is always the hereditary princess with whose hand in marriage will go the kingdom, to the deprivation of her male relatives, who therefore seek to keep her single. The equally prevalent fairy-tale theme of the landless young prince who woos the princess and with her wins the kingdom is also a memorial to matriliny. The landless young prince is the disinherited scion of a matrilineal dynasty who must go and seek his fortune elsewhere through marriage to an heiress, while his sister stays at home upon the throne and chooses among competing suitors for her hand and for her lands.

Strabo, writing in the first century of our era, reports that the Cantabrians, like the Egyptians, limited inheritance to the daughters, who "had the obligation to supply their brothers with dowries." [36] And Diodorus Siculus, a few years later, stated that in his time "only the daughters inherit in Egypt." [37] In Lydia, Lycia, and Caria, also in late historical times, the daughter inherited, no matter how many brothers she may have had. In Lycia, King Bellerophon was succeeded by his daughter Laodamia, to the exclusion of his many sons. And in Lydia, in the sixth century B.C., Candaules' queen murdered her husband and put her lover Gyges on the throne, proving once again that the throne went with the queen and not with her consort. The Trojan War was fought over Helen, not because Menelaus was a jealous husband but because Helen was the hereditary queen without whose consent no King could reign in Lacedaemon.

As late as the fifth century B.C. Persian kings were made by marriage to the royal princess. Herodotus tells us that the great King Cyrus was "the son of a common father" and "a Persian subject lowly in all respects yet he had married the royal daughter of the king, Astyages," and had thus become king of Persia.[38] His successor, Darius, also won the title by virtue of marriage—to Atossa, the daughter of Cyrus. When Darius died in his turn, it was not *his* eldest son, Artabazanes, who became king but the boy Xerxes, son of Queen Atossa by a former, unroyal husband.

Candace was the name, or title, of the hereditary queen of Nubia from the time of Herodotus to the time of Dio Cassius, a span of nearly eight hundred years. Strabo, writing in the year 7 B.C., describes the Candace of his time, whom he had actually seen, as "a masculine sort of woman, blind in one eye." [39] Strabo goes on to report that this one-eyed queen personally led ten thousand troops in battle against the Roman governor of Egypt, Publius Petronius. Candace is mentioned by Pliny the Elder and by Seneca in A.D. 62. Seneca's Candace is no doubt the one mentioned in the Acts of the Apostles, where Philip's conversion of "an eunuch, a great authority under Candace the Queen" is discussed. Nubia, ancient Ethiopia, modern Sudan, in ancient times was a colony of Egypt populated by Egyptians.

It was a Phoenician queen, Dido, who founded the great city state of Carthage and reigned over it until her death, followed by a succession of queens descended in direct line from her. Legend and Virgil say that one of her queen daughters was fathered by Aeneas on his way to Italy after the Trojan War and that it was Aeneas' refusal to remain in Carthage and become her consort that caused the beautiful Dido to throw herself from the walls of her city. However that may be, the gynarchy of Carthage some centuries later may have been the cause of Cato's obsession with the idea that Carthage must be destroyed: *Carthago delendum est,* with which vow he closed his every Senate speech. Cato was a rabid antifeminist and was responsible for the Voconian laws of the late republic which temporarily deprived Roman women of some of their ancient rights and privileges.[40] Temporarily, because the laws were repealed under the empire and were not reinstated until the Christian era, but then in a much harsher form.

In modern Ghana, neighbor to ancient Carthage, "like Dido the queens of the Akan have wielded power since times beyond memory; and like the Phoenician and Carthaginian goddess Tanit, the Akan goddess Nyame gave birth to the universe without a male partner." [41]

In Egypt, as in the rest of the ancient world, the throne descended through the female line, the husband of the heiress becoming pharaoh. It was for this reason that brother-sister marriages were the rule rather than the exception in the Egyptian royal family. But the brother reigned only with the consent of the heir, his sister-wife. Occasionally the legitimate heir refused to give her consent, as was the case with Nitocris of the sixth dynasty who, Manetho tells us, reigned as absolute monarch; and as was probably the case with the unknown lady of Sakkara whose recently discovered tomb proclaims her to have been a powerful and mighty pharaoh in her day.[42]

Such also was the case with Queen Hatshepsut, daughter of Thutmose I, who was married first to her older brother and then, on his death, to her younger brother. During both of these marriages Hatshepsut reigned supreme as pharaoh, and her long and glorious reign is recognized to have been one of Egypt's finest hours. Velikovsky very interestingly and persuasively identifies her with the queen of Sheba who visited Solomon.[43] Upon Hatshepsut's death, her brother-husband ascended the throne as Thutmose III, perhaps having married his niece, and immediately launched his country into a series of bloody wars of conquest.

Rawlinson and James Breasted, both of whom should have known better, consider the reign of Hatshepsut to have constituted an act of usurpation. Breasted calls her "aggressive" and her seizure of the throne "an enormity." [44] And Rawlinson describes her as "a woman of great energy, of masculine mind, clever, vindictive, and unscrupulous." [45] Yet the evidence for matrilinear succession was plain and unequivocal even in their day. Both of these Victorian scholars, bred in the patriarchal tradition of the incapacity of women, to paraphrase a famous lady,[46] were incapable of recognizing it, naturally assuming that women had always been the nonentities the Victorian male had molded them into and that therefore the Thutmoses II and III had been wrongfully bilked of their rights by their sister. Twentieth-century scholars, however, have seen the truth and have openly acknowledged it—as did the ancients.

The very last of the pharaohs, Cleopatra, queen of Egypt in the century just preceding the Christian era, was also married to her brother, but it was she who was recognized as pharaoh and absolute ruler of her nation. It was with her that Antony and Caesar dealt in their attempts to win Egypt over to their opposed causes in the Roman civil war. And it was she, who incidentally was a pure-bred blond Macedonian Greek and not the sultry half-breed which modern sociologists and cinema moguls would have her, who led her fleet at the battle of Actium. Octavian, who won that battle and for the victory was proclaimed emperor as Augustus, was the cognatic nephew (on the female side, that is) of Julius Caesar. And Augustus himself was succeeded years later on the imperial throne by the descendants of his wife, Livia, his own agnatic relatives being left out of it.

Livy tells us that the first Roman tribes were headed by women,[47] and Tacitus that the great Claudian imperial family was descended from a glorious ancestress, Claudia Quinta, whose shrine was revered in his own time.[48] Marcus Aurelius became emperor through marriage to Faustina, daughter of Faustina the Elder and Antoninus Pius. The younger Faustina was a great adulteress, but Marcus Aurelius refused to take the advice of the Senate and divorce her because, he said, "if I part from Faustina I shall have to part from her dowry, which is the Roman Empire." [49]

It is a sad commentary on the "improvement" in morals introduced by Christianity that only two centuries after Marcus Aurelius the first *Christian* emperor, Constantine, boiled his innocent young wife alive on mere suspicion of adultery. And Constantine's misogyny is a long leap indeed from ancient Sumer, when it was decreed that a man caught in adultery must die but that the woman should go free. "She shall make affirmation of her innocence and shall return in peace to her house," reads the text, "and her husband shall welcome her," as the law decrees.[50]

Constantine himself, like Marcus Aurelius, was a beneficiary of matriliny, having won the empire by virtue of his marriage to Fausta, the daughter of the Emperor Maximian.

Matriliny prevailed in Europe among all ranks of the people until the late Middle Ages, when Teutonic and/or church law finally triumphed over the older Celto-Roman legal system. Henry Hallam points out that daughters succeeded to lands and titles on an equal basis with sons as late as the fourteenth century in France, despite the Salic law of the Teutonic Franks that excluded females in direct descent.[51]

Montesquieu suggests that the Salic law has been misread by modern historians. "If daughters had been generally debarred by the Salic law from the inheritance of land," he writes, "it would be impossible to explain the histories, formularies, and charters which are continually mentioning the lands and possessions of the females." [52] It is significant that even under the Salic

law, which favored sons over daughters, sisters took precedence
over brothers and *mothers'* sisters over fathers' sisters. "The sister
of the mother," writes Montesquieu, "was a tie that had in it
something most tender." [53]

Thus we see that sister priority, which we have found prevailing
from modern Polynesia to ancient Celtic Europe, prevailed also
among the "barbarous Germans," as Montesquieu dubs them. If
the sororal relationship was endowed even in historical times by
the antifeminist Germans with an aura of sanctity, how much
more sacred must have been that of the mother and the daughter
before these lineally closer relationships had been found to
threaten the property rights of the male.

Among the Franks and the Saxons, Teutonic peoples both,
daughters inherited when there were no sons, and the daughter
had precedence over the son's son.[54] Patrilinear inheritance and
female exclusion, so taken for granted in modern society, are in
reality very recent innovations. Yet the heartbreak they have
caused is incalculable. The lasting grief of Victoria Sackville-West,
who in 1925 could not inherit her beloved ancestral home, Knole,
because the law decreed that a distant male relative of her father's
had precedence over the daughter, has been mentioned often.
This injustice was accepted by most as an immutable law; yet
only a few hundred years ago, under Saxon law, Lady Victoria
would have been considered the natural and rightful heir of her
father and of his title and estates.

In the United States, where we have never had entailed estates
(the Virginia Declaration of Rights banned them in colonial times),
it is nonetheless customary for the son to inherit the bulk of his
father's wealth and property as the scion who will "carry on the
name"—an absurdity unequaled in the long annals of human
absurdities. For what is this "name"? The daughters as well as the
sons are born with it, and in a just society the daughters and their
children could retain and perpetuate it, as they so often did in the
Middle Ages and as far back in history as one cares to go.

Even as late as the eighteenth century, the great name of Churchill was perpetuated through the *daughter,* not the son, of the
first Duke of Marlborough. It was *her* children who retained and
carried on the ducal title and the Churchill name, their father's
name of Spencer taking second place and finally being virtually
dropped by the greatest of Churchills, Sir Winston.

Modern law of the past few centuries has diminished the status
of women even below that of the Teutonic women of the barbarous
Germans of the late Middle Ages and far below that of the Celts,
among whom, as Tacitus wrote, *"no distinction of sex was made in
their successions."* [55] Even among the Hebrews, matriliny prevailed into historical times, as the Old Testament, albeit unintentionally, reveals.

Matriliny in the Bible

"Sarah ranked higher than her husband, Abraham," say the
legends of the Jews. Abraham owed his flocks and his herds, as
well as his position as tribal chief, to his wife Sarah.[56] It is clear
from the legends, though not so clear from the book of Genesis,
that Sarah was a Chaldean princess who conferred status on
Abraham by marrying him. That she was the more important
personage is hinted at in the Old Testament and made abundantly
clear in the legends. *The Legends of the Jews* is a compilation of
old Jewish traditions that survived in the minds of the people after
the Pentateuch had been submitted to drastic editing by the later
patriarchs and presents, therefore, a far more accurate view of early
Judaism.

In the legends it is said that "the death of Sarah was a great loss
to her country. So long as she was alive all went well in the land.
After her death confusion ensued." [57] And confusion does not en-
sue on the death of a mere consort.

The fact is that Abraham was the "mere consort." His tribe
was originally the tribe of Sarah, and it was to her that the alleged
promise of God was given—that she would found a great nation.
According to the legends, when Sarah was informed that Abraham
was up in the hills preparing to sacrifice Isaac, or Israel as he came
to be called, "she turned to stone" and died on the spot.[58] Thus
she never knew that God had stayed the hand of Abraham and
that her son lived. The Jews acquired their name "Israelites" not
from father Abraham but from Sarah's son Isaac, or Israel. In a patrilinear society the son's name would not have replaced the father's,
and the Hebrews would have been known as *Abramites,* not *Israelites.* It was only in matrilinear societies that the mother's name
was later superseded by the son's.

Talmudic scholars, Jewish rabbis all, have long acknowledged
that the matriarchs, Sarah, Rebecca, Rachel, and Leah, were more

important persons than their consorts, Abraham, Isaac, and Jacob.[59] Yet postexilic patriarchal editors of the Old Testament concealed the fact very successfully. For that reason it is curious that at least one important queen of Israel was allowed to retain her rank and importance in the Old Testament: Deborah was left as she had always been, "with dominion over the mighty."

In the Old Testament Book of Judges, Deborah is a judge in Israel, and she herself proclaims her status as head of the tribe: "I, Deborah, arose a mother in Israel." "The children of Israel came to her for judgment," says the Book of Judges 4:4. She sent for her general, Barak, and ordered him into battle at the head of ten thousand against Sisera the Canaanite. She was thus not only judge and chief of the tribes of Israel, but she was also commander in chief of the armies and reigning queen of her people. This portion of the Old Testament probably gives an accurate picture of the ancient queendoms; yet Deborah's reign occurred well within historical times—in the first millennium B.C.

Christian Bible commentators, horrified at the idea of a reigning queen in historical Israel, have transferred the judgeship to Barak and have made Deborah a mere "prophetess," subservient to Barak. But that is not the way the Bible tells it. And in this case, at least, the Bible can be trusted to be accurate.

And so, why was Deborah's story unchanged by the patriarchal editors? The answer is simple: the story of Deborah is left whole and unedited because it contains the Jew's most prized literary gem, the *Song of Deborah,* the earliest artistic product of a semi-literate people. The later editors would no more have tampered with this poem than modern editors would alter a word of the Hamlet soliloquy. Other, and perhaps more important, queens might be sacrificed to the cause of male supremacy—but not Deborah and her song.

Sigmund Freud was "astonished" (his word) to hear that as late as the fifth century B.C. a Jewish colony in upper Egypt near Elephantine was still worshiping the ancient and original Jewish deity, the goddess 'Anat.[60] If Freud had been acquainted with his own national literature he may have been even more astonished to have read in the Book of Judges that about the time of Homer a queen had ruled in Israel.

With all their horror of incest, the Jews yet married their female relatives for dynastic reasons, as in the cases of Nahor and

Jochebed, who married their respective aunts—their father's, not
their mother's, sisters, be it noted. For among the early Hebrews,
as in all ancient societies, kinship was counted only through the
mother. The paternal kin were not considered blood relatives.
For this reason marriage between siblings of the same father but
different mothers was not considered incest. As Demosthenes, the
great orator of classical Greece, said of one of his clients: "He
legally married his sister, she *not* being his sister by the same
mother." [61]

In the New Testament, as well as in the Old, matriliny again
rears her august head, in spite of all the editors' efforts to lop it off.
For it is obvious that the genealogy of Jesus offered in the Gospel of
Matthew was originally and correctly the genealogy not of Joseph
but of Mary. Jesus owed his authority and his royal blood to his
mother, Mary, who was "a descendant of the tribe of Judah and the
royal house of David." [62]

Only Luke's Gospel mentions Mary's lineage, the other Gospels
having transferred Mary's genealogy to Joseph. Yet Joseph, in
Christian belief, had no part in Jesus' conception. How then could
Jesus have traced his Davidic ancestry through Joseph, who was
not his father? The elaborate genealogy of Joseph as reconstructed
in Matthew, seeming to outline the descent of Jesus and ending
lamely with "Matthan begat Jacob and Jacob begat Joseph the
husband of Mary of whom was born Jesus," reminds one of the
old "rube" joke: The rube is directing a lost traveler to his hotel,
and after intricate and lengthy directions the rube ends lamely,
"there is a hotel there, but it ain't it."

Neither was Joseph "it." According to the lore of the New
Testament, the legends of Jesus and Mary perpetuated by word
of mouth by their own neighbors: "Matthan begat Anna, who
bore Mary, of whom was born Jesus who was called the Christ."
And this genealogy makes a great deal more sense than the Biblical one which traces David's descendants to a dead end in Joseph
"the husband of Mary."

In the legends, Herod is blamed for having destroyed *Mary's*
family records in order to conceal the royal blood of Jesus. [63]

It is far more likely, however, that the transference of Mary's
family tree to Joseph is the result of later editing by scribes ordered
to "play Mary down" in accordance with the new Pauline Christian
doctrine of the unimportance and expendability of women.

Part II
The Patriarchal Revolution

*It is, perhaps, in a spirit of
revenge that man has for so many
centuries made woman his slave.*
—EDWARD CARPENTER

8

Ram Versus Bull

The strictness of the patriarchal
system points to an older system that
had to be combatted and suppressed.
—J. J. BACHOFEN

The Taurian and Arian Ages

In India in the eighteenth century after Christ there existed
a megalith, reminiscent of ancient gynocratic woman's mysterious
ways with stone, carved in the form of a gigantic bull. Richard
Payne Knight, an eighteenth-century traveler in India, describes
this megalithic bull as he saw it at Tanjore late in the 1700's:

> It is a statue of a bull lying down, hewn with great accuracy
> out of a solid piece of hard granite which must have been con-
> veyed by land from the distance of some hundred or more miles,
> although its weight in its present reduced state must have been at
> least one hundred tons. Even the flexible perseverance and ha-
> bitual industry of the natives of that country could scarcely have
> erected it without *far greater knowledge* [author's italics] in prac-
> tical mechanics than they now possess.[1]

The bull and phallus, symbols of generation, are infallible indications of the presence of gynarchic societies. For even if men
in ancient times knew nothing about the male role in procreation,
it is obvious that women did. Both Malinowski and A. M. Hocart
say of the Trobrianders that although the men did not connect
intercourse with impregnation, the women evidently did and kept
the secret from the men in order to preserve their independence.[2]

That the largest likeness of a bull yet discovered should have
been found in India is curious, for according to myth and tradition India was the first civilized nation to switch from mother-

right to father-right. The bull of Tanjore, then, must have been extremely ancient, dating from a time before Rama.

Rama, the dissident Aryan, we are told by Fabra d'Olivet, converted India from gynarchy and goddess worship to patriarchy and god worship about three thousand years before our era.[8] Before Rama all women were regarded as divine beings in whose province fell law and justice, religion, philosophy, poetry, music, and all the finer aspects of life. Rama, however, the first patriarchal hero, resented the power and authority of the women and, unable to overthrow them in his native land—somewhere in Anatolia or southern Europe—he departed his country and wandered into India.

Perhaps Rama came from Thrace, that mysterious center of the ancient civilization whence Orpheus was later to bring the long-lost knowledge of the plurality of worlds and the sun-centered universe and where Philip of Macedon was to find evidence, in the fifth century B.C., of a great forgotten technology far surpassing anything the Greeks were capable of. If Rama had been an early rebel against the original gynocracy and had been expelled from his homeland for this reason, the Rama myth in both Europe and India would be explained. In European myth Rama sought to abolish the ancient priestess (Druid) colleges and establish a male priesthood. In this effort he set up the ram as his symbol and made it the rallying point for his masculist followers. The Ramites then warred against the people of the bull, the feminist people, but were defeated; and Rama led his people out of Europe into India.

Throughout the ancient world the ram became the symbol of patriarchy, just as the bull was that of matriarchy. It is a curious fact that according to astrology the age of the bull, the Taurian Age, coincided historically with the last two thousand years of the gynarchates—4000 to 2000 B.C., while the Arian Age, the age of Aries the ram, coincided with the age that immediately preceded the Christian era, the time of the patriarchal revolution. The Piscean Age, the age of the fish, embraced the Christian era, the two-thousand-year period from which we are just now emerging, and it is therefore appropriate that the fish became the symbol of Christianity.[4]

But the fish was also the symbol of the Great Goddess, Tiamat, and of her cities, Ur and Nineveh. May we surmise from this that a previous Piscean Age, 26,000 or 52,000, or even 104,000 years ago[5] saw the birth of civilization under the goddess? And that an equally remote Taurian Age had seen the flowering of Atlantis? For Plato says that in Atlantis the bull was sacred, and that the Atlanteans performed a bull dance similar to that celebrated in Crete, where the bull was also revered. Further, the chief city of Atlantis, according to Plato, was Poseidonia, named for the god who was son of Potnia, the Great Goddess of Crete. And, of course, Crete was the last surviving world power of the gynocratic Taurian Age.

The ram symbolized the patriarchal unsettled society of herders and hunters—the rejects of the civilized queendoms. It is not by chance, therefore, that the shepherd analogy abounds in the Old Testament or that the "golden calf" was the object of such anathema to the prophets of Israel, symbolizing as it did the feminine power with which the nomadic peoples were at war. Even in the New Testament the ram analogy is carried on, for Jesus is called a shepherd and his followers sheep.

It was these Ramites, the nomadic shepherds, as we have seen, who overthrew the established agricultural communities in the Near East and ushered in the first historical dark age; and it was the shepherd kings, the Hyksos, who destroyed the advanced civilization of ancient gynocratic Egypt. It was the shepherd king David who finally conquered the intellectually superior Philistines. And it was Abel, the keeper of flocks, who was the real hero in the eyes of the Semitic authors of Genesis, while Cain, the husbandman and settled tiller of the soil, was the villain.

In a queer twist of allegory, the Genesis writers allowed the shepherd hero to be slain by the villain farmer—in total contradiction of the facts. For in history it had been the uncivilized shepherds, the Abels, who had slain the civilized husbandmen, the Cains —not the reverse.

Cain and Abel

The Biblical story of Cain and Abel reflects the changeover from the previous age of peace and nonviolence to the barbarism of the patriarchal age. Under the goddess, as Bachofen says, "Special cul-

pability was attached to the physical injury of any living creature"
—man or beast.[6] So in accepting Abel's offering of meat, "the first-
lings of the flock and the fat thereof," and rejecting Cain's offering
of the "fruits of the ground," the new male God was announcing
his law: that thenceforth harmony among men and beasts was out,
and killing and violence were in.

The story may be a garbled version of an older Sumerian account
wherein the goddess accepted Cain's gift and punished Abel's
bloodlust with death. The mark of Cain may have been originally
a sign of the goddess' favor, bespeaking her approval of the older
frugivorous agricultural race over the new meat-eating gangs represented by Abel. On the other hand, the myth may have been
invented by the Semites to justify their overthrow of the civilized
Cainites (Sumerians) by the pastoral and nomadic Abelites, the
Semites. There can be no doubt that Abel is the hero in the Semitic
account. Though favored by God he is slain by Cain, who was his
elder, as the Sumerians were the elders of the Semitic peoples. If
the original Sumerian account of this allegory is ever found it will
probably feature Cain as the hero and Abel as the villain. And that
there was an earlier account can hardly be doubted in face of the
evidence that the Genesis authors invented nothing else in their
distorted compilation of old Babylonian legends.

The form in which the myth has come down to us does not
make sense. Flavius Josephus tries to explain it, but he only com-
pounds the nonsense by saying that God was "more honored by
Abel's offering of what grew naturally and of its own accord than
what was gotten by forcing the ground." [7] Here the word "force"
is ridiculously misapplied, as though tilling the ground were a
more violent act than murdering an innocent lamb. Louis Ginzberg writes that in the old tradition the mark with which Cain
was branded was leprosy, which is probably a later Jewish attempt
to make Cain seem dangerously unclean, further to justify their
elevation of Abel.

After the murder of Abel, says Ginzberg, "the earth changed and
deteriorated, and the trees and plants refused to yield their fruits." [8]
This may be a clue to the cause of the "mutation" of man from
agricultural pacifist to beast of prey.[9] If a worldwide drought had
occurred, as suggested in the legend and as postulated by Velikovsky in *Earth in Upheaval*,[10] man may have been forced to kill in
order to survive. "At the end of the pluvial period," writes Eisler,

"man driven by hunger to aggression, learned to hunt in common,
devouring alive the run-down booty." [11] This theory accords with
the ancient Babylonian-Semitic legend that it was not until the
time of Noah, when the earth had been depleted by the flood, that
God gave man permission to eat his fellow animals.[12] With the
transition from peaceful tillage to rapine and murder may have
come the revolt of man against a disapproving goddess and the
enthronement of a murder-approving, bloodthirsty male god.

Whatever happened, "The primitive food-gathering peaceful
man characterized by Plato and other ancient philosophers, must
have suffered a radical change in diet and modus vivendi—a mutation such as is remembered in mankind's widespread tradition of a
fall, or original sin, with permanently disastrous consequences." [13]

The killing and eating of animals by man is a recent phenomenon and is related in time to the patriarchal revolution. Greek
myth records that it was not until the Bronze Age, almost within
human memory, that man defied the matriarch and learned to eat
meat. Lucretius, as well as Plato, tells us that early man lived on
roots, berries, acorns, grain, and fruits; and Porphyry that our
ancestors sacrificed only fruits and vegetables.[14]

Cain and Abel personify the war of the Bull and the Ram, and
their conflict is the first event recorded in the Bible after the Creation.

Violence characterized the patriarchal revolution. "Again and
again, in examining ancient sites, one finds evidence of the violent
destruction of once peaceful city-states." [15] At the site of the ancient
city of Ur in modern Iraq, the oldest building excavated up to 1927
was discovered to be the goddess temple. The temple had been
guarded by four copper bulls, which had evidently been the object
of the invading Ramites' fury. For the bull images had been thrown
down in a heap at the base of the walls, and then the walls had
been undercut and toppled over so as to shatter and crush the
offending bull symbols of the goddess.[16]

Counterrevolution

Occasionally archeological evidence is found of what appears to
be a counterrevolution, when the Bull, as it were, turns on the
Ram and fights back. Sir Leonard Woolley describes one such incident in the long Bull-Ram war in his account of the ancient city

of Alalakh. For in this long-buried city of Anatolia, which showed evidence of having changed hands frequently over a period of thirteen hundred years, the bull and the ram images alternate on the different archeological levels in such a manner as to indicate when the matriarchs and when the patriarchs were in control. The top, or latest, level, dated about 1200 B.C., showed that the patriarchs had won the last battle: "A much defaced limestone figure of a seated goddess," writes Woolley, was found thrown down in the forecourt of the temple "among the remnants of a smashed bull image." At the same level was found a carved ram's head, "the only object left whole . . . the white limestone head of a ram." [17]

Alalakh, near modern Atchana in Turkey, was excavated between 1936 and 1949. The archeologists at the site, headed by Woolley, found evidence that the city had been an extremely ancient matriarchal city-state that must have been first conquered by invading nomads in the third millennium. But in the nineteenth century B.C., after many years of patriarchal rule during which the goddess shrines had been converted to god shrines and the bulls' heads replaced by rams' heads, there was a violent uprising of the original matriarchal inhabitants. The temple of the new gods was razed to the ground, and the palace of the patriarchal king was destroyed by fire.

"In this studied break with everything that stood for the hated kingdom of the conquerors," [18] we have a clear picture of a Taurian counterrevolution, in which the defiling god of the conquerors is replaced violently by the ancient goddess, and the palace of the patriarchal king is burned to the ground, its site becoming an abomination of desolation to the counterrevolutionaries.

It is a matter of history that Egypt in the eighteenth century B.C. staged a counterrevolution in expelling the patriarchal shepherd kings, the Hyksos, and restoring its ancient matriarchal way of life. Herodotus, writing in the fifth century B.C., twelve hundred years after the expulsion of the Ramite Hyksos, reports that in Egypt in his day the women attended to the mercantile business, conducting trade and providing for the family, "while the men sit at home at the loom." And he adds, "in Egypt sons need not support their parents, but daughters must." [19] As late as the first century Egyptian girls, as heirs of the family property, had to supply their brothers with dowries so that they could attract wives. From such evidence it seems indubitable that the Egyptian counterrevolution had been thoroughly successful.

In distant Indo-European India, however, the outcome of the Ramite revolution, led by Rama himself, was more successful for the patriarchs. Rama attacked from within, so to speak, first winning the hand of the hereditary princess Sita, and then proceeding to dominate her, to mistreat her, and finally to usurp her position as monarch.

The vile treatment of Sita by Rama, as recorded in the *Ramayana*,[20] and her patient endurance and steadfast loyalty under his cruelty, are obvious attempts by the late revisionists of the *Ramayana* to intimidate women and teach them docility, just as the *Pentateuch* is an obvious attempt on the part of its authors to belittle and degrade women. The lesson of both documents is to impress upon the female sex the fact that all women, even goddess-queens such as Sita, must meekly accept abuse and injustice as their lot in life.

Rousseau's ideas of woman's place and destiny, as expressed in his *Émile,* are reminiscent of the legendary treatment of Sita at the hands of Rama five thousand years ago: "Formed to obey man, woman must learn to suffer injustice and bear the tyrannies of a cruel husband without complaint. . . . Meekness on the woman's part will often bring a husband back to reason if he is not absolutely a brute." [21]

In other words, woman should be a docile victim, even to a brute. Yet this same Rousseau in *The Social Contract* says of slavery and the immorality of enforced obedience: "Force is a physical power; and I do not see what morality can result from its effects. . . . No man has any natural authority over his fellow human beings, and force produces no right to any." [22]

Obviously, in Rousseau's philosophy, " 'human being' has been struck from the definition of woman," and only man is human.[23]

Rama died in India five thousand years ago, and his reign was followed by centuries of warfare between the matriarchal people of the Bull, the Kourava, and the patriarchal Ramites, the Pandavas. It was not until the coming of Krishna (Vishnu) that the Ramites finally won out and India settled down to unrelieved, unadulterated patriarchalism.

Indian religion, however, did not completely abolish women

from its hierarchy as did the Jewish and Christian religions with
their all-male trinity. For in the Hindu trinity there are father,
mother, and son; and the virgin mother of Krishna, Devaki, is the
second person in the trinity. She is worshiped as "Goddess of the
Logos, Mother of the gods, One with Creation." The prayer to
Devaki reads:

"Thou art Intelligence, the mother of science, mother of courage;
the firmament and the stars are thy children; from thee proceeds
all that exists, Thou hast descended to the earth for the salvation
of the world." [24]

Babylon and the Jews

"Pastoral nomadism can be proved to have post-dated the
agricultural age, and marked a definite cultural depression in the
history of man. . . . The pastoral-nomadic age, as the Children
of Israel who belonged to it show clearly enough, was a warlike
and destructive one." [25] In the nineteenth century it was firmly believed "that men became shepherds before they advanced to the
state of tillers of the soil," as a curator of the British Museum
wrote a hundred years ago.[26] But this is no longer the theory accepted by modern scholarship, and the believers in the steady upward progress of mankind have had to revise their conceptions.
For settled agricultural gynarchic societies preceded the nomadic
pastoral stage and were in fact destroyed by semibarbaric nomads.

Until quite recently nearly all the ancient civilizations of the
Near East were thought to have been Semitic. Even *The Mythology
of All Races* (1916 edition, reprinted in 1964) still includes Sumerian myth in its Semitic volume. Modern scholarship, however,
has quite definitely concluded that all the early civilizations of the
Near East were non-Semitic and belonged either to the Indo-European or to a pre-Indo-European family—such as the Sumerian,
through the Hittite, Iranian, Mitannian, Ionian, Minoan, Ugaritic,
Phoenician, and so on. And recent Anatolian archeology has shown
that the people who colonized and civilized Mesopotamia, the Near
East, and the Aegean from their base in Anatolia were primarily
Indo-European. The ancient Egyptians, like the ancient Nubians
(Ethiopians) and the pre-Greek Pelasgians, belonged to a fair-
skinned so-called Mediterranean race which was certainly non-
Semitic, as their murals and wall paintings clearly show.

The Semitic peoples of old were confined to the Arabian Peninsula, whence, presumably, the later Hebrew tribes emerged. The
Semites never achieved a civilization of their own (unless the great
Moorish Islamic civilization of the eighth to thirteenth centuries
after Christ can be classified as Semitic), the modern desert Arabs
being true to the ancient Semitic pattern of unsettled semibarba-
rism. The Moslem Arabs today still worship the ancient goddess of
Semitic Arabia in the shape of a black stone enshrined in the
Kaaba at Mecca. "To this day," writes Reik, "pilgrims go to Mecca
to kiss this ancient image of the Great Arabian Goddess." [27]

The Hebrews imbibed a modicum of culture from their long
sojourn in civilized Egypt; and they were later shrewd enough to
adopt the civilization of Canaan, but to this already established
culture they contributed nothing.[28] The Babylonian captivity was
another civilizing episode in the life of the Hebrews, and it was
during this period in the sixth century B.C. that the Old Testament,
based on Sumerian-Babylonian history and legend, was conceived
and partially written, but not without great distortion and bowd-
lerizing.

Yet it was these people, cultureless and semicivilized, who first
upset civilization in the ancient East by overthrowing the city states
and later by dethroning the ancient goddess and enthroning male
strife in the form of Yahweh. "It was stated and proved long ago
by the historians," writes Reik, "that the Hebrew tribes, like their
neighboring nations, worshipped a . . . goddess . . . and that
only the severe regime of Yahwism suppressed the ancient cult of
which traces still survive in the Old Testament." [29]

During their captivity in Babylon the Jews heard the legend of
Tiamat and the account of the creation of the world as written in
the *Enuma Elish*. In the oldest advanced civilization yet discovered,
the Sumerian, the creator of the universe is Tiamat, the goddess
who later became Ishtar. The Jews decided to include this myth
in their national literature, with the one difference that Tiamat
must become a god and their own ancient goddess Iahu, or 'Anat,
must be completely abolished.

And so, on their return from Babylon, the Jewish priests set to
work to bowdlerize the ancient truths. They took the lines of the
Enuma Elish: "In the beginning Tiamat brought forth the heaven
and the earth. . . . Tiamat, the mother of the gods, creator of
all," [30] worked them over in their patriarchal minds and came out

with: "In the beginning *God* [author's italics] created the heavens and the earth," etc., a close paraphrase of the original account—yet how vastly different.

"The first four chapters of Genesis," writes Graves, "are an extremely late literary product." [31] The creation legend, including the story of Adam and Eve, "was written not earlier than the end of the fifth century [B.C.] by a post-exilic priest who lived in Jerusalem, and was based partly on a slightly earlier account penned by a Judaean prophet," both priest and prophet stealing copiously from the *Enuma Elish*. These differing accounts were incorporated into the final book of Genesis, to the confusion of everyone. In one account of the creation of Eve, she is created at the same time as Adam: "Man and woman created he them." In the later account God creates Adam, then the animals, and finally, as an afterthought, makes woman out of Adam's rib!

Adam and Eve

"A tale such as the Genesis account of Eve's creation from Adam's rib is in its whimsicality a piece of grotesque fantasy—a monotheistic masquerade," writes Reik.[32] The Adam and Eve myth has been completely reversed from its original meaning; Eve is not born from Adam's rib, but Adam from Eve's. "The tradition that Adam gives birth to Eve is a reversal of the *original* version that Adam was born from . . . the Great Earth Goddess." [33]

"It must be borne in mind, while reading the Old Testament, that when the Jews decided to disown their own old Goddess-religion and adopt male monotheism, they were obliged to recast all the popular myths concerned with the Goddess—which was no light task." [34] All myths of the creation, including the original Hebrew one, substantiate the earliest social stage, "the unqualified matriarchates," [35] in which a goddess performs the act of creation. Yahweh himself had been created by the goddess 'Anat, Mother of All Living, who was Eve (in Hebrew *Hawwah*, "Mother of every kindred"). Eve then created Adam, and he became her consort, just as in all early religions the goddess elevated her son to the kingship and he ruled by her consent. Adam thus stood in relation to Eve as Marduk to his mother Tiamat.[36]

This is in line with all other creation myths, in which the goddess gives birth to a son who later becomes her spouse, as in the myths of Marduk, Zeus, Tammuz, Osiris, Attis, Adonis, Poseidon, and many others. Even in the central Christian myth this theme is faithfully carried out, in that Mary gives birth to Jesus who is both God the father and the Holy Ghost—in other words Mary marries the God *before* she creates him.

The Garden of Eden in the Genesis story represents the lost golden age of the Great Goddess, Eve. "Jehovah did not figure in the original myth. It is the Mother of All Living [Eve], who [creates Adam and then] casts him out of the fertile dominions because he has usurped some prerogative of hers." [87]

"Eve constitutes three-quarters of the God's essence," writes Schuré, "for the name of the god is composed of the prefix *Jod* (j) and the word *Eve*. Once each year the high priest uttered the divine name, spelling it out letter by letter: Jod, he, vau, he." [88] The "E-Vo-E" of the Bacchantes and the cry of the maenads may be echoes of this ancient Eve cult that predated Yahweh by untold millennia.

"The story of Eve's creation from Adam's rib is equalled in perversity only by the post-Homeric myth of Athene's birth from the head of Zeus . . . a grotesquerie that Harrison calls a desperate theological expedient to rid Athene of her Matriarchal condition" [89] and to demote her from her age-old position as chief of the immortals and creator of the race of Greeks. "According to all myth, the female, not the male, gives life." [40]

In the Biblical myth, "the natural course of events, that women give birth to men, is reversed," writes Erich Fromm. "Eve is born from Adam's rib. . . . God creates the world. Women's creative powers are not necessary. But the purposed elimination of matriarchal memories is not complete." [41] In spite of the story's anti-feminist objective, "we see in Eve the woman who is superior to the man. She takes the initiative and does not consult Adam." [42] Moreover, she nobly takes the blame for her husband's weakness and emerges the stronger of the pair, in contradiction to the purpose of the myth which is to degrade the woman and make of her a vicious troublemaker. It is interesting that in the *Legends of the Jews* Eve is said to have remarked late in her life: "I promised him that I would protect him from God. And so he blamed me when we were ejected from the Garden," [48] which certainly implies that the woman was expected to be the protector—the stronger of the couple, and the liaison with God.

The whole intention of the distortion manifested in the Hebrew tale of Adam and Eve is twofold: first, to deny the tradition of a female creator; and second, to deny the original supremacy of the female sex. It is significant that only the Jews strove to deny the feminine creation. Even after patriarchy had succeeded in suppressing the tradition of female supremacy, the belief in a feminine creator persisted throughout the world. In Greece, Rome, Egypt, Syria, and even in India, the creation of the world and of men continued to be attributed to the Great Goddess as Rhea, Bona Dea, Isis, Tiamat, and Devaki far into the Christian era.

"Jewish culture as recorded in the Old Testament is outspokenly patriarchal," writes Karen Horney. "Only by being aware of this fact can we recognize the male bias in the Adam and Eve story." First of all, continues Horney, woman's capacity to give birth is first denied, and then devalued. In the second place, in tempting Adam, Eve appears as the sexual temptress who plunges man into misery. "I believe these two elements, the first born of [man's] resentment, and the second born of [his] anxiety, have damaged the relations between the sexes from the earliest times." [44]

That the story was invented for just such a purpose can hardly be denied. Inspired by what Jane Harrison calls "patriarchal malice," [45] the cruel myth of Eve's guilt has succeeded in its purpose. The Christian Church has used it for two thousand years to chasten women, and women themselves have accepted it as proof of their unworthiness. This gigantic hoax was perpetrated by men with the deliberate intention of placing women in a subservient, penitential, and guilt-ridden position.

It is time the church absolved women of Eve's "sin," as it has absolved the Jews of their "crime." In both cases, the "sin" and the "crime" were fabricated lies promoted by the church to gain its own ends—one, the end of keeping women in subjection, the other, the end of giving the early Christians who did not want to become Christians a scapegoat race upon whom they could vent their rage against the church.

Zeus and Athene

Just as the Jews of Palestine transmogrified their ancient goddess from bearer and giver of life to mere accipient, born of the bone of man, so the Dorians transmuted the role of the ancient creator-goddess of the earlier Greeks—Athene. In pre-Hellenic myth, as well as in the memories of Hesiod and Plato, Athene had created the race of Greeks from Hellen, the son (originally the daughter) of the first couple—Pyrrha and Deucalion. From the four sons of Hellen—Ion, Achaeus, Aeolus, and Dorus—had sprung the four branches of the historical Greeks, the Ionians, Achaeans, Aeolians, and Dorians.

Athene remained the supreme deity of the three older branches until the Dorians, the youngest and least civilized of the family, invaded Greece at the beginning of the first millennium B.C. Somewhere in their two-thousand-year wanderings in the wilds of Europe, they had learned a new god-religion and had adopted Zeus as their deity. After their conquest of their elder brothers, they sought to impose on them their new god, in which endeavor it became necessary to demote the Great Goddess, in the persons of Themis (Justice), Metis (Intelligence), Hera (Courage), and Athene (Wisdom). The Dorians therefore married Zeus to the first three goddesses, relegating them to secondary roles as mere consorts of the new god. But with Athene the problem was more difficult. Athene was the eternal and blessed virgin, and her devotees would not permit her to become a wife of Zeus. And so the Dorians determined that she must become his daughter. Zeus thereupon got Metis with child. When he was warned by the Delphic Oracle that the child in Metis' belly would wrest the world away from him (that the goddess would depose the god), he swallowed Metis.

Metis remained in Zeus' belly "giving him knowledge," [46] while the child Athene, insisting upon being born even from a belly within a belly, as it were, burst from her father's head. This miracle, no more absurd than Eve's birth from Adam's rib, reflects the effort of patriarchal society to denigrate the importance of women even in the procreative role. "The outrageous myth of the birth of Athene from Zeus' head," writes Harrison, "is but the emphasis and over-emphasis of a new patriarchal social structure." [47]

Despite Zeus' precautions, Athene remained the primary deity of Athens, and was always worshiped by the Ionian Greeks with more ardor and more devotion than was Zeus. [48]

In the Orphic religion, Metis was the Creator of All. She had borne Zeus, who, like Christ, had existed from the beginning of time. When Zeus swallowed his wife-mother Metis, he destroyed the world of "men who were not of our race"—the men of the Golden and Silver ages—and re-created the world with the aid of her intelligence, "having the body of all things in the hollow of his belly." [49] Zeus' new world was a man's world. After Zeus' triumph over his mother, she, Metis, became Phanes and was no longer all female but was "of both sexes," and her masculine aspect gradually took precedence over the feminine. [50]

In this respect, Orpheus was the St. Paul of the ancient world—a misogynist, "the foe of the whole female sex." [51] His antifeminism occurred from his having been spurned by Eurydice, as Paul's antifeminism is said to have been the result of his rejection by a rabbi's daughter. According to Konon, writing in the first century of our era, it was Eurydice's cavalier treatment of Orpheus, choosing to remain apart from him in her underground world, that turned him into a woman-hater. Like Paul after him, he barred women from participating in his new male religion, "and for this cause," says Konon, "the women, filled with anger at the slight put upon them, seized weapons, slew the men who attempted to overpower them, and rending Orpheus limb from limb, cast the scattered remnants into the sea." [52]

Zeus-worship, however, was not Orpheus' greatest crime in the opinion of the Thracian women. According to A. J. Symonds[53] Orpheus was an ardent exponent of male love and was the first to promote the Doric habit of pederasty that became the accepted form of romantic love in later classical Greece.

Greek pederasty, writes Symonds, was a Doric custom and was brought to Greece by the invading Dorians. Symonds offers the conjecture that the habit of pederasty originated in south-central Europe in prehistoric times when the Dorians were a band of those marauding beasts, the adult males ejected from the matriarchal tribes, doomed to wander homeless and womanless through the forests of primeval Europe. [54]

From the omission in Homer of any suggestion of homosexuality, we must infer that pederasty was not a custom of the pre-Dorian Greeks of whom Homer wrote with such fidelity to truth. Plato reports of the Ionians of his own day that they "counted pederasty a disgrace," a peculiarity of the Ionians that mystified the homosexual Plato. In Homer's delineation of the friendship of

Achilles and Patroclus there is no hint of physical passion. Yet the later Greeks were to use the love of Achilles for Patroclus as a justification, even a religious sanction, for the open pederasty which came to be known as "Greek love."

When the great Cretan culture was revived in Athens after the dark age that followed the Dorian invasion, it emerged with a strong Doric cast, which manifested itself primarily in the new attitude toward women. Gone was the Great Goddess of the Minoans and Mycenaeans, and gone was female supremacy. In Hellenic Greece pederastic love became the ideal of romantic love. "The new patriarchy turned Greek society into a game that men could play without women," and as in India where Rama had relegated once-dominant woman to the hearth, so in Greece "the hitherto intellectually superior Greek woman degenerated into an unpaid worker and bearer of children wherever Zeus was the ruling deity." [55]

When the Romans conquered Greece, they appropriated all the Greek culture they were capable of absorbing, but they did not perpetuate Greek love as a legal institution as the Athenians had done. It cannot be denied, nonetheless, that homosexuality was openly practiced in the last days of the Republic and throughout the period of the Empire. [56]

The early Christian fathers were almost as shocked by the prevalence of pederasty in the Roman Empire as they were by the freedom and dignity of the Roman women. But the church was not nearly so successful in eliminating pederasty as it was in degrading women. "There is nothing more common than pederasty among the monks and priestlings," Robert Burton was to write in the early seventeenth century. "So great a number of gilded youth, catamites, boy things, pederasts, sodomites, Ganymedes, etc. was found in every one of them [the English monasteries] as to constitute a new Gomorrah." [57]

Our English word for the practice of pederasty comes from a corruption of the word Bulgar, the early church having found that the reluctant Christians of southeast Europe were great offenders in this respect. Interestingly enough, it was from these same wilds of Europe that the Dorians had brought pederasty and patriarchy —and Zeus—to Greece a thousand years before Christ.

9

The Sexual Revolution

Every change in the relation between
the sexes is accompanied by bloody events.
—J. J. BACHOFEN

The Need to Punish

Man became so thoroughly conditioned to the idea of his own inferiority through the long ages of feminine supremacy that he built up in his subconscious mind an everlasting resentment against women. From the time when he was first permitted to deputize for the queen and was forced to wear false breasts and female attire in order to exert his authority, man has feared woman, resented her, and hated her. His hatred has led to a systematic code, sanctioned by law and custom, of cruelty toward women—a cruelty that he would never consider inflicting upon his own sex. "The strictness of the patriarchal system points to an earlier system that had to be combatted and suppressed," as Bachofen says.[1]

In their new-found physical superiority after the patriarchal revolution, men reacted understandably. They sought to wipe out all traces of their former condition of servitude and to give women "a little of their own back." The effort to conceal their original subservience took the form not only of rewriting history and of destroying all records that could not be reinterpreted from a masculist point of view but of resort to physical abuse as the norm in male-female relations. The bitter need to retaliate against their former masters led to the sexual sadism that has characterized man's relations with women in these later centuries and has even become accepted by male psychologists as "natural" and "normal."

In patriarchal law sexual abuse of a man is a far more serious crime than abuse of a female. As recently as 1969 a young woman was tried and convicted in France for "seducing" a young man. Yet how many men have ever in modern history been convicted, or even brought to trial, for seducing a young woman? "The clemency with which the seducer of a girl is judged," writes Edward Westermarck, "contrasts strikingly with the moral condemnation of his unwilling victim" and with "the harshness with which similar attacks on boys are punished." [2] "Is the seduction of a male youth fraught with so much more terrible consequences for the victim than that of a girl," he asks, "as to justify the enormous difference in the treatment of the seducer?" [3] In Europe until quite recently the seducer of a boy was hanged, while the seduction of a girl was looked upon as a charming peccadillo to be boasted of openly "even though the seducer's behavior may have inflicted a life-long [not to say a mortal] injury upon the girl." [4] The difference of course is in the sex of the victim. In the Judeo-Christian creed the male body is the temple of God, while the female body is an object made for man's exploitation. When the enlightened nation of France did for a brief time at the beginning of the present century make forcible rape a capital offense, the law was deplored as "positively inhuman" by Anthony Ludovici in England.[5] He passed over the inhumanity of the forcible rape and its consequences as of no importance. What, after all, were women made for?

"Our whole modern civilization," writes Georg Simmel, "is a masculine civilization: the State, the laws, morality, and religion are institutions created by men and *for* men." [6] "Sex morals," adds Margaret Sanger, "have been fixed by male agencies which have sought only to keep women enslaved" and to use women solely as instruments of man's whim. Thus, "any attempt on the part of women to live for themselves has been attacked as 'immoral' by these selfish agencies." [7]

"As long as physical love is man's favorite recreation," observes Mary Wollstonecraft, "he will endeavor to enslave women. . . . Yet how eager men are to *degrade* women, the sex from whom they claim to receive the chief pleasure of life." [8] "Behind man's insistence on masculine superiority," says Erik Erikson, "there is an age-old envy of women." [9] "The realization that the dogma of female inferiority had its origin in an unconscious male tendency to envy women," says Horney, "could only dawn upon us after a doubt had arisen as to the truth of the fact [of female inferiority].

Behind this conviction of feminine inferiority lies a very powerful . . . impulse . . . to depreciate women." [10]

"Yet," continues Horney, "the man has very obvious strategic reasons for keeping his fear and envy of women quiet; he also tries by every means to deny it even to himself. . . . Relief is sought and found in the *disparagement* of women that men often display ostentatiously in their speech and attitudes. . . . This way of allaying his fear has a special additional advantage: it helps to support his masculine ego, which is more threatened by the admission of a fear of women than of men." [11] He also takes refuge in the gigantic masculist myth of feminine masochism (see Chapter 21) and in the ego-soothing canard of female "penis envy."

Penis Envy Versus Womb Envy

Sigmund Freud is responsible for the "penis envy" fallacy, as well as for the term itself. For a few decades his theory of the "castration complex," from which all women were supposed to suffer, was accepted at face value by psychologists as well as by laymen. But soon differences of opinion arose. Such great post-Freudian psychologists as Horney, Jung, Fromm, Reik, Harold Kelman, and Gregory Zilboorg found on studying women themselves, as Freud had not done, that penis envy was a figment of Freud's imagination. "Quite in contrast to Freud's assumption," writes Fromm, "there are better reasons for assuming . . . pregnancy envy in the male" than penis envy in the female. [12]

In his book on Freud, Fromm remarks: "Freud's prejudices against women were all those . . . of the male who needs to dominate because of his *fear* of women." Because of his strong and compelling need "to put women in an inferior category . . . he looked upon them as castrated men, always jealous of men," and particularly jealous of the penis, which to Freud was the symbol of male superiority. [13] Of Freud's belief that woman was no more than a castrated male, Erik Erikson remarks that Freud could have had no understanding of the matriarchal foundations of history and "missed the whole substratum of matriarchy in man." [14]

"Freud," says Harold Kelman, "was brought up in a traditionally Jewish home where the man was lord and master, and women were looked upon as lesser beings," mere satellites to the men, created only to serve and obey.[15] His idea of penis envy was therefore based not on research but simply on his belief that no sane creature could be satisfied to be a woman, therefore every sane woman must wish to be a man; and since to Freud the penis made the man, every woman must logically wish to have a penis. Freud stated that penis envy was inspired in all little girls at a very tender age and served to blight and cripple the child for the remainder of her life.

Before we proceed to the scientific facts of the argument, let us first ask: How many well brought up little girls are even *aware* of the human penis? Some females never have the great privilege of viewing a penis until their wedding night, although for those little girls who have baby brothers this opportunity does come earlier. What normal human being, however, could be envious of the poor little devices of boys? Simone de Beauvoir records that her first glimpse of a boy's penis left her with a slight feeling of nausea, as if she had witnessed something faintly disgusting, "like a wen or a wart." Other women have expressed more active disgust, even comparing the sight to a monstrous deformity.

This feminine disgust bears out Reik's conclusion from his studies of the psychology of women that, contrary to the belief that little girls feel deprived upon discovering the boy's penis, "we have good psychological evidence that the sight . . . leads to the first manifestations of feminine *vanity!*" The little girl feels that her body is more esthetically beautiful than the boy's[16] and that her private equipment is far less repulsive—though, perhaps, not so convenient on a picnic. Horney brings out this point when she says that "the disadvantage on the side of women exists only at the pregenital levels [urination]. On genital levels the advantage in not having a penis is all on the side of the woman," for her sexual activity is not dependent upon the whim of an organ over which she has no control. "Woman's capacity for coitus and its enjoyment is certainly not less than man's." [17]

Gregory Zilboorg writes that womb envy on the part of man is far older and far more fundamental than penis envy on the part of women.[18] And Horney says: "When one begins to analyze men only after a long experience of analyzing women, as I did, one is surprised by the intensity of their envy" of women.[19] "Is it not really remarkable . . . that so little recognition and attention are paid to the fact of man's secret dread and envy of women? It is almost more remarkable that women themselves have so long overlooked it!" [20]

The psychological nucleus of this dread of women lies in the fact that "during coitus the male has to entrust his genitals to the female body, that he presents her with semen, and interprets this as a surrender of his vital strength to the woman, similar to his experiencing the subsiding of erection after intercourse as evidence of having been weakened by the woman." [21]

The penis is the only muscle man has that he cannot flex. It is also the only extremity he cannot control. Be his will however strong, the penis rises and falls on its own terms. Man cannot command it. This all-important and highly regarded organ, so necessary for his pleasure and his self-esteem, is a thing apart from him, with a mysterious life and will of its own. This fact in itself, the possession of an external anatomical part which seems in no way to be connected to his brain, is a disconcerting and humiliating phenomenon in itself. But even worse, as it affects the dignity of its owner, is its seeming obedience to that inferior thing—woman. It rises at the sight, or even at the thought, of a woman. This helplessness on the part of man to control his most cherished possession, his penis, infuriates him to the point of wishing to punish the sex that has such power over "what belongs to him."

Woman possesses no such defiant appendage. Her clitoris, so often equated with a vestigial penis, is a mysterious little thing, apparently put there exclusively for the woman's pleasure. Unlike the penis, it neither urinates nor creates. It is a purely gratuitous sexual adjunct which causes her no discomfort and no humiliation. Man resents woman's independence of her "penis," the unipurposed clitoris, and his dependence on his multipurposed penis. Nature seems to him to have practiced a niggardly economy when she came to designing man, in contrast to the munificence she lavished on the making of woman.

In civilized societies today this clitoris envy, or womb envy, takes subtle forms. Man's constant need to disparage woman, to humble her, to deny her equal rights, and to belittle her achievements—all are expressions of his innate envy and fear. In earlier times, and still in primitive societies where the instinctive dread and awe of women has not yet turned to fear-plus-hate, men have sought to imitate the dreaded object. "The basic theme of the [male] initiatory cult" among primitive tribes, writes Margaret Mead, "is that women . . . hold the secrets of life, and that man is perhaps unnecessary." So "man has hit upon a method of compensating his basic inferiority" by imitating the functions of women.[22]

Men go through all the motions of giving birth, of menstruating, and of penis mutilation to make the penis more closely resemble the female vulva. In a previous chapter we presented a brief sampling of the evidence for male envy of women. We know of no comparable evidence in history or in legend for penis envy, no sacred rituals based on woman's imitation of the functions of the male, no incident in which women have sought to mutilate their genitals to resemble man's, and no play-acting in which women have pretended to produce seminal fluid as men have pretended to produce menstrual blood.

Sexual envy is exclusively a masculine phenomenon.

Female Circumcision

Modern man's womb envy is most forcefully expressed in his resentment of woman's pleasure in sex. The famous argument between Zeus and Hera as to which of them received the greatest pleasure from sexual intercourse was settled by old Tiresias, who, having been both man and woman in his time, was deemed best qualified to judge. He promptly agreed with Zeus that woman's pleasure was ten times that of man.

Men dislike the idea of women's enjoying sex because it suggests to them the treasonous thought that perhaps man was made for woman's pleasure and not woman for man's convenience, as his ego has made it necessary for him to believe. It is this gnawing doubt that has motivated man "in a kind of *revenge*, for so many centuries to make woman his slave." [23]

The simple fact was, and is, that the masculist man resents the necessity for sharing even sex with a woman. Thus we have the paradox of patriarchal man regarding woman as merely a sex object and yet wishing to deny her any pleasure in sex. It is significant that matriarchal peoples "pleasure" the woman, while patriarchal peoples "ride" her!

Some time back in the later years of the patriarchal revolution, some extreme patriarch devised a method of reducing woman's pleasure in sex without affecting man's. If the clitoris was the seat of woman's pleasure, as Aristotle said, then away with it! The invention of clitorectomy, or female circumcision, was accredited in tradition to Gyges, the Lydian. But since Lydia was still female-dominated in Gyges' time (he had won the throne by murdering the queen's consort and marrying her himself at *her* insistence, as Herodotus tells us), this seems very unlikely. It is far more likely that the Islamic legend that Hagar, Abraham's concubine and Ishmael's mother, was the first victim of female circumcision is the correct one. The odds are that it was a Semitic innovation originally, as the Arabs became, and continue to be, the most enthusiastic exponents of it. "Son of an uncircumcised mother" is the worst epithet one Arab can hurl at another.

The "reasons" offered by the Arabs for the practice of female circumcision are as numerous as those offered for male circumcision by the ancients. The chief reason concerns female chastity. Women who are uncircumcised, say the Arabs, are oversexed and are therefore apt to be unfaithful and unchaste. Sir Richard Burton, however, who knew the Arabs well in the nineteenth century, says that the excision of the clitoris and the labia rendered women more lascivious but far less easily satisfied. "The moral effect of female circumcision is peculiar," writes Burton. "While it diminishes the heat of passion it increases licentiousness and breeds a debauchery of mind far worse than bodily unchastity." [24]

The prevention of ardor is another reason cited for female circumcision. It is believed in some quarters that orgasm in women prevents conception, the heat of her passion serving to destroy the semen. "She burns," writes Davenport, "and as it were, dries up the semen received by her from the male, and if by chance a child *is* conceived it is ill-formed and does not remain nine months in the mother's womb." [25]

A bizarre reason offered for the practice is that in the women of Egypt, Arabia, Abyssinia, and adjacent areas, the clitoris grows so large that it interferes with coition. "From climate or some other cause, a certain disproportion is found generally to prevail among them," writes Davenport, quoting one Bruce in his *Travels in Abyssinia*. The clitoris if allowed to grow uncropped becomes as long as a goose's neck, he goes on, "and men have sought to remedy this deformity by the amputation of the redundancy." [26]

When the Christian missionaries forbade the Copts to crop their daughters' clitorides, Davenport relates, "the converts obeyed. But the consequence was that when the daughters grew up men found that in marrying a Coptic wife they were subjected to a very disagreeable inconvenience, and therefore they married heretical women free from this encumbrance, with whom they relapsed into heresy." [27] "The missionaries, therefore, finding it impossible that their congregations would ever increase, laid their case before the college of cardinals at Rome. They took it up as a matter of moment, which it was, and sent over visitors to make a report upon the case as it stood. They, on their return to Rome, declared that the heat of the climate or some such cause did in fact alter the formation of woman's clitoris in such a way as to impede the consequences for which matrimony was instituted. The college upon receiving this report ordered that, because it disappointed the ends of marriage, the imperfection was by all means to be removed, so that the Catholics as well as the Copts and other Egyptians have undergone excision ever since." [28]

Overdevelopment of the clitoris is not confined to women of Egypt and Arabia, however, as a case reported in 1789 in Paris seems to prove: "A man was greatly surprised on his wedding night, while fondly caressing the naked person of his bride, at feeling a member as stiff as his own virile one. In the utmost confusion he got out of bed, imagining that he was bewitched, or that a trick was being played upon him by substituting in the marriage bed a man in place of his beloved spouse. No sooner, however, had he procured a light than he recognized the countenance of his wife, who fondly entreated him to return to bed. . . . He no sooner cast his eye on his wife's pudenda than a penis as long and stiff as his own presented itself to him. Questioning his wife upon this subject, she as delicately as possible in the circumstances, informed him that she had supposed all women to have been formed like herself in these parts. She again implored him to return to bed, and overcoming his surprise and bewilderment he renewed his amorous attack, only to find his genital organs refused to lend their assistance. To his further surprise, his newly acquired wife then turned him over beneath her, and by a strange metamorphosis the man became, as it were, a woman, while the woman played the part of one of the male gender. . . ." Davenport does not report on the end of this humiliating experience of a wedding night. He quotes thus much only from the *Annales Medicales et Physiologique* (1789).[29]

Still another reason offered for female circumcision is the prevention of "women's abuse of each other."[30] T. Bell writes: "It [the clitoris] sometimes acquires an astonishing magnitude, and we have the proof on record of women with large clitorides who have seduced young girls. . . . It is to avoid such unnatural connections that the Asiatic nations, especially the Arabians, are in the habit of removing the clitoris."[31]

All these are interesting but unconvincing reasons. The true and basic reason for the mutilation of the female vulva is male envy and sadism, which seeks to punish women merely for being women. The operation is performed on little Arab girls at puberty —the clitoris and the labia majora being excised down to the bone with a sharp razor. It is a far more dangerous, painful, and bloody operation than male circumcision and serves no purpose other than to deny the girl her full measure of future sexual enjoyment.

That the operation is merely a patriarchal form of revenge for female sexual superiority is suggested by the fact that it is performed only in countries where uncompromising patriarchalism has existed longest—that is, in Semitic lands. The Jews, before the Republic of Israel, denied that they practiced it upon their daughters, but there is evidence to the contrary. Richard Burton says the rite was practiced by the Jews until the days of Rabbi Gershom (A.D. 1000), who denounced it as a scandal. Burton goes on to say: "I believe it is still the rule among some out-lying tribes of Jews. The rite is the *proper complement* of male circumcision, evening the sensitiveness of the genitories by reducing it equally in both sexes: an uncircumcised woman has the venereal orgasm *much sooner and oftener* than a circumcised man, and frequent coitus would injure her health."[32] (Author's italics.) This was the supermale Sir Richard speaking for all patriarchal men. He is not at all worried about the health of the woman but only about the injustice of her greater sexuality and her superior pleasure in sex. He himself admits that the circumcised women of his acquaintance were almost incapable of orgasm, which, however, being unattainable, they doubly yearned for.

Sir Richard Burton gives a vivid first-person account of the re-

sults of female circumcision on Arab women: "The prostitutes of
Aden all had the labia and clitoris completely excised and the skin
showing scars and the traces of coarse sewing." [33]

Sewing was resorted to to insure the chastity of young girls and
unmarried women. After the operator has cut out the clitoris and
the lips of the labia, "she then sews up the parts with a pack needle
and a thread of sheepskin, while a tin tube is inserted for the passage of urine. Before marriage the bridegroom trains himself for
a month on beef, honey, and milk; for if he can open the bride
with his natural weapon he is a mighty sworder. If he fails, he tries
penetration with his fingers, and by way of last resort, whips out
his knife and cuts the parts open. The sufferings of the bride must
be severe." [34] One cannot help suspecting that the latter statement
sums up the whole reason for female circumcision of the brutal
kind practiced in some parts of the East: male sadism combined
with sex envy.[35]

The Italian anthropologist Mantegazza, writing in 1885, says that
female circumcision is practiced in Egypt because "Egyptian men
do not care for any sensual participation on the part of the woman
in the act of coitus. The circumcised women therefore are left with
the desire for a pleasure that must go forever unsatisfied. . . . It
would be hard to imagine a more selfish form of perversion, when
one stops to think that love is a joy meant for two, and that to
suppress our companion's pleasure in the act is cruel and barbarous, representing a species of pleasurable refinement which must
be paid for at usurious rates." [36]

10

Patriarchy and Hymenolatry

*A great over-valuation of virginity is
found only in communities that treat their
women as if they were chattels.*

— E. WEXBERG

The Hymen and the Blood Taboo

Another by-product of the patriarchal revolution was the development in the human female, through sexual selection, of the hymen, a membrane which she shares only with the elephant, the ass, and the pig. Like female circumcision, regard for the hymen occurs only in certain very restricted areas of the world—primarily in Semitic and Christian countries. The more universal any custom or belief is, the more ancient we find it is. The ubiquity of penis multilation, the couvade, and male circumcision testifies to their antiquity; while the spatial restrictiveness of female circumcision and hymenolatry testifies to the recency of their origins.

It has long been observed, by sailors, missionaries, and other travelers, that maidens of primitive societies are hymenless at a very early age. Many a ribald song has resulted from this observation of the apparent lack of virginity among peoples of the Pacific and the Far East. The assumption was, and is, that these girls had all lost their virginity through sexual intercourse at a tender age, indicating the rampant sexuality of the "native" peoples. The song that sailors sing about "the virgin in the Island of Cebu"—"there's a virgin I am told, but she's only three years old"—is typical of the bawdy that has arisen from the assumed absence of virgins in areas once remote from Western, Judeo-Christian civilization.

The truth, however, is that these girls have lost their virginity not through sexual intercourse but by deliberate defloration at an early age. In China, Japan, Siam, Cambodia, the Moluccas, the Philippines, and adjacent islands, "the hymen was ruptured in early child-hood by an old woman who was employed for this purpose." [1] Among the Toda a man of another tribe comes and stays in the village and deflowers all the young girls approaching puberty.[2] Since in primitive tribes puberty in girls occurs in the ninth or tenth year, the result is that most girls are deflowered by the age of eight. This defloration "must take place *before puberty* [author's italics], and there are few things regarded as more disgraceful than that this ceremony should be delayed." [3] Obviously, the hymen fetish does not exist in the Far East and in the islands of the Pacific, as it certainly would if the hymen and hymenolatry were of ancient lineage. The worship of the hymen is restricted to the few peoples among whom patriarchy was enforced literally with a vengeance—that is among the Semitic peoples of the Near East and their cultural descendants of later Christian Europe.

The hymen is an acquired adjunct. Just as the shape and size of the penis were the result of sexual selection on the part of prehistoric women, so the hymen is the result of a far later pattern of selection on the part of patriarchal men in historical times. When the concept of paternity led to notions of father-right and property rights, men became the selectors of their sex partners, and virginity in women became a thing of value.

"The virgin's hymen seems to be a late acquisition of human females, produced by the sexual selective action of the possessive male," writes Eisler, "after the transition from matriarchal to patriarchal values," wherefore very late in human history.[4]

The development of the hymen in women, however much men approved and encouraged it, led to new problems, new taboos, and new guilts on the part of men in their relations with women. Woman's blood had always, ever since time began, been dangerously taboo. Menstrual and postpartum blood, as well as the venous and arterial blood of women, was powerfully sacred, a thing to be avoided at all costs. But now it became necessary to shed woman's hymenal blood in the sex act. So man was beset on all sides by that mysterious and dangerous creature, woman.

The forcing by many patriarchal peoples of virgins to give up their hymens to the god may also have served by way of retaliation for the mountains of foreskins, penises, and testicles that men had in times past showered upon the goddess. In nearly all early pa-

triarchal societies the virgin's first coition was performed as a sacrifice—by the god himself in the person of the priest or by any
stranger or wayfarer who chose her in the temple. The offspring
of such unions were considered sons of the god, especially if they
later became great heroes. Thus Theseus considered himself the
son of Poseidon, as his mother Aethra had given herself in the
temple of Poseidon at Troezen; and Romulus was the son of Mars
by virtue of the cohabitation of his mother, Rhea Silvia, in the
temple of Mars in Alba Longa. Hercules, the hero of heroes, was, of
course, the son of the king of the gods, Zeus, who had ravished his
mother Alcmene in the Temple of Zeus at Thebes.

The rupture of the hymen was regarded as a sacrifice to the god
equal to the sacrifice of the foreskin to the goddess of old in the
rite of circumcision.

Herodotus gives us a vivid picture of temple prostitution as he
witnessed it in Babylon in the fifth century B.C.[5] The naïve traveler
did not attempt to understand the meaning of the practice. Strabo,
in the first century, reported that the Armenian virgins offered up
their hymens to the god Amiatus; and in patriarchal India the actual
membrane itself was offered as an adornment to the idol of the
sacred lingam. We know that Roman matrons of the empire were
wont to seat themselves upon the erect phallus of Priapus—but this
was not strictly speaking hymen sacrifice so much as it was a fertility charm, Priapus, like Saint Foutin, having had the power to
make women fecund.

In the eighteenth century, when Captain Cook visited the South
Seas he witnessed a ceremony in which a ten-year-old virgin was
publicly deflowered by the chief of the tribe. This, however, was
not, as Captain Cook supposed, a ritual hymeneal sacrifice but a
therapeutic measure designed to render the girl fit for marriage,
hymens being held in low esteem by matriarchal peoples. In fact,
"so little value is placed upon virginity that the culling of the
first flower is considered a servile duty, and girls who retain the
membrane past puberty are looked down upon."[6] In many cultures the custom was adopted of having a bride deflowered by a
third party, in some cases the priest, in some a midwife, and in
some present-day primitive societies by the sister or father of the
bride.[7] (The medieval *droit du seigneur,* in which the baronial
bride was deflowered by the lord of the manor, was not a cruel

appropriation of the husband's "right," as modern sociologists assume, but a survival of the custom of removing the danger of the hymenal blood from the husband to one whose power was better able to withstand the menace.)

"The object of the custom is clearly to remove the danger from the husband," writes Crawley.[8] Yet in "The Taboo of Virginity," Freud attributes the custom of defloration by the father to the "Electra complex," which, like penis envy, all girls are supposed to suffer from: that is, the wish to be raped by their fathers. "This primitive custom," writes Freud, "appears to accord some recognition to the existence of the early sexual wish [the wish to be raped by her father] by assigning the duty of defloration if not to the father, to an elder, a priest, or a holy man, that is, to a father substitute." [9]

The only thing wrong with this hypothesis is that it is not true. And, anyway, the girl does not choose her deflowering agent. The actual reason for premarital defloration, by whomever performed, goes back to man's ancient fear of woman and the shedding of her blood. "In the defloration of the virgin, the fear that comes into play is not merely that of woman in general, but also the fear of shedding [her] blood." [10]

Thus man sought to avert from himself the consequences of the very bloodshed that his own sexual selection had made necessary. Man suffered already from an ancient guilt, the sense of original sin, that was the result of his overthrowing the goddess, after defying her to become a killer and eater of animals. The goddess had always forbidden the shedding of any blood, even that of animals. In Greek legend it was not until the early Bronze Age, the period of the patriarchal revolution that followed the long millennia of the golden and silver ages of matriarchy, that man first began to eat the flesh of animals. And in *The Legends of the Jews,* Ginzberg places the innovation of meat-eating in the time of Noah's descendants—after the Flood of the fifth millennium B.C. "God accorded permission to Noah and his descendants after the Flood to use the flesh of animals for food, which had been forbidden from the time of Adam until then." [11]

Carnivorousness may have become necessary as a consequence of the great catastrophe that overwhelmed the world at that time. The myth of Cain and Abel, as we have pointed out heretofore, implies a great drying up of the vegetation and a famine of the fruits of the ground. The Cain story is an allegory, misplaced in time, of the drastic change in man's habits from vegetarian, agricultural gynarchy to hunting and preying, nomadic patriarchy.

The institution of sacrifice was a product of man's shame and guilt at these drastic innovations. Whereas the goddess had been satisfied with offerings of fruits and vegetables[12] and the foreskins of circumcised males, the new male god demanded sacrifices of blood. "When frugivorous man became a carnivore," writes Eisler, "he felt compelled to ameliorate his guilt by animal sacrifices, and even human sacrifices to the new gods." [13] The blood spilled in these sacrifices was masculine blood, the sacrifice itself being a shameful secret between bloodshedding man and his bloodthirsty gods.

Woman's blood remained strictly taboo. Even after the demise of goddess worship and of matriarchy, woman's blood must not be shed. Smother her, poison her, drown her, burn her, or boil her in oil, but do not shed a drop of her blood! In medieval Christian Europe, when men no longer understood the atavistic reason for the ban on woman's blood, women were never beheaded or drawn and quartered as were men. Burning alive was the accepted form of execution for women. A great inquisitor, on being asked why this was so and himself not being aware of the true reason, replied that "a bloodless death was more agreeable to women"! Paracelsus, the famous sixteenth-century physician, perpetuated the ancient belief in the mysterious sanctity of woman's blood when he wrote in his book on diseases: "Only a common boor thinks that the blood of a woman is the same as that of a man. It is of a different substance, a spiritual substance, more refined than man's." [14]

So, from the shedding of woman's blood in the sex act arose the feeling of guilt connected with sex, to be added to man's other great guilts: meat eating and goddess dethroning. "Sex guilt," says Eisler, "could not have existed in the matriarchal stage, before the possessive patriarch had succeeded in breeding, from a highly-prized *accidental mutation* [author's italics], a strain of maidens provided with a hymen, an anatomical abnormality analogous to webbed feet—which has since been identified with a woman's honor." [15]

As the patriarchal revolution progressed, however, the consciousness of sin in the shedding of blood began to dim, and man became more and more convinced that he was indeed the lord of all creation. As he gained in confidence and power, the *hymen intacta* became the criterion in his sexual selection. Male emphasis on the absolute essentiality of virginity in marriageable females led eventually to such evil practices as female infibulation and the use of chastity belts. In patriarchal Christian Europe the hymen became so important that the prospective bride was expected to submit to an intimate examination by the relatives of her betrothed before being accepted into his family. In important dynastic families, this insulting examination was performed by a priestly representative of the pope. Of this examination, the great French naturalist Georges Louis Buffon wrote in the eighteenth century, "Indeed the physical evidence of virginity is often lost in the very search for it. And the indignity which causes the pure and modest girl to blush [*rougir*—to bleed] with shame is the true defloration of her purity." [16] (Author's translation.)

Hymeneal sexual selection went so far eventually as to produce a few high-bred ladies with hymens so impenetrable as to render them perpetual and unwilling virgins—which may have been the case with Queen Elizabeth I, the Virgin Queen of England.

Infibulation

The development of hymenolatry led eventually to the infibulation of women and girls. As Eric Dingwall says, "The infibulation of mares has long been known to the veterinary profession, and there is no difference between it and the means of infibulating women. The two are identical, and consist of fastening together the labia majora by means of a ring, a buckle, or a padlock." [17]

The method of infibulation which Dingwall describes was the European Christian form—mild and merciful by comparison with the Semitic form which was practiced in the Arab countries of Africa and Asia. According to Mantegazza, it was "one of the first Christian kings who first introduced the practice of infibulation into Nubia." [18] Yet after the Crusades, when the idea was brought back from the East along with the chastity belt, the practice was attributed to the Moslem "infidels," from whom the Crusaders, no doubt to their delight, had learned it.

The European form of infibulation was undoubtedly painful in its imposition and vastly uncomfortable in its duration. As late as 1871, less *than one hundred years ago*, a woman of Europe complained to her doctor that the weight of the padlock which her husband had imposed on her was tearing the lips of her vagina and causing her great pain and bleeding. On examination the doctor found that the husband had bored holes in her labia, through which he had inserted two metal rings, similar to curtain rings, which he had then drawn together and locked securely with a padlock.[19] A similar case involving a German immigrant couple was reported in New York in 1894 and another in Eastern Europe in 1906! [20]

This sort of thing was probably a great deal more common in Europe than is generally supposed, the few cases which have come to light having been discovered purely accidentally. The sewing up of the labia over the vaginal opening, which we discussed above in connection with clitorectomy, also occurred spasmodically in Europe, though probably less frequently than the padlock type of infibulation. A case of the former was discovered in England in the eighteenth century.[21]

All in all, European women escaped the most atrocious form of infibulation—that which consisted in scraping the labia raw and fusing them together over the vagina. This form of torture was performed on young girls of the Moslem countries of Africa and Asia in order to protect the hymen from casual encounters with the unlicensed. The excruciatingly painful operation was performed, and may still be, on little girls without benefit of anesthesia. Mantegazza gives an eyewitness account of such an operation as performed in the nineteenth century:

> Infibulation is done in this manner. The greater labia on their internal surface are scraped with a razor, and then there is placed in the urethra a small funnel like a catheter for draining off the urine; thereafter the feet are bound together, and from the malleoli up there is a regular bandaging continuing to the middle of the thighs, all of this with the object of keeping the thighs so close together that the greater labia will come to adhere together. For eight days the patient must remain lying down, after which the girls are permitted to rise; but for eight days more they must keep their feet and thighs close together so that the labia will not

tear apart. When the operation has healed, there remains but a small orifice for the draining of the urine and the menstrual fluid, corresponding with the position of the fork.

When an infibulated girl comes to take a husband, the midwife arms herself with a knife, and before the bride is turned over to her husband, she rips the scar as much as is necessary, reserving to herself the task of making a larger cut before parturition takes place, so that the narrowness of the parts may not occasion any obstacle to the emergence of the head of the child.

In the Pegu region girls in infancy are sewn up in such a fashion that there remains only a tiny hole, and when they marry the bridegroom makes the aperture as large or as small as suits him, often leaving the threads in place so that when he goes on a long journey he may draw the stitches together again.[22]

This barbaric and heartless cruelty to women, perpetrated with the ostensible purpose of keeping them chaste, had been undreamed of in the pre-Christian, pre-Jehovah, pre-Allah civilizations of Greece, Rome, and Persia. For in those countries, when frail woman's virtue was not to be trusted, it was not she but the men around her who were tortured. Their penises were simply cut off. There is an analogy here in the present-day customs of birth control. For in Christian countries it is the woman's health, comfort, and safety which are sacrificed in the name of population control; while in non-Christian India, it is the men who are sterilized.

The Chastity Belt

In Europe, infibulation was resorted to by the lower classes, while the chastity belt was supplied to the upper classes "who can afford such luxuries, and who are aware that bodily cruelty is punished more heavily than the imposition of mental torture." [23] It is certainly true that the chastity belt caused a great deal less pain than infibulation, but its discomfort and inconvenience, not to mention its humiliating aspects, were fully equal to that of infibulation.

The idea of the chastity belt, like that of infibulation, was brought from the Semitic East by the Crusaders and was a fad in Europe from the thirteenth century on.

The device consisted of an iron or silver corset with, curving

between the legs, a tight-fitting metal bar perforated with a narrow opening surrounded by rows of sharp teeth. Into this instrument of torture the woman was locked, the key carried only by
her husband. It was bad enough, no doubt, when the husband
was at home to unlock the contraption occasionally and allow the
poor woman to relieve herself and wash up. But at times when
the lord and master was off to the wars, and months and even
years went by, the accumulated filth can hardly be imagined.
Many were the medieval ladies who threw themselves from the
castle battlements in despair at the unrelieved agony caused by
this invention of the misogynists.

Henri Fleury, who in 1860 saw in the ducal palace in Venice
the very chastity belt that a fourteenth-century duke of Carrara
had imposed on his wife, wrote (in *En Italie,* 1861): "This monstrous apparatus was devised by the ferocious jealousy of the husband in order to insure the material fidelity of his wife, and made
her who was subject to it a victim of permanent and truly atrocious
torture." [24]

The Abbé de Brantôme, in his sixteenth-century book, remarks
that the chastity belt came into France from Italy, where in the
Middle Ages a provost of Padua invented an iron device "which en-
cased the whole of the lower part of his wife's body." In France,
some years later, during the reign of Francis I, a popular song referred to this all-embracing form of belt, as Brantôme relates:

> The man who wants to keep his wife
> From whoring if she's once begun,
> Would have to barrel her for life
> And take his pleasure through the bung.[25]

Of his own time, the reign of Henri II, Brantôme recounts an
incident at the annual Saint Germain Fair in Paris, when an
ironmonger offered for sale "a dozen contraptions for bridling
a woman's parts." Several jealous husbands bought them up, and
at once proceeded to lock their wives in them. Unfortunately,
some of these were ladies of the court, where chastity in women
was *outré.* So, "a number of estimable nobles of the court threatened that ironmonger that if he ever dared to bring any more
such rotten goods to market they would kill him." [26]

Brantôme describes the ironmonger's invention as being "made of iron, and consisting of a belt and a piece which came up under and was locked in position, so neatly made that once a woman was bridled it was out of the question for her to indulge in the gentle pleasure, as there were only a few little holes for her to piss through." [27]

That example of the chastity belt was a sixteenth century one. Three hundred years later, in 1880, a French merchandising house distributed the following prospectus on its product *la camisole de force:*

> The advantages are manifold. Not only will the purity of the virgin be maintained, but the fidelity of the wife exacted. The husband will leave the wife without fear that his honour will be outraged and his affections estranged. Fathers will be sure of their parenthood, and will not harbour the terrible thought that their children may be the offspring of another, and it will be possible for them to keep under lock and key things more precious than gold.[28]

That the purpose of the belt was not solely to prevent the conception of illegitimate children, however, can be inferred from the fact that the most common type of the device protected both the anal and the vaginal openings. The same French firm mentioned above, wrote in answer to a customer's request for a *camisole de force* of the double type:

> The apparatus can be made in the way you desire affording protection both in front and behind. But I must inform you that there is a drawback to the latter, namely that in order to go to stool it is necessary to remove the apparatus, which otherwise need not be done, as urination is accomplished with the apparatus in position. It closes with a safety lock.[29]

Hymen Worship Through the Ages

So important had the hymen become by the sixteenth and seventeenth centuries in Europe that women, in order to save their very lives as well as their fortunes and their sacred honor, were forced to simulate a hymen when none existed. The "proof of the bed linen" was universal in Europe at one time and continues to exist in some peasant communities today. In this rite, the bridegroom proudly displays to the assembled and eager wedding guests the bloody bed sheet as evidence of his bride's virginity, as well as of his successful rupture of it. When hymeneal blood was not likely to flow naturally, the bride saw to it that the sheet was spattered beforehand with pigeon's blood, the blood of the dove having been considered almost indistinguishable from that of the virgin. (Shades of the Great Goddess and the Dove of Rhea!)[30]

The ruse of the pigeon's blood may have fooled the trusting bridegroom, but for the suspicious and sophisticated something more realistic and drastic was demanded. When the bride or her mother feared that the pigeon's blood would not suffice, the bride-to-be, months before the nuptial night, sought to create an ersatz hymen in place of the missing membrane. In Brantôme's words: "They take leaches and put them on the part so they suck the blood, till by their sucking they have caused and leave small embolisms, blisters full of blood, so that when, come the wedding night, the gallant husband proceeds to tackle, he bursts these blisters, out of which the blood pours, making him all bloody, which is a great delight to both parties." [31]

By the nineteenth century, which might be called the heyday of the hymen, this matter of virginity had assumed such proportions that manuals were published on the art of identifying virgins.

A Dr. T. Bell, in 1821, published for the masculine trade a book in which he sought to instruct innocent young men in the very important art of selecting a wife whose "honor" was intact. After conceding that the only absolutely sure evidence of defloration was the rupture of the hymen, which, alas, could not be ascertained in time to avert the fatal step of marriage to a fallen woman, the good doctor goes on to describe some of the outward symbols of degradation in women: "It is certain that, in virgins, the mamma is firm and round and no irregularity of the surface is visible to the eye. It is not less certain that after defloration its surface exhibits some irregularity." [32] One pities the poor virgins who had not been blessed with the glorious rounded globes so much admired throughout the ages by the patriarchs. They must have resorted to all sorts of tricks to give their sagging, flat, or immature bosoms the "virginal" look of opulence. In Roman usage, the virgin bosom, contrary to the opinion of Dr. Bell, was expected to be smaller than that of the nonvirgin. As a matter of fact, the breast was believed to expand *immediately after* defloration, as witness the Roman custom of measuring the bride "before and after." In Rome, where virginity was not nearly the sacred cow it became under the Christians, still a bridegroom rejoiced when the morning-after measurement of his wife's bosom exceeded that of the wedding day. He had married a virgin, whatever the evidence offered by the presence or absence of the hymen. Catullus refers to this evidence of virginity in the lines *Non illam nutrix, oriente luce revisens hesterno collum poteret circumdare filo,* which, roughly translated, mean, "by the morning light the thread that but yesterday encompassed her breasts, no longer meets." [33]

But back to Dr. Bell and the nineteenth century in Christian England. His second hint to young men on the identification of nonvirgins has to do with the glands of the neck: *"The sudden swelling of the neck in young women is a sign of defloration* [author's italics]." [34] One wonders how many engagements were precipitously broken off by young men whose fiancées came down with mumps or colds in the neck glands. Poor girls, they probably never suspected that their condemnation to a life of spinsterhood was the result of having caught cold at the boating picnic that wonderful day on the Cam.

Bell's next *cave* is not too clear: *"Defloration alters the tones of the voice* in such a manner that the change is easily discovered by a good *ear."* [35] (Author's italics.) Unfortunately, the worthy doctor does not tell us in what way the voice changes, except to add darkly that "in prostitutes who daily abandon themselves to men, this change is great and obvious."

But his last warning is all embracing: "Intelligent and attentive observers will, on such an occasion [*i.e.,* on the defloration of a virgin] discover a change of expression, of complexion, of look, of demeanor, and of *conversation, by which much is implied."* In other words, if the girl suddenly becomes bolder, more outspoken, less modest and shy, the careful bachelor will at once become suspicious and retreat to the nearest exit. He is in the presence of a fallen woman.

Dr. Bell is not satisfied to warn away wife-hunters. He also seeks to disabuse those already caught who may entertain some doubts as to their wive's premarital chastity. "Although it is true that the hymen is often relaxed in virgins, or broken and diminished by accidents independent of all coition, *such accidents are very rare, and the absence of the hymen is assuredly a good ground of strong suspicion* [author's italics]." Moreover, the good doctor warns suspicious husbands: "The slight tendency of the hymen to regenerate when the habits of sex have been abandoned for years or *from the use of astringents, can deceive only the most inexperienced husband* [author's italics]." [36] So men, beware.

"With all these guides," concludes Dr. Bell, "the skilful observer will never be deceived."

And the prospective husband who follows them will never run the risk of having palmed off on him a used virgin as a wife.

If we had any doubts about the accuracy of Dr. Bell's diagnosis, they are confirmed by his statements on sex determination in children. In the same book, he advises husbands who wish to beget sons to concentrate on their own organ and its pleasures during intercourse; whereas, if they want a daughter, they need only concentrate on the sexual parts of the wife and on *her* pleasure." [37] (It is a fact that a far larger percentage of boys than girls is conceived and born, but with Dr. Bell's explanation of sex determination one would expect the proportion of boys to be even larger.) "The imagination of the *male* parent," goes on the doctor, may determine not only the sex of the child, but also its beauty and perfection. "But the manner of accomplishing this latter cannot be unfolded with sufficient delicacy for the public eye. . . ." [38] So we are left in the dark as to the doctor's prescription for determining the looks and talents of the child-to-be. Perhaps his male readers were expected to seek him out in his chambers in Harley Street for further elucidation, at a price, on this point.

Davenport, writing shortly after Bell, warns against assuming that the absence of the hymen proves lack of chastity in a woman. "The chastest and most moral of her sex," he writes, "might have her hymen destroyed by preceding illness, and thus be incapacitated from giving her husband the proof of her purity. It should also be remembered that there are persons, in whom the hymen is so indistinct, that several anatomists have doubted its existence altogether. With what eloquence does Buffon, who shared this incredulity, inveigh against the absurd importance attached to this membrane by us lords of creation." [39] Davenport then goes on to quote, in the original, Buffon's opinion: "Primitive man and all generations since have made a great case for exclusive ownership of all they possessed; and this folly has been best expressed by his insistence on virginity in his women. This virginity is a purely physical thing, and has nothing to do with the purity of the heart." [40] (Author's translation.)

Hippocrates, the father of medicine, wrote in the fifth century B.C. that "women who cohabit with men are healthier than those who do not." [41] Whatever the truth of this dictum, and modern vital statistics would seem to deny it, it was believed for many centuries. Yet, under the influence of patriarchy, women themselves came eventually to worship the hymen.

Zenobia, the great third century A.D. queen of Palmyra, "availed herself of the liberties of her wedded state only for the procreation of children." [42] Isabella of Gonzaga, a duchess of Urbino, remained a virgin for two years after her marriage, receiving her husband's embraces "through the back door"—a compromise probably happily accepted by her part-Moorish husband, the duke—before she realized that frontal intercourse was permitted to married women. "She had imagined all married women did likewise. At length, however, the scales fell from her eyes and vanished away," [43] as, no doubt, did her hymen.

The *pièce de résistance* in hymen worship is recorded in the 1608 Bull of Canonization of Saint Francisca Francis. This noble lady, having taken the veil, was so tormented by the demands of the flesh and was yet so determined to meet her bridegroom, Christ, with hymen intact, that "she used to check the solicitations of the flesh by pouring scalding wax or grease upon her pudenda." [44] And for this she was canonized.

So we see that just as early man had taken over from women the worship of the phallus so eventually women adopted the worship of the hymen. And where virginity is exalted, women are subjugated; where the hymen is valued, woman is devalued.

All these products of the patriarchal revolution—sexual sadism, infibulation, hymenolatry, and the degradation of women—were far in the future for the women of Europe. The masculist revolt spread very slowly westward from the Semitic East into the Aegean only in late historical times. But even then in a corner of Anatolia, that nursery of civilizations, there was preserved the seed of the gynarchates. This minute corner of the world, whence had sprung the great civilizations of Sumer, Egypt, and Crete, was destined once again to revive a flagging civilization. For it was from the tiny Ionian nations of western Anatolia—Lydia, Lycia, and Caria—that the great pre-Christian civilizations of Athens, Rome, Ireland, and Celtic Europe were to spring.

Part III
Pre-Christian Women
in the Celto-Ionian World

*The women [of Classical times] associated
with men as equals; brave, outspoken, courageous
and practical, they shared the virtues as well
as the faults of their husbands.*

—AGNES SAVILL

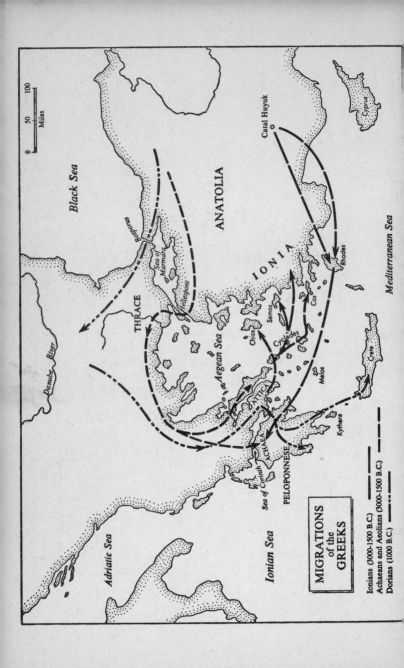

MIGRATIONS
of the GREEKS

Ionians (3000-1500 B.C.) ————
Achaeans and Aeolians (3000-1500 B.C.) — — —
Dorians (1000 B.C.) —·—·—·—

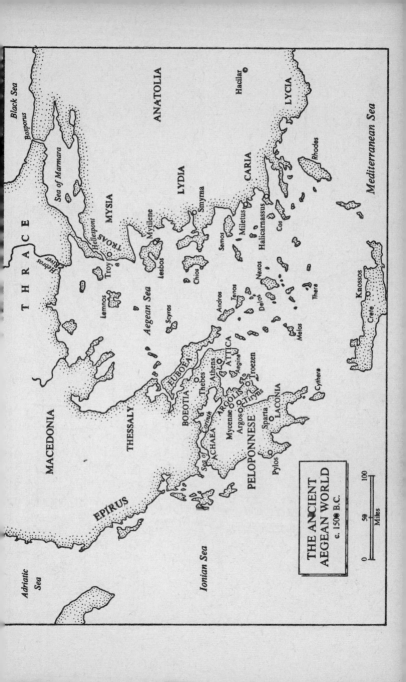

THE ANCIENT
AEGEAN WORLD
c. 1500 B.C.

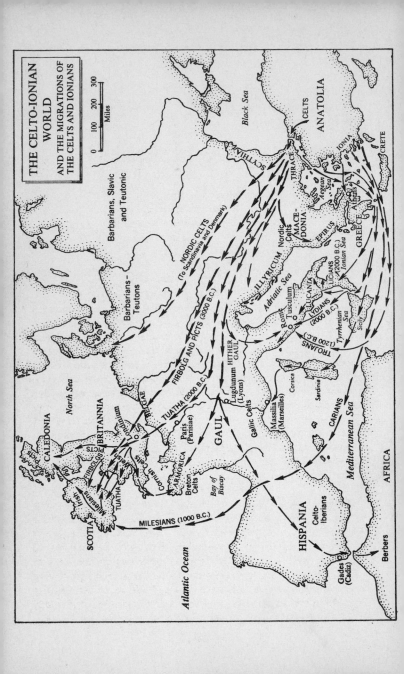

11

The Pre-Hellenes

*In the religious and civic
primacy of womanhood, it [the pre-
Hellenic world] possessed the seed
of noble achievements which was
suppressed and often destroyed by
later developments.*

—J. J. BACHOFEN

The great universal civilization of the ancient world reached its apogee in the flowering of Crete in the second and third millennia B.C. The supremacy of women in the organization of Cretan society from 3700 B.C. to Crete's absorption by the Mycenaeans around 1400 is well known and has been well documented by archeological research. What is less well known is that the indigenous people of pre-Mycenaean Greece, the Pelasgians, were also a gynocratic people "dominated by the female principle; men were but the servers of women in the chase, in the fields, in love, and in war." [1] Now archeology has revealed that the Mycenaeans themselves were a gynarchic people. Digs at the great Mycenaean palace sites reveal that these early Greeks were as truly female-dominated as were their Pelasgian predecessors and the Cretans whom they absorbed.

Pictorial artifacts dug up at Pylos, Mycenae, Tiryns, and other early Greek sites, like those found on the island of Crete, bear out Charles Seltman's observation that "men were but the servers of women." Women are shown driving chariots, leading hunts, occupying the best seats at the theater, presiding in the halls of justice, and receiving homage from men. On a gold signet ring dug up at Mycenae a woman is shown "raising an admonitory finger to a man standing before her." Archeologists label this lady "the goddess" but she bears none of the usual regalia of the Minoan-

Mycenaean goddess—the long pleated skirt, the snake coiled round her arm, or the double ax. She is seated on a stool, her skirt is mini length, her arms are bare, and she resembles a modern woman "boss" rather than a goddess. The man she is reprimanding carries a long spear. Apparently he is a hunter or a warrior who has been derelict in his duty and has been "called on the carpet" by his chief.

On another ring from Mycenae a woman stands, arms akimbo, supervising a man kneeling at an altar. Her facial expression as well as her stance bode no good for the culprit before her, who has probably been ordered by her to do a penance at the altar as punishment for some minor act of insubordination.

The origin of the Mycenaeans is still debated, but evidence points more and more to an Anatolian origin. They were an Indo-European people, like the people of Catal Huyuk, and when they seeped into Greece about five thousand years ago, they brought with them two exclusively Anatolian artifacts—their pottery and their house style, "both peculiar to the central parts of Anatolia" and unknown elsewhere.[2] After about 1,500 years, these expatriate Anatolians met up with the Minoans of Crete, adopted their customs, learned their arts and crafts, including the craft of modern plumbing, and established what we now call the great Minoan-Mycenaean civilization.

The Mycenaeans, Homer's Achaeans, expelled their Ionian cousins, whom they found occupying the Peloponnese, and drove them up into Attica and back across the Aegean into Anatolia. When, some five hundred years later, the Dorians swept down from the north and destroyed the glorious era of Mycenae, Ionian Attica alone on the Greek mainland retained the seeds of the lost culture, and it was here, in Attican Athens, that the classical Greek renaissance was to take place about 600 years after the Dorian conquest.

The Ionians seem to have been the vital chromosome in the Greek genetic complex. For it was these Ionians, the ancestors of the grandeur that was classical Greece, who returned unknowingly to their ancient homeland, Anatolia, and founded there the states of Ionia—those small nations of western Asia that became the founders of European civilization—Lydia, Lycia, and Caria.

For even after Athens had ceased to be a gynarchy, her daughter states in Anatolia remained gynocratic and were able to pass on the great Minoan-Ionian culture not only to classical Greece, but to Rome, to peninsular Italy, to Europe, and to the British Isles.

The Lydians occupied a portion of Ionia in what is now Turkey, ancient Anatolia, west and south of the modern Turkish city of Izmir (Smyrna). When the incoming Ionians brought their goddess Athene to Lydia, they found there, carved in a rock niche at the base of Mount Sipylus beyond Smyrna, a colossal image of a goddess whom they at once identified as their own Great Goddess, Athene, but who was actually the prototype of Athene, the Great Goddess Potnia-Tiamat, goddess of the aboriginal Anatolians and of the later historical peoples of the Near East, from Sumer to Palestine.

Of Lydia, Herodotus writes that the most remarkable thing about the country in his time—the fifth century B.C.—was "a structure of enormous size, hardly inferior to the huge monuments of Egypt, the base of which is formed of immense blocks of stone, the whole being six furlongs and two plethron in circumference" (about one mile).[3] Here we have another survival of the engineering work of the ancient mariners, whose ways with stone cannot be duplicated even by present-day builders. A further echo of the lost civilization was the tradition among the Lydians of Herodotus' time that the huge monument had been built "by the women of old,"[4] an obvious memory of the ancient power of women to build walls and move stones by mysterious means.

Lycia has even today a similar megalith—a columnar block of stone weighing eighty tons—whose origins are lost in the mists of time.[5] In the sixth or fifth century the Hellenic Greeks carved figures in the column, but they had no knowledge of the history or origin of the megalith.

Herodotus affirms the strength of the survival of the ancient matriarchates in Lycia up to his own time: "Ask a Lycian who he is and he gives his own name and that of his mother and of his mother's mother, but never his father's name. Moreover, if a free woman marry a slave their children are free citizens; but if a free man marry a slave, even though he be the first citizen of the state, his children forfeit all the rights of citizenship."[6] This was without doubt the universal custom among the ancient matriarchates, a custom that was carried to the far corners of the world by the ancient mariners, and still prevails in Oceania and Polynesia.

That the Carians had been a mighty people in ancient times is proven by the tablets excavated at Ugarit (Ras Shamra in Syria) in the 1920's. In these texts the Carians are referred to as the Khr, and they were a mighty people at the time the tablets were inscribed in the fifteenth century B.C.

Herodotus writes of the Carians that they were great sailors and were "in those days the most famous *by far* of all the nations of the earth." [7] Even in historical times the Egyptians called the Mediterranean Sea "the Sea of Kharu" after the Carians. It was these Carians, says Herodotus, with whom the displaced Greek Ionians mated when they were driven from the Peloponnese around 1400 B.C. And it is significant that some of the greatest names of later classical Greece, from Thales, Anaximander, and Pythagoras to Aspasia and Herodotus, were descended from these Carian-Ionian marriages of an earlier time.

Caria became famous also for the women she produced. Artemisia of Halicarnassus was a Carian, and she won fame in history as a great admiral in the Persian wars. "Her brave spirit," writes Herodotus, "sent her forth to war" at the head of the men of Cos and Halicarnassus. "Her navy was superior to any on the Persian side except that of the Sidonians [Phoenicians]. . . . And she likewise gave Xerxes sounder counsel than any other of his allies." [8] Five hundred years after the Persian wars, Apollonius of Tyana was to hold Artemisia up as an example of courage to the wavering Athenians of his own day, referring to her as "that woman admiral in whom nothing was womanish." [9]

The closely related Mysians also had a famous woman warrior in the person of Hiera, who fought at the head of her armies in the Trojan War. Philostratus, in the *Heroicus,* says of Hiera that Homer omitted reference to her in the *Iliad* because "this greatest and finest of women, general of the Mysian troops before Troy, would have outshone his heroine, Helen." [10]

These women are prophetic of the Celtic women of later Europe, and it is impossible not to conjecture that they may have been the direct ancestors of the Celtic warrior queens of Britain, Europe, and Ireland of a later day. Not only were the Carian women valiant, they were gifted also with brains. For Aspasia, whom Pericles and Socrates considered the most intelligent Greek of her time, was a Carian from Miletus.

The Carians apparently were not only sea-kings and adventurers but were true citizens of the world. Their ubiquity was so notorious that in the first century Strabo, the historian-geographer of Rome, wrote of them "the emigrations of the Carians are not matters of knowledge." [11] It is known that Carians accompanied the Phoenician queen Dido when she fled Tyre in the thirteenth century and founded the city of Carthage in northern Africa. There were Carians not only in Queen Nefertiti's bodyguard but in that of Queen Athaliah in Jerusalem at the time of Jehoshaphat. The stem "Car" in so many place names of the ancient world testifies to the influence these people had on ancient geography and history. From Carchemish to Carthage they gave their name to famous cities. It is even possible that the "Caer" incorporated in Celtic place names of Wales and Ireland is this same "Car"— Caerleon, Caernarvon, or Carnarvon as it is now called, Caerphilly, and Caermarthen.

Irish legend says the Milesians, the early Celtic settlers of Ireland, were from Miletus in Caria. This has always been thought a baseless myth, but is it baseless? The Carians were kings of the sea, and like the Phoenicians, who have received all the credit, they made frequent visits to the tin mines of Cornwall. Why not also to Ireland?

It is quite reasonable to suppose that the Carians reached the British Isles by sea at some time early in the second millennium, after they had become blended with the Ionians. But long, long before that time, these blond Carians had wandered overland northward and westward from their ancient homeland in Anatolia into Europe proper. In the eons of their wanderings in uninhabited southern and central Europe they forgot their ancient heritage, retaining only the sacred relics of the glorious past, the golden relics that had fallen from the sky, whose meaning they had long forgotten.

And could these Celts have been the last survivors of the ancient race—the red-haired people whose memory was sacred to the most ancient Egyptians, the red-gold strangers who sailed the world in ancient times and left their image forever engraved in the memory of all peoples?

The Ionians of Anatolia, wrote Herodotus, "were the first of the Greeks who performed long voyages," and it was they who made the Greeks acquainted with the Adriatic, and with Tyrrhenia [Italy], with Iberia [Spain], and the city of Tartessus [Tarshish, Cadiz].[12] They also founded the modern city of Marseilles (ancient Massalia) in France, and the great city of Elia in Italian Lucania, where Jason had earlier built his Temple of Hera.

Prior to the founding of these places, however, the Ionians had colonized Corsica, Sardinia, Sicily, and the entire foot of the Italian boot. Before the Trojan War a colony of Lycians had settled in Italy, as Virgil writes in the *Aeneid*. They were the Volscians, whose queen, Camilla, was chief of the Italian united forces which challenged Aeneas' invading Trojans after the fall of Troy.

> To crown them comes Camilla, Volscian-bred,
> Heading her horse troops, squadrons bright with brass,
> A warrior maid, her hands unused
> To loom or basket of Minerva's wool,
> But strong to bide the battle, and on foot
> Outrace the breezes. . . .
> At her, astonished, youths and maidens all
> From house and field throng, gazing as she goes,
> Agape with wonder at the royal pomp
> Of purple draped about her shoulders smooth,
> Her tresses intertwined with clasp of gold,
> To mark the Lycian quiver that she bears,
> And pastoral wand of myrtle tipped with steel.[13]

Camilla was a prototype of the Celtic warrior queen of later Celtic Europe and the British Isles, and she carried a "Lycian quiver." That the early Latins were closely related to the Celts of Europe is indicated by their language. The historian Mommsen writes: "There is a close philological affinity between the Celts and the ancient Italians—closer than that between the latter and the Hellenes [who were mostly Doric]. The branch of the great tree from which the Indo-European peoples of south and west Europe have sprung, divided first into Greeks and Italo-Celts, and the latter, after a time subdivided into Celts and pre-Roman Italians. History must be brought into harmony with this theory, because what has hitherto been called 'Graeco-Roman' civilization *may well have been 'Graeco-Celto-Roman'* [author's italics]."[14]

But since both the Roman and Greek civilizations were ultimately derived from Ionian Anatolia, Mommsen's "Graeco-Celto-Roman" civilization might more simply and more accurately be called Celto-Ionian.

The Lycians and the Carians, however, were not the first of the Anatolian Ionians who colonized Italy. Even before them, and before Jason and Medea, had come the Lydian Etruscans. Driven from Lydia by famine in the remote past, says Herodotus, these people had taken ships from Smyrna (Izmir) under Tyrrhenius, had gone ashore in western Italy on the Tyrrhenian coast, and had there established one of the most civilized nations of the ancient world.

"Who could have dreamed," asks Grimal, "of the might of an empire on the Italian peninsula that rivalled the greatness of classical Rome—an empire in fact that imposed its political structure on great Rome itself" and whose culture was the seed of Roman civilization. When they confronted the Etruscan civilization in Latium, the "Latin peoples experienced an evolution similar to that which transformed the Greek immigrants when they came into contact with the Cretan civilization on the shores of the Mediterranean. . . . From all this we see that the chain of circumstances which led to the Roman miracle was not so different from that which produced the miracle of classical Greece." [15]

Both the Cretan and the Etruscan civilizations had surpassed the civilizations of Greece and Rome; yet both of these great predecessors had been utterly forgotten by their cultural descendants, and their very existence had remained unsuspected until only yesterday. The Hellenic Greeks may have had some excuse for their ignorance of their Cretan heritage, owing to the long dark age that separated the flowering of Crete from the flowering of Athens. But the Romans had no such justification. By the time Etruscan civilization had begun to languish in the fourth century B.C. Rome was already well on her way to greatness. There was no dark age in Italy until the universal darkness of medieval Europe fell across it in the fifth century of our era. "The oblivion to which the Etruscans were consigned," writes Grimal, "was due to human agency, to a kind of conspiracy of silence" on the part of the Romans.[16] The world leaders of the Pax Romana chose to think of their civilization as *sui generis,* owing no debt to anyone. For this reason the Roman historians and poets of the classical age ignored their Etruscan educators, and Virgil in his great Roman epic depicted the early Etruscans as semibarbarians, much as modern historians have pictured the Celts.

The Etruscans contributed to later Rome "its constitution, its language, arts, customs, and religious practices." [17] And yet for thousands of years these people were all but unknown.

When Aeneas and his Trojans reached Italy after the fall of Troy toward the end of the second millennium B.C., they found there the descendants of the Lydians, the Etruscans—or Tyrrhenians as they called themselves—firmly entrenched and enjoying a very high degree of civilization.

According to Livy as well as to Virgil, Aeneas married Lavinia, the hereditary Etruscan princess of Latium, thus becoming king of Latium, as was the way all kings were made in ancient times. On Aeneas' death, according to Livy, Lavinia in true gynocratic style remained as reigning queen, while her son by Aeneas, Ascanius, was forced to leave home and found a new city at Alba Longa.

The great Julian and Claudian families of later Rome claimed descent from Ascanius, the son of Aeneas; yet there are no Juliuses or Claudiuses in ancient Rome. To explain this discrepancy, Virgil says that Ascanius changed his name to Iulus, but Livy says nothing of this. And it still, even if true, does not account for the Claudians. The names Julius and Claudius must, therefore, refer to Etruscan matriarchs, Julia and Claudia, who gave their names to Roman tribes when Romulus divided up the people into *curiae* and named them for the women, as Livy states.[18]

Tacitus, in the *Annals,* reveals the existence of a very early Claudia, "Claudia Quinta, whose statue had been dedicated by our ancestors in the Temple of the Mother of the Gods; *hence the Claudian line had been accounted sacred* [author's italics] and numbered among the deities." [19] No doubt there was also an early Julia whose name has been forgotten, as would Claudia's have been except for that one brief passage in Tacitus.

Romulus himself was rightful king of Rome only because of his mother, Rhea Silvia, an Etruscan princess. To prevent her from ruling on her rightful throne or from bearing children who would be the rightful heirs, the usurper Amulius had incarcerated her among the vestal virgins. But despite all Amulius' precautions, the god Mars somehow got to Rhea, and she bore the twins Romulus and Remus. And so by right of matrilinear succession, Romulus became the king of Rome.

This tale is reminiscent of that of King Acrisius of Argos in the Greek myth. For this king, to prevent his daughter Danaë from marrying and depriving him of the throne he had acquired through marriage to the queen, had Danaë incarcerated in a bronze tower. But Zeus visited her in a shower of gold, and she became the mother of Perseus. Now Perseus is no more mythological than is Romulus. Although both kings border on the legendary, they were no doubt actual historical persons, Perseus having reigned in Mycenae in the fourteenth century and Romulus in Italy in the eighth. Both legends have been mythologized to conceal their real significance: the absolute right of the daughter to inherit the throne and the machinations perpetrated by her male relatives to deprive her of this right.

12

The Women of Greece
and Italy

*Sex has not [yet] made too great inroads
upon her. She is not merely woman, but a
human being.*

—EMILY JAMES PUTNAM

The Women of Classical Greece

According to Marcus Terentius Varro (116–27 B.C.), Athens toppled woman's power in a pique of male jealousy in the reign of Aegeus, about three hundred years before the Trojan War. It was only then that the men of Athens, asserting their physical superiority, decreed that women should no longer be elected to the Assembly, that children should no longer bear their mother's names, but their father's,[1] and that the proud name "Athenian," child of the goddess, should no longer apply solely to female Athenians. The men of Athens, of course, retained Athene as their patron deity; but much later, after the Doric conquest and the invention of Zeus, they were to invent for Athene a monstrous, motherless birth from Zeus' head, and they were to make of her that heinous anomaly: a "man's woman," a traitor to her sex.

According to Aeschylus, writing in the fifth century B.C., it was not until *after* the Trojan War that father-right won out over mother-right in Athens. When Agamemnon returned from that war and was murdered by his queen, Clytemnestra, Orestes, as everyone knows, killed his mother to avenge his father. He was pursued by the ancient goddesses, the Erinyes, but defended by Apollo, who represented the new male gods. In the *Eumenides*, Aeschylus dramatizes the struggle between these Erinyes (Eumen-

186

ides) and Apollo over Orestes' revenge murder of his mother. The Eumenides see no wrong in Clytemnestra's murder of her husband, for "the man she killed was not of blood congenital." But Orestes' murder is heinous and unforgivable. "Do you forswear your mother's intimate blood?" they ask and demand the age-old punishment for the matricide.

Apollo then speaks and voices in his brand-new policy of father-right, a genetic fallacy that was believed down to the time of the rebirth of scientific eugenics in the twentieth century A.D.:

> The mother is no parent of that which is called
> her child; but only nurse of the new-planted seed
> that grows. The parent is he who mounts.

Despite this fallacious but effective reasoning on the part of Apollo, the Erinyes would still have won out if Athene herself had not switched sides:

> It is my task to render final judgment here.
> This is a ballot for Orestes I shall cast.
> There is no mother anywhere who gave me birth;
> and, but for marriage, *I am always for the male* [author's italic].[2]

The cad! The traitor! Pretending to believe that fairy tale about her birth from Zeus' head! "Always for the male," indeed! Yet even in this vital moment she acknowledges that she'd *never marry* one.

This is probably the first recorded instance of man's use of the brainwashed enemy to brainwash her fellows. Television-commercial writers and women's magazines have made an art of it.

Yet, although Aeschylus places Athene's treachery back in Mycenaean times (long before Zeus, actually, and long before the myth of the strange birth of Athene had been invented), the fact is that Greek women did not lose their prestige and power until after the Dorian conquest. Their position even then remained high, until Rome succeeded in Christianizing Greece in the fifth century A.D. —sixteen centuries after Orestes' trial for murder.

As a matter of historical fact, Greek women of the classical age enjoyed rights and privileges under Athenian law that are still denied women of the United States in these last years of the twentieth century A.D. Among these rights were:

1. The right of abortion and birth control. Plato, in the *Laws*, recommends that Greek women should bear at least two children, "the number regarded as adequate by law" to maintain the population. And in the *Politics* Aristotle advises women practicing abortion to do so "before the foetus receives life," that is, before the sixth month. These two passages prove the legality and availability of both birth control and abortion.

2. The right to unilateral divorce. "Athenian law," writes Montesquieu, "gave the right of repudiation [one-sided divorce] without penalty to the woman. But for a man to repudiate his wife he had to hand over one-half of all his wealth to the wife, and the other half to the goddess Ceres." [3] Which obviously influenced him to put up with wifey until *she* was ready and willing to divorce *him*.

3. The right to own and administer her own property. "According to Athenian law, the wife's money and property did not pass into the control of her husband, but there was nothing to prevent her giving it to him." [4] This law differs from that of Rome, where the husband was not permitted to touch his wife's money even *with* her consent.

The canard of the inferiority of Greek women in the Classical age is repeated by Robert Flacelière in 1959,[5] as if it were a lesson he had learned by rote at his professor's knee. After reciting the old formula that Greek women were on a par with slaves, he goes on to illustrate, unconsciously as it were, how *free* Greek women must actually have been.

To begin with, he makes the statement that "by the fifth century the traditional seclusion of women was giving way to numerous exceptions." [6] If it was "giving way" in the fifth century, when was it holding sway? Certainly not in the seventh century, when Sappho flourished, and certainly not in the heroic (Mycenaean) age, when, as Flacelière himself asserts, "women enjoyed all the freedom and privilege" of Cretan women. So what was this "traditional seclusion," and how traditional was it? We have here a distinct case of the professorial syndrome—a parrotlike repetition of "facts" propounded by the scholars of the prearcheological nineteenth century.

Flacelière does concede, in the light of his own studies and in open defiance of his teachers, that "perhaps there may be some truth in the supposition that the Greek woman altogether lacked

that humble and self-effacing character" that has been attributed
to her.[7]

The Oxford Companion to Classical Literature, under "Women,
position of," takes the same devious route to the same conclusion:
first, the statement that Greek women of the classical age had lost
the "position and independence" they had enjoyed in Heroic times;
and then an apparently unconscious unfolding of their actual
status.

"In historical times," says the *Companion,* "the women of Sparta
had independence and authority. . . . In Athens the wife could obtain a divorce by judicial decision. . . . In the fifth century new
ideas sprang up tending to emancipate women. . . . During the
Hellenistic Age women played an important role. . . . Education
was in the reach of women, and we hear of women among the
pupils of the great philosophers." There were "women scholars,
painters, 'poetesses' " (how Victoria Sackville-West hated that monstrous word!). "Women were granted honorary citizenship of cities
other than their own for services rendered; and a woman was Chief
Magistrate of Priene." [8] If this is not female emancipation, it comes
closer to it than anything we have experienced in the United States
since the settlement of Jamestown in 1607.

In Greece, as in Rome, marriage was permitted between brother
and sister who had different mothers, but it was considered inces-
tuous for brother and sister of the same mother to marry, even
though the fathers were different. This, of course, was a survival
of the ancient taboo against sexual relations with the matriarch
and her daughters.

Paternity did not constitute kinship in Greece any more than it
did in Rome, or Palestine, or in the Polynesian Islands before the
advent of the Christian missionaries of the nineteenth century.

Flacelière, with remarkable obtuseness, explains the fact of the
legality of agnatic brother-sister marriages as owing to the "urge
to ensure the continuity of the family cult," especially in cases
where the female was the heir.[9]

This is the same explanation given in 1842 by one Charles Anthon "professor of the Greek and Latin languages in Columbia
College," American editor of *A Dictionary of Greek and Roman
Antiquities.* "Brother and sister by the same mother," states this
dictionary, "were forbidden to marry; but marriage between col-

lateral (agnatic) relations was encouraged in order to keep the property in the family," when "the female relative was the heiress." [10]

Thus does scholarship progress.

It seems impossible that the Greeks, among the most civilized of people, could have failed in this "one most important mark of civilization, the elevation of women." [11] And the writings of the ancient Greeks themselves do not indicate any suppression of the rights of women. The contemporary Greek writers, as well as Plutarch a little later, betray the essential freedom of Greek women in their casual revelations of daily life. From these writings the evidence is inescapable that Greek women enjoyed a high degree of independence.

Greek wives attended salons with their husbands, held "stag" drinking parties at which their husbands grumbled but dared not object,[12] and made up large segments of the audiences at the performances of the bawdy plays of Aristophanes. These facts do not accord with the picture of subservient, house-bound Greek wives portrayed by scholars of the nineteenth century.

The common belief in the subjection of women in classical Greece must go the way of all theory based on misinterpretation. "The subservience of Greek women," writes Jacquetta Hawkes, "has been greatly exaggerated through the bias of nineteenth-century scholarship." [13] The misconception seems to have arisen because of the high incidence of homosexuality. The syllogism in the nineteenth century went something like this:

> Women are nothing without the love of men;
> Greek men loved Greek boys to the exclusion of women;
> Ergo, Greek women were nothing.

But, as A. J. Symonds points out, pederasty was primarily a fad among the students, the intellectuals, and the military, the average citizen being unaffected by it. "It does not follow from the facts of Greek love among men," he writes, "that women were excluded from an important position either in Athens or in Sparta. The women of Sophocles and Euripides and the noble ladies of Plutarch, warn us to be cautions in our conclusions on this topic." [14]

The comedies of Aristophanes express feminist sympathies with a rich and sexual humor. "Women," observes Hawkes, "who were

free to enjoy this kind of thing were in no state of dire frustration" [15]—or, one might add, of haremlike subjection. The rollick-
ing and determined women in *Lysistrata* certainly do not portray
suppressed or intimidated wives!

In Greek art, Symonds continues, Aphrodite, the goddess of
romantic love, holds her own place beside Eros, the god of pederastic love, or sodomy. And Artemis, the eternal divine virgin, is as
prominent as is Ganymede, the god of passive pederasty, beloved
of Zeus.

When two such prominent men as Socrates and Plato proclaimed
the equality of women, it would have been hard for the mere citizen
to confute them. "The feminism of Plato and Pythagoras," says
Hawkes, "could not have helped but be widely influential." [16] Plato,
in the *Republic,* says: "No calling in the life of the city belongs
to woman as woman or to man as man; by nature the woman has
a share in all practices, and so has the man. For a woman to hold
the guardianship [public office] she will not need special education.
We will be dealing with the same nature in woman as in man and
the same education will be required for both." [17] For the only difference between the sexes is that "men beget and women bear
children." [18]

This confidence in female ability, unbelievable by nineteenth-
century scholars, was voiced by a Greek who was not only himself
a lover of boys but who gave his very name to a form of homosexual love. So it does not follow that physical love for boys neces-
sarily predisposes a man to despise women, the nineteenth-century
syllogism notwithstanding. Pericles loved boys, but he also loved
and admired Aspasia, whom he considered his wisest adviser. "He
loved her with a most wonderful affection," writes Plutarch. "Aspasia was courted by Pericles because of her great knowledge and
skill in politics; Socrates also consulted her for her wisdom and
brought his students to visit her. Men who frequented her salon
brought their wives [author's italics] with them to listen to her." [19]

Most modern reporters on Greek life omit this last passage in
Plutarch, the fact of wives accompanying their husbands to literary
salons being uncongenial to the accepted myth of their intellectual
inferiority.

The immortal funeral oration delivered by Pericles over the
Athenians who lost their lives in the Peloponnesian War was actu-

ally composed by Aspasia, according to Plato in *Menexenus,* who quotes Socrates to this effect. Socrates avowed himself a pupil of Aspasia, and it was at one of her salons that he first met the boy Alcibiades, the ward of Pericles, and fell in love with him. "Aspasia saw how intensely Socrates admired the boy and wittily counselled him in verse in the art of pederastic love." [20] The brilliant Aspasia was, significantly, an Ionian from Miletus in Caria (a Celt?). Alcibiades, who was so passionately loved by the great Socrates himself, loved his wife Hipparete. Plutarch tells us of Alcibiades carrying off Hipparete and winning back her love on the occasion of her divorce proceedings against him—and that he succeeded so well that she spent the rest of her life with him.[21]

Despite their romantic love for boys, both Socrates and Plato welcomed girls as students, as did Epicurus and Pythagoras. Pythagoras had many girl pupils, the most famous having been Theoclea, the head of the priesthood of Apollo at Delphi. Theano, a brilliant mathematician of Italy, he considered his finest student and named her his successor at the famous institute of philosophy he founded at Croton. In his old age he married her, and she thus became the head of the Pythagorean order.

The Pythagorean prayer speaks more vocally for the Greek attitude toward women than all the nineteenth-century scholarship combined:

> Honor be to woman on earth as in Heaven, and may she be sanctified, and help us to mount to the Great Soul of the world who gives birth, preserves, and renews—the divine Goddess who bears along all souls in her mantle of light.[22]

It was the Christians, not the pagan Greeks, who debated whether women had souls, as was done in all seriousness at a sixth-century council at Macon. At this infamous council, incidentally, it was the Celtic bishops of Britain, the pre-Augustinian, apostolic prelates of Celtic Glastonbury, who saved the day for women, thus saving the souls of half the human race.

Sparta is acknowledged to have been a more feminist city than its sister Athens. It was a Spartan lady who, on hearing that the Spartan women had the reputation of ruling their men, replied that they also gave birth to men! A fine retort. In Sparta girls and boys were brought up together from birth, swimming, exercising, and learning together. Plutarch tells of the training of children in Sparta in his *Life of Lycurgus.* "The girls, like the boys, go naked in the processions, at the dances, at the solemn feasts, and in athletics. Nor is there anything shameful in this nakedness of the young women; modesty attends them and all wantonness is excluded." [23]

In Ionic Attica (Athens) as well as in Doric Lacedaemon (Sparta) girls and women ran, wrestled, hunted, and competed in the games with boys and men. At the Olympic games they had their own events, sacred to Hera, which more often than not stole the limelight from the men's events.

The modern craze of "sexual identity" that decks little girls out in pink ribbons and little boys out in cowboy hats and gun holsters had fortunately not been adopted as a disguised effort to accentuate not the sex difference but the "caste" difference between modern male and female—a plot to instill feelings of superiority in the boy and inferiority in the girl.

As the nineteenth-century French scholar Schuré observed: "Away behind official Greek history and philosophy appear many half-veiled though luminous woman forms. There was Theoclea who inspired Pythagoras; Corinna the rival of Pindar among the greatest of Greek poets; there was the mysterious Diotima who appeared at Plato's banquet to give the supreme revelation of love." And there were also Aspasia, Theano, Sappho, Aristoclea, Nausicaa and Erinna among many now forgotten, whose names, had they been men, would be as truly "household words" as the names of Homer and Plato. By the side of these exceptional women, the ordinary Greek woman exercised a veritable priesthood at the family hearth and in the gynaeceum. "Indeed, she created those great poets and artists we so greatly admire, for their education was entirely in her hands." Up to the age of eight years Greek boys and girls were confined to the women's households, where no man might enter, not even the husband and father. "The wisdom of antiquity looked upon the child as a sensitive plant who needed the great encircling love of a mother and protection against the influence of the father whose coarser nature might adversely affect the child's development and stunt the awakening and growing soul." [24]

"Nobody can deny that Hellenic civilization showed the highest respect for the feminine principle. The Great Mother and the other aspects of the Goddess received far more devotion and worship than Zeus—even as the Virgin Mother does in Catholic lands today. Over the city, Athena presided. The finest things of life were personified as Graces, Muses, Justice, Wisdom, Peace—all, all feminine. No other people has paid a higher tribute to the feminine principle." [25] And certainly no people of modern Christian times has paid so high a tribute.

Etruscan Women

When in the sixth century B.C., about two hundred years after Romulus, the Etruscan princes, the Tarquins, rode into Rome to visit Lucretia, the Roman wife of one of them, they found her "employed at her wool, sitting in the midst of her maids." [26] They were struck by the contrast between this domesticated Roman matron and their Etruscan sisters and wives whom they had left behind in Latium "whooping it up" at a cocktail party in true Cretan style, without a domestic care in the world.

It was this tale, no doubt, and the contrast between the prudent and prudish Roman matron and the merry wives of Tusculum, that gave the latter their bad name in Roman society. Everyone knows what happened to poor Lucretia as a result of this famous midnight visit of her husband and his kinsmen—how one of her Tarquin in-laws later returned and raped her, and how she killed herself for very shame. William Shakespeare tells the sorry tale in *The Rape of Lucrece*, as does Thomas Macaulay in *Lays of Ancient Rome*.

Jacques Heurgeon writes: "In the opinion of the Romans, Etruscan women had a rather bad reputation." Yet "the Etruscan woman was invested in her own country with an authority that was sovereign. Artistic, cultivated, interested in Hellenic refinements, she was the bringer of civilization to her homeland. Finally venerated in the tomb as an emanation of divine power, she held a privileged position which recalls that of Ariadne in Minoan Crete." [27]

The Etruscan woman was very active, both socially and politically. In the frescoes and bas reliefs of Umbria she is portrayed always in the forefront of the scene. Like the women of Mycenae and Crete, she is depicted attending public functions, seated in the best seats at sports events, reclining at banquets with men, enjoying herself at concerts and the theater, always poised, sure of herself, as women can be only in a woman-dominated society.

Back in the 1820's, long before the remarkable "preconception-shattering" discoveries of recent twentieth-century archeology, when the Etruscan tombs alone had pointed to the truth about the buried past, J. A. Cramer wrote: "It is singular that two customs peculiar to the Etruscans, as we discover from their monuments, should have been noticed by Herodotus as characteristic of the Lycians and Lydians. The first is that the Etruscans *invariably* describe their parentage and family with reference to the mother, and not the father. The other is that they admitted their wives to their banquets and public events." [28]

In 1964, nearly a hundred and fifty years later, Heurgeon wrote: "One of the most certain facets of ancient civilization was the eminent dignity and authority of the mater-familias, the head of the family. . . . The feminism of the Etruscan civilization, strange as it may seem to us, is not an Etruscan phenomenon, but is a survival of an ancient and worldwide modus vivendi," when woman was dominant.[29]

As in other modified gynocracies of historical times, kings reigned in Italy, but they reigned as viceroys of women. They ruled by permission of the wives or mothers who were the hereditary heirs to the throne, as in Egypt, Persia, and Mycenae in late historical times, and even in pre-Republican Rome. Livy tells in shocked tones of Tullia, the wife of Lucius Tarquinius, who, "driving into the Roman Forum in her chariot, unabashed by the crowd of men present, called her husband out of the Senate house and was first to greet him 'king.' " [30] Tullia, an Etruscan lady, was only performing the expected function of a royal wife; for she was the daughter of the old king and queen, and therefore it was in her power to make a new king. But Livy, first-century patriarchal Roman that he was, unaware of earlier customs, was shocked by the incident.

"These words, 'she was first to call him king,' " observes Heurgeon, "are one of those fossils, buried in a very ancient tradition . . . an immemorial usage in which the Etruscan woman, as in Cretan and Egyptian society, had the status, incomprehensible to Livy, of 'king-maker'—as if the legitimate monarchy depended on the queen's designation and consecration of the monarch," as it had in all ancient societies.[31]

Raymond Bloch writes: "The position occupied by the women among the Etruscans was a privileged one and had nothing in common with the humble and subordinate condition of the Greek woman. This is, however, a mark of civilization which we also observe in the social structure of Crete and Mycenae. . . . Inscriptions confirm the status enjoyed by the Etruscan woman; frequently the person dedicating the inscription mentions, with or more often without mentioning the name of his father, that of his mother. There is evidence of this use of the matronymic [the mother's name] in Anatolia, and particularly in Lydia. . . . Perhaps," hedges Bloch, "we can see traces in it of an ancient matriarchy." [32] Perhaps, indeed.

Contrary to Bloch's caution, Heurgeon sees an outright gynocracy lingering in the customs of the Etruscans—a gynocracy inherited from the ancient civilization from which they were directly descended by way of Anatolian Lydia. The burial customs of the Etruscans, as a matter of fact, bring forcibly to mind those burials at Catal Huyuk, where the tombs were all women's, and men's bones were heaped in a charnel house. In Etruria, however, the male status had improved to the point where men were entombed *with* their wives and mothers, although not in the place of honor. The large sarcophagus in each tomb opened in Umbria has been found to be that of a woman. Around her may repose the bodies of her husband and children—but *her* name alone is on the tomb. Occasionally a baby daughter may share with her the honor of the sarcophagus, but never a son.

"It was as if," writes Heurgeon, "the Etruscans had considered women to be of a superior essence. . . . Woman by her very nature was considered to participate in that of the divinity who reigned in all the temples." [33]

Claudius, the most gentle and most feminist among the imperial Caesars, was married in his boyhood to Urgulanilla, an Etruscan girl. It was because of her that the scholarly Claudius became interested in the Etruscan people and wrote his twelve-volume history, regrettably now lost, about them. There can be no doubt that this study accounted for Claudius' noble concept of women and his lifelong deference to them. It was possibly his expression of this philogyny in his great work that accounts for the disappearance of the entire mammoth history in early Christian times.

It was Claudius' Etruscan mother-in-law, Urgulania, incidentally, about whom Tacitus writes in the *Annals* as having had great influence with the emperor Augustus. During the reign of Tiberius this imperious old lady had wordlessly sent a dagger to her own Roman grandson as a hint to him to kill himself rather than stand trial for the suspected murder of his wife. The grandson, Marcus Plautius Silvanus, meekly stabbed himself to death with the dagger —but whether to avoid the trial or out of fear of disobeying his grandmother, no one will ever know.[34]

Even into the days of the empire, when the Etruscan nation no longer existed and when its past greatness had already been forgotten by the Romans, the Etruscan dowager still inspired terror in the Roman male.

Roman Women

We have the authority of Livy that the original Roman tribes, or Curiae, were named for the women. Romulus, the founder of Rome in the eighth century B.C., "when dividing the people into thirty Curiae, called the Curiae after the women's names." [35] There could be no more convincing proof than this that the Romans were originally a collection of matriarchal tribes who bore the names of their mothers.

Further evidence of the gynarchic social structure of early Rome is found in the very words denoting kinship: *cognate* kinship, relationship through the mother, was *co-gnatus*—born *within* the tribe; while *agnate* relationship, that through the father, was *ad-gnatus*—added to, or born outside, the tribe. This indicates an active exogamy, when the husbands were added to the wife's tribe and forfeited by virtue of their marriage all connection with their own. Roman law of the republic continued this differentiation between cognate and agnate relationship by legalizing marriage between cousins and even siblings on the father's side but banning it between half-brother and sister who had the same mother and between cousins related on their mother's side. In Rome, one could marry one's father's niece or aunt or daughter but not one's mother's, the belief being that relationship through the mother was the only tie—that origin in a common womb was the only kinship.

Malinowski, the distinguished anthropologist, was oddly surprised when he found this same custom still operating in the twentieth century A.D. in the Trobriand Islands in the remote Pacific: "They have only one word for kinship, and this is *veiola*. Now this term means kinship in the maternal line only, and does not embrace even the kinship between a father and his children, nor between any agnatically related people. . . . Thus the line of demarcation between paternal [agnatic] relationship . . . and maternal [cognatic] kinship, *veiola*, corresponds to the division between those people who are of the same body . . . and those who are not of the same body." [36]

The very name of the great Claudian family of the emperors was derived, according to Tacitus, from Claudia Quinta,[37] a great lady of early Rome, not from any "Claudius," as we have seen.

Originally, as among the Etruscans in historical times, Roman children bore the names of their mothers, and only later in the republic was the father's name, the agnomen, added. To this day in many Latin countries, notably Spain and Latin America, children bear the family names of both parents, as they once did throughout the civilized world.

As in Greece, Roman women were the sole educators of their young children. Tacitus, Plutarch, and Cicero all mention the important part played by the Roman matron in the education of her children. Cornelia, the mother of the Gracchi ("these are my jewels") was a typical example; but Aurelia, the mother of Julius Caesar, and Atia, the mother of Augustus, devoted their lives to the education of their fatherless sons. It is an arresting fact that most great men who have left their mark on history have been the products of feminine rearing. Among certain branches of the Celts, the education of the boys as well as the girls was entrusted to academies run by women, who taught not only all the arts of peace, from philosophy to poetry, but also the arts of warfare, equestrianism, swordplay, use of the lance, etc.[38]

As in Greece, the women of Rome took an active part in all fields of athletics; and Juvenal, that inveterate scold, is unsparing in his criticism of women who "join the hunt in men's clothes" and of those who "devote themselves to fencing and wrestling." "What modesty can you expect in a woman," he asks, manlike, "who abjures her sex and delights in feats of strength?" [39]

Voluntary birth control and legal abortion, always indicative of feminine emancipation, were practiced by the Roman women, as by the Greek, as Martial's praise of Claudia Rufina implies.[40]

Here it might be well to unmask the lie of infant exposure among the Romans. Our textbooks teach that those perfidious pagans habitually abandoned their unwanted babies, especially their girl babies, and left them to die of hunger and neglect. Female students in ancient history classes are wont to shrivel in their seats at this proof of the unworthiness of their despised and miserable sex, while the males preen themselves and cast pitying glances at their less valuable classmates.

Yet this canard has no more validity than the similar one of wife-immolation among the ancient Europeans. Both fairy tales were invented by masculist historians of the Christian era whose purpose was to discredit the two greatest obstacles to the acceptance of Christianity: contented paganism and the high value the pagans placed upon women. So thoroughly had the lie of infant exposure been accepted, however, that in the eighteenth century the *very* Christian Lord Montesquieu, in compiling his classic history of the law, was surprised to find no legal or historical evidence for it. "We find *no* Roman law," he writes, "that permitted the exposure of children." [41]

What Montesquieu did find was a Roman law of 485 B.C. (Year of Rome 265) requiring that *all* children be educated equally, regardless of sex or social condition.[42] In 450 B.C. (Year of Rome, or A.U.C., Ab Urbe Condita, 300) a statute of the Twelve Tables permitted the "stifling" at birth of monstrously deformed infants, provided five disinterested persons were able to testify to the child's hopeless deformity.[43] And this is a far cry from "exposure."

Recent writers on Roman social customs acknowledge that the exposure of female infants had long been presumed from the fact that there were so few daughters in Roman families of the republic and the empire. But so were there very few *sons* in Roman families. And the reason is simple: birth control and legal abortion limited family size to an average of less than two children per family. We have seen Plato pleading with the women of Greece to produce at least two children; and Martial praised to the skies a Roman matron who bore the unprecedented total of three.

It was without any doubt the disgruntlement of the early church "fathers" at this evidence of feminine privilege in Rome that prompted Constantine, the first Christian emperor, in the fourth century to make voluntary abortion a *criminal* offense. Ever since then, the church, and with it modern society, has insisted that the unformed, unborn, and lifeless fetus is more valuable to society than the life of the woman on whose body it is battening.

Punishment for abortion became so popular a form of woman torture among the Christians that in the eleventh century the Holy Roman Emperor Henry II (973-1024) made it a criminal offense for a woman to miscarry even *unwillingly*, and any woman who lost a child through miscarriage was condemned to death by burning.[44]

We no longer burn them alive, but today's laws in most states demand that women jeopardize their lives in order to bring to fruition any and all seed that is carelessly deposited within them, however socially undesirable the matured organism is certain to be or at whatever risk to the physical and mental health of the mother. In *Look* magazine of November 4, 1969, a woman whose life was legally put into jeopardy by the medical profession in order that her fetus might survive asks "why was the foetus' life so much more important to them than mine?" It is an old question among Christian women, and its answer lies in the barbaric and gynophobic minds of the church fathers and in our accepted Judeo-Christian "morality."

The more civilized Romans, like the Greeks, considered the woman's body her own property and hers the right to bear or not to bear, as she saw fit.

For many reasons Greek and Roman women preferred small families, and with birth control and safe abortion easily available they were able to indulge this preference. The ancients considered the education of their children as important as their lives, and the offspring of small families could receive better educations than those of large families. In Rome the daughters were as carefully educated in the classics and in philosophy, rhetoric, history, and logic as were the sons.

Pliny the Younger, in his *Letters,* admires the erudition of his friends' wives and lavishes praise on his own wife, Calpurnia, for her taste in literature and for the lack of pedantry in her learning. Gaius Musonius Rufus, a lecturer and philosopher in the reigns of Claudius and Nero, like Plato in Greece, proclaimed the moral and intellectual equality of the two sexes and insisted on the right of all women to individual dignity and independence.

Divorce laws, another bellwether of feminine emancipation, were as favorable to women in Rome as in Greece. Plutarch refers to the ease with which women could divorce their husbands in Athens of the fifth century B.C.,[45] and in Rome the laws were no less lenient. Juvenal rails against the woman who, after "lording it over her husband for years," divorces him at the slightest whim and leaves him alone and helpless in his old age.[46] Grounds for divorce were numerous, among them being the age or poor health of the husband and even his absence on army duty at the front, none of which is grounds for divorce today in even our most enlightened states.

"Women attained great power and influence in the Roman Empire," writes P. Donaldson. "They enjoyed freedom of intercourse in society; they studied literature and philosophy; they took part in political affairs; they defended their own law cases if they wished; and they . . . engaged in the government of provinces and the writing of books. . . . But all this was swept away in the rising tide of Christianity." [47]

It has been the custom of Christian historians for eighteen centuries to bewail the freedom of Roman women and to hold them responsible for the decline of the Roman Empire. But the facts do not bear out this accusation. Rome did not fall until *after* it had adopted Christianity, a fact which suggests the "heretical" belief, voiced by Dante, Gibbon and others, that Christianity itself caused the decline and fall of the empire and the Dark Ages that followed, "when this power of destruction and decay sat like a ghost on the throne of the Caesars." [48]

The extreme patriarchalism of the Paulist-Semitic Christians was wounded to its core by the freedom and power of the Roman women. The Semitic women had for centuries been the slaves and chattels of men, and it was the intention of the church fathers to put all women in similar subjection, as decreed by Paul, "the little,

202 &#128 THE FIRST SEX

bald, bandy-legged renegade Jew" of Tarsus, as James Cleugh describes him.[49] Paul's antifeminism amounted to an active phobia
of all things female. Modern psychologists have attributed Paul's
misogyny to everything from homosexuality to resentment of
women's repugnance at his own misshapen body and ugly features.[50] Whatever the cause, Paul's contempt for women led to
disastrous results just when the patriarchal revolution was beginning to level off toward a true equality of the sexes. Western women
and Western civilization are still suffering from the rabid misogyny
of Paul and the church fathers. One has only to read the fulmina-
tions of these early "fathers" to realize the vitriolic unease with
which the Christian Church regarded women and to plumb the
depths of the church's psychopathic determination to degrade the
female and annihilate her soul.

A modern French historian of ancient Rome, who certainly cannot be regarded as a feminist, has written the deserved epitaph of
these Roman women whom the early church so hated and feared:

> One of the fairest examples of human greatness was the woman
> of Imperial Rome. Thanks to her, proud and free as Arria, an-
> cient Rome, in the very years she was about to receive . . . the
> bloody baptism of Christianity, scales one of the loftiest moral
> heights humanity has conquered.[51]

But the most fitting epitaph for Roman and all pre-Christian
women was written by a Roman poet of the empire, speaking for
all women of all time:

> Clames licet et mare caelo
> Confundas! Homo sum![52]

Which, freely translated, means:

> You men may raise all the hell you want to about it!
> I, too, am a human being!

The empresses of Rome, commencing with the very first of them,
Livia, the powerful consort of Augustus, were among the earliest
targets of the Christian fathers. With their liberated libidos they
were in the vanguard of the "feminist" movement of imperial

Rome. They sought and easily won equality with men, especially in the intellectual and political fields and in the realm of sex. Their republican predecessors, Augustus' notorious daughter Julia and the renowned Clodia, Catullus' beloved "Lesbia," had paved the way, and from the very first there was never any double standard in imperial Rome. The older surviving conservatives such as Seneca and Juvenal might rail at the "new woman" and praise the old-fashioned virtues of Cornelia and Aurelia, but the new men, like the younger Pliny, sang with Ovid and Catullus of the charm and the intellectual beauty of the liberated woman.

"It is certain that the Roman woman [of the empire] enjoyed a dignity and an independence at least equal if not superior to those claimed by contemporary feminists." [53] The empresses of the first three centuries, just prior to the triumph of Christianity, stand out like beacon lights of resurgent womanhood, reincarnations of the noble women of Etruria whom they numbered among their ancestors. Plotina shared the glories and responsibilities of her husband Trajan (A.D. 98–117) and even accompanied him throughout the Parthian wars. On Trajan's death it was Plotina who steered the empire through the turmoil of the succession and saw to it that Hadrian, Trajan's choice as his successor, entered his new reign peacefully and without civil war.

Julia Domna, first lady of the empire from 197 to 217, first as wife of Septimius Severus and then as mother of Caracalla, "in her son's reign administered the affairs of the empire with a prudence that supported his authority, and with a moderation that corrected his wild extravagances. . . . Julia Domna possessed even in advanced age [she died by suicide at fifty] the attractions of beauty, and united to a lively imagination a firmness of mind, and strength of judgment, seldom bestowed on her sex. . . . She applied herself to letters and philosophy, with some success, and with the most splendid reputation. She was the patroness of every art, and the friend of every man of genius." [54] Thus Gibbon. It is to Julia Domna that we owe all we know of Apollonius of Tyana, the great philosopher of the first century and rival of Christ. For it was Julia who commissioned her protégé Philostratus to research and write his biography.[55]

When in 217 Caracalla was murdered by the usurper Macrinus and the empire was plunged into chaos, it was a woman, Julia

Maesa, the sister of Julia Domna who "took the initiative" [56] and restored order. She deposed the tyrannical Macrinus and placed her own grandson, Elagabalus, son of her daughter Julia Soaemias, on the throne in what Gibbon calls "a conspiracy of women, concerted with prudence, and conducted with rapid vigor." [57] In Elagabalus' reign, his mother sat in the Roman Senate and held the office of consul.[58] When Elagabalus was murdered by the Praetorian guard in the year 222, Maesa again stepped in to guide the empire through a chaotic interregnum, naming her young grandson Alexander Severus, son of her daughter Julia Mammaea, emperor under the regency of his mother.[59]

Julia Mammaea stands out as one of the great sovereigns of all time. Like the reign of Queen Hatshepsut in Egypt, the reign of Mammaea in Rome (222–35) marked an era of peace and justice and prosperity rarely precedented in all of Roman history. While her son, the titular emperor Alexander Severus was still a minor, this remarkable woman, niece and daughter of remarkable women, established a strong democratic form of government over the empire, a government that remained effective throughout most of the later reign of her son.

> The general tenor of her administration was equally for the benefit of her son and of the empire. With the approbation of the senate, she chose sixteen of the wisest and most virtuous of the senators as a perpetual council of state, before whom every public business of moment was debated and determined. . . . The prudent grimness of this aristocracy restored order and authority to the government. As soon as they had purged the city from foreign superstitions . . . they applied themselves to remove worthless creatures from the administration, and to supply their places with men of virtue and ability. Learning and the love of justice became the only recommendations for civil offices.
>
> But the most important care of Mammaea and her wise counsellors was to form the character of the young emperor, on whose personal qualities the happiness of the Roman world must ultimately depend. . . . An excellent understanding soon convinced Alexander of the advantages of virtue, the pleasure of knowledge, and the necessity of labor. . . . His unalterable regard for his mother . . . guarded his unexperienced [sic] youth from the poi-

son of flattery. . . .[60] She exacted from his riper years the same dutiful obedience which she had justly claimed from his unexperienced youth.[61]

And Alexander developed into a wise and just ruler, succumbing to the avarice, cruelty, and lust that were the occupational hazards of Roman emperors only after the death of his esteemed mother.

Perhaps Rome's close association with the Celts of Gaul and Britain, induced by the conquests and defeats of Julius and Claudius Caesar and the generals Agricola and Cerialis, helped to restore the women of imperial Rome to the freedom and dominance they had known during the kingdom and in the republic before Cato. For the Romans excessively admired the Celtic women and were impressed by their *audax muliebris,* their capability in all fields, and by their untrammeled freedom and nobility of soul.

13

The Celts

Their wives are to every man
the most sacred witness to his bravery.
Tradition says that wavering armies have
been rallied by women. . . . They believe
that the sex has a certain prescience,
and they do not despise their counsels
or make light of their opinions.

—TACITUS

The Emerging Celts

⋞§ We first meet the modern northern Celts, Tacitus' blue-eyed giants, around 900 B.C., when the Greeks called them "Keltoi"— which Professor Powell thinks may have been the name of their royal family.[1] Where had they been since the fall of the ancient civilization? Where had they dwelt through those long ages in which the Sumerian civilization had bloomed and died and the patriarchal revolution had upset and changed the society of eastern Asia and the Aegean?

Wherever they were, they had kept the mores and customs of their ancient heritage. Classical writers invariably wonder at the strange ways of the Celts and their various branches: they had no slaves; they had no capital punishment; they observed complete equality of the sexes, with the balance slightly weighted on the feminine side; women attended, and often presided at, the tribal councils; their chief men were elected, while the monarchy was hereditary and that in the female line. Only in this last respect, matrilinear succession, did they resemble the rest of the ancient world.

By the time the classical world had become aware of them they had spread all over Europe. "In the third century B.C.," write Dilion and Chadwick, "one could travel from Galatia in Asia Minor northwest to Scotland and Ireland, and south again to Andalusia in Spain, without leaving Celtic territory." [2] They were one people, with one culture. And everywhere they retained their ancient democratic institutions and their traditional reverence for women.

They were by no means the barbarians that modern history has made them out to be. Archeology, combined with the more open-minded approach of later twentieth-century scholarship, is finally revealing the ancient pre-Christian Celts as they actually were before they, like the Cretans and the Etruscans before them, had become the victims of a "conspiracy of silence," a conspiracy designed to underrate their achievements in order to overrate those of their conquerors. The conquerors of the Celts were the barbaric and savage Teutons, the modern Germans, who emerged from their dense Baltic forests as the Vandals and the Goths in the fifth century of our era and aided unwittingly the Christian effort to destroy both the Celtic and the Roman empires. Together these mammoths of masculism—Teutonic barbarism and Semitic Christianity—annihilated the ancient civilized world and imposed in its place the Dark Ages of medieval Europe, from which degrading and retrograde experience Western civilization has not yet recovered.

Contrary to the prevalent belief that Western Europe was an uncivilized wasteland until its colonization by Rome in the last three centuries B.C., the findings of very recent archeology "indicate that Europe was inhabited in prehistoric times by peoples of more advanced culture than has heretofore been supposed. Also, their achievements had been steadily progressing for *thousands of years even before the Etruscan period* [author's italics]." [3]

The Celtic age of prehistoric Europe, writes Stuart Piggott, "was a Heroic Age, akin to Homer on the one hand, and on the other to Beowulf and the Sagas; and behind it all lay Hesiod's Works and Days!" [4] That is to say, behind it lay the gynocratic substructure memorialized by Hesiod, "the poet of the Matriarchies." "Celtic art was one of the great . . . arts of Europe," continues Piggott. [5] The technology of the ancient Celts formed the basis on which European technology rested until the age of steam, less than two brief centuries ago. The blacksmiths and the potters of the eighteenth century used the same techniques and the same material used by the Celts of the fourth millennium B.C. [6]

The technology and the farming economy of medieval Europe
were but a continuation of the Celtic technology and farming
economy of the sixth millennium B.C.—eight thousand years ago!
"The basic structure of the Mediaeval farming economy had been
in existence in prehistoric Celtic Europe for five thousand years
prior to our era," writes Piggott. "The traction plough and the
rectangular field system had been employed in Celtic Britain
since the third millennium. Crop rotation and manuring to obvi-
ate land exhaustion were evolved by prehistoric Celts." [7]

Contrary to popular belief, the Celts were not illiterate. They
had a literature of their own, a literature that has survived in the
medieval lays and later romances of Ireland, Britain, and Western
Europe. In the age of chivalry, writes W. W. Comfort, "the French
poets took over a great mass of Celtic folklore and made it the
vehicle to carry a rich freight of chivalric customs and ideals." [8]
And Lady Charlotte Guest writes: "It is remarkable that when
the chief romances of all European literatures are examined, the
names of many of the heroes and their scenes of action are found
to be Celtic. . . . The loss of their language by the great mass
of the Celtic peoples makes us wonder how stories, originally embodied in the Celtic dialects of Great Britain and France, could
so influence the literature of nations to whom the Celtic languages were utterly unknown." It can only be presumed, she goes
on, "that when driven out of their homes by the later nations,
the names and exploits of their heroes and heroines, and the
compositions of their poets, spread far and wide among the in-
vaders, and affected their tastes and their literature for many
centuries, and that Celtic literature has strong claims to be considered the cradle of European Romance." [9]

Lady Charlotte wrote these words in 1849, when the high civilization of the Celts was as completely unsuspected as were their vast
numbers, and they were thought of merely as small, scattered, un-
lettered tribes, inhabiting only southwest Europe and the British
Isles.

It can be deduced from the observations of Comfort and Guest
that the age of chivalry, which briefly brightened the medieval
gloom and for all too short a time restored medieval women to
their ancient glory, was but a revival of Celtic feminism.

Piggott, in his recent book (1968) on the Celts, says that they "showed a scholarly concern for standards of literacy" and that "there is presumptive evidence for the importation of papyrus as a writing material in early Celtic Britain. This would clearly imply literacy," he goes on, "as do the coin inscriptions and the graffiti on early Celtic pottery." [10]

That the Celts must have known the art of writing since earliest times is suggested by the fact that their script, "Ogham," "seems to have originated in *Anatolia*," [11] a region they had migrated from so far back in the misty past as to have forgotten it themselves.

But memorable as were their art, their literature, their eloquence, and their love of beauty, the distinguishing characteristic of the ancient Celts was their love of liberty. They were unique in later antiquity for their concepts of justice, sexual and social equality, democracy, and humanitarianism. They abhorred capital punishment. Henry Hallam writes that "capital punishment was contrary to the spirit of the ancient people of Europe. Instead, compensation was paid to the family of the victim," [12] certainly a more humane and socially beneficial method of punishment than execution.

The Women of Gaul

We have no more magnificent portrait from ancient times than that of the Celtic woman. Tall and noble in bearing, red-gold hair rippling down her back or caught in a loose knot at the base of her neck, blue eyes shining, we see her leading troops in battle, presiding over tribal councils, nursing her wounded on the battle-field, fighting bravely at her husband's side, and tenderly instructing her children. A later Camilla she appears, free as Artemis, and glorying in her freedom.

This splendid creature, this Celtic woman of old, we glimpse only a few centuries later, in the Dark Ages of Christian Europe, cringing at her cottage door, a whimpering slave, branded by the church as a thing of evil, sans soul, sans rights, sans humanity. No longer arbiter of her people or priestess of her goddess, she is debarred from the courts of justice, debarred from serving at the altar of the new God, deprived of her right to own property, even deprived of her rights over her own body. Jules Michelet gives us an unforgettable picture of this once proud woman, humbled to her knees, blue eyes sodden with constant weeping, golden hair matted and unkempt, limbs bruised and discolored from whip and club. Enslaved by law, abused and exploited by her husband, made sport of by her Christian liege-lord, tricked and soiled by priest and friar, she has become an overworked, beaten, hopeless object— prototype of generations of Christian women yet to come! [13]

But in the countless millennia before Christianity, this subhuman slave had been the glory of the world, an object of worship among her people, a source of awe to the conquering Romans. As late as the fourth century A.D. the Roman historian Ammianus Marcellinus wrote of the Celtic women of pagan Gaul: "Nearly all the Gauls are of lofty stature, fair, stern of eye, and of great pride. A whole troop of foreigners would not be able to withstand a single Gaul if he called his wife to his assistance, who is usually very strong, and with blue eyes." [14] Julius Caesar records that the Celtic women comprised the joint chiefs of staff of the Celtic people. "It was for the matrons to decide," he wrote in *The Gallic Wars* in 58 B.C., "when troops should attack and when withdraw." [15] And in A.D. 68, Tacitus records that it was the queen, Veleda, of the Celtic tribe of Batavi, to whom the Roman general Cerialis had to appeal for the surrender of his flagship, which the Batavi "had towed up the River Lupia as a present to Veleda." [16]

The continuing supremacy of women in Celtic government is attested by Tacitus; for when this same Roman general, Cerialis, exhorted the tribes to come over to the Romans, "the lower classes murmured that if we must choose between masters, we may more honorably bear with the Emperors of Rome than with the women of Gaul." [17] From this vignette we can imagine the Romans appealing to the masculist elements among the Celtic lower classes in a way that modern Black Power advocates and unscrupulous white politicians appeal to the racist elements among lower-class Americans.

In the third century B.C., the would-be conqueror of Rome, the Carthaginian king Hannibal, had learned to respect and fear the Celtic women, whose realms he traversed in his march across the Alps into Italy. In Spain, in Gaul, and in northern Italy he was accosted by women, with whose permission only he was allowed to continue his march unmolested. In the treaty drawn up between the Celts and Carthaginians it was stipulated that: "If the Celtae have complaints against the Carthaginian soldiers, the Carthaginian commander shall judge it. But if the Carthaginians have anything to lay to the charge of the Celtae, it shall be brought before the Celtic women." [18]

Edward Gibbon, in the eighteenth century, took the typical masculist view that femininity equals pusillanimity and denounced the Celtic woman of pre-Christian Europe as "unfeminine." Those "high-spirited matrons," as he dubbed them, "must have resigned that attractive softness in which consist the charm and weakness of woman." [19] But the idea that softness and weakness in women is attractive is a Judeo-Christian concept and had no place in the thought of the pre-Christian Europeans. Like the ancient people of Italy, the Celts admired *audax*—audacity—especially in women, which the Etruscans called *audacia muliebris*—a phrase which modern scholars have pondered over as a contradiction in terms. "Feminine audacity," they say, "is certainly not an admirable thing. Feminine timidity and submissiveness, yes. Feminine daring and courage, no." As Carpenter observes: "Nowadays the notion that women require strength and courage is regarded as very heterodox. But the truth is that qualities of independence and courage are not agreeable in a slave, and that is why man in all these later centuries has consistently denounced them, till at last the female herself has come to consider them 'unwomanly.'" [20]

But the Celts believed in *audacia* and even their marriage ceremony was designed to assure the bride that she would lose none of her independence by marrying—that she would be equal partner with her husband in the pursuit of honor and glory, "to share with him and dare with him, both in peace and in war," as Tacitus reports.[21]

Tacitus takes approving note of the fact that the Celts, like the Romans and Greeks, were monogamous and "were content with one wife." [22]

"No part of their manners is more praiseworthy than their marriage code. The wife does not bring a dowry to the husband, but the husband to the wife. His marriage gifts are not such as a bride would deck herself with, but oxen, a caparisoned steed, a shield, a lance, and a sword. Lest the woman should think herself to stand apart from aspirations after noble deeds she is reminded by the ceremony that she is her husband's partner in danger, destined to share with him and dare with him both in peace and in war. The yoked oxen, the harnessed steed, the gift of arms proclaim this fact." [23]

As mothers, the Celtic women also won Tacitus' approval: "In every household the children grow up naked with those sturdy frames and limbs we so much admire. Every mother suckles her own child and never entrusts it to servants and nurses." [24] "The soldier brings his wounds to his mother, who shrinks not from counting them." [25]

The feminism of the Celts in the first century A.D. is further proved, if further proof be necessary, by their religious customs and by the importance of cognatic relationships. "All the tribes have a common worship of the Mother of the Gods and the belief that she intervenes in human affairs and visits the nations in her care. . . . It is a season of rejoicing, and festivity reigns wherever she deigns to go. They do not go to battle or wear arms; every weapon is under lock; peace and quiet are known at these times, until the goddess, weary of human intercourse, is at length restored to her temple," which is on an island in the ocean amidst a grove of sacred oaks.[26]

Sisterhood is sacred, and the children of one's sister are more highly esteemed than one's own. "Indeed the sororal relationship is regarded as more sacred and binding than any other." [27]

Tacitus had obviously forgotten or was unaware that in his own country not so long before his time, the same custom had prevailed, the cognatic, or sororal and maternal, bonds being the only ties that bound.

The Warrior Queens

All the written records we have of the early Celts originated with men whose countries were enemies of the Celts—from Herodotus in the fifth century B.C. to Ammianus Marcellinus in the fifth century A.D. Yet all speak admiringly of the Celtic woman, of her nobility, her courage, her pride, her independence.

"Unlike modern critics, these ancient writers do not question, much less alter the tradition because of the anomaly they seem to find in it," says Bachofen.[28] In a word, "matriarchal conceptions had not yet ceded to the requirements of patriarchal theory." [29]

And these ancient authors are therefore far more reliable than are their modern interpreters, whose "conscious hostility to the old" has changed the very substance and texture of ancient history and ancient society.[30]

Herodotus, in the fifth century B.C., whose Greek homeland by his time had succeeded in imposing patriarchy over its original matriarchy, wrote admiringly of Tomyris, the Celtic queen who slew the mighty Cyrus the Great, king of Persia. Herodotus saw nothing "anomalous" in this fact. He does not berate her as an "unnatural, unfeminine virago," as modern historians have done, but presents her as a woman of high nobility and integrity.

When Cyrus threatened the Massagetae, "Tomyris, their queen, sent a herald to him, who said: "King of the Medes, cease to press this enterprise. . . . Be content to rule in peace thy own kingdom, and bear to see us reign over the countries that are ours to govern.' " But Cyrus refused this plea, and Tomyris sent her son Spargapises at the head of an army to expel the Medes and Persians from her land. The Persians won the ensuing battle and captured Spargapises, who promptly killed himself rather than submit to slavery. Tomyris, on hearing that her son was taken captive, sent to Cyrus saying: "Thou hast ensnared my child. Restore my son to me and get thee from my land unharmed. Refuse, and I swear that, bloodthirsty as thou art, I will give thee thy fill of blood."

"Tomyris," continues Herodotus, "when she found that Cyrus paid no heed to her advice, collected all the forces of her kingdom, and gave him battle. . . . Of all combats, this was the fiercest. The Massagetae, under the personal generalship of Tomyris, at length prevailed. The greater part of the army of the Medes and Persians was destroyed; and Cyrus himself fell. . . . On learning that her son was dead, Tomyris took the body of Cyrus, and dipping his head in a skinful of gore, she thus addressed the corpse: 'I live, and have conquered thee in battle; yet by thee am I destroyed, for thou hast taken my son by guile. But thus I make good my threat, and give thee thy fill of blood." [31]

It is most revealing that in spite of Herodotus' factual account of the death of Cyrus the Great, written within a very few years of the event, modern historians pretend not to know how Cyrus died. He died in 529, say the encyclopedias, with slight variations in wording, *probably* on some expedition. It would seem that the masculist writers of Christian ages find it impossible to report that this great king, Cyrus, founder of the Persian Empire and conqueror of the East, might have been slain by a woman's hand in battle. If she had treacherously slain him, by poison or by trickery, as he had slain her son, Tomyris would live in history as one of the notorious women, one of "the monstrous regiment," as Toynbee characterizes them, whose memory has been preserved by male historians as examples of the perfidy of the female sex.

Tomyris' words of defiance are reminiscent of another Celtic queen, Boadicea of Britain, who some six hundred years later was to slay *seventy thousand* of the invading Romans, as the Romans themselves dolefully reported. Boadicea's challenge to her people in A.D. 60 has the same proud ring as that of Tomyris to Cyrus in 529 B.C.:

> It is not as a queen descended from noble ancestry, but as one of the people that I avenge our lost freedom. Roman lust has gone so far that not even our very persons are left unpolluted. If you weigh well the strengths of our armies you will see that in this battle we must conquer or die. This is a *woman's* resolve. As for *men*, they may live, and be slaves! [32]

Dio Cassius has left us an impressive picture of Boadicea:

> She was tall of person, and of a comely countenance; apparelled in a loose gown of changeable colors, the tresses of her yellow hair hung to the skirts of her dress. About her neck she wore a chain of gold, and in her hand she bore a spear. And so for a while she stood surveying her army, and being regarded with a reverential silence she addressed to them an eloquent and impassioned speech.[33]

This is Agnes Strickland's translation. It is fascinating as evidence of the continuing war of the sexes that G. R. Dudley's translation is far less flattering to Boadicea. To him she was *"huge* of frame," *"terrifying* of aspect." She wore a *"tunic* of many colors," and her *"great mass* of *bright red* hair fell to her *knees."* She wore about her throat "a *great twisted* golden necklace," and in her hand "she *grasped* a *long* spear." And she was regarded by her army not with *"reverence"* but with *"fear."* [34]

Unfortunately both of these translations are fairly accurate. The differing words are given as alternate definitions of the Latin originals in most Latin dictionaries—as in "revere, fear," for the verb *vereor*.

It is all a matter of choice, and the masculist chooses one definition, the feminist another. The psychoanalyst might find interesting material, however, in the masculist's choice of frightening, terrifying words to describe this warrior queen, as though the very thought of a woman warrior conjured up atavistic visions of male helplessness in the presence of feminine power. Like James Thurber's classic cartoon of the tiny man being pursued by a gigantic, terrifying wife ten times his size, it reveals man's innate and primeval fear of woman.

Boadicea not only routed the armies of mighty Rome but she captured the Roman cities of London, Colchester, and St. Albans before she was finally faced with capture by the reinforced legions under Suetonius Paulinus. Rather than submit to the indignity of display in a Roman Triumph, this magnificent queen put an end to her life in A.D. 62.

How different had been the behavior of her fellow Briton Caractacus, captured in A.D. 51, only eleven years earlier, by the Roman general Publius Ostorius. Taken to Rome in chains, Caractacus was displayed in a Triumph to all the citizens; and on reaching the imperial box he cravenly pleaded for his life: "My death would be followed by oblivion; but if you save my life, I shall be an everlasting memorial to your clemency." [35] The soft-hearted Emperor Claudius forgave him but forbade his return to Britain; and Caractacus spent the remainder of his inglorious life a captive in Rome.

Tacitus records the amazement of the Romans when Caractacus, on this occasion, true to his Celtic upbringing, made his first obeisance to the empress and "did homage to Agrippina in the same language of praise and gratitude as he addressed the Emperor." [36]

It is interesting that Caractacus remains a heroic figure, a name to be reckoned with in world history, while the far braver and more noble Boadicea has been forgotten except as the "unnatural virago," the "anomaly," the "unfeminine freak" of early British history.

Cartismandua has been even more shamefully forgotten than Boadicea, yet she is another British Celtic queen who was a true hero to her people and a scourge to their enemies. "Cartismandua," write Dillon and Chadwick, "is one of the outstanding rulers of Celtic antiquity, comparable to Queen Boadicea of the Iceni, and with the heroic Queen Maedb of Connacht. It is indeed impossible to have any true understanding either of Celtic history or of Celtic literature without realizing the high status of Celtic women." [37]

"Queen Cartismandua ruled the Brigantes," writes Tacitus, "in virtue of her illustrious birth." [38] In other words, Cartismandua was queen by inheritance and was, like Boadicea, "a woman of kingly descent, for they make no distinction of sex in their royal successions." [39]

Cartismandua's first successful battle was against her husband, Venutius, who had somehow displeased her. Having defeated him, she took on the Roman Empire. It was only the great Roman general Agricola who finally, in A.D. 77, put down the Brigantes, who "under a woman's leadership might well have thrown off the yoke of Rome." [40]

Not only the queens were valiant, however. Valor seems to have been a common trait of Celtic women, both on the continent and in the isles. "The British women hardly fell short of their Gaulish sisters in force of personality and political and military prestige." [41] When Paulinus sought to take the island of Mona in the Irish Channel, sacred since earliest Druidical times, he was confronted by ranks among whom "dashed women in black attire waving brands," a sight "which so scared our soldiers that they stood motionless as if their limbs were paralysed. . . . Then urged by their general not to quail before a troop of women, they bore the standards onward." [42] Again, when the Romans faced the armies of Boadicea, the soldiers lost their nerve and were exhorted by their general: "There you see more women than warriors. . . . Close up the ranks and discharge your javelins." [43]

Tacitus correctly calls the Britons of whom he writes Celts and remarks their resemblance to the Celts of Europe: "Their language differs but little from that of Gaul, and there is the same boldness in challenging danger; their large limbs and red hair point clearly to a 'german' origin." [44] But where Tacitus refers to "Germans" he is speaking of the Celtic people, "the Germany of his day being Celtic Germany, not yet invaded by the patriarchal square-heads whom we call Germans nowadays," as Graves writes.[45] And Terence Powell adds: " 'Germani,' as used by Tacitus, was a Celtic tribal name. . . . The Teutonic people we know as the Germans of today did not emerge into the full view of history until the fifth century A.D. Then they appeared as the Vandals and the Goths." [46]

"Tall and Beautiful and Fair"

In line with our belief that the gods and goddesses of mythology were originally real-life heroes and heroines is the statement of Dillon and Chadwick that the Irish gods were neither little people nor fairies but were "tall and beautiful and fair. . . . They recall the descriptions of the Gauls [Celts] which we find in classical writers." [47]

These gods and goddesses, "tall and beautiful and fair," who so resembled the classical descriptions of the Celts, were originally the Tuatha De Danann, the People of the Goddess Dana, who reached Ireland about the time of Moses. This goddess Dana, or Danu, was according to one version the ancient pre-Achaean Aegean goddess Danaë, whose name by Homer's time had been masculinized into Danaus, "matriarchal conceptions having ceded by Homer's time to the requirements of patriarchal theory, when the feminine name is so often replaced by a masculine one." [48] Danaus, in Greek myth, was the father of the fifty Danaids who murdered their fifty husbands at their wedding feast. This wholesale mariticide may have symbolized an antipatriarchal counterrevolution in early Dorian times, when the women rose up against the men and killed them, after the fashion of the Lemnian women.

Nennius preserves the legend that Albion, the Roman name for Britain, was derived from the name of the eldest of the mariticidal Danaids, Albina, the White Goddess,[49] which indicates that this daughter migrated with her mother at least as far as England. The influence of the goddess Dana, as well as the diffusion of her worship, can be traced through Europe from the Danaans and the rivers Don and Danube in the east to Denmark and the Danes in the west—all of which peoples and localities were named in her honor. The city of London, which according to John Stow was

founded in 1108 B.C.—"about the year of the world 2855," he adds
for clarity—was also named for the Celtic goddess Dana.[50] Thomas
Fuller, writing in 1654, hands on the tradition that the city took
its name from a "temple of Dana [Diana], in Celtic *Lan Dian,*
which once stood where now St. Paul's doth stand." [51]

It was long long before the founding of London, however, that
the "tall and beautiful and fair" people of the goddess Dana reached
Ireland. Whence they came is unknown, but it is impossible not to
identify them with the people of the ancient civilization—the
golden strangers of worldwide legend who sailed the seven seas
and mapped the seven continents 10,000 years ago.

"The Tuatha De Danann," writes the Irish historian Sheumas
MacManus, "were a cultured and highly civilized people, so skilled
in the crafts that the Firbolgs named them necromancers; and in
course of time both the Firbolgs and the later-coming Milesians
created a mythology around them." [52] "Later generations of the
Milesians to whom were handed down the wonderful traditions of
the wonderful people, lifted them into a mystic realm, their great
ones becoming gods and goddesses who supplied their successors
a beautiful mythology." [53] Their queen, Eire, gave Ireland its
name; for it was she who led the armies of the Tuatha against the
invading Milesians. It was the Milesian queen Scota, who was
killed in the battle against Queen Eire, for whom the Irish people
were long named, the Scots of the ancients having been the Irish.
Eventually, at Tailte, modern Teltown, Queen Eire herself was
slain in battle, and the Milesians, "tall and red-blond of hair" like
the Tuatha De Danann[54] became masters of Ireland.

Tradition links the Milesians with Miletus in Caria, as we have
said, and Caria could well have been the cradle of the Gaelic Celts,
just as Lydia and Lycia had been the cradle of the Italo-Celts, the
ancient Latins whom Mommsen found to be so strangely similar
to the northern Celts of Europe. Could these Celts of historical
Europe have been the last remnant of the great lost civilization
whose existence is becoming more and more of a reality and of
which Sumer was a last faint dying echo? Perhaps the gods and
goddesses of Greek mythology, also "tall and beautiful and fair,"
had been the heroes and heroines of that lost civilization, just as
the gods of later Celtic Ireland had once been the heroes and
heroines of the Tuatha De Danann.

The Brehon Laws and Christianity

As an example of the just and intelligent laws of the Celtic peoples, we still have in existence copies of the Brehon laws, a body of law handed down since prehistoric times to the Celts of Ireland. "These laws show the existence of a complete legal system among the Celtic races at a very early period," and they throw "an important light on ancient Celtic civilization." [55] And, more important still, as Powell observes, *"They are a mirror of ancient Celtic society at large* [author's italics]." [56]

Among the Brehon laws affecting women were their right to inherit great landed estates and the noble titles that went with them, only being obliged, in much later times, to provide a surrogate warrior when a military levy was made. This custom still prevailed in France until the fourteenth century A.D. According to Hallam: "Until the Fourteenth Century in France great fiefs might universally descend to women, and the Crown resembled a great fief." "The great fiefs of the Crown descended to females, and Burgundy had always been considered a feminine fief until the Fifteenth Century." "Women were admitted to inherit even military fiefdoms." [57]

"It is a curious circumstance," concludes Hallam from his nineteenth-century patriarchal perch, "that *no* hereditary kingdom of Europe appears to have excluded females from the throne in the Middle Ages." [58]

The church found its efforts toward the subjugation of women among royalty and the nobility uphill going, compared to the relative ease with which they finally effected the subjection of the women of the people. Still, even this latter effort took a very long time, the church's complete victory over women not having been achieved until the seventeenth century, and then only with the enthusiastic help of the new Protestant Christians, the Puritans.

Under the Brehon laws the husband and wife were equal and had equal rights under the law. As in pagan Rome, "it is only a contract that is between them. . . . Roman law treated marriage as a contract, dissoluble at the will of the parties." [59] But Christian canon law under Pope Leo III (A.D. 796–816) decreed "that marriage was an indissoluble bond" from which there was no escape except through death.[60]

The wife not only remained sole owner of her own property after marriage, as in Greek and Roman law before Christianity, but she also acquired an equal share in her husband's property, which he could not dispose of without her written consent. Under Celtic law, women were not only permitted in court, as they were not under Christian law, but they could represent themselves in suits at law and sue even their own husbands to recover for debt—a heinous crime in Christian law. With cause, a wife could divorce her husband, as in ancient Greece and Rome, and on the separation she had the right to retain her own property as well as her husband's dowry and all other marriage gifts. In addition, she could demand one-third to one-half of all her husband's private wealth.[61]

The Brehon laws concerning women were soon challenged by the church and were gradually attrited away in Europe. In England, the Brehon laws—at least those that affected and benefitted men, such as peer-jury trial—were preserved in the English common law. Martia Proba, a Celtic queen of Britain in the third century B.C., incorporated Brehonic law in the code she gave her people, the Martian Statutes. It was on these statutes that King Alfred the Great, a thousand years later, based his code of laws, the origin of our common law.[62]

In Ireland the church had to adapt itself to the people, not the people to the church. It took the wily Saint Patrick of the slippery tongue to magnify men and diminish women in obedience to the Christian doctrine. We read in the *Senchus Mor,* a sixth-century A.D. revision of the Brehon laws, that "the man has headship in the marriage union. It is proper to give superiority to the noble sex, that is, to the male, for the man is the head of the woman. Man is more noble than the woman." [63]

This has the suspiciously Semitic ring of a certain gynophobic author of the New Testament, where we read: "Wives, submit yourselves to your husbands, for the husband is the head of the wife" (Ephesians 5:22-23). And "The man is not of the woman, but the woman of man; neither was the man created for the woman, but the woman for the man" (I Corinthians 11:8-9).

And our suspicions of plagiarism are justified when we find, on consulting the authorities, that the *Senchus Mor* was penned by no other hand than that of *Saint Patrick* himself! [64] The wily dissembler!

During the Christian Dark Ages of the Western world, when only Celtic Ireland kept alight the lamp of learning, women were in the forefront in law, scholarship, and poetry. Celtic girls attended academies with the boys, and the heads and instructors in these academies were nearly all women.[65]

In the fifth and sixth centuries, Saint Bridget was noted for her classical learning as well as for her brilliance in the law; and her influence and example lasted for centuries after her death. But she was by no means unique in the annals of Irish-Celtic women. Women poets, heroes, physicians, sages, lawyers, warriors, judges are referred to often in the old records, as Sheumas MacManus and Edmund Curtis affirm. Among Ireland's greatest poets were the Lady Uallach, who died in A.D. 932, and Liadan of the seventh century.[66]

Irish Celtic women, like their sisters in Britain and on the continent, went to war and acquitted themselves heroically. It was Saint Adamnan, a Christian bishop, who as late as A.D. 697 forbade the women of Ireland to indulge in the active sport of arms. Meekly they obeyed, semibrainwashed already by the Christian myth of their inferiority. And so ended the long and glorious age of the Celtic battle heroine and warrior queen, which began, as far as history has yet learned, with Camilla, queen of Latium in the thirteenth century B.C.

In England it was not until A.D. 936 that Celtic women began their long and painful descent into chatteldom. For it was not until 936 when "the British Celtic Bishop Conan submitted to the Roman Catholic Archbishop Wolfstan of Canterbury"[67] that the status of women in Britain, in Celtic Britain at any rate, began to decline. For nearly five hundred years the Celtic Christians had held out against the woman-hating Roman Christians who had been converted by Saint Augustine. For Augustine did not bring Christianity to the Celts, only to the Saxons of England. And what he brought was the Paulist brand of Roman Catholicism, which had been inimical to women from its inception.

The Celts of southern Britain had been exposed from early times to another sort of Christianity, an Apostolic brand untainted by Paulism. Tradition avers that the Celtic Church of Glastonbury was founded "in the last year of Tiberius Caesar" (A.D. 37), as Gildas writes.[68] Ancient historians from Tertullian to Eusebius acknowledge that Christianity had been introduced into Celtic Britain during Jesus' lifetime or, at the latest, only a few years after his Crucifixion, brought there by a true Apostle, Philip.

Even Saint Augustine, writing to Pope Gregory in 600, acknowledges that the "neophytes of Catholic law" (himself and his followers) found already established in England a church "constructed by the hands of Christ himself," in other words, established during Christ's lifetime.[69] Since we do not know the date of the Crucifixion, A.D. 37—the date given by Gildas for the founding of Glastonbury—may well have been within Christ's lifetime. It certainly predated the "conversion" of Saint Paul.

The antiquity of Celtic Christianity in England has been overlooked for the reason that the chroniclers of the English church, from Bede on, have been Saxons who preferred to equate Christianity with the Paulist Roman Catholicism introduced by Augustine, the missionary to the Saxons. The triumph of Paulist Christianity ended, in the tenth century A.D., the traditional freedom and supremacy of women, which Celtic Christianity had accepted and perpetuated.

John Lloyd writes that Pope Gregory, in sending Augustine to Britain, "made a serious error and miscalculation." Gregory assumed that these ignorant Celts would welcome, honor, and revere "this new light from the seat of St. Peter and St. Paul," and thus he gave Augustine authority over the Celtic bishops. But alas, the Celts were neither honored nor reverent, nor did they intend "to be treated as of no account and accept a subordinate position in an upstart missionary church." [70] Augustine's ill-temper, "be it confessed," says Lloyd, did not render his job any less difficult; and the battle waged for four hundred years. The Romish Church, of course, and probably regrettably, finally won out over the more tolerant and certainly more Christly Celtic Church.

Lugh and the Great Goddess

Herodotus says that the chief deity of the Celts of his time was the goddess, Tabiti.[71] Could this have been the Great Goddess, Tiamat, Tabirra, or Tibir, the great civilizer worshiped by the early Sumerians and translated into "Tubal," the inventor of civilized arts, by the Hebrews? Perhaps Tabiti, or Tabirra, was an ancient queen of the lost civilization who had become a goddess to the remnant of that civilization, Sumer, and the Celtic nations.

Another possible connection between the Sumerian and Celtic offshoots of that great civilization exists in the word *Lugh*—in the Sumerian language the word for "son," and in Celtic mythology the name of the greatest of Celtic heroes, the son of Queen Ethne.[72]

The fact that the Irish Tailtean games were established by Lugh[73] brings closer the link between the Celts, ancient Sumer, and the lost civilization. For the similarity of the Irish Tailtean games to the funeral games of the Etruscans has been noted by scholars.[74] And the Etruscans, as is known, brought with them the games from Lydia in Anatolia, the ancient home of the Celts and the source of the Sumerian civilization.

"The Lydians," writes Herodotus, "declare that they invented all games, about the time when they colonized Tyrrhenia" [Etruria]. For the eighteen years of the famine that finally forced Tyrrhenius to set out on his colonizing expedition to Italy, the Lydians amused themselves with games, fasting and playing, and feasting and resting, on alternate days. "Various expedients were discovered by various persons," Herodotus explains.[75] But more probably, the dim memory of ancestral games was brought forward by necessity and, little by little, the pastimes of their remote ancestors were reconstructed.

It does not seem preposterous that these very games, which were exported to Italy in Lydian times, were carried also to the British Isles by Celts migrating at an earlier date from Anatolia. The fact that in Celtic Britain and Ireland the games had been inaugurated by Lugh—"son," adds weight to the hypothesis—the Goddess-son duality being far older than any trinity.

Lugh's death day on the first Sunday in August was called Lugh-Mass and was a period of mourning among the Celts. The church, in its expedient fashion, unable to stamp out this pagan festival, incorporated it into the calendar and called it Lammas, a celebration later combined with All-Saints' Day but still called Lammas in parts of England, Wales, and Ireland.[76]

It is an interesting sidelight on religious history that Lugh's mother, Ethne, has been identified with the Celtic goddess Oestre, whose spring festival was taken over by the church as the day of the risen Lord and was called Easter after the goddess, as it had been called among the Celts since the beginning of time.

Cuchulain, the great Irish hero of early historical times, is believed to have been the reincarnation of Lugh, his soul having flown as a mayfly into the mouth of his mother, Dichtire. Could Dichtire have been an echo of Dictynna? Dictynna was the patron goddess of Aegina, and it was from Aegina that some say the Tuatha De Danann first emerged from the mists of time. The island of Aegina, in the Saronic Gulf between Attica and the Peloponnese, was colonized in the fourth millennium by Ionian Greeks from Anatolia; and it was on Aegina that Herodotus saw the golden drinking cup sacred to the goddess. This golden cup was one of the Celtic relics that had "fallen from the sky" in the remote past; and Plutarch, in his *De Defectu Oraculorum*, says that it was still in use in Druidic ritual as late as the second century A.D.[77]

Its prototype, an oaken chalice carved in the shape of a trophy cup, has recently been unearthed at Catal Huyuk in Anatolia. The wine-glass shape of this cup is unusual, if not unique, in early archeology. Cups with stems but no bases have been found, as have cups with bases but no stems. Most often ancient cups, like modern coffee cups, rest on their own flattened bottoms. But the unique shape of this *ninetieth*-century (B.C.) chalice from Catal Huyuk somehow found its way to modern Europe and became the model for altar cups in the Christian Church.

And it, itself, the sacred drinking cup of the ancient Celts, metamorphosed into the Holy Grail of Christian legend. The similarity between imaginative depictions of the Holy Grail in medieval art and the oaken cup from "prehistoric" Catal Huyuk is startling.[78] In popular legend, the Holy Grail was brought to Glastonbury in southern Britain by Joseph of Arimathea in A.D. 37. It was supposed to be the cup from which Jesus had drunk at the last supper and in which Joseph had caught the blood of Jesus at the Crucifixion.

There is no historical evidence, even of the flimsiest nature, that anyone ever saw this cup at Glastonbury. In the sixth century, however, the legend was resuscitated, and the quest for the Holy Grail, originating at Camelot in southern Britain, spread, like the "chivalry" of the Celtic knights of King Arthur, throughout Chrisendom and grew into the noblest—perhaps the *only* noble—aspect of medieval European life.

But the grail that Arthur's knights sought was not the Holy Grail of the Christian myth. It was the golden cup of the ancient Celts that the Celtic knights of King Arthur's court went in search of.[79] In Welsh literature there survives a pre-Christian tale of Arthur and his men seeking the sacred chalice in a sort of mysterious initiation rite, no doubt a Druidic ceremony, in which a journey over water and under ground is involved.[80] It was Chrétien de Troyes in the twelfth century who first substituted the Holy Grail for the original golden chalice of Camelot.

And thus we have seen the sacred ax, the labyris, travel from ninth millennium Catal Huyuk to Stonehenge in England, the sacred horns of Catal Huyuk evolve into the golden torques of Celtic graves in second-century Britain,[81] and the sacred drinking cup of ancient Anatolia end up as the Holy Grail of Christian legend. All of these were relics sacred to the Great Goddess. All date back at least to ninth- or tenth-millennium Catal Huyuk in Anatolia. And all were imbued with a deep and mystic significance in the great Celtic civilization of Europe.

"The civilization revealed at Catal Huyuk shines like a supernova among the dim galaxy of contemporary Near-Eastern cultures. Its most lasting effect was not felt in the Near East, but in Europe; for it was to this new continent that Anatolian culture introduced . . . the cult of the Great Goddess, *the basis of our civilization* [author's italics]."[82]

Part IV
The Tragedy of Western Woman

Men have looked on at the destruction of women like dumb oxen on a riverbank, placidly chewing the cud, while the ox-herd drowns before their eyes, not even dimly aware that they are in any way involved in her tragedy.
                                        —EDWARD CARPENTER

14

The Advent of Christianity

*Christian ideology has contributed
no little to the oppression of women. . . .
Through St. Paul the Jewish tradition,
savagely antifeminist, was affirmed.*
—SIMONE DE BEAUVOIR

The Early Fathers

If the power and importance of Western women had been somewhat diminished in classical Greece and republican Rome, feminism had revived in imperial Rome, and in Celtic Europe it had never languished. It required the combined power of the Christian Church and the later empire to degrade Western woman. To those who have accepted the myth that the church improved the status of women, it will come as a startling revelation to learn that, on the contrary, it was the Christian Church itself which initiated and carried forward the bitter campaign to debase and enslave the women of Europe. The status of Western women has steadily declined since the advent of Christianity—and it is still declining. The female in the Western world today is valued less than she was even in the early Middle Ages, when the church had had only three or four centuries to accomplish its mission rather than the sixteen centuries it has now devoted to the cause.

The Christians found the women of Europe free and sovereign. The right to divorce, to abortion, to birth control, to property ownership, to the bearing of titles and the inheritance of estates, to the making of wills, to bringing suits at law, all these and many other ancient rights were attrited away by the church through the Christian centuries, and not yet have they all been restored. The deliberate suppression of the evidence for the former condition of European women and the promotion of the myth of its betterment by the Christian Church are revealed unconsciously in the words of the Celt authority Terence Powell: "It is generally assumed "that the right of a wife to hold property or of a daughter to inherit, is a late development. But a more liberal practice seems to have been operative in Roman and Celtic legal custom." [1] Like all who study the past, Powell is surprised to find that women were more highly esteemed as persons by the pagans than they have ever been by the Christians.

The Semitic myth of male supremacy was first preached in Europe to a pagan people to whom it came as a radical and astonishing novelty. We must not forget that the leaders of the early church were Jews, bred in the Hebraic tradition that women were of no account and existed solely to serve men. Orthodox Judaism of the time, like Saint Augustine of Hippo, taught that women had no souls, and then as now the Jewish prayer of thanksgiving included the words: "Blessed art thou, Lord, that thou hast not made me a woman." The Jew, Saint Paul, first spokesman for the Christian Church (and without whom there would have been no church) stressed over and over again in his letters the accepted Jewish concept: "Let woman be silent," "The man is the head of the woman," "The man is the servant of God, but the woman is the servant of man," "Woman was made for man," "Wives, submit to your husbands," and so on ad nauseam.

All this sounded very strange and wild to Celtic men and women who had for millennia before the founding of the Hebrew race been taught to revere and honor their sisters and their wives above their brothers and their fathers. And now to learn that these very special people had no souls! Were not of God! Were the servants of mere men!

As the Jewish disciples, like Paul, radiated out of Palestine into the more civilized worlds of Greece, Rome, and southern Gaul, their Semitic souls were outraged at the freedom and authority granted to Western women. They were stunned by the respect women received at all levels, but the imperiousness of the Roman matron and the authority of the Celtic woman especially infuriated them. Paul said sternly: "Suffer not a woman to teach, nor to usurp authority over a man." [2] And the author of Saint Peter warned slaves to submit to their masters and wives to their husbands.

As a result of the antifeminism of the disciples, Saint Clement, as early as the second century A.D., announced that "Every woman should be overwhelmed with shame at the very thought that she is a woman." [8]

These and similar rantings, however, went unheeded by the majority of the civilized world. Nobody who was anybody read Paul or Peter or Clement, or any of the Christian writers of the first three centuries. The civilized world looked upon the Christians as a rather silly group of harmless fanatics (although Tacitus called them "the vilest of people"). "The names of Seneca, the two Plinys, Tacitus, Plutarch, Galen, Epictetus, and the Emperors Marcus Antoninus and Marcus Aurelius adorn the age in which they flourished," writes Gibbon. "Their days were spent in the pursuit of truth. Yet all these sages overlooked or rejected the 'perfection' of the Christian system. Their language, or their silences, equally discover their contempt for the growing sect. Those among them who condescended to mention the Christians consider them only as obstinate and perverse enthusiasts [fanatics] unable to produce a single argument that could engage the attention of men of sense and learning." [4]

The Christians were not taken very seriously by anyone, and they were tolerated benignly by the imperial Roman government. The so-called persecutions of the Christians by the Romans have been highly exaggerated by Christian writers. "The total disregard of truth and probability in the representation of these primitive martyrdoms was occasioned by a very natural mistake: the ecclesiastical writers of the Christian centuries ascribed to the magistrates of Rome the same degree of implacable and unrelenting zeal which filled their own breasts against the heretics and idolators of their own times." [5]

And a medieval Christian of the twelfth century, the learned and orthodox Petrus Cantor (Peter the Precentor), complained that the church of his time dealt "more harshly with heretics than the pagans had dealt with the early Christians." [6] Thus, while the Romans had slain their hundreds, the Christians had slain their hundreds of thousands.

The first question that must present itself to the innocent observer from the non-Christian world is, "Why?" How could this localized, fanatical little religion of despised Jews and pitied Gentile slaves have attained such power as to set civilization back 2,000 years?

Helena and Constantine

The answer, I believe, lies with Helena, the mother of Constantine. Helena was a lady of Britain, perhaps a queen. And she was undoubtedly a Christian, a member of that small Celtic Christian community that predated Roman-Paulist Catholicism in Britain by some six centuries. The Celts of southern Britain had known a brand of eastern Apostolic Christianity since about the year 37 (Year of Rome 791), as Gildas, Tertullian, Eusebius, and even Augustine affirm. (It must be remembered that the Western World, up until the tenth century, continued to date from the founding of Rome, *ab Urbe Condita,* in 754 B.C. It was not until the tenth century that the church, at the suggestion of Dionysius Exiguus, a Scythian priest and canon lawyer who had died in the year 544 of our era, started dating from the Incarnation of Christ, a date picked arbitrarily as having been in the Year of Rome 754. Thus, all the early writers prior to the year A.D. 1000 use the Roman chronology, and Augustine arrived in England to convert the Saxons not in 597 but in 1351 A.U.C. We shall here, however, adhere to the new Christian chronology, even though the personages of whom we write did not.)

Christianity, brought to Glastonbury by the Apostle Philip and, legend says, by Joseph of Arimathea, was well established in Celtic Britain by the time of Helena's birth, around the middle of the third century after Christ. Helena was undoubtedly a member of the Christian community, and her influence on Constantius, the Roman governor of Britain, probably accounts for his "softness on the Christians," a weakness for which he was reprimanded by the Emperor Diocletian.

The venerable Bede, writing in the eighth century of our era, reports that "Constantius who governed Gaul and Britain under the Emperor Diocletian, died in Britain leaving a son by Helena, Constantine, who was created Caesar and Emperor in Britain." [7] Bede does not say who Helena was, but his reference implies that she was too well known to his readers to require further identification. Geoffrey of Monmouth, writing in the twelfth century, says that Helena was the daughter of King Coel ("Old King Cole was a merry old soul") and was his heir to the throne of Britain.[8] This fact offers further proof that Helena was an early Christian, for William of Malmesbury writes that King Coel was *buried at Glastonbury,* the seat of Celtic Christendom in Britain.[9] According to the same writer, Coel's ancestor the Celtic king Arviragus gave land to the founding of the church there in the first century A.D., and although he himself did not become a Christian, his descendants Marius and Coel apparently did and continued to support the church into the third century. Helena was born around the middle of the third century, only five or six generations after the founding of Glastonbury. "She was the Queen," writes Geoffrey, "and possessed this kingdom by hereditary right, *as none can deny.*" [10] Furthermore, "after her *marriage* to Constantius she had by him a son called Constantine." [11] Both of these statements of Geoffrey have been discredited by later historians; yet John Stow, of the sixteenth century, a careful and accurate reporter if there ever was one, seems to accept the royalty of Helena: "As Simon of Durham, an ancient writer, reporteth, Helena, the mother of Constantine, was the first that enwalled the city of London, about the year of Christ 306." [12]

Legend held, with Geoffrey, that Helena was rightful queen of Britain; but eighteenth- and nineteenth-century scholarship consigned her to a very low status, that of a public courtesan. Gibbon guesses that she was a Dacian courtesan, ancient Dacia having been where modern Romania is. But why a Dacian courtesan should "enwall the city of London," he does not explain. Historians, lay as well as church, have also insisted that Constantine was the *illegitimate son* of Constantius by this courtesan, Helena, contradicting the statement of Geoffrey of Monmouth that they were married.

Constantius was a soldier who had come up through the ranks of the Roman legions to the top of his profession and had been rewarded by the emperor with the hand of his stepdaughter in marriage and by being named Caesar of the West. At this time Rome had two emperors (Augustuses) and two governors (Caesars), one each for the eastern and western empire. Constantius was governor of the West, comprising Gaul, Britain, and contiguous territories. Constantius had already had children by Theodora, the emperor's stepdaughter, when he met Helena. Yet it was his son

234 &◆ THE FIRST SEX

by Helena, illegitimate or not, who became Caesar and emperor on
his death, not his legitimate children by Theodora, who were the
grandsons of the emperor Maximian.

Helena's son was born in London (A.D. 275) and was brought up
there by his mother, while his father traveled over the empire,
another indication that Helena was more than a courtesan, for
in Roman times fathers claimed their bastard sons and separated
them at an early age from undesirable lower-class mothers. In
later years, Constantine the emperor was to tell his biographer
Eusebius, "I began in Britain." [13] Yet still the place of his birth
is debated in some circles.

On becoming Caesar of the West on his father's death in 306,
Constantine continued his father's policy of softness toward the
Christians. This attitude, as well as his preferment over the emperor's son Maxentius, led in 312 to Constantine's march on Rome.
Maxentius resented his father Maximian's favoritism of Constantine, and on the old emperor's death Maxentius defied Constantine
and charged him with coddling Christians.

As early as 298, Constantine had been married by proxy to
Maximian's infant daughter Fausta, and this marriage probably
accounts for the emperor's much resented preference of Constantine over his own son Maxentius. The matrilinear idea was
very deeply ingrained in the Roman imperial mind, the daughter's
husband always in olden times, even up to the time of Marcus
Aurelius, having taken precedence over the sons.

It was on Constantine's march toward Rome in 312 that the
famous vision at the Milvian Bridge took place. Constantine told
Eusebius in later years that at the Milvian Bridge over the River
Tiber he saw in the setting sun the sign of the Cross inscribed with
the words *in hoc signo victor eris* ("In this sign you will be victor"). The next day Constantine met and defeated Maxentius and
was proclaimed emperor of the West. And four years later he
made the Cross the symbol of the empire, and Christianity his
chosen religion.

But *was* Constantine converted by the vision at the Milvian
Bridge, as historians and churchmen still claim? Or had he always
been a Christian, son of the Celtic Christian Helena? The historian
of the Roman Empire H. M. D. Parker writes: "The belief had
grown in Constantine that the Christian God was the greatest

supernatural power in the world. . . . And *even before* he left
Gaul [to march on Rome] in A.D. 312 he had become convinced
that under the banner of Christ he would be victorious over his
enemy. *In the strength of this belief he marched on Rome* [author's
italics]." [14]

It would seem, therefore, that the famous vision at the Milvian
Bridge, of which Christians have made so much, was a result and
not the cause of his conversion to Christianity.

As a matter of cold truth, it is doubtful that there ever was a
vision at the bridge. Constantine told Eusebius the incident occurred as described above. But he also told Lactantius, a Christian
apologist whom he admired and who was the tutor of his son,
that there had been no vision but a dream. The night before the
battle, he told Lactantius, he had dreamed that he saw *not* the
Cross with its Latin inscription but the Greek letters *Chi Rho* in
the shape of a cross. [15]

The whole story was probably a later invention put into the
mind of Constantine by his mother, Helena. All the evidence seems
to point to Helena as the real agent in Constantine's conversion—a
conversion that took place in his infancy, at the maternal knee,
and not at the Milvian Bridge—evidence universally overlooked,
or scrupulously ignored, by masculist historians.

That Helena was a domineering woman of great influence over
her son is attested to by the fact that it was she who maneuvered
his marriage to the infant princess Fausta, thus assuring his preferment and eventual rise in the imperial government. It was also
Helena who, later, when the adult Fausta was of no further use to
her son, engineered her downfall and cruel death at the order of
Constantine.

The Most Christian Emperor Constantine

Sufficient attention has not been given to the fact that Constantine, the first *Christian* emperor, was the first to order the
execution of his own wife. He had Fausta, through marriage to
whom he had secured the empire, boiled alive on suspicion of
adultery, and this precedent set the pattern for the next fourteen
centuries. Thirteen centuries later, the Abbé de Brantôme was to
deplore the freedom with which "our Christian lords and princes

murder their wives. To think that the pagans of old, who did not know Christ, were so gentle and kind to their wives; and that the majority of our lords should be so cruel to them." [16] He was thinking, perhaps, of, among other "pagans of old," the pagan emperor Marcus Aurelius, who had refused even to divorce his wife, Faustina, whose crimes made Fausta's seem like mere peccadillos.

Under Roman law, men and women caught in adultery shared a like punishment—banishment from Rome and confiscation of part of their property. But whereas the man must forfeit half of his worldly goods, the woman was required to give up only one-third of hers. And with both parties there was always the chance of recall and pardon. Under the later *Christian* Roman Empire, "a husband was justified in *killing* his *wife* so caught, but he might kill the adulterer only if he was a slave." [17]

The opinion voiced by Will and Mary Durant that "Medieval Christendom was a moral setback" [18] is universally accepted outside the Catholic Church. Yet the *Catholic Encyclopedia* explains Constantine's conversion to Christianity in these astonishing words: "In deciding for Christianity, Constantine was no doubt influenced by reasons resulting from the impression made on every unprejudiced person by the *moral* force of Christianity." [19]

The *Catholic Encyclopedia* fails to mention the fact that Constantine scalded his young wife to death in a cauldron of water brought to a slow boil over a wood fire—a protracted and agonizing death indeed. Nor does it mention Saint Helena's part in this crime. Helena, who was later to find the "true cross" in Jerusalem and was for this reason to be canonized by the church that she had established, was idolized by her son Constantine. He conferred on her the title Augusta, a title once held by the deified Livia, wife of Augustus Caesar and mother of Tiberius. Constantine also ordered that all honor should be paid his mother throughout the empire, had coins struck during her lifetime bearing her image,[20] and built a city, Helenopolis, in her honor. All these things bespeak the tremendous influence this Christian woman had over her son. I think we need inquire no further into the origins of Constantine's "conversion" to the new religion.

Yet in the face of all this evidence of Helena's influence over Constantine, the author of the article on Helena in the *Catholic Encyclopedia,* unwilling to grant that even a mother, because she is female, can influence a man, says of Helena: "She, his mother, came *under his influence* [author's italics] such a devout servant of God that one might believe her to have been from her very childhood a disciple of the Redeemer." [21]

As, indeed, she had been.

Once adopted officially by the emperor, Christianity became the state religion of the Roman Empire, and treason to the one became treason to the other. With heresy to the church now a treasonous act punishable by torture and death, the Christian leaders went wild in a bloody orgy of revenge for the three centuries of humiliation and ridicule they had suffered at "pagan" hands. Constantine made things easier for them by proclaiming in 318 that the bishops of the church could set aside judgments of the civil courts anywhere in the empire—which, we must not forget, included the European realms of the democratic Celts with their ancient heritage of law and justice. In 333 Constantine reinforced the power of the church in civil matters by ordering all courts to enforce the judgments of the bishops, so that the civil courts became mere law enforcement agencies of the church and were no longer allowed to weigh evidence and mete out justice as of old.

The *Catholic Encyclopedia,* acknowledging that the early church was "not the defender of individual freedom, nor of freedom of conscience *as understood today* [author's italics]," explains: "Religious freedom and tolerance *could not continue* [author's italics] as a form of equality; the age was not ready for such a conception." [22]

The author of the above astounding rationale overlooks the fact that in Celtic Europe, as in Rome, individual freedom, freedom of conscience, religious freedom and tolerance, and equality had existed since before the memory of man. What the author really meant to say was that the *church* was not ready for any conception of freedom and tolerance. Nor is it now, where women are concerned.

The emperor himself set the pattern for Christian conduct. After his "conversion," he not only boiled his wife alive, but he also murdered his son Crispus and his brother-in-law Licinius, after having guaranteed to the latter his personal safety. Licinius' son, Licinianus, he had whipped to death for no reason other than that he was his father's son. This last horrible deed is excused by Christian writers on the grounds that "because Licinianus was not

the son of Constantine's sister, Licinius' wife, but of a slave woman,
Constantine treated him as a slave and subjected him to a slave's
death." [23] The matriarchal overtones in this "excuse" seem to have
escaped its patriarchal authors, for, in regarding Licinianus as the
child of his mother primarily and endowing him with *her* status,
it avows the priority of mother-right over father-right, a doctrine
the church claims to abhor.

Needless to say, matriarchal traits did not reveal themselves in
the majority of Constantine's actions. He was the defender *par
excellence* of patriarchal Christian values and, after Paul, was the
chief exponent of masculist theories of male supremacy and the
inferiority of women. In the century following Constantine, Augustine, bishop of Hippo, denied that women had souls; and this
infamous tenet was actually debated at a Council at Macon in the
sixth century. It was the Celtic bishops from England who saved
the day for half the human race at that council.

After Constantine, in the later Middle Ages, Saint Thomas Aquinas was to place women lower than slaves: "Woman is in subjection because of the laws of nature," he pontificated in the thirteenth century, "but a slave only by the laws of circumstance. . . .
Woman is subject to man because of the weakness of her mind as
well as of her body." [24] And Gratian, the great canon lawyer of the
twelfth century, wrote: "Man, but not woman, is made in the
image of God. It is plain from this that women should be subject
to their husbands, and should be as slaves." [25]

One wonders what the millions of people throughout the empire who still believed that God was a woman, a female deity, a
goddess, thought of all this.

Descent into Barbarism

Christianity—official, federalized, state Christianity—spread like
a bloody stain from Constantinople up through southern Europe,
into France and Italy, westward into Spain and the Low Countries,
and finally across the channel into Britain and Ireland—"a torrent
of rapine impelled by the spiritual rulers of the Church." [26] Wherever it went it was stubbornly resisted and openly defied, until

cruel experience had shown that defiance and resistance were of no avail.

"Historians," as Henry Thomas says, "have sought to hide the crimson stains of blood that bespatter the record of the Middle Ages, with the golden glow of romance." [27] Yet the stains remain. "The Europeans were never persuaded, never convinced, never won by the appeal of the new doctrine; they were either transferred by their kings to the Church like so many cattle, or beaten down into submission after generations of resistance and massacre. The misery and butchery wrought from first to last are unimaginable. . . . Christianity was truly a religion of the sword and of the flame," writes Robertson in his *History of Christianity.*[28]

Ideologically, the church endorsed slavery and promoted to a new high the sanctity of property and property rights, comforting the poor and propertyless with promises of an afterlife in which the church itself did not believe. It established firmly the concepts that "might makes right" and "wealth makes the man," thus leading to the terrible materialism that marks and mars our present civilization. It branded all the finer sentiments with that worst of epithets, "womanlike," and turned woman's very virtues against her. It glorified "manly" aggressiveness in the cause of the church and surpassed even the Nazis in contrived cruelty and organized terror.

"Cruelty and barbarity were more frequent in the Christian Middle Ages than in any civilization prior to our own," write the Durants.[29] And the venerable *Cambridge Mediaeval History* says: "The laws of mediaeval Europe represent a *barbarization* [author's italics] of the old laws" that prevailed in Rome and Celtic Europe prior to the sixth century A.D.[30] "Christian law is more injurious than useful to the state. . . . I know of nothing more destructive to the social spirit," writes Rousseau. The good Christian is necessarily and by definition "harsh, and lacking in compassion for his fellow creatures . . . for to love the unfortunate would be to hate God who punishes them." [31]

Not satisfied with brutalizing the souls of men and hardening their hearts, the church proceeded methodically to blight their minds by suppressing all information that did not emanate from the church itself. They first closed down the ancient Greek academies and then set about burning the books of the great classical poets, philosophers, and scholars, setting knowledge back fifteen hundred years and necessitating the painful *rediscovery* in modern times of truths and facts well known even to the early Greek sages.[32]

In the fifth century they turned their wolfish attention to the great library at Alexandria, the last repository of the wisdom and knowledge of the ancients. They burned the books and razed the buildings and carried off to Constantinople whatever they thought might be of monetary value. Among the antique treasures thus saved was the map of the ancient sea kings mentioned earlier—but its real value was undreamed of by its abductors.

At Alexandria they also pillaged the great School of Philosophy, from which had emanated one of the last lights of learning in the gathering darkness of the brave new Christian world. The head of this great school of Neoplatonism was Hypatia, "a remarkable woman of great learning and eloquence, the charm of whose rare modesty and beauty, combined with her great intellectual gifts, attracted to her lectures a large number of disciples." [33] This great woman, mathematician, logician, astronomer, philosopher, naturally inspired the fanatical hatred of Cyril, the Christian bishop of Alexandria, and he resolved upon her ruin.

After a defamatory and Paulistic sermon on the iniquity of women in general and of Hypatia, who presumed to teach *men,* in particular, he urged his congregation not to allow such an un-feminine, un-Christian monster to live. Fired with Christian zeal the congregation poured out of the church and, finding Hypatia alone with but one pupil, Synesius of Cyrene, they tore off her clothes, cut her to pieces with oyster shells, and then burned her body piece by piece. Synesius saved himself by professing to be a Christian—and he later became bishop of Ptolemaïs.[34]

As a result of such persecutions of the intellectual community there began a gigantic "brain drain" from Christian Europe to the non-Christian Near East, a "flight of the bright" equaled only by that of the Jewish writers, scientists, and scholars—the brains of Germany—from Nazi-threatened Europe in the 1930's. Montesquieu, quoting Agathias as his authority, says that most of the brains of Greece and Rome migrated to Persia rather than live under Christianity; and "whole countries [of Europe] were desolated and depopulated by the despotic power and excessive advantage of the clergy over the laity." [35] This flight of the intellectuals to the East no doubt contributed to the flowering of Arabic culture between the eighth and fourteenth centuries, when only the Moors and Moslems could boast any geniuses equal to the geniuses of ancient Greece and Rome. Christian Europe during these dark centuries produced not one soul who contributed anything at all to the sum of human knowledge.[36]

Wherever Christianity went it carried with it the deadly germ of antifeminism, forcing civil governments to adopt the harsh and woman-hating laws of the church. Men, of course, accepted the new ideas more readily than women, who resisted longer and more tragically than their brothers. Women, as James Cleugh observes, had been the revered sex in Europe, and "they were as determined to remain so as the Church was to demote them." [37] Yet their determination was of no avail. Men had always harbored in the depths of their subconscious a fear and dread of women, and to turn this dread into active hatred and contempt became the mission of the all-male Christian hierarchy.

"Abuse was lavished upon the sex," writes Jules Michelet. "Filthy, indecent, shameless, immoral, were only some of the epithets hurled at them by the Church." Woman, announced the Christian clergy, were naturally depraved, vicious, and dangerous to the salvation of men's souls—a commodity women needed not to worry about as they were possessed of none. "Woman herself," continues Michelet, "came eventually to share the odious prejudice and to believe herself unclean; . . . woman, so sober compared to the opposite sex . . . was fain to ask pardon almost for existing at all, for living, and fulfilling the conditions of life." [38]

The miracle is not that the church finally succeeded in its purpose of degrading women. With the might of the empire behind it at first and the even greater might of the pope behind it after a while, it could hardly have failed. The miracle is that it took the church so *long* to humble the once stronger sex. For it was not until after the Protestant Reformation of the fifteenth and sixteenth centuries and the triumph of Puritanism in the seventeenth that woman's status reached the low point at which we find it today. After the church had succeeded in its mission of teaching men to regard women as brute and soulless beasts, the civil law stepped in and placed woman in the absolute power of men. Her enemy became her master, and the obscene design of the Christian fathers was finally and completely achieved.

"Our curiosity is naturally prompted to inquire by what means the Christian faith obtained its remarkable victory," writes Gibbon. "It appears that it was most effectively assisted by the inflexible and intolerant zeal of the Christians, derived from the Jewish religion." [39] And the Jewish religion, as expressed in the Old Testament, says John Stuart Mill, is "a system in many respects barbarous, and intended for a barbarous people." And this barbarous religion, steeped in woman-hatred and superstition, continues Mill, is the basis of so-called "Christian morality." [40]

15

Mary and the Great Goddess

> *What ails Christianity is that the old*
> *Mother-Goddess religious theme and the new*
> *Almighty-God theme are fundamentally irreconcilable.*
> —ROBERT GRAVES

The Discovery of Mary

"And so," as Rousseau writes, "what the pagans had feared actually came to pass." With their new power, and the blessing of the imperial government, "the humble Christians changed their language, and their pretended kingdom of the other world became the *most violent despotism* in this."[1] In the implacable enforcement of the Christian faith, spies were everywhere alert to inform against the humble as well as the mighty. Lip service to the church became the only safety. Europe became a world of hypocrites, paying overt homage to the new church while covertly worshiping the old divinities.

Simulating a reverence for the strange religion that confused ethics with morality in a way that hitherto only a small and unknown Jewish sect in Palestine had done, the real religion went underground. The Black Mass and the Sabbat were far more widespread than the church cared to admit; yet witches' covens comprised only a small fraction of the secret protest against the authority of the church.[2] Like overly restrained children who dare not defy father to his face, the people of Europe formed secret societies at every level, figuratively and literally to thumb their noses at Christianity.

The church seemed doomed to failure, destined to go down to bloody death amidst the bleeding corpses of its victims, when the people discovered Mary. And only when Mary, against the stern decrees of the church, was dug out of the oblivion to which Constantine had assigned her and became identified with the Great

243

Goddess was Christianity finally tolerated by the people. Saint Patrick, a Dale Carnegie of the early church, was the discoverer of this secret of winning willing converts.

Saint Patrick, although he had been trained for the priesthood in Rome, had originally been a Celtic Christian of Britain, and he carried with him into the Catholic priesthood an understanding of the desire of the Celtic peoples for their own goddess. The story is told that when, in his new Romish robes of authority, he landed on the Irish coast, he found the Irish gathered together worshiping an image of Brigante, the mother of the gods. Patrick of the nimble wit and nimbler tongue soon convinced them that the mother of the gods was really Mary, the mother of God. The always ingratiating Irish politely agreed to call the goddess *Mary*, and immediately resumed their worship of her. Ireland to this day is a Mary-centered rather than a Jesus-centered land, as are all the remnants of the Celtic peoples throughout Catholic Europe.

In Ireland, writes Graves, "Christianity had been introduced by eloquent and tactful missionaries, not, as elsewhere, at the point of the sword; and the college of Druids accepted Jesus and his Mother as completing, rather than discrediting, their ancient theology. The Irish bishops, appointed at first by the kings, and not by the popes, were expected to sing low, and they did sing low. They Christianized the Goddess as St. Bridget, patroness of poets, and her immemorial altar-fire at Kinsale was still alight under Henry VIII." [3]

Christ's greatest rival throughout the Roman Empire, as E. O. James writes, was the Great Goddess, "the Goddess of many names yet only one personality." And it was Patrick's discovery that the pagans would accept Christ if they could have Mary that changed the official policy toward Mary in the church. Constantine had ordered the destruction of all goddess temples throughout the empire and had sternly forbidden the worship of Mary, "fearing Her worship would overshadow Her Son." [4] Yet despite the authority of the church, the last surviving goddess temple was not closed until the year 560.[5]

"Can the Eternal One Be Female?"

How are we to account for the victory of Christianity over the beautiful Greek pantheon? asks Jane Harrison. She finds the answer to consist in a disturbing element in the classical Homeric gods and goddesses. "They are *too* beautiful, too artificial to have been natural outgrowths of a people's yearning for immortality. . . . The Olympian gods seemed to me like a bouquet of cut flowers whose bloom is brief because they have been severed from their roots. . . . To find these roots we must burrow deep into a lower stratum of thought, into those chthonic cults which underlay their life, and from which sprang all their brilliant blossoming."

To find these roots, Harrison delved deep into Greek religion and wrote her great work, *Themis,* tracing the Olympians back to their ancient source in the original and primordial worship of the goddess *Themis,* Justice, the earliest aspect of the Great Goddess. "The Great Goddess," she found, "is everywhere prior to the masculine gods." When her assumptions were later proven by archeology, Harrison was delighted: "I found to my great joy that my 'heresies' were accepted by the new generation of scholars as almost postulates . . . matters of historical certainty, based on definite facts. . . ." [6]

In Harrison's time, a half century ago or more, archeology was still in its infancy, and yet it had already toppled many of man's cherished beliefs and biased preconceptions about prehistory: primarily, the preconception that human society had always been male-dominated and that the deity, by whatever name, had always been masculine.

In the sixty years that have passed since Harrison penned her jubilant words, our concepts of history, sex, and religion have been so thoroughly discredited by the proof and testimony of archeology that all our history books, all our theological theories, and all our ideas about sexual differences and limitations have become obsolete. Yet the textbooks have not caught up with the new knowledge —nor have the theologians, nor the sociologists, nor the politicians.

Robert Graves, writing of the similarities of Greek, Celtic, and Jewish religions, arrives at Harrison's conclusion in the vast priority of the goddess, though by a different route. "The connection," he writes, "is that all three races were civilized by the same ancient Aegean people whom they conquered and absorbed." [7] These lost people, the ancient race, were goddess worshipers and were woman-oriented, regarding the Female Principle as the primary one and femininity superior to masculinity. This last concept the new people could not endure, and in the process of humbling femininity they at the same time overthrew the female deity and set up in her place a male-dominated hierarchy of gods and goddesses. The reason, therefore, for the artificiality and rootlessness of the Olympian gods, as of the Jewish and Christian God, is that they are *contrived*—deliberately invented by patriarchs to replace the ancient Great Goddess. Thus the only reality in Christianity is Mary, the Female Principle, the ancient goddess reborn.

It was because of their lack of authenticity that the classical gods fell to Christianity. Yet not, says Graves, to *masculine* Christianity —not to Jehovah or Jesus—but to Mary.

The ancient prevalence of goddess worship, writes Graves, "is not merely of antiquarian interest, for the popular appeal of modern Catholicism is, despite the all-male priesthood and the patriarchal Trinity, based rather on the ancient goddess and the Aegean Mother-Son religious tradition to which it has reverted in the adoration of Mary, than on its Aramaean or Indo-European . . . god elements." [8]

"Since it was claimed that the Logos became flesh through a human mother," writes James, "when the Jewish sect at Rome became the Catholic Church . . . the ancient cult of the goddess and the young god was re-established in a new synthesis." [9]

In short, Christianity succeeded ultimately because it represented a return to the original goddess worship, which the Olympian gods had temporarily replaced but which had never been totally replaced in the minds and hearts of the people.

Montesquieu, quoting Cyril's *Letters*, says that when the people of Ephesus were informed by the bishop in the fifth century "that they might worship the Virgin Mary as the Mother of God, they were transported with joy; they kissed the hands of the clergy, they embraced their knees, and the whole city resounded with acclamations." [10]

And because of Mary and her identification in the medieval mind with the primordial Great Goddess of the Celts, Christianity was able eventually to triumph over the "artificial and rootless" male gods who had been consciously invented in patriarchal ages to conceal the Eternal One.

"Can the Eternal One be female?" asks Gide and does not wait for an answer. [11] Yet, it is an interesting fact, as stated earlier, that it is always the Virgin Mary who is seen in visions—never God, never the Holy Ghost, and very rarely Jesus. The great Christian mystics to a man, and woman, claim to have seen Mary in the flesh at one time or another. And hardly a week passes that some simple peasant or padre somewhere in the world doesn't have a visitation from "our Blesséd Lady."

Those interested in psychical research may wonder whether these people actually do see something—the astral or etheric body of a real woman. But of what woman? King Numa saw her in the grotto at Nemi and called her Egeria. Bernadette saw her in the grotto at Lourdes and called her Mary. Who can say she is not the materialization of a real "Blesséd Lady," the Great Goddess herself, "the multitudinously named White Goddess, relic of matriarchal civilization, or, who knows, the harbinger of its return." [12]

Mary in the Middle Ages

Thus the church, which in its fanatical patriarchalism had set out to annihilate goddess worship, found itself forced by popular demand, and in order to assure its own survival, to recognize Mary. They could not go to the extreme of including her in the Trinity, where by ancient religious tradition she belonged, but they did finally and reluctantly, nineteen hundred years later, admit her to a seat in heaven with her son and endow her, like him, with a sinless and superhuman purity.

"The Church refused for centuries to pronounce upon the sinless birth of Mary, an immaculacy that would have placed her, Mary, on a par with Jesus, as the only person born without sin. The great schoolmen were against it and the learned monks fought it to the last. Yet the great masses of the people favored it so strongly that the Church was finally forced to give in." [18]

From the very beginning, the exclusively masculine character of the new religion was resented and resisted by the pagans. From Rome to Greece, from Egypt to Anatolia, and particularly in Europe, abortive attempts were made to throw off the yoke of Christianity, to "restore the old order, and reestablish the ancient system; but without success: Christianity prevailed over everything." [14]

The last image of the goddess in Rome, the gold statue of the goddess as *Virtus* (Virtue), fell in 410. And with her, writes Zosimus bitterly, "finally vanished all that was left in Rome of courage and worth." [15]

This remark raises the question, once raised by Dante, whether Constantine did not do more harm than good by establishing the church, and the related question, raised by many scholars and thinkers including Gibbon, whether Christianity was not responsible for the fall of the Roman Empire and for the chaos of social and intellectual retrogression that resulted therefrom. "In exterminating Excellence," writes Otto Seeck, the church deliberately turned its back on progress and plunged the Western world into the long misery and oppression of the Dark Ages.[16]

But in the darkness a faint light glimmered—a light that gradually grew into a flame that warmed men's hearts and revitalized their hopes. The light was Mary. Men and women flocked to her in droves, and her cult soon rivaled that of Jesus. By the eleventh century she had *eclipsed* Jesus as the savior of mankind. "The Holy Virgin," writes Briffault, "called by Albertus Magnus the Great Goddess, had well nigh replaced the male Trinity in the devotion of the people. God the Father was unapproachable and terrible. Christ had the stern office of a judge. The Queen of Heaven alone could show untrammelled mercy. She wrought more miracles than all the divine and saintly males in Heaven. She had, in fact, entirely regained her original position as the Great Goddess, the divine prototype of magic womanhood." [17]

Henry Adams, traveling in Europe seventy years ago, made what was to him, a nineteenth-century patristic American male, a startling discovery: the magnificent cathedrals of medieval Europe, those "paeans in stone," were built not to the glory of God, as the church had intended them, but as expressions of the adoration of Mary. "He loved their dignity, their unity, their scale, their lines, their lights, their shadows, their decorative sculpture; and he was conscious of the Force that had created it all—the Virgin, the Woman—by whose genius the stately monuments were built, through which She was expressed. . . . All the steam power in the world could not, like the Virgin, build Chartres. . . . Symbol or energy, the Virgin has acted as the greatest force the Western world ever felt, and has drawn men's activities to herself more strongly than any other power, natural or supernatural, has ever done." [18]

Adams did not seem to realize that this mystic power of the Virgin Mary, the woman, the goddess, was a thing as old as time, that it had been this very power which in the primeval eons had held the world together and had started mankind on its long and frequently interrupted journey toward humanhood. But medieval man, in whose memory the Great Goddess still survived, knew it; and as he chiseled in stone or raised the flying buttresses on the great cathedrals, he was remembering and honoring her as his ancestors had of old, with his greatest efforts and his loftiest conceptions.

The most beautiful and reverent sculptures are those of Mary. The most perfect paintings are of her. And the most tender and most beautifully executed stained glass windows represent the mother and child. [19] In spite of the pope and the secular power of the local padre, medieval man still worshiped the mother of the gods.

Mary and the British Celts

The New Testament has nothing to say of Mary after the Crucifixion. In the *Lore of the New Testament*, however, Mary is said to have been buried by Peter and some of the other Apostles in a cave tomb at Jehoshaphat. Eight days after the burial, her tomb was opened and found to be empty. Whereupon Thomas, who had just arrived on a cloud from India, announced that he had witnessed the Assumption of Mary from the top of Mount Ararat, where his flying cloud had briefly deposited him en route from India. Jesus himself, said Thomas, had descended from heaven and had conducted his mother upward. On this testimony Thomas was finally forgiven for having doubted various previous supernatural happenings, and the Apostles fell down and worshiped him. Afterward, twelve clouds alighted and bore the united twelve back to their respective ministries.[20]

But there is another legend about Mary's later years that is more acceptable to earthbound mentalities. And this is the legend, still current in southern France and England, that Mary died in Marseilles.

According to this version, after the stoning of Saint Stephen in A.D. 35, several of his friends and relatives, fearing for their own lives, resolved to flee Jerusalem and put as much space as possible between themselves and the Sanhedrin. Joseph of Arimathea thereupon purchased a ship, and in it a small band of Christian Jews sailed for Europe. Aboard the ship were Joseph of Arimathea, his niece Mary, who was the mother of Jesus, her cousins Lazarus, Martha, and Mary, and a young orphaned girl named Thekla.

They sailed along the northern coast of Africa, up through the Tyrrhenian Sea, and landed at Marseilles in the year 36. "Marseilles still gossips," writes Lionel Smithett Lewis, "about these refugees of two thousand years ago." [21]

Marseilles was a great seaport, the gateway to Europe in Roman times, and from it fine Roman roads led to all parts of the empire. The established trade route to the British Isles from the Mediterranean world led from Marseilles up through Armorica, and across the channel to southern Britain. Joseph of Arimathea was thoroughly familiar with this route, and Marseilles was chosen as his place of refuge for the reason that he was well known and highly regarded there.

For Joseph of Arimathea was a metal merchant, a tin tycoon, with tin and copper mines in Cornwall and in Somerset in the south of England. He was in the habit of making frequent visits to these mines, and he had many friends among the British Celts, of whom the Celtic king, Arviragus, was one.

Shortly after the arrival of the Jerusalem refugees at Marseilles, the Apostle Philip visited them there on a missionary expedition. Soon finding, however, that the people of Marseilles were too sophisticated and too Romanized to fall into the Christian camp, Philip resolved to go farther afield. He decided to go into Britain with Joseph of Arimathea. And accompanied by Mary and perhaps Thekla, Martha, and the other Mary, the two men set out for Somerset in the spring of the year.[22]

Finding the Celts of Britain hospitable to new ideas, Philip left Joseph and some of the women there to found a church at Glastonbury, which, according to Gildas, they did in that very same year, 37, while Philip accompanied Mary back to Marseilles. There she later died and was buried.

That is the Marseilles legend. In Somerset and Cornwall the legend goes back to the childhood of Jesus. In this delightful story, the boy Jesus had accompanied his great-uncle, the rich merchant Joseph of Arimathea, on at least one business trip to Britain and had so won the hearts of the Celts with his bright and questing mind that they had never forgotten him. Thus when some thirty years later his mother visited them with Joseph and they learned of the sad fate of the promising boy, they were eager to build a wattle church in his memory at Glastonbury. Thus did Christianity come to Celtic Britain nearly six hundred years before Augustine.

Blake's poem "Jerusalem" is obviously based on this lovely legend:

> And did His feet in ancient time
> Walk upon England's mountains green?
> And was the holy Lamb of God
> In England's pleasant pastures seen?
> And did the countenance divine
> Shine forth upon our clouded hills?
> And was Jerusalem builded here
> Among those dark Satanic mills?

"Perhaps there is some truth in the strange tradition, which still lingers, not only among the hill folk of Somerset but of Gloucestershire, that St. Joseph of Arimathea came to Britain first as a metal merchant seeking tin from the Scilly Isles and Cornwall, and lead and copper and other metals from the hills of Somerset, and that Our Lord Himself came with him as a boy. There is also a tradition in Ireland that Our Lord came to Glastonbury as a boy." [23]

The Celtic King Arviragus, the direct ancestor of Queen Helena and thus of the Emperor Constantine, was the old friend of Joseph, and he memorialized this friendship by donating to the infant church at Glastonbury the land on which it was built.[24]

There can be very little doubt that Joseph was well known in ancient Britain. And that he left more than mere memories and traditions behind him is attested by the fact that the Celtic King Arthur in the sixth century claimed to be eighth in direct descent from Joseph of Arimathea.[25]

It is also significant that the Celtic Christian knights, beginning with King Arthur, invariably carried the likeness of the Virgin on their shields. And at the Battle of Castle Guinnion, according to Nennius, Arthur carried on his shoulders into battle "an image of St. Mary, the Ever-Virgin." [26]

But *was* this the image of Mary "the Ever-virgin"? Or, rather, was it the image of the Eternal One, the Ever-Goddess of the ancient Celts?

16

Women in the Middle Ages

If Christianity turned the clock of
general progress back a thousand years,
it turned back the clock two thousand years
for women. . . . The Churchmen deprived her of
her place in and before the courts, in the
schools, in art, in literature and society.
They shut her mind from knowledge . . . [and]
they chained her to the position into which
they had thrust her.

—Margaret Sanger

Domestic Chastisement

"Last of all, but by no means least, in the heart of the country the people, the *pagi,* retained their love of their old festivals, the worship of their old gods and goddesses of field and fold. They loved the old ways, and were content to leave the new religion to the cities."

But the ubiquitous church would not let them be content with the old ways, any more than it had let the Roman Senate "remain undisturbed in its error." [1] Everyone must be baptized with the blood of the lamb. Everyone, Celtic peasant and Roman senator, must conform to the harsh new morality and participate in the new barbarism.

Men were exhorted from the pulpit to beat their wives and wives to kiss the rod that beat them. In a medieval theological manual, now in the British Museum, under the word *castigare* the example for its use is given as "a man must castigate his wife and beat her for her correction, for the lord must punish his own as is written in Gratian's *Decretum.*" [2] "The unnatural restraint of the women

252

in Mediaeval illustrations," writes Eugene Mason, "was induced by the lavish compulsion of the rod; parents trained their children with blows, and husbands scattered the like seeds of kindness on their wives." [3]

The deliberate teaching of domestic violence, combined with the doctrine that women by nature could have no human rights, had taken such hold by the late Middle Ages that men had come to treat their wives worse than their beasts.

Wife beating, at the church's instigation, had become so popular by the fifteenth century that even a priest was moved to protest. Bernardino of Siena in 1427 suggested in a sermon that his male parishioners might practice a little restraint in the punishment of their wives and treat them with at least as much mercy as they treated their hens and their pigs. "You men have more patience," he said, "with the hen that befouleth thy table but layeth a fresh egg daily, than with thy wife when she bringeth forth a little girl. Oh, madmen, who cannot bear with a word from their wife who beareth such fine fruit but forthwith taketh thy staff and will beat her. . . . Dost thou not see the pig again, squealing all day and always befouling thy house, yet thou bearest with him. Yet seeing thy wife perchance less clean than thou wouldst see her, smiteth her without more ado. Consider the fruit of the woman, and have patience; not for *every* cause is it right to beat her." [4]

Even the well-meaning Bernardino did not consider the woman as a person, worthy of respect for her own sake. "Consider the fruit of the woman," he said. Woman was a breeder, a sex object, a slave worthy of her keep.

Under late medieval law in effect in Christian Saxony any squire could whip any woman of his domains who displayed pride and self-respect, euphemistically called "immodesty" in the wording of the law. "The same affront is shamefully and unjustly inflicted on honest women, tradesmen's wives, beginning to show overmuch spirit, whom the men wish to humiliate," writes Michelet.[5]

The lord of the manor, with his household of men, considered the women of his feudal realm fair game for every outrage. "Men at arms, pages, serving men, knights, formed hunting parties, . . . their pleasure consisting in outraging, beating, making women cry. . . ." The French court was convulsed with mirth "to hear the Duke of Lorraine describe how he and his men raided villages, ravishing, torturing, and killing every woman, old women, included." [6]

Before the village church stands a lady, "proudly dressed in fine green robe and two-peaked coif. . . . Milord draws a poniard and with a single slash of the sharp blade, slits the green robe from neck to feet. The half-naked lady is near-fainting at the cruel outrage. The lord's retainers one and all dash forward to hunt the prey. Swift and merciless fall the lashes; the poor lady stumbles, falls, screaming shrilly. But the men are remorseless, and whip her to her feet again." All the way to her own doorstep they pursue her with their whips, and she falls bleeding and faint against her door. But her husband has locked and barricaded the door against her, and he cowers shamefully within, unwilling to interfere with milord's sport.[7]

As Michelet points out in his *Origines,* the above episode was of daily occurrence in the Middle Ages. It was a form of punishment that any man could inflict on any woman who displayed pride and self-assurance. One can easily imagine the gleam in the avenging male's eye and the smirk on his brutal face as he inflicts this punishment on woman.

The squires and noblemen of the Middle Ages were no more reluctant to beat their own wives than to beat their serfs and the common women of their baronies. A moral tale told in medieval times and preserved by Geoffrey de la Tour de Landry for the instruction of his daughters points out the wickedness of a nagging wife: "Here is an example to every good woman that she suffer and endure patiently, nor strive with her husband nor answer him before strangers, as did once a woman who did answer her husband before strangers with short words; and he smote her with his fist down to the earth; and then with his foot he struck her in her visage and brake her nose, and all her life after she had her nose crooked, the which so shent [spoiled] and disfigured her visage after, that she might not for shame show her face, it was so foul blemished. And this she had for her language that she was wont to say to her husband. And therefore the wife ought to suffer, and let the husband have the words, and to be master, for that is her duty." [8]

The peasants followed faithfully the example set by their lords. There is a record preserved of a serf who beat his wife severely

every morning before going into the field, in order, he said, that
she would be so busy all day weeping and nursing her injuries that
she would have no time or inclination for gossip.

The church approved these methods of keeping women in subjection and only advised the abused wives to try to win their husband's goodwill by increased devotion and obedience, for meek
submissiveness was the best way to dispel a husband's displeasure.
Rousseau in the eighteenth century was still giving wives the same
advice. Unfortunately, this habit of looking upon women as creatures apart, without the same feelings and the same capacity for
suffering that men have, became so inbred in the thought of the
Middle Ages that it has not yet been eradicated. Most men today
still feel that women can stand more pain, more humiliation, and
more disdain than men can. And male judges and doctors are still
more willing to let them.

Next to beating, the most prevalent form of approved punishment was hair pulling. In convents and monasteries it was the rule
that there should be no form of physical chastisement for novices
and oblates except beating with rods and pulling of hair: "Be it
known," decreed the *Custumal* of the Abbey of Bec, "that this is
all their discipline, either to be beaten with rods, or that their hair
should be stoutly plucked." [9]

Berthold, a friar of Regensburg in the thirteenth century, exhorted husbands whose wives were wont to dress their hair "with
crimple-crispings here and cristy-crosties there" to pull it out. "*Tear*
the headdress from her," he admonished his male parishioners,
"even though her own hair should come away with it. Do this *not
thrice or four times only*," he advised, "and presently she will for-
bear." [10] One would think so, since after thrice or four times she
could have had but little hair left to dress!

A grim and gruesome playfulness was not entirely unknown to
the young married couples of the medieval world. Sir Thomas
More reports a fifteenth-century case of a woodsman who was chopping wood on the village green, where many of the villagers had
gathered to watch him work and to pass the time of day. The re-
partee was brisk and clever, jokes followed fast on each other's
heels, and the laughter was merry. All this jollity brought the woodchopper's wife out to join the fun. When her good man had laid
down his ax, the good wife playfully knelt and laid her head on

the chopping block, and her good husband playfully chopped it off.

When questioned by the bishop as to the reason for this grisly joke on his wife, the woodchopper explained that his wife had long been deserving of punishment because she had been a "scold." As proof of his allegation, witnesses to the head-chopping testified that even after the poor woman's head had rolled bloodily from the body, "they heard the tongue babble in her head and call 'villain, villain' twice, after her head was severed from her body." This testimony proved the husband's claim of provocation, since, of course, any woman whose tongue automatically called her husband names after death had incontestably been a scold in life. Sir Thomas does not say whether the woman's small children witnessed their mother's head rolling playfully from the blade of their father's ax.

The woodchopper, needless to say, was completely exonerated by the bishop. There was one dissenter among the witnesses for the defense, however, "only one, and that was a woman who said she heard the tongue not." But since she was only a woman, her testimony was disregarded by the bishop.[11]

Ribald Priest and Bawdy Friar

François Rabelais, Giovanni Boccaccio, and Marguerite of Navarre are fertile sources for tales of the crimes against women perpetrated by the churchmen of the Middle Ages. And it is revealing that to Rabelais and Boccaccio these true episodes are comic, while to the queen of Navarre they are tragic. "It hath been shown," wails Elisa in the *Decameron,* "in sundry of the foregoing stories how much we women are exposed to the lustful importunities of the priests and clergy of every kind." [12]

And, indeed, women were in double jeopardy, for if they succumbed to the clergymen's desires they were apt to be killed by their husbands, and if they refused, they were liable to be reported as heretics and end their lives roasting in a slow fire at the stake. "Moreover," wrote Petrus Cantor in 1190, "certain honest matrons, refusing to consent to the lasciviousness of priests, have been written by such priests in the Book of Death, and accused as heretics and *condemned to the fire.*" [13]

Women were burned with remarkable lack of compunction throughout the Middle Ages. If statistics were kept they have been very successfully concealed; but evidence indicates that the proportion of women to men who were burned alive from about 800 to *1800* was as much as ten thousand to one. Men were sometimes burned as heretics after having been mercifully strangled to death. But women were burned *alive* on countless pretexts: for threatening their husbands, for talking back to or refusing a priest, for stealing, for prostitution, for adultery, for bearing a child out of wedlock, for permitting sodomy, even though the priest or husband who committed the sodomy was forgiven,[14] for masturbating, for lesbianism,[15] for child-neglect, for scolding and nagging, and even for *miscarrying*,[16] even though the miscarriage was caused by a kick or a blow from the husband. We read in the old chronicles of women in the last weeks of pregnancy being burned until the heat burst their bellies and propelled the fetus outward beyond the flames. The infant was then picked up and flung back into the fire at its mother's feet. We read of the little daughters of burnt women being forced to dance with bare feet one hundred times around the smoldering stake, through their mothers' ashes and through the still glowing embers—in order to "impress upon them the memory of their mothers' sins." And all of this in an age when the only law of the land was the law of the church, when civil courts were merely the agents of the Christian hierarchy.

"The most sly, dangerous, and cunning bawds are your knavish priests, monks, Jesuits, and friars," wrote Robert Burton in the seventeenth century. "For under cover of visitation, auricular confession, comfort, and penance, they have free egress and regress, and corrupt God knows how many women. Women cannot sleep in their beds for necromantick friars. Proteus-like, they go abroad in all forms and disguises to inescate and beguile young women and to have their pleasure of other men's wives. Howsoever in publick they pretend much zeal and bitterly preach against adultery and fornication, there are no verier Bawds or Whoremasters in a Country." [17]

Bearing out Burton's summing up of priestly morality are such facts of history as that Pope John XII in the tenth century kept a harem in the very Vatican itself, and Pope John XIII "found nunneries as amusing to visit as brothels." At the Synod of London in 1126, the Vatican's representative, Cardinal Giovanni of Cremona, eloquently denounced fornication in the ranks of the clergy and the same night was surprised in bed with a prostitute. In 1171 Clarembald, Abbot of Canterbury, openly boasted that he had seventeen bastards in one parish alone, and the Bishop of Liège fathered fourteen illegitimate children in his diocese in the space of twenty months.

Brother Salimbene, a Franciscan monk of Parma, in 1221 warned his young niece of "the common habit of confessors who take their little penitents behind the altar in order to copulate with them." [18] The same monk recounts a true story of a lady who confessed to a priest that she had been forcibly raped by a stranger in a lonely spot, and "the priest, excited by her confession, dragged his weeping penitent behind the altar and raped her himself," as did the next two priests to whom she confessed. Bishop Faventino bribed his little parishioners, the small girls of his diocese, to lie in bed with him, "where he contemplated and fondled their naked flesh by daylight for hours on end, decorating their little privates with gold coins which the little girls, on being released from the old satyr's bed, were allowed to keep." [19]

The depravity of the clergy was well known to the hierarchy, yet their crimes were overlooked and their inviolable sanctity was protected: "Albeit the life of many clerics be full of crimes," decreed Saint Bernardino in the fifteenth century, "yet there resideth in them a *holy and venerable authority*." [20] The bishop of Orléans, when he had raped the small daughter of a prominent knight of his diocese, was absolved of guilt by his superiors, even though the knight himself had reported his conduct to Rome. In Brussels in the thirteenth century a poor girl was ordered on a walking pilgrimage, barefoot, to Rome, as penance for having reported a priest who had raped her. The saintly Thomas à Becket, when a priest was brought before him for raping and murdering a young girl, simply had the guilty priest transferred to another parish. [21]

The priest went unpunished for rape and seduction, even though the victim might be punished with death by her husband with the full sanction of the law and the church. By contrast, in pagan Rome in the reign of Tiberius, two "pagan" priests (perhaps Hebraic and perhaps Christian) were crucified for seducing a Roman matron, while the matron was held entirely guiltless. [22] Josephus, the

Jewish reporter of this incident, cites it as an example of the Romans' distorted idea of justice.

The precedent for the Christian idea of justice for women is to be found in the Old Testament Book of Judges 19:23 ff., where the story is told of "a certain Levite" visiting in Gibeah, who is beset by a group of sodomists. "They beat at the door, and spake to the master of the house saying, Bring forth the man that came into thy house, that we may know him. And the master of the house went out to them and said unto them, Nay, brethren, do not do so wickedly, seeing this man is my guest. Behold, here is my daughter, a maiden, and his concubine; *them* I will bring out, and humble ye them, and do with them what seemeth good to you: but unto this *man* do not so vile a thing. So the man took his concubine and brought her forth unto them; and they knew her and abused her all the night until the morning, when they let her go. Then came the woman in the dawning of the day and fell down [dead] at the door of the house where her lord was. . . ."

We see here the source of the Christian evaluation of women, an evaluation that it took the Christians over a thousand years to inculcate in the minds of Western men.

By way of justification for their brutality to women, priests cited the Bible, both the New and Old Testaments. Proverbs 9:13 and 30:16 and 21 ff. were very popular, but of course Paul's epistles, especially I Corinthians 2 and Ephesians 5, as well as I Timothy 1 and II Timothy 1, were considered the best points of departure for the antifeminist sermon.

Eve was presented over and over again as the source of all evil, the sinful creature who had brought sorrow to the whole world by disobeying her husband.[23] Jezebel's horrible death and the consumption of her body by curs was offered as an example of what would happen to women who might seek to influence their husbands. Delilah's betrayal of Samson was presented to husbands as a warning not to trust or confide in their wives.

Chastity and virginity and the importance of their preservation were preached from the pulpit, but many a virgin went to the fiery stake for obeying these very exhortations. Ralph of Coggeshall tells the story of one such virgin—and he tells it without indignation at the cruel injustice done this virtuous maiden. In the days of Louis VII of France (1137–1180) the Archbishop William of

Rheims was riding one day outside the city, attended by his clergy, when one of the latter, Gervase of Tilbury, saw a fair maid and rode aside to speak to her. After a few brief pleasantries he suggested "amour," and the virgin, blushing, replied: "Nay, good youth. God forbid that I should be your leman; for if I were to be defiled and lose my virginity I should suffer eternal damnation." The poor innocent, unused to the double talk of the clergy, was probably only prating what she had been taught in church.

But the archbishop, coming up at that moment and seeing the angry disappointment on Gervase's face, took the girl's refusal as insolent defiance of her betters. After all, what would happen if all young women took their chastity seriously and refused their favors to the clergy? What would become of priestly pleasures? The girl still refusing after the archbishop's intervention, the latter ordered that she be carried with the party back to Rheims, where she was, predictably, accused of heresy. "No persuasion," continues Ralph the Chronicler, "could recall her from her foolish obstinacy; wherefore she was burned to death, to the admiration of many who marked how she uttered no sighs, no tears, no laments, but bore bravely all the torments of the consuming flames." [24]

The Cruel Destruction of Women

The Christian evaluation of women as expendable sexual conveniences was adopted with varying degrees of enthusiasm by laymen to whose ancestors the doctrine would have been incredible. Sir John Arundel, in 1379, on his way to the war in France, raided a convent at Southampton and carried off sixty young nuns to provide recreation for his men during the campaign.

"Raping started immediately, aboard the ships. But a storm springing up in the English Channel, in order to lighten the ships, Arundel had all the wretched captives thrown overboard" into the raging torrent of the sea,[25] where they all drowned. Lest this outrage be brushed off as a uniquely medieval atrocity, be it known that in the nineteenth century the American crew of a U.S. merchant ship, *Pindos,* treated some fifty Polynesian women and girls in the same fashion. After the crew had had their fill of them on board ship, the girls were thrown overboard into the Pacific Ocean. Our United States merchant mariners, however, added a refinement to Arundel's precedent: when the mate, one Waden, saw that some of the women, expert swimmers that they were, seemed likely to reach the distant safety of Easter Island, "he shot them with his rifle, the entire crew cheering him on each time he made a hit." [26]

By the sixteenth century even the kindly and feminist Abbé de Brantôme accepted the Christian doctrine of the worthlessness of women and of man's unquestioned right to abuse, torture, and murder them at his pleasure. Yet Brantôme's basic instincts were bothered: "There is much to be said on the matter, which I refrain from setting down, fearing my arguments may be feeble beside those of the great [of the church]. . . . But however great the authority of the husband may be, what *sense* is there for him to be allowed to kill his wife?" [27]

He then tells a true story of a knight of his acquaintance—a story that can be compared for horror only to the Biblical story of the cowardly Levite:

> A certain Albanian knight I knew at the Court of Venice, so irked that his wife did not love him, to punish her went to the trouble of seeking out a dozen riotous fellows, all great wenchers reputed to be well and lavishly fashioned in their parts, and very able and hot in the execution too, hired them for a fee and locked them in his wife's bedroom (she being very lovely), and left her absolutely in their hands, requesting them to do their duty at it. And they all set upon her, one after another, and so handled her that in the end they killed her. . . . That was a terrible sort of death.[28]

Boccaccio's account of Romilda, Countess of Forli, is so similar to this that one is forced to wonder how prevalent this particular form of wife murder might have been in the late Middle Ages. One Caucan, recounts Boccaccio, had married the Countess Romilda for her vast property, but not caring to be burdened with her once the property had become his, by right of marriage only, he decided to kill the fair Romilda. "Summoning twelve of his toughest, strongest soldiers he handed Romilda over to them to take their pleasure of her, and they spent a night so doing to the best of their ability, and when day came he summoned Romilda to him and after reproving her sternly for her infidelity, and insulting her greatly, he then had her impaled through the privy parts, by which she died." [29]

Brantôme's gossipy stories of murder and mayhem all concern gentlemen of the French court with whom he was acquainted but whom he dared not name. No doubt his more contemporary readers knew of whom he spoke, but to us they remain faceless and unidentified.

Except for Father Bernardino in the fifteenth and the Abbé de Brantôme in the sixteenth century, no man spoke out in defense of women in the Christian era before the late nineteenth century. The male, however cruel and brutal, was always right, and the church was ever at his side, ready to support him in the vilest crimes against the "lesser" sex. "The cruel destruction of women in the Middle Ages," writes Horney, "has implications of an underlying anxiety . . . for woman poses a danger to man." [30] And "the priest," writes Michelet, "realized clearly where the danger lay— that an enemy, a menacing rival, is to be feared in woman, this high-priestess of Nature he pretends to despise." [31]

"The Church has always known and feared the spiritual potentialities of women's freedom," observes Margaret Sanger. "For this reason male agencies have sought to keep women enslaved, . . . to use women solely as an asset to . . . the man. Anything which will enable women to live for themselves first has been attacked as immoral." [32]

By the twelfth century, writes Roger Sherman Loomis, "the natural depravity of Eve's daughters was an accepted fact, and woman had become the Devil's most valuable ally. She was not only inferior, she was *vicious;* and as Chaucer wrote in the *Wife of Bath*, 'It is impossible that any cleric wol speke gode of wyves.' " [33]

That the churchmen of the Middle Ages even exceeded their model, Saint Paul, in their violent hatred of women is frighteningly evident in all their writings that have come down to us. Johann Nider, a distinguished Dominican of the fifteenth century, describes without any observable degree of compassion or remorse the torture of a poor old woman whose only crime was her mobility. "She often changed her abode," writes Nider, "from house to house and city to city, and this had gone on for many years." Supposedly this mobility smacked to the church of unfeminine independence, an anomaly that could not be tolerated. They put a watch on the unsuspecting old lady, and finally one day in Regensburg that for which they had hoped and waited came to pass. In the hearing of their spy, "she uttered certain incautious words concerning the Faith, on which she was immediately accused before the Vicar and clapt into prison."

On being questioned by the inquisitor, who was none other than Father Nider himself, "she answered very astutely to every objection made to her, and stated that she refused obedience to the Pope *in matters which he had ill disposed*." (One wishes that Nider had seen fit to name these papal errors!) Here obviously was a thinking woman, a woman of mental independence and the courage of her convictions—an anomaly despised and feared by the church. For these very reasons, she did not have a chance. It was decided that "she be racked by the torture of public justice, *slowly*, in proportion as her sex may be able to endure it." In plain words, Nider ordered that her torture be prolonged as long as possible, as extra punishment for her sex, her independence of mind, and her unwomanly "astuteness." Her age was not considered an ameliorating factor.

"Having been tortured for a while," goes on Nider complacently, "she was much humbled by the vexation of her limbs; wherefore she was brought back to her prison-tower where I visited her that same evening. She could scarce stir for pain," says the good father with righteous satisfaction, "but when she saw me she burst into loud weeping and told me how grievously she had been hurt." When the good inquisitor "induced many citations from Holy Scripture to show how frail is the female sex" (!) and after he had threatened her with further torture, the poor old woman "declared herself ready to revoke her error publicly, and to repent." Which, as soon as she was able to walk again, she did "before the whole city of Regensburg." [84]

Thus were "pagans" attracted to the banner of Christ and encouraged to adopt Christianity in the Middle Ages. Yet children are taught in school even today to believe that the Christian religion brought mercy and enlightenment and justice to a world where people had formerly lived in the darkness of heathendom. They are taught to believe that Christianity saved the world from barbarism; yet it actually created a barbaric culture such as the Western world had never seen before. And most heinous of all, it had found Western woman free and independent, revered, honored, and respected, and had plunged her into an abyss of serflike hopelessness and despair from which she has not yet been able to extricate herself.

As Michelet writes: "She who from her throne had taught mankind, [and who] had given oracles to a kneeling world, is the same woman who, a thousand years later, is hunted like a wild beast, reviled, buffeted, stoned, scorched with red hot embers! The Clergy has not stakes enough . . . for unhappy Woman." [35]

17

Some Medieval Women

*How many glorious deeds of womankind
lie unknown to fame!*

—SENECA

Saint Joan

Our Johann Nider, the inquisitor who described so dispassionately the agony of the poor nameless old woman whose limbs he had broken and whose joints he had dislocated on the rack, was once permitted to "question" Joan of Arc. And here is what he says of her:

There was lately in France, within the last ten years, a maid named Joan, distinguished, as was thought, both for her prophetic spirit and for the power of her miracles. For she always wore man's dress, nor could all the persuasions of the Doctors of Divinity bend her to put aside these and content herself with woman's garments, especially considering that she openly confessed herself a woman, and a maid. "In these masculine garments," she said, "in token of future victory, I have been sent by God, to help Charles, the true King of France, and to set him firm upon his throne from whence the King of England and the Duke of Burgundy are striving to chase him"; for at that time the two were allied together and oppressed France most grievously with battle and slaughter. Joan, therefore, rode constantly like a knight with her lord, predicted many successes to come, and did other like wonders whereat not only France marvelled, but every realm in Christendom.

At last this Joan came to such a pitch of presumption, that layfolk and ecclesiastics, Regulars and Cloisterers began to doubt of the spirit whereby she was ruled, whether it were devilish or divine. Then certain men of great learning wrote treatises concerning her, wherein they expressed adverse opinions as to the

Maid. After she had given great help to Charles the King and placed him securely upon the throne, she was taken *by God's will* and cast into prison. A great multitude were then summoned of masters both in Canon and Civil law, and she was examined for many days. She at length confessed that she had a familiar angel of God, which, by many conjectures and proofs, and by the opinion of the most learned men, was judged to be an evil spirit; so that this spirit rendered her a sorceress; wherefore they permitted her to be burned at the stake by the common hangman.[1]

"They permitted her." One supposes from this that the common hangman insisted upon burning her at the stake and that the churchmen and the most learned men of the canon and civil law permitted him to have his way. If a male knight had secured the throne of France for its rightful king and had confounded an enemy that was "oppressing France most grievously with battle and slaughter," would the common hangman have had his way so easily? One wonders.

While no man (save one) rose to the defense of Joan—not even the king whose throne and country Joan had secured for him—two women *did* and were tortured and burned for their trouble.

The one exception to the indifference of her male beneficiaries to Joan's fate was the original Blue Beard, the infamous Gilles de Rais. This nobleman had been Joan's lieutenant in her wars against the English and had developed a strong and steadfast devotion to her as his leader and captain. He used all his influence to save her from the flames, but to no avail. When he walked away from Joan's smoldering pyre, his cause lost, he changed into the fiend he is known as in history. He was finally arrested for multiple murder, after having killed by the most horrible tortures literally hundreds of little girls and little boys for the gratification of his perverted sexual desires. The thing that is interesting about his case is that, although he shared the saint's fate of burning at the stake, his death had occurred *before* the fire was lit. As was the case with all male criminals, he was granted the mercy of strangulation prior to burning, while Saint Joan, like all women, was burned "quick"—that is, alive.[2]

Nider voices only one regret in connection with the entire Joan affair. And this regret was caused by the escape from the power of the inquisitor a few years later of a maid who claimed to be the reincarnation of Joan of Arc. Women must have been greatly agitated by the horror of Joan's fate, so many of them seem to have behaved so aberrantly—so like a flight of doves when one of their number has been brought bleeding to the ground by the huntsman's arrow. Yet we have no contemporary account by any woman of the time. Reams were written by men and discovered four centuries later, all damning Joan and exulting over her well-deserved fate, but not one line by a woman.

The church, almost immediately after Joan's martyrdom, inaugurated an intensive campaign to mythologize her. So successful was this campaign that by the eighteenth century Joan had become a semimythical character, only partly believed in by the general public and vehemently denied by the faithful. It was not until the nineteenth century when the actual transcripts of her trial were rediscovered in Paris that Joan became generally acknowledged as the actual historical personage she was. Finally, in 1920, five hundred years after her immolation, the red-faced church reluctantly, and in obedience to popular demand, canonized her.

Pope Joan

The attempted relegation of Joan of Arc to the realm of myth recalls another Joan who has been *successfully* mythologized by her church—the Pope Joan. So successfull indeed has the church been in its endeavor to wipe Pope Joan out of history that the vast majority of people living today have never even heard of a female pope. And to those few who have heard of her she is an established myth, just as the Catholic Church claims her to be.

But *is* Pope Joan merely a medieval myth? If so, it seems very odd that the church waited nearly 800 years so to declare her. Throughout the long centuries from 855, when she died, to 1601, when she was annihilated and anathematized, Joan was accepted as genuine. Through all these centuries, says the *Catholic Encyclopedia,* "Joanna was a historical personage whose existence no one doubted." [3] The church numbered her among the popes as John VIII, and erected statues to her among the images of the popes at Siena Cathedral and at St. Peter's in Rome.

It seems that Joan, a "handsome" young English girl, made her

268 &~ THE FIRST SEX

way to Athens disguised as a monk. "In Athens," says the *Catholic Encyclopedia,* "she excelled so in learning that no man was her equal." Armed with a degree in philosophy, she came to Rome, where the pope, Leo IV, made her a cardinal. Upon Leo's death in the year 853, Joan was elected pope by her fellow cardinals. The *Catholic Encyclopedia* goes on to say: "She served as Pope two years, four months, and eight days, when she was discovered to be a woman and was stoned to death." [4]

Legend says that Joan's sex was discovered when she gave birth to a child during a papal procession and that her baby was stoned to death in her arms. In corroboration of this tradition, the *Catholic Encyclopedia* says that for a long time during the centuries before 1600 there was a statue in the street where Joan's stoning was believed to have taken place of a figure in papal robes and miter, holding an infant in her arms. This sculpture has been long lost, but for many centuries the route of papal processions was changed to avoid the street where it had stood.

Whatever happened, however, the name of "John VIII a Woman from England" graced the papal list from 855 to 1601. In that year, Pope Clement VIII officially declared Joan mythical and ordered all effigies, busts, statues, shrines, and records of her utterly demolished and her name erased from the papal rolls. It was the jibes and taunts of the German Reformation at the "absurdity" of a woman pope, says the *Catholic Encyclopedia,* that influenced Clement to take these extreme measures.

It can only be hoped that the church was as remiss in destroying all records of *Pope* Joan as it was to be in the case of *Saint* Joan and that someday written proof of her existence will be unearthed.

There are two unexplained mysteries about the case of Pope Joan that have not been satisfactorily explained by the officials. The first is: where *was* Pope John VIII through all the centuries until 1601? For the Pope John (872–882) who is *now* numbered eighth was for seven centuries listed as number nine. There was a Pope John VII from 705 to 708, then no more Johns before Leo IV was consecrated in 847. According to the official *Annuario Pontificio* of the Catholic Church, Benedict III was consecrated in 855. But *Leo had died in 853,* two years before the consecration of Benedict. The church glosses over this gap by mumbling that Leo lived until 855, but the truth of this statement is easily refuted by anyone with sufficient interest to look up the facts.

The next official John to become pope was John IX in 872. Where, then, was John VIII? And why was John IX suddenly renumbered VIII when the church officially mythologized Joan seven hundred years later? By that time there had been no fewer than fourteen popes John since John IX, and all of them had to move back one number, so that John XX (1024–1032) became John XIX, and number twenty was simply dropped. For the next John (1276–1277) remained John XXI and was followed by the twenty-second and twenty-third *before* 1600.

Then, marvelous to relate, we have another John XXIII in 1958! Does that mean that the *Annuario Pontificio* has quietly moved them all back one notch to fill up the vacancy of John XX who was left out in the first go-round?

The second unexplained mystery is that from the time of Pope Joan, and *not before*, all candidates for the papacy for seven hundred years had to undergo a physical examination to prove their sex. Why?

The reason given by the church for this examination is to avoid having a eunuch as pope.[5] But it is very revealing that the examination went into effect in 855, the year Benedict was elected, and Benedict himself was the first of the popes to submit to the test. If Benedict followed immediately after Leo, as the church now claims he did, why was no pope prior to Benedict subjected to the examination? It could be only Benedict's immediate predecessor, Joan, who was the cause of the innovation.

Pope Joan is included by her contemporary Anastasius the Librarian in his *Lives of the Popes*. Other references to her were not completely expunged in the general "dump Joan" campaign of the seventeenth century. She is listed as an actual person and a historical pope in the writings of Marianus Scotus in the eleventh century. And Otto of Friesing, Gottfried of Viterbo, Martinus Polonus, William of Ockham, Thomas Elmham, John Hus, Gulielmus Jacobus, and Stephen Blanch all include her in their papal histories of the next four centuries as a genuine pope.

Johann Lorenz von Mosheim, in his *Ecclesiastical History* written in the sixteenth century just prior to the official annihilation of

Joan, writes: "Between Leo IV and Benedict III, a woman who concealed her sex and assumed the name of John, opened the way to the Pontifical throne by her learning and genius, and governed the Church. She is commonly called the Papess John. During the five subsequent centuries the witnesses to this event are without number; nor did anyone prior to the Reformation by Luther, regard the thing as either incredible or disgraceful to the Church." [6]

Sabine Baring-Gould of the last century, who wrote the words of the reprehensible militaristic hymn "Onward Christian Soldiers," believed that Pope Joan was the Antichrist. "I have little doubt myself," he declares, "that Pope Joan is an impersonification of the Great Whore of Revelation seated on the seven hills." [7]

Thus is history rewritten by the masculists.

"Gynikomnemonikothanasia"

The zeal of the masculine historians and encyclopedists in destroying even the memory of great women (which is the intended meaning of the above word) has rendered the pursuit of feminine historical research extremely difficult. There are so few names! If the *sense* of history demands the inclusion of a female, she is referred to merely as somebody's wife, or mother, or daughter, or sister, and is never included in the index. Archeology has recently revealed the historical existence of once great women whose names have been as completely wiped from the history books as if they had never existed.

George Ballard, in the eighteenth century, wondered why so many of the great women of England had been overlooked by the historians, while so many *lesser men* had won lasting places in their country's annals.[8] The oversight is, of course, deliberate. Men have written history not, as Dingwall complains, "as if women hardly counted" [9] but as if women hardly existed. Yet the role of women in molding history and their influence on the events that have shaped man's destiny are incalculable. Scholars are aware of this fact and yet, when they are bound by the necessity for accuracy or logic to include a woman's *name* in the unfolding of a national event, her name is invariably coupled with a belittling adjective designed not only to put down the woman herself but to assure their feminine readers that such women are undesirable and "un-feminine." Thus all outstanding women become in the history books "viragos" (Boadicea), "hussies" (Matilda of Flanders), "hysterics" (Joan of Arc), "monstrosities" (Tomyris), or merely myths (Martia and Pope Joan).

Arnold Toynbee, whose *A Study of History* a generation ago was accepted as a great work of genius but which has now been consigned to the dustbin as outmoded and whose philosophy has been disavowed even by Toynbee himself, voiced the masculist view of great women in that work. In attempting to explain the dominance of women in the Minoan-Mycenaean culture of Greece, for example, he inadvertently acknowledges the basic equality of the sexes by explaining that in that "socially unorganized age . . . individualism was so absolute that it over-rode the intrinsic differences between the sexes"; and this "unbridled individualism bore fruits hardly distinguishable from those of a doctrinaire feminism." [10]

In short, Toynbee is saying, where society has not subjected one sex to the other, the sexes develop equally: equality of treatment and of self-expression abolish the apparent inequality—"the intrinsic differences"—between the sexes. But, of course, this is an undesirable state of affairs from the masculist viewpoint. The "*a priori* logic*," continues Toynbee, of weak woman's "inability to hold her own against the physically dominant sex" is confuted "by the *facts of history."* Women *were* dominant, he admits—but how could this have been? How could futile, weak woman ever, in any period of history, have dominated man, the muscular lord of creation? Victorian-minded, Biblical-bred Toynbee, a true product of masculist materialism, is pathetically baffled by the conundrum. To Toynbee, woman's former dominance can be attributed to only one source, her greater "persistence, vindictiveness, implacability, cunning, and treachery." [11]

He, like the majority of his nineteenth-century-educated contemporaries, had learned well the lesson dinned into Western man for nearly two thousand years of the viciousness of Eve's daughters and of "the absolutely incurable infirmities and inferiority of the female sex," to quote the revered Scottish-English Christian philosopher David Hume. One wonders how such men as Hume and Toynbee could ever have brought themselves to mate with such loathsome creatures!

Emily James Putnam about sixty years ago wrote of the "ever-recurrent uneasiness of the male in the presence of the insurgent female." [12] Over two thousand years ago the Roman senator Cato warned his fellow senators against the insurgent females of republican Rome: "The moment they have arrived at an equality with you, they will become your masters and your superiors," he stormed. And in the eighteenth century of our era, the great Dr. Samuel Johnson confided to James Boswell that the reason men denied education to women was that men knew that if women learned as much as they, they, the men, would be "overmatched." [13]

The basic reason for man's reluctance to admit women to the mysteries of learning is this same fear of "insurgent," or "resurgent," woman: if women were to be permitted to roam at will in the paths and bypaths of scholarship, they might uncover man's most closely guarded secret, the fact of woman's greater role in the history of the race and the truth of man's deliberate concealment of that fact.

The malicious erasure of women's names from the historical record began two or three thousand years ago and continues into our own period.

Women take as great a risk of anonymity when they merge their names with men in literary collaboration as when they merge in matrimony. The Lynds, for example, devoted equal time, thought, and effort to the writing of *Middletown,* but today it is Robert Lynd's book. Dr. Mary Leakey made the important paleontological discoveries in Africa, but Dr. Louis Leakey gets all the credit. Mary Beard did a large part of the work on *America in Midpassage,* yet Charles Beard is the great social historian. The insidious process is now at work on Eve Curie. A recent book written for young people states that radium was discovered by Pierre Curie with the help of his assistant, Eve, who later became his wife.

Aspasia wrote the famous oration to the Athenians, as Socrates knew, but in all the history books it is Pericles' oration. Corinna taught Pindar and polished his poems for posterity; but who ever heard of Corinna? Peter Abelard got his best ideas from Héloïse, his acknowledged intellectual superior, yet Abelard is the great medieval scholar and philosopher. Mary Sidney probably wrote Sir Philip Sidney's *Arcadia;* Nausicaa wrote the *Odyssey,* as Samuel Butler proves in his book *The Authoress of the Odyssey,* at least to the satisfaction of this writer and of Robert Graves, who comments, "no other alternative makes much sense." [14]

Nefertiti, the Egyptian queen of the fourteenth century B.C., could well have been the author of the 104th Psalm; and the Apostle Thecla may have written the Epistle to the Hebrews. Yet how many people in the past thousand years have even so much as heard of a female Apostle?

The Apostle Thecla is perhaps the outstanding example, after Pope Joan, of "gynikomnemonikothanasia" in the Christian Church. Saint Thecla of Iconium was a historical personage, and according to the *Catholic Encyclopedia* she was accepted as a "bona fide Apostle" by the early church and is still accepted as such in the Eastern Church. She was a companion of Saint Paul, who ordained her as a preacher of the Gospel and an Apostle of Christ. A book called the Acts of Paul and Thecla was widely read in the first four Christian centuries, and even as late as 590 it was referred to as an authentic document of the apostolic age. It is now included among the Apocrypha.

No one questioned its authenticity, even though Tertullian had attempted to cast doubt upon it in the third century, until it was barred from the official canon of the New Testament in A.D. 367. Seventeen years after that date, however, Saint Jerome, "the most learned of the Latin fathers," still vouched for its authenticity as well as for the undeniable historicity of Thecla herself, the female Apostle. So much is fact.

Philippa the Feminist

"Philippa, as is usual with the brightest specimens of female excellence, was the friend of her own sex," writes Agnes Strickland.[15] And indeed, Philippa, the fourteenth-century queen of Edward III of England, was one of the few active feminists of the Middle Ages. She was in a position to honor not only women but to elevate men who honored women. It was because of Philippa's appreciation of his championship of downtrodden women that the French knight Sir Bertrand Du Guesclin was freed after his capture at the Battle of Poitiers. She paid his immense ransom herself, out of her own pocket, because, "though an enemy of my husband, a knight who is famed for his protection of women, deserves my assistance." [16]

Philippa was famed throughout Europe for her beauty and the beauty of her many sons and daughters and for the gallantry of her eldest son, Edward the Black Prince, the epitome of medieval knighthood and the model for generations of knights to come. But more than this, she was famed for her great innovations in social welfare and her successful efforts to improve the condition of the poor, particularly of the women of the poor.

One of her first acts after her coronation as queen at the age of sixteen was to found the woolen industry at Norwich, which became, with the coal industry she was later to inaugurate at Tynedale, the basis for centuries of England's wealth and the foundation of her economy. As part of her dowry, Philippa had been given Norwich, a center of sheep growing and the production of wool for export. Too many people, Philippa found on her first visit there a few months after her marriage, were forced to subsist on this one source of income. She immediately sent to Flanders, her homeland, for wool kempers (combers), weavers, and dyers to instruct the people of Norwich, particularly the women, in the art of making cloth from raw wool.

Predictably, later historians, including Henry Hallam, Charles Dickens, and those of the *Cambridge Mediaeval History*, attribute the English wool industry to Edward III and do not so much as mention Philippa's name in connection with it. But her own contemporaries John Froissart and the unnamed monkish chronicler quoted below, as well as the *Foedera*, give Philippa sole credit for this boon to England.

"Blessed be the name and memory of Queen Philippa, who first invented English clothes," wrote a monastic chronicler later. [17] For thanks to Philippa the average Englishman was forever after able to wear good woolen, "made in England" clothing, at great savings to himself and to the lasting benefit of the English economy.

Philippa's wool factories were a far cry from the sweat shops they degenerated into in the eighteenth and nineteenth centuries. These fourteenth-century Norwich "factories" were pleasant, open places where men and women worked happily without benefit of machinery at their combing and weaving and dyeing. "Like a beneficent queen of the hive, Philippa cherished and protected her working bees. Nor did she disdain to blend all the magnificence of chivalry with her patronage of the productive arts." She arranged for tournaments and jousts of arms to be held at Norwich, at which the nobles and knights entertained the working people with pageantry and feats of equestrianism and swordplay. "These festivals displayed the defensive class and the productive class in admirable union, while the example of the Queen promoted mutual respect between them. At a period of her life which is commonly considered mere girlhood, Philippa enriched and ennobled her realm." [18]

To show their appreciation of their queen, the merchants and workers of Norwich were later voluntarily to raise among themselves the vast sum of 2,500 English pounds sterling to redeem Philippa's "best crown," which she had pawned in Cologne to raise money for the Scottish wars.

It was while King Edward and the sixteen-year-old Black Prince (so called because, although he was blond like all the Plantagenets, he wore black armor) were engaged at the Battle of Crecy in 1346 that the Scots led by King David Bruce descended from the north and threatened England. Philippa was serving as regent in the absence of the king, and "it was now her turn to do battle royal with a king," and she did not flinch. She rallied her army at Neville's Cross and, riding among the men on a white charger, she urged them "for the love of God to fight manfully for their King." They assured her, as Froissart reports, that "they would acquit themselves loyally, even better than if the King had been there himself." [19] And the battle was joined. In a few hours it was all over. The Scottish king had been captured, and his troops were fleeing back over the border in a complete rout. Philippa was again the hero of the hour to the English people.

As a result of Philippa's military success, "out of compliment to the Queen's successful generalship, the English ladies began to give themselves the airs of warriors." Hats shaped like knights' helmets became the fashion, and the ladies decked themselves with jeweled daggers. "The Church was preparing suitable remonstrances against these fashions, when all pride was at once signally confounded by the plague which approached the shores of England in 1348." [20]

Philippa's second daughter, then aged fourteen, the beautiful Joanna, was one of the first to die in that terrible Black Death that was to more than decimate the population of Europe in the next few months. According to the *Cambridge Mediaeval History*, one-third of the people of England perished in the plague.

Philippa was the mother of twelve children—all handsome, all tall (Lionel and Edmund each measured nearly seven feet in early manhood), and all unusually gifted and intelligent. Eight of them survived her, including her favorite child, Edward, the Prince of Wales. Yet none of them ever occupied the English throne. Merlin the Wizard had prophesied eight hundred years earlier that none of the children of Edward and Philippa would reign. And Merlin proved to be right. Edward the Black Prince, "learned, elegant, and brilliant, and strongly marked with the genius . . . of the Provençal Plantagenets [Celts]," [21] died before his father; and so upon the king's death the small son of the Black Prince, Richard, became King of England.

Philippa died in 1369, in her mid fifties, and Froissart, her secretary and protégée, wrote: "I must now speak of the death of the most courteous, liberal, beloved, and noble lady that ever lived, the Lady Philippa of Hainault, Queen of England." [22]

Philippa had been the patron not only of Froissart the Chronicler but, more notably, of Chaucer, who, it is reported, was so deeply grieved at her death that he withdrew into retirement, "and not even the marriage of his wife's sister to the Duke of Lancaster [Philippa's son] would draw him from his retirement." [23] (It was the son of this duke who was to wrest the crown from young Richard in the next generation and found the House of Lancaster as Henry IV.) Philippa founded and endowed Queen's College at Oxford and was the patroness, as well as the patient, of the renowned Caecelia of Oxford, the outstanding physician of her day.

Philippa had turned the Scots out of England, had established the great wealth-producing industries of clothmaking and coal mining, had patronized the greatest men and women of her day, and had founded a college at Oxford. But in the strange medieval mind she was most remarkable and longest remembered for the simple fact that she had nursed her son, the Black Prince, at her breast. The Madonna and Child of the religious art during and after her lifetime "were modelled from Philippa with the infant Prince of Wales at her breast." [24] Philippa was tall, well proportioned, and stunningly lovely in her youth; and the infant Edward was a young Hercules: "The great beauty of this infant, his great size, his fair complexion, and the firm texture of his limbs, filled everyone with admiration who saw him." [25] He can still be seen as the Infant Jesus in many of the stained-glass windows of medieval churches and cathedrals in England and on the Continent in the arms of his mother, Queen Philippa of England.

An odd coincidence is the fact that this good queen, model for so many depictions of the Virgin Mary, died on the anniversary of the Assumption of the Virgin into heaven, August 15. And like Mary, writes Froissart, "when this excellent Lady, who had done so much good and who had such boundless charity for all Mankind . . . gave up her spirit, it was caught by the Holy Angels and carried to the glory of Heaven." [26]

Queen Philippa was spared the lingering illness of her beloved son, the Black Prince, who died "of a dropsy" seven years after his mother's death. Her husband, Edward III, deteriorated mentally and morally after her demise, squandering state money on his paramour, Alice Perrers, and even ordering all the beneficiaries of his queen to give over their legacies to Alice.[27]

"The close observer of history," writes Strickland, "will not fail to notice that with the life of Queen Philippa, the happiness, good fortune, and even the respectability of Edward III and his family departed, and scenes of strife, sorrow, and folly, distracted the court, where she had once promoted virtue, justice, and well-regulated munificence." [28]

The Social Reformers

Britain has been very fortunate in her queens. Whether as monarchs or as consorts, they have shown greater talent for rule, as Mill noted, than kings; and since time immemorial British queens have been in the forefront of the struggle for social and civic reform. The English common law, on which our legal system is based and which provides the germ of the United States Bill of Rights, was first devised and promulgated by a queen, a Celtic queen, Martia Proba, who reigned in Britain in the third century B.C.

"Martia, surnamed Proba, 'The Just,' " writes Raphael Holinshed, "perceiving much in the conduct of her subjects which needed reform, devised sundry laws which the Britons, after her death, named the Martian Statutes. Alfred the Great caused the laws of this excellently learned princess . . . to be established in the entire realm of England." [29] Geoffrey of Monmouth, writing in the twelfth century, says of Martia: "On the death of King Guithelen, Martia, a noble woman who was skilled in all the arts and who was extremely intelligent yet at the same time most practical, ruled over this entire land. . . . Among the many extraordinary things she used her natural talents to invent was a law she devised which was called the Lex Martiana by the Britons. King Alfred translated this along with other laws. In the Saxon tongue he called it the Mercian Law." [30]

Thus the common law, generally attributed to King Alfred the Great, was originally promulgated a millennium before his reign by a Celtic queen of the Britons whose name no longer appears in the encyclopedias. Among her great reforms, many no doubt borrowed from the Brehon laws of the Celts, was the right to trial by jury— a concept unknown in Roman law. It is ironic that the idea of peer-jury trial, so sacred in modern jurisprudence and first promulgated by a woman, has been denied to women almost since its inception. To this day, women of England and the United States are still tried and sent to their deaths by jurors who are not their peers. Only woman receives more law than justice; but in the case of peer-jury trial woman receives neither law *nor* justice. Even today, women jurors do not preponderate at the trials of women, as according to the law they should.

Another neglected queen of early England was Aethelflaed, the daughter of this same Alfred the Great who perpetuated the laws of Martia. On his death in A.D. 906, Alfred bequeathed to his son Edward his kingdom of Wessex and to his daughter Aethelflaed his kingdom of Mercia. According to William of Malmesbury, "Aethelflaed for a generation gave Mercia a most conscientious and effective government." [31] The *Anglo-Saxon Chronicle* credits her with the building and settling of nearly a score of towns, of planning military excursions, and of winning back from the Danes all of Leicester, Derby, and York, which had been captured in King Alfred's time. Most of her victories she obtained peaceably, according to the chronicle, *by persuasion rather than by force*. At the time of her death in 918, "all of the people of York had promised her that they would be under her direction. But very soon after they had agreed to this she died twelve days before Midsummer in Tamworth, in the twelfth year in which with lawful authority she was holding dominion over the Mercians. And her body is buried in Gloucester in the east chapel of St. Peter's Church." [32] Her brother Edward then descended upon Mercia, and "all the people which had been subject to Aethelflaed submitted to him . . . and the daughter of Aethelflaed was deprived of all authority in Mercia and taken into Wessex. She was called Aelfwyn." [33] And so the little queen was deposed by her wicked uncle Edward, who had not dared interfere with the kingdom in Aethelflaed's lifetime.

Aethelflaed is memorable for a remark she is reported by William of Malmesbury to have made at the court of her father, Alfred, shortly after her marriage to Ethelred, her future consort in Mercia. On being asked why she refused the embraces of her husband, Aethelflaed replied that "it was unbecoming in a king's daughter to give way to a delight which produced such unpleasant consequences." [34] Yet her daughter Aelfwyn constitutes proof that at some time this king's daughter did give way to a delight that produced consequences.

It was a queen, also, who reestablished the civil rights of the English people after the Norman Conquest. The Normans had brought with them to England in the eleventh century the Franco-Christian legal system of the continent, a far less democratic and egalitarian system than that of those two great lawgivers Celtic Martia and Saxon Alfred. The English chafed at the attrition of their liberties under the first two Williams—the Conqueror and his son Rufus, the latter of whom, says the *Anglo-Saxon Chronicle*, "was hateful to all his people." [35] When William Rufus was mysteriously shot to death while hunting in the New Forest, his younger brother, Henry, the first of the Norman heirs to have been born on English soil, ascended the throne as Henry I. It was this king's love for a princess and his willingness to be influenced by her that brought about the restoration of their ancient liberties to the English people.

This princess was Matilda of Scotland, daughter of the Saxon heir of England, Margaret the Aetheling. Margaret, fleeing England after the conquest with her mother and brother, had married Malcolm, Macbeth's adversary, and had thus become queen of the Scots. She had sent her eldest daughter, Matilda, or Maud, to Wilton, where the English royal family had for centuries sent their daughters to be educated, and there Henry had seen her. On his accession to the throne he at once asked Malcolm and Margaret for the hand of their daughter in marriage—a proposal that met with the approval of the parents. But Matilda unaccountably refused the offer. Matilda had remained true to her English roots, and the suffering of her people under the Normans had deeply impressed and disturbed her. At the urging of her parents, however, and in the belief that she might, as Queen of England, alleviate the oppression of her people, she finally consented to Henry's suit, on condition that he promise as king to "restore to the English Nation their ancient laws and privileges, as established by King Alfred and ratified by King Edward the Confessor." [36]

On Henry's solemn oath to accept these conditions, "the daughter of the royal line of Alfred consented to share his throne." [37] Henry immediately repealed all the astringent civil laws imposed by his predecessors, the two Williams, and caused a digest of the laws of Alfred to be made and copies sent to all the towns of England "to form a legal authority for the demands of the people." [38] Upon this initial act of good faith on the part of King Henry, Princess Matilda married him on November 11, 1100.

"Many were the good laws made in England through Maud the Good Queen," wrote the chronicler, Robert of Gloucester. She caused regular welfare benefits to be extended to pregnant women of the poor and founded two free hospitals for the underprivileged, St. Giles in the Fields and Christ Church. She repaired and improved the roads and bridges throughout the land that had fallen into disrepair under the Normans. And, as a contemporary chronicler wrote:

> She visited the sick and poor with diligence.
> The prisoners and women eke with child
> Lying in abject misery ay about,
> Clothes, meat, and bedding undefiled
> And wine and ale she gave withouten doubt,
> When she saw need in counties all throughout.[39]

But above all, in Strickland's words, "to this queen of English lineage, English education, and an English heart, we may trace all the constitutional blessings which this free country at present enjoys. It was through her influence that Henry granted the important charter that formed the model and the precedent of that great palladium of English liberty, Magna Charta. And it was this princess who refused to leave her gloomy convent at Wilton and to give her hand to the handsomest and most accomplished sovereign of his time, till she had obtained just and merciful laws for her suffering country, the repeal of the tyrannical imposition of the curfew, and a recognition of the rights of the common people." [40]

This good queen, known to generations of Englishmen as Saint Maud, died in 1118, at the age of forty-one. And with her died many of the hard-won benefits she had bestowed on her people. For after her death, Henry reverted to type—the Norman tyrannical type of his father and his brother. In the reign of King John, a hundred years after the time of Good Queen Maud, when the digest of the laws of Henry and Matilda was sought, only one copy could be found. "It was thought that after the death of his queen, Henry I destroyed all the copies he could lay his hands on of a covenant which in his later years he regretted having granted. On this one extant copy, Magna Charta was framed." [41]

Thus Magna Charta, that eminent milestone in human advancement, like the English common law, was a direct descendant of the Martian Statutes of the Celtic Queen Martia, by way of Alfred the Great, Edward the Confessor, and the "digest" of Henry and Matilda. And the ultimate source of the Martian Statutes was the Brehon laws of the ancient Celts, those determined champions of liberty and justice. According to the *Anglo-Saxon Chronicle* and the genealogies included in Dorothy Whitelock's edition of it, there was a great deal of Celtic blood in the royal Saxon line of Alfred, and so in his direct descendant, Matilda. All the descendants of Matilda, therefore, derived Celtic genes from her. More Celtic blood was injected into the English royal line when Matilda's daughter, the Empress Matilda, married Geoffrey Plantagenet, "the Provençal Celt." The son of Geoffrey and the younger Matilda, who became Henry II of England in 1154, was thus more Celtic than either Norman or Saxon, as were all the "golden" Plantagenets.

The Celtic influence remained a force to be reckoned with, and the Celts were then and are now by no means a dead or dying breed.

18

Women in the Reformation

Since a woman must wear chains,
I would have the pleasure of hearing
'em rattle a little.

—GEORGE FARQUHAR

Brief Flowering—The Sixteenth Century

The Protestant revolution promised in the beginning to lighten the burdens of women by relieving the stultifying and crippling stresses so long applied by the church to the despised sex. The Reformation might be said to have brought on the Renaissance, for that revival of intellectualism and of ancient learning required the violent breaking of the chains with which the church had for so long bound the minds of men. With the Reformation too came an end in Protestant lands to the Inquisition, that bloody blanket under whose all-covering fiat so many women had been cruelly destroyed for so many reasons not connected with heresy. The Puritan witch-hunts which were to replace for the female sex the horrors of the Inquisition were still in the future; and the despotism of the clergy, with the dangers it had for so long represented for women, was no more. For millions of women this reprieve meant a release from fear and tension, and for a short while it seemed that the general Renaissance would be extended permanently to include the feminine half of Europe's population.

But the brief period of enlightenment was suddenly ended in Protestant countries by the ascendancy in the seventeenth century of fanatical and woman-repressing Puritanism and in the Catholic countries by a strengthened papacy, bled to new health by the defection from its ranks of the doubters, the intellectuals, and the better educated. However, in the brief period between Luther and Calvin, women enjoyed a life-giving respite from the abuse and bondage of the past thousand years. The ban on women's brains was also for a time lifted, with the result that the sixteenth century witnessed a remarkable blossoming of brilliant women—a true renascence of feminine intellectualism and creativeness that far out-shone, relatively, the Renaissance itself.

"Never since the women poets, philosophers, and thinkers of ancient Greece and Rome," writes John Augustus Zahm, "had women greater freedom of action in things of the mind than in the sixteenth century. Everywhere the intellectual arena was open to them on the same terms as men." [1] And sixteenth-century women, like long-deprived plants brought out of the darkness into the sunshine, responded to the unaccustomed light and warmth in a way that can be described only as miraculous.

In less than a generation from the time when girls had not been allowed to learn to read, "Every city of importance had women whose renown was a source of civic pride. . . . Women attended the great universities, and even occupied important chairs in the most distinguished faculties." [2]

The feminine Renaissance reached Spain before it reached England. Late in the fifteenth century, Queen Isabella of Spain had two distinguished lady scholars at her court who taught her daughters and herself the revived learning of the ancient Greeks and Romans. One of these instructors was the noted Beatrix Galindo, professor at the University of Salamanca; and the other was Francisca de Lebrixa of the University of Alcalá. These two women created a learned and intellectual environment at the Spanish court, a stim-ulating atmosphere in which the queen's daughter, Catherine of Aragon, grew to womanhood. This brilliant girl, dubbed by the great Desiderius Erasmus *egregia docta* ("a very learned lady"), was sent to the English court to become the consort of the then Prince of Wales. To England she brought with her the learning and intellectual curiosity of the Spanish court of Queen Isabella, and by 1501 learning for ladies had become as fashionable in England as in Spain.

By the time of Queen Mary, the daughter of Catherine and Henry VIII, learned and brilliant women were rife in England. One of the most brilliant was Queen Mary herself, granddaughter of the learned Isabella, whose translation of Erasmus' *Paraphrase on the Gospel of St. John* won international acclaim. Anne Bacon, a contemporary of Mary, daughter of Sir Anthony Coke and mother of the great Elizabethan genius Sir Francis Bacon, was chosen by King Henry VIII as chief tutor of his son Edward, Mary's half-brother. Little Jane Grey, the granddaughter of Henry VII, who succeeded young Edward as queen for nine short and tragic days, was a brilliant scholar. By order of Henry VIII she received instruction together with her cousin Edward, the future King Edward VI, who was reputedly a fine scholar and manifestly wise beyond his years. Yet, according to the teachers of the two children, "the Lady Jane was superior to King Edward VI in learning and in languages." [3]

But the greatest of pre-Elizabethan Tudor women of learning was Margaret Roper, daughter of Sir Thomas More. Sir Thomas was a firm believer in education for women, and his daughters were given all the advantages his son John received. "I cannot see why learning in like manner may not equally agree with both sexes," he wrote, echoing the words of Plato two thousand years earlier. And Sir Thomas proved his theory by producing daughters whose great learning was acclaimed far and wide, patently exceeding the accomplishments of their only brother, John.

The foremost scholar among More's brilliant daughters was Margaret, his "sweete Megg," whom he chided gently in a letter for "asking money too fearfully of your father, who is both desirous to give it to you, and that thou hast deserved it." [4] In another letter he sympathized with her in that age-old problem from which brainy women today still suffer, "that men that read your writings suspect you to have had help from some man therein." [5]

In the next century, Thomas Fuller, writing in 1661 when women had been thrust back into bondage by the new Puritanism, feels it necessary to apologize for including Margaret More Roper among the worthies: "Excuse me, reader," he was to write, "for placing a woman among men . . . but Margaret Roper attained to that skill in all learning and languages that she became the miracle of her age. Foreigners took such notice hereof that Erasmus hath dedicated some epistles to her. . . . She corrected a depraved place in St. Cyprian's works, and translated Eusebius out of the Greek." [6] Needless to say, Margaret's Eusebius was never printed, as one "I. Christopherson," explains Fuller, "had done the same" and had beaten her into print. [7]

In 1524 Margaret's translation of Erasmus' *Treatise on the Lord's Prayer* was printed, with an introduction by Richard Hyrde, who used Margaret's achievements as an argument for the higher education of women—"the first reasoned claim, written in English, for university education for women." [8]

Hyrde was followed before the middle of the century by many distinguished men who advocated the higher education of women, among whom were Edward Coke, the Earl of Arundel, the Duke of Somerset, More, and King Henry. Even Erasmus was finally won over, persuaded, as he said, by the numerous examples of wit and learning among the young ladies of England. In attempting to demolish the general male objection to learned women, he advised men to try to accustom themselves to the new ideas, much as Hamlet advised his mother to accustom herself to virtue, so that eventually that which "now seems unpleasant will become pleasant, and that which seems unbecoming will look graceful." [9]

Queen Elizabeth was one of the foremost scholars of the later sixteenth century. Her tutor Roger Ascham, among the greatest scholars of all time, considered Elizabeth even as a young girl more learned than any six gentlemen of the Court.[10] She spoke and wrote Greek and Latin, as well as French, Italian, and Spanish, with ease, and was the translator of Plato, Aristotle, and Xenophon. She wrote passable poetry, among her sonnets, ironically, being one addressed to that "lovely daughter of debate," her cousin Mary, Queen of Scots, whom she was later to treat so cruelly.

Some great contemporaries of Elizabeth were Jane Weston, ranked among the best poets of her day; Elizabeth Danviers, authority on Chaucer; Elizabeth Melville, poet; and above all, Mary Sidney, Countess of Pembroke, sister of Sir Philip Sidney and mother of that William Herbert who was loved by Shakespeare and was possibly the subject of the most amorous of the sonnets. Mary Sidney was not only a poet in her own right, but it is to her that we owe most of the works of her brother, Sir Philip Sidney, Queen Elizabeth's "perfect knight." For after his early death it was Mary who gathered his works together and edited, polished, and published them. His *Arcadia*, the greatest of his long poems, she is said to have largely written herself, as her brother had left it unfinished.

It is quite possible that the entire *Arcadia* was the work of Mary

Sidney and not of Philip. The title page of the first edition of the *Arcadia*, when it appeared in 1590, clearly indicates that it is the work of the Countess of Pembroke, Mary Sidney Herbert. It was only in later editions that more and more of the credit was given to Sir Philip. In their minor poems there is not much to choose between Philip and Mary; thus either of them could with equal credibility have written the *Arcadia*. But, of course, in English literature courses today, Sir Philip is *the* author.

John Aubrey, the seventeenth-century gossip and author of *Brief Lives*, says that Mary Sidney was a "Chymist of note," whose knowledge of chemistry won the admiration of Adrian Gilbert, the foremost "chymist in those days." [11] Mary Sidney, Countess of Pembroke, was not only a brilliant and learned lady but she was long remembered for her great charm and beauty. She was the patron of Ben Jonson and, through her son, of William Shakespeare. Ben Jonson's tribute to her is still included in all the anthologies, in some of which, however, it is attributed to William Browne:

> Underneath this sable hearse
> Lies the subject of all verse—
> Sidney's sister, Pembroke's mother.
> Death, ere thou hast slain another,
> Learned and fair and good as she,
> Time shall throw a dart at thee.[12]

Mary Sidney Herbert, Countess of Pembroke, who died in 1621, was the last survivor of a pageant of great and witty, learned and charming women who graced sixteenth-century England. "There are no accounts in history," wrote William Wotton in 1697, "of so many truly great women in any one age as are to be found between the years 1500 and 1600." [13]

And then suddenly, almost at the century mark, the interlude of feminine resurgence ended. Queen Elizabeth died, Puritanism reared its ugly head, learning was eclipsed, and women were thrust back into the darkness from which the Reformation had rescued them for so brief a time.

Back into Bondage—The Seventeenth Century

It has been suggested that Puritanism should, because of its stress on individualism, have lightened the ordeal of women and contributed to their emancipation. The very fact that male writers so casually speak of "emancipation" in connection with women, one-half the human race, is revealing in itself; for emancipation implies slavery. The suggestion that Puritanism emancipated women has been made by many men. But it is difficult to follow such reasoning. For Puritanism was a reversion to that Old Testament antifeminism which had brought about the enslavement of Western women in the first place. Individualism was stressed by the Puritans but, like the American Declaration of Independence with its "all *men* are created equal," the Puritan declaration applied only to males. Puritan women were triply denied equality—by secular law, by established church law, and now by the Puritan stress on Judaic "morality" which decreed that women must always be in subjection to men.

If the Catholic Church had overstressed the Old Testament under the mistaken impression that it was a moral document, the Puritans were far more gullible. So enamored were they of the harsh inhumanity and compassionless opportunism of the ancient Hebrews that they considered the ritual of the Anglican Church, as of the Catholic Church, wicked and sinfully frivolous. "The rituals connected with our Lord's life and death were left blank by the Puritans," says the *Catholic Encyclopedia*, "who observed only the Sabbath in a spirit of Jewish legalism." [14] Christmas was never celebrated in seventeenth-century Puritan England or in the Plymouth Colony of the revered pilgrims of North America, in the country where today it is the most important commercial carnival of the year. And as for the Virgin Mary, the mother of Jesus, the less said about *her* the better!

Women had had a brutal experience under Catholicism, and their plight did not improve under Protestantism. First, it was the Protestants who initiated the witch-hunts which caused the violent deaths of untold thousands of innocent women, young and old, in the seventeenth century. Witch-burning, as contrasted to heretic-burning, was not a fad of the Middle Ages. It was a modern Protestant innovation, and though many "witches" did suffer in Catholic countries during the witching era, the mania originated and was largely pursued in Protestant Germany, that cradle of extremism and of violence.

Contrary to popular belief, no witches were ever burned in England or in England's colony of Massachusetts. In England some men and women were hanged as witches, and in Massachusetts exactly five women and fifteen men were hanged and one man was crushed to death between boards. The popular American legend of old women being burned by the hundreds in Salem is pure myth. Of the twenty-one people executed for witchcraft there, over seventy-five percent were men; and none, male or female, was burned.

Even though in England execution for witchcraft was rare, the searching out of possible witches forced too many women of all ages to the pain and indignity of examination for "witch marks." These examinations were conducted by laymen appointed by the government, and far more often than was necessary they extended to the woman's most private and most sensitive parts. Bad enough to be stuck all over with long pins in the endeavor to find insensitive spots, "witch marks," but far worse was it to have the large, filthy, and callused hand of the examiner thrust up one's vagina on the pretext of searching for concealed witch paraphernalia. Just as the priests and friars of the Middle Ages had taken advantage of this privilege in their pretended search for female fornicators, so did the Puritan witch-hunters of the seventeenth century.[15]

The women of seventeenth-century England, from the street waif to the lady of the manor, were forced to submit to this degrading and painful examination at the whim of the witch-hunter. And one may be sure these men were no more gentle about it than they had to be.

There was also in women's lives of this dark century a new and soul-destroying ugliness of environment, which women and artists are always more sensitive to than are men.

With all its cruelties and repressions the Catholic Church had at least allowed dancing and merry-making on the village green and had permitted the enjoyment of sex, within bounds, between man and wife—perhaps the only bright spots in the dull drudgery and misery of the medieval woman's world. But now even these minor pleasures were prohibited by the stern and puritanical pastors of the Reformation.

Moreover, the worshipers in the Catholic churches, whether willing communicants or not, had found momentary uplift and solace in the beauty of the church itself, in the colorful costumes of the priests, the bright pictures in the stained-glass windows, the aroma of incense, the gleaming altar furnishings, the painted images of the saints, and the mumbo jumbo of the Latin service. But now what little beauty their tragic lives had been permitted was all wiped out. Dancing was prohibited, sex was frowned upon, husbands were exhorted to indulge in sex only with procreation in mind and never, never, by all that was holy, to permit their wives to reach orgasm.

In the chapels and churches all beauty and mystery were abolished as things of the devil. Gone were the colorful vestments of velvet and satin and gold, gone the stained-glass windows, gone the statues of the saints, the incense, the silver altar furnishings, the crosses with their limp and bleeding Jesuses and, above all, the Madonna in her blue cape, her rosy babe at her exposed and rosy breast. And gone was the mumbo jumbo of the Latin service that had once hidden the vacuity and barbarism of the traditional words. Now *Nunc dimittis* meant "You are dismissed" and there was no more mystery. The Reformation had done away with the one redeeming feature of organized Christianity, the mystic, pagan Greek beauty of its ritual.

But perhaps the most soul-shattering aspect of the new Calvinist Protestantism was the dictum of predestination—that man's fate was fixed and that not all his piety nor wit could cancel out a line of it. For women especially this new hopelessness must have been devastating. Trained for a thousand years to the conviction that they were God's basest creatures, born sinners, cursed forever by the disobedience of Eve, women had looked forward to heaven where their sins would be forgiven by the merciful and compassionate Virgin. But now there was no more hope. The Virgin had been annihilated, and woman's fate was fixed and horrible. She could never be redeemed. Saint Paul's hortations to women were more closely studied than ever before, in the forlorn hope that by obeying to the letter Paul's stern admonitions, she, each woman, might be more kindly treated in man's heaven than she had been on man's earth.

One unexpected result of all this Paul-studying was that Mary, Princess of Orange, daughter of James II, when recalled to England to occupy the throne in 1688 refused the crown. And all because she had taken to heart Paul's dictum: "Suffer not a woman to have authority over a man." The pleadings of the English government, the Parliament, and the newly reinstated Church of England did nothing to move her from her Paulist stand. She finally consented to become Queen of England only if her insufferable little husband, William of Orange, was allowed to share the throne with her on an equal basis but with precedence over *her*, the heir. The authorities had to consent to her terms; and so, for the first time in their long history, the English were possessed of two co-equal monarchs, William and Mary.

At the beginning of the seventeenth century Mary's great-grand-father James I, influenced by the woman-hating Puritan fanatic John Knox, who had driven James' own mother, Mary Queen of Scots, to her death, had stated the reinvigorated antifeminism of the time. A man owed nothing to his mother, he announced, ex-cept his existence. The father was the only parent, the mother merely an incubator. This was an abrupt return to the medieval belief, descended from Aristotle, that man's sperm contained a "homunculus," a perfect and complete little man who needed only the proper environment to mature into a finished human being. This superstition is prophetic in a way of the genetic truth that the new human being at conception contains all the makings and ingredients that will form the man, or woman. The error lies in the old belief that only the father's sperm contains the building materials, that, in Aeschylus' words, "the parent is he who mounts." It is known now that the mother contributes a great deal more to the unborn child than does the father. Not only does she contribute a larger number of genes on an equal number of chromosomes,[16] but having the child in her body for nine months enables her to contribute certain intangibles to the new person—intangibles of psyche, temperament, nervous stability, physical health, tendencies and preferences—that the father cannot match.

All through the Dark Ages it was so firmly believed that only the father could determine the child's nature and appearance that many a wife was killed on grounds of infidelity when her son turned out to resemble her cousin or some unknown ancestor instead of being the "spit and image" of its father. Women, themselves, secure in the knowledge that they had committed neither incest nor adultery, acquiesced in their own punishment for such lapses in the belief that some incubus resembling brother, father, or cousin, had had intercourse with them in their sleep. Many women even "confessed" to such strange psychic seductions.

"Woman furnishes the soil in which the seed of man finds conditions required for its development," had written Theophrastus Bombast (Paracelsus). "She nourishes and matures the seed without furnishing any seed herself. Thus man is never derived from woman, but always from man." [17]

So thoroughly was this fallacy believed that a seventeenth-century scientist, Count Johann von Kueffstein, was reputed to have created actual living beings from sperm kept for nine months in a warm damp place and fed on menstrual blood.[18]

The most sterile retrogressive move of the century, however, was the renewed vigor with which female intellect was anathematized. Like the Jewish Christians of the first and second centuries who on beholding the freedom and power of the Roman women determined to humble and enslave them, so the Old Testament Puritans of the seventeenth century now resolved to curb the sixteenth-century trend and restore women to their proper, God-ordained position of servitude.

"The sixteenth and seventeenth centuries seem more than a hundred years apart in tone and temper," writes Myra Reynolds. "We turn from the eager intellectual life of the women of Tudor England, from their full and rich opportunities, and we find that in the seventeenth century there was no provision at home or in the schools for any but the most desultory education for girls." [19]

The spirit of the great medieval gynophobes, from Saint Clement to Gratian, was revived. The foremost poet of Puritanism, John Milton, echoed thirteenth-century Saint Thomas Aquinas, who had called woman a "monster of nature," in his lines from *Paradise Lost*:

> Ah, why did God,
> Creator wise that peopled highest Heaven
> With spirits masculine, create at last
> This novelty on earth, this fair *defect*
> *Of nature*, [*Woman*]? [author's italics] [20]

In a book published in 1631, the author, one Thomas Powell, exhorts women to leave music and books alone and "learn cookerie

and laundrie and the grounds of good huswifery." Richard Braith-
waite, in 1633, warns wives to "be inquisitive only of new wayes
to please" their husbands and "to sayle her wit only by his com-
pass," looking upon him "as conjurers do the circle, beyond which
there is nothing but Death and Hell." Sir Ralph Verney, in his
Memoirs of the Verney Family, rejoices that his daughter "Pegg is
very backward," as "she will be scholar enough for a woman." [21]

Anne Clifford, Countess of Pembroke, wife of the fourth earl,
who was a grandson of the great Elizabethan Countess of Pembroke,
Mary Sidney, suffered cruelly for her possession of intellect in this
dark century. She had had the misfortune of an education after
the Elizabethan tradition of her mother and grandmothers, and
her subsequent marriage to a nobleman who, being a man of his
times, detested and reviled all learning, in men as well as in
women, was "an arbor of anguish." In 1638 this pitiful woman
wrote to a friend that she feared to visit her without her husband's
consent "lest he turn me out of this house as he did at Whitehall,
and then I shall not know where to lay my head." [22] Yet this
daughter of an earl had brought a huge dowry in land and in
money to her brutal husband.

Another pathetic learned lady of this century was Elizabeth
Jocelyn, granddaughter of Sir Anthony Coke's friend, the bishop
of Lincoln. The bishop had shared Coke's belief in education for
women and so had taken great pains with the education of his
most promising and intelligent grandchild, little Elizabeth. That
all his care and interest brought her only misery in this age of
anti-intellectualism is attested by a letter she wrote on her death-
bed at the early age of twenty-five. She had just given birth to a
baby daughter, and her last letter to her husband expressed her
anguished concern over the future happiness of this poor little
female: "I desire her bringing up to bee learning the Bible, good
huswifery, and good workes; other learning a woman needs not,"
she wrote. "I desired not so much my owne, having seen that a
woman hath no greater use for learning than a mainsaile to a flye
boat, which runs under water." [23]

By the end of the seventeenth century it could have been said,
as indeed it *was* said by Hannah Woolley, the "mother of home
economics," in 1675, that "a woman in this age is considered

learned enough if she can distinguish her husband's bed from that of another." [24]

In the 1670's there appeared *The Ladies' Calling,* a man-authored book which foreshadowed the thundering antifeminism of the eighteenth, nineteenth, and twentieth centuries. Among its gems was this: "Since *God* has determined subjection to be women's lot, there needs no other argument of its fitness, or for their acquiescence." [25]

And with this unanswerable *argumentum ex deo,* the masculine debate over women's rights and capacities was closed, not to be reopened for two hundred years.

So well, indeed, had the "suppress the wretch" campaign accomplished its purpose in this retrograde century that at the very end of it one J. Richards, whose manuscript, dated 1699, now reposes in the British Museum, could write of the women of his day: "These miserable creatures, who have no other knowledge than that they were made for the use of man!" [26]

19

The Age of Reason— The Eighteenth Century

So long as physical love is man's favorite recreation, he will endeavour to enslave woman.
—MARY WOLLSTONECRAFT

"Restricted, Frowned Upon, Beat"

By the dawn of the eighteenth century, Puritanism in England was a thing of the past. It had been a nightmarish episode in the nation's history, an error that England wished only to forget. But its brief reign had had a lasting effect on the position of women in England. Now, at last, patristic Christianity had accomplished its thousand-year-old purpose, and woman herself had come to acquiesce in her debasement and to accept the myth of her own inferiority.

The seventeenth century had taught women a harsh lesson, and the mothers of the next generation, such women as Anne Clifford and Elizabeth Jocelyn, saw to it that their daughters should not suffer as they had suffered for their brains. Thus woman's education was limited for the next two hundred years to needlework, singing, drawing, and playing the harpsichord.

But there were dissenting voices, and these voices, for the first time, were women's. Until the eighteenth century no Christian woman—except the frenzied defenders of Joan of Arc—had dared publicly or in print to speak up for her sex. But in 1706 Mary Astell, a brilliant, self-educated woman, threw the first large pebble into the pond of male complacency in a book entitled *Reflections on Marriage*: "Boys have much time and care and cost bestowed on their education; girls have little or none. The former are early initiated in the sciences, study books and men, have all imaginable encouragement: not only fame, but also authority, power and riches." (Over two hundred years later, Virginia Woolf was to note the deficiencies in the physical appurtenances of the woman's college at Oxford as compared to the luxurious comforts in the men's colleges and write—in *A Room of One's Own*—"The safety and prosperity of the male sex, and the poverty and insecurity of the other!")

"The other sex," continues Mary Astell, "are restricted, frowned upon, beat. . . . From their infancy they are debarred those advantages for the lack of which they are afterwards reproached; and are nursed up in that feminine pettiness which will hereafter be upbraided to them. . . . No man can endure a woman of superior sense; and no man would treat a woman civilly but that he thinks he stands on higher ground, and that she is wise enough to take her measures by his direction." [1]

In the same book Astell, with tongue obviously in cheek, advises wives as follows: "She who marries ought to lay it down for an indisputable maxim that her husband must govern absolutely and entirely, and that she has nothing else to do but Please and Obey! She must not dispute his authority, for to struggle against her yoke *will only make it gall the more*. She must believe him Wise and Good in all respects. She who cannot do this is in no wise fit to be a wife." [2]

Maurice Ashley, with typical male obtuseness, quotes this paragraph, which he mistakenly attributes to Damaris, Lady Masham, as *proof* that even intelligent women agreed with men's ideas of the role suitable to wives, and "acquiesced in their own inferiority." [3] But it is evident that Astell was satirically pointing out to women the incongruities and utter absurdities expected of them in marriage and subtly warning them against it.

Jonathan Swift, although he loved and admired his brilliant and learned Stella, wrote: "A very little wit is valued in a woman, as we are pleased with the few words of a parrot." And Samuel Johnson compared a preaching woman to a dog walking on its hind legs: in either case we ask not how well it is done, but marvel that it can be done at all. Women were expected to take all these public insults and belittlements, as they are today, like good sports, never retaliating and never showing their hurt or anger but smiling bravely and never wavering in their loyalty and devotion to their persecutors.

Johnson's contempt for women was inspired by the age-old woman-dread that has plagued men since the patriarchal revolution first began; for he is reported by Boswell to have said, in an unguarded moment: "Men know that women are an over-match for them. If they did not they would not be so afraid of women knowing as much as they themselves." [4]

Alexander Pope was a great feminist when he was in love with Lady Mary Wortley Montagu, but when she rejected him he became a rabid misogynist. "Most women have no character at all," he wrote; and "Every woman is a rake at heart."

Like Bishop Burnet, a despiser of intellectual women who yet married three of them in succession, these men all loved and admired individual women of intellect but "depreciated any scheme for the education of women in general," as Myra Reynolds points out.[5]

By far the most enthusiastic male promoter of women in the eighteenth century or, for that matter, in the entire history of Christian Europe, was George Ballard. He was a poor boy, son of a tailor, without any sort of formal education; but somewhere in his family background existed genes of great intelligence, for both he and his sister made of themselves scholars of national consequence. In 1752 Ballard, by then a don at Cambridge, published a two-volume book called *Memoirs of Several Ladies of Great Britain*. In the introduction to his book, upon which he had spent many years of dusty research in the forgotten files and documents of British history, he wrote:

> This age . . . hath produced a great number of excellent biographies; and yet, I know not how it hath happened, that very many *women* of this Nation who . . . in their own time have been famous, are not only unknown to the public in general, but have been *passed by in silence* by all our greatest biographers.[6]

"Passed by in silence," indeed. How naïve and unworldly this tailor's son must have been not to have known the ways of the patriarchal world and not to have known "how it hath happened" that so very many great women had been "passed by in silence" by the masculist historians and biographers of Christendom.

"I Have Thrown Down My Gauntlet"

By far the most noteworthy of eighteenth-century feminists was Mary Wollstonecraft Godwin. "I have thrown down my gauntlet," she challenged in her book *A Vindication of the Rights of Women,* in 1791.[7] "It is time to restore women to their lost dignity, and to make them . . . part of the human species." [8]

Wollstonecraft's book had a surprisingly large readership. This writer found, during research for a paper on Midwestern culture, that in 1796 her book was one of only ten or twelve titles ordered by the first bookstore west of the Alleghenies, that of John Bradford in Lexington, Kentucky. It came by sail, by barge, and by horse-drawn wagon across Cumberland Gap into the wilderness, accompanied by Gibbon's *Decline and Fall of the Roman Empire,* the Bible, and Thomas Paine's *The Rights of Man.* Today Wollstonecraft's demands seem mild. The remarkable thing about her book is that she recognized back in the eigheenth century the fact of man's essential fear and resentment of women—a psychological truth that was not scientifically established until the twentieth century. She asked why men, who profess to derive "their primary pleasure" from women, should hate them so much. Modern psychology has not only endorsed her perceptive discovery but has explained it: men do resent women, and partly for the reason of their dependence on women for "their primary pleasure."

Across the English Channel in France, the philosopher Jean Jacques Rousseau had just published his *Emile,* a book saturated with Old Testament patriarchalism and Judeo-Christian misogyny. The book infuriated Wollstonecraft, and part of *her* book is devoted to refuting Rousseau's:

Rousseau (in *Emile*): "The education of women should be always relative to men. To please, to be useful to us, to make us love them, to render our lives easy and agreeable; these are the duties of women at all times, and what they should be taught in infancy." [9]

Wollstonecraft: "Woman was not created merely to be the solace of man. . . . On this sexual error has all the false system been erected, which robs our whole sex of its dignity. . . . Whilst

man remains . . . the slave of his appetites . . . our sex is
degraded by a necessity." [10]

Rousseau: "Girls must be subject all their lives to the most constant
and severe restraint, . . . that they may the more readily learn
to submit to the will of others. . . . But is it not just that this
sex should partake of the sufferings which arise from those
evils it hath caused *us*?" [11] (Eve again?)

Wollstonecraft: "How can a woman believe that she was made to
submit to man—a being like herself," her equal? [12]

Rousseau: "Women ought to have but little liberty: they are apt to
indulge themselves excessively in what little is allowed them.
Girls are far more transported by their diversions than are
boys." [13]

Wollstonecraft: "Slaves and mobs have always indulged themselves
in excesses when once they broke loose from authority. The
bent bow recoils with violence, when the hand is suddenly
relaxed that forcibly held it." [14]

Rousseau: "Boys love sports and noise and activity: to whip the
top, to beat the drum, to drag about their little carts; girls on
the other hand are fond of things of show and ornament—
trinkets, mirrors, dolls." [15]

Wollstonecraft: "Little girls are *forced* to sit still and play with
trinkets." Who can say whether they are fond of them or
not? [16]

Mary Wollstonecraft saw clearly two hundred years ago what
this sort of training had done to the feminine psyche; yet modern
psychology is just beginning to be aware of it.

What Mary Wollstonecraft most bitterly resented was the effect
man's dominance had had on the *minds* of women: "Men have
denied reason to women; and instinct, sublimated into wit and
wiles for the purpose of survival, have been substituted in its
stead." [17] In 1860, John Stuart Mill observed that *all* the apparent
differences between men and women, "especially those which imply
inferiority in the female," are the result of the social demands of
men on women. "There remain no legal slaves [anywhere in the
British Empire]—except for the woman in every man's home." [18]

To Wollstonecraft far more shameful than the enslavement of
woman's body had been the fact that man had imposed upon her a

slavish personality—a necessity to please "master" at whatever cost to her own integrity or her pride. And this was slavery at its most obscene.

"How," she asks, "can men expect virtue from a slave—a being whom [masculine] society has rendered weak?" [19] "Be just, o ye men, and mark not more severely what women do amiss than the vicious tricks of the horse, and allow her the same privilege of ignorance to whom you deny the rights of reason." [20]

Mary Wollstonecraft, who married William Godwin[21] after she had finished her *Vindication*, has not received the acclaim she deserves. She is the Tom Paine of her sex, with the one great difference that Paine's book on *The Rights of Man* helped to free a colony of Englishmen in the New World who were already far freer than their sisters had been for a thousand years. And Mary's book did not accomplish, and has not yet accomplished, its purpose. Even in the New World the founding fathers turned deaf ears to the women who pleaded—and there were many even in 1789—to be included in the new constitution and to be granted citizenship in the new republic.

Let us say, then, of our antifeminist founding fathers, as Mary Wollstonecraft said of her enemy Rousseau:

"Peace to their shades! We war not with their ashes but with their 'sensibility' that led them to degrade woman by making her, and keeping her, a slave of sex." [22]

Crime and Punishment

Wollstonecraft's half-serious plea that women, since they were regarded as mute beasts, should have the same privilege of immunity from punishment granted irresponsible mares is a sensible one. Why should those noncitizens, who had no civil rights, who could not vote, own property, make wills, testify in court, serve on juries, or obtain divorces, whose children belonged exclusively to the fathers, who could not even sign their names to checks or maintain bank accounts—for to such an extent had women's rights been attrited away by the eighteenth century—why should these chattels have been subject to the same laws that governed the citizens, the males?

Yet they were. And the law was a great deal more implacable in

its demand for punishment of women than of men. We have mentioned the preponderance of legal executions of women over men
in medieval Europe, and this preference for punishing women violently and mercilessly did not end with the Middle Ages.

In eighteenth-century England, the Age of Reason, the age of
newspapers, coffeehouses, scientific discovery, mechanical invention,
street lights, Tom Paine, Ben Franklin, and the *Encyclopaedia
Britannica,* women were still being burned alive.

In the enlightened year of our Lord 1752, only two hundred years
ago, one Anna Whale, aged twenty-one, was burned alive in England. Her crime was the most heinous crime of all in masculist eyes
—complicity in the death of her own husband. As Havelock Ellis
said of husband-murder in the nineteenth century, it was considered
by the law to be *more* than murder—it was a form of treason combined with deicide, God-murder. (It is strange that the English
language, which has a good word for wife-murder—uxoricide—has
no word for husband-murder. Was it too vile and "unnatural" a
crime to be given a name?)

Anna Whale was an innocent young girl whose husband abused
her so outrageously that a neighbor, Sarah Pledge, was moved to
protest and to plead with the husband to treat his wife with less
violence. This well-meant intervention merely exacerbated the
man's brutality to his wife. Knowing that there was no recourse in
law, since wife-torture was no crime, Sarah Pledge determined to
take matters into her own hands. A few days later Mr. Whale died
rather suddenly. The suddenness of his death and the common
knowledge that his wife had good reason to wish him dead aroused
the suspicion of the local coroner. The corpse was examined, and
a large quantity of arsenic was found here and there in his interior.
So, on August 14, 1752, little Anna was tied alive to a stake, the
fire was ignited, and the girl went slowly and agonizingly to an
undeserved death.

Sarah Pledge, who admitted having performed the murder un-
assisted, was hanged by the neck until dead—spared the worse fate
because the victim had not been *her* husband.[23]

In the very same year that Anna was innocently executed by fire,
another innocent young English girl was hanged for complicity in
the murder of her father. The guilty party in this case was ad

mittedly the girl's sweetheart, a young medical student to whom Mary Blandy, for that was her name, had given her heart but to whom her father objected. In spite of his objections to the youth, Mr. Blandy did not object to taking medicines prescribed by him, and one of these medicines, administered by the hand of Mary, killed him. The servants and neighbors swore to the devotion of Mary to her father, she herself disclaimed any knowledge of the poison in the medicine she had given him, the young medical student suspiciously fled the country, and "justice" took its course. Mary Blandy, aged eighteen, went to the gallows on April 6, 1752. Her sweetheart was allowed to reenter the country with no charges against him, and he lived out his life as a physician with no felony attached to his name. Yet he admitted having put the arsenic in Mr. Blandy's medicine without Mary's knowledge.

An even sadder case, if possible, than those of Anna and Mary was that of Margaret Harvey, hanged July 6, 1750, at the age of seventeen. Married very young to a brutal older husband, she soon ran away from him and sought refuge with her parents. But her father, in true patriarchal fashion, refused to take her in and ordered her to return to her husband. Rather than commit this form of suicide, she repaired to the city to seek work. She very soon was driven by hunger to steal a small coin from a man on the street. The man called the constable, the girl was caught, justice took its course, and Margaret paid for her petty theft with her life.

Martha Tracy, sixteen, driven from home by her father because she had become pregnant, followed her faithless lover to London, was repudiated by him, became hungry, picked a man's pocket, was caught, and was hanged, pregnant, at Tyburn in 1745.[24]

Then there was the case of Mrs. Brownrigg, an elderly matron who for years had "adopted" orphans from the workhouse and given them lodging, food, and employment. Never a complaint was filed against her untill her son returned from the sea and took up his abode with her. Then rumors began to spread that the Brownriggs were abusing the young girls in their care. Stories of sadistic tortures, whippings, dark closets, and worse reached the authorities, and the Brownriggs were haled into court. Mr. Brownrigg and his son put all the blame on their wife and mother, Mrs. Brownrigg. The abused girls blamed the young Mr. Brownrigg, the son. Nonetheless, *Mrs.* Brownrigg, dignified to the last, was hanged at Tyburn, 1767. The two Mr. Brownriggs got six months each and were then released.[25]

In that same decade Mrs. Sarah Meteyard and her daughter, haberdashers of Bruton Street, were both hanged for causing the death of a boy apprentice in their shop. Only a few years earlier, James Duran, a ribbon-weaver, had been *acquitted* after he had beaten his thirteen-year-old apprentice to death with a mop handle; and John Bennett, fisherman of Hammersmith, got off with a light sentence after he had beaten his eleven-year-old apprentice to death with a rope. "The lad died of wounds and want of looking after and hunger and cold together," read the medical testimony at John Bennett's trial.[26]

These cases of apprentice-murder reveal not only the lack of concern for the children of the poor in the eighteenth century but, more to our purpose, they illustrate the double standard of justice for male and female offenders. A case that testifies to both of these deficiencies in the social order of the eighteenth century is that of little Mary Wotton, who stole trinkets from her mistress and was hanged therefor in 1735. Mary was just nine years old.[27]

20

Not Quite People—The Nineteenth Century

All that is distinctly human is the male.
The males are the race.

—GRANT ALLEN

A Special Kind of Property

Having succeeded in enslaving her mind and degrading her body, patriarchal society in the nineteenth century proceeded to annihilate woman's very identity as a human being. In the battle up to now she had been taken into some account if only as a dangerous element in society. But now came the final reduction to absolute zero of her value as a person.

Throughout the Christian centuries, up to and including the early eighteenth century, although women had been mercilessly persecuted and cruelly singled out for "special treatment," still the luckier ones had clung to certain traditional privileges. The old records of England show that all through the Middle Ages women continued to be licensed to practice law and medicine; and a woman, Caecelia of Oxford, was accounted the outstanding physician of the fourteenth century.

Even in the dark and retrograde seventeenth century, women's contributions to the economy were not wholly spurned. "Women actually owned and managed businesses requiring a considerable amount of capital," writes Alice Clarke. "They not infrequently acted as money lenders. The names of women often occur in connection with the shipping trade and with contracts. Women's names appear in lists of contractors to the Army and Navy." [1] But these feminine enterprises were sternly frowned upon by the more masculist elements of society, and by the end of the century they had largely been abolished. Even in the eighteenth century, however, as M. Dorothy George reports, many women still owned their own shops in London.[2]

Fewer and fewer women of independent means mar the records of England as the eighteenth century wears on, and by the nineteenth century they are practically nonexistent. In the United States, still strongly influenced by the Puritan perversion even in the twentieth century, such "anomalies" as independent women had always been extremely rare.

The French and American revolutions had been fought and won at the close of the eighteenth century in the names of liberty and equality for all people; and in both wars there had been multitudes of valiant and heroic women fighting on the side of liberty. Yet when the dust had finally settled and the victors had sat down at the conference tables to form the new governments, the women found that they themselves had been left out. There were no women at the Constitutional Convention in Philadelphia, no women in the first Continental Congress, no women at the polling places when George Washington was elected first President of the United States. Worst of all, women had been left out of the Constitution and remained unmentioned in the cherished Bill of Rights of individual freedoms. In spite of the influential Abigail Adams' reiterated plea to her powerful husband to "remember the ladies," the ladies had been utterly forgotten. Despite all the courageous assistance they had given in the fight for freedom, the ladies were still chattels.

They were a special kind of property, not quite like houses or beasts of burden, yet not quite people. They could not be party to law suits, could not offer legal testimony, could not make contracts, could not own property, and could not buy or sell goods or land.

"All that is distinctly human is the male," announced a spokesman for the human race in the nineteenth century. "The males are the race; the females are merely the sex told off to reproduce it." [3]

Woman was no longer to be considered either dangerous or threatening or vicious; she was simply not to be considered at all. She was not a member of the human race. Her place in the scheme of things, if she was fortunate, was that of a household pet. The very name with which she was christened branded her as an amusing and diverting plaything. Such names as Flossie, Kitty, Mandy, names formerly given only to lapdogs and kittens, were bestowed upon her at baptism. For what need had she of a name?

Psychologists today know the importance of their names to all children; what affect must her single, meaningless pet name have had on the American girl of the past few generations? She could not help observing the weighty consideration given to the selection of names for her brothers—names they would carry through life and in which they were expected to take pride. And *her* name only confirmed her in the belief that she was of no account in the scheme of things and of no value to the world or to the race, except as a breeder of men.

Contrary to ancient custom, the little girl was taught from infancy to revere the male, even including her own younger brothers, whom she was exhorted to look upon as creatures of a superior and sacred breed. "Always bear in mind," cautions *The Young Lady's Friend,* "that boys are naturally wiser than you. Regard them as intellectual beings, who have access to certain sources of knowledge of which you are deprived, and seek to derive all the benefit you can from their peculiar attainments and experience." [4] "Sisters should be always willing to attend their brothers, and consider it a privilege to be their companions. . . . Consider the loss of a ball or a party, for the sake of making the evening pass pleasantly for your brothers at home, as a small sacrifice." [5]

This early training in deference to all things male was designed to develop in the little girl the desired attitude of the wife to her future husband—a sort of knee-jerk submissiveness, an automatic Pavlovian response of homage and obedience to anything in trousers. Her destiny was wifehood, and for this honorable estate she was rigorously prepared, except in the sexual way, almost from the day she was born. The woman of the nineteenth century, and for nearly half of the twentieth, had no respectable alternative to marriage; for her, it was either marriage, work at starvation wages, spinsterhood, or prostitution. And it is hard now to decide which of the four was the worst of the evils.

For the vast majority of women "work" meant only slavery in a factory or sweatshop. Women in the shoe factories of New England earned all of sixty cents a week for an eighty-four-hour week, fourteen hours a day, six days a week—less than one cent per hour. In the cotton mills working women fared better. The going wage there was a flat fifty dollars a year for fifty-two eighty-four-hour weeks, which figured out to one and one-tenth cent per hour.[6]

But even these pitiful wages were not paid to the women who earned them but to their fathers if they were unmarried (and an outrageous percentage of these working "women" were mere children) or to their husbands if they were married. For of course the husband was legally entitled to every cent his wife earned.

For the woman who was a little higher in the social scale, work meant hiring herself out as governess in some gentleman's family or giving music or drawing lessons to the children of the affluent. But this form of independence brought with it a decided demotion in social status. In the democratic, classless society of the United States of the nineteenth century, "ladies would on no account invite her [the lady teacher] to their houses as a guest; for she is considered by them of inferior rank because she has attempted to render herself independent by the exercise of her talents." [7]

The masculine establishment saw to it that work should offer no inducements to any woman who might "anomalously" yearn for freedom.

The second alternative, prostitution, could hardly be classified as a choice, since nearly all the women who practiced the profession were thrust into it by the harsh vindictiveness of society and the law and did not choose it. Prostitutes were allowed to pursue their trade for the benefit and convenience of the male population, but they were considered outlaws. In the eyes of the church they were excommunicants *per se* and could not be buried in hallowed ground. In civil law they had no rights whatever. Men could maul them, rob them, beat them, even murder them, with impunity. No laws protected them, and no penalty accrued to their assailants.

"Women who have submitted to public prostitution are so corrupt that they can have no protection from the law," wrote Montesquieu in the previous century,[8] and the same incredible attitude was held throughout the nineteenth century. T. Bell, in an 1821 book, repeated Montesquieu's pronouncement with approval and with embellishments. Attempting to explain to his readers the "justice" and "logic" of society's brutality to prostitutes and "fallen women," Bell expounds, quoting Montesquieu: "Illicit conjunctions contribute but little to the propagation of the race. The father is not known, and the mother, with whom the obligation to raise the child remains, finds a thousand obstacles from shame, remorse, the constraint of her sex, and the rigour of the laws; and besides, she generally lacks the *means*." [9]

"Even women who have *slightly erred* must fall into the class of prostitutes," continues Dr. Bell with satisfaction; "for cast upon the world, unable to provide for herself, she must preserve her life by the *complete surrender of her delicacy and modesty*." [10] "If the husband is the criminal [the adulterer], he escapes with little or no injury either to fame or fortune," proceeds Bell. "If the wife be the criminal, the persecutions of the world and her incapacity to make honorable provision for herself, compel her to join the ranks of prostitutes. She becomes the Sport of society, and her innocent children, deprived of a mother's love, are also deeply tainted with their mother's disgrace." [11]

And then Bell goes on to warn any loving or compassionate husband who may be reading his book that forgiving the erring wife will only make matters worse. *He* will then be the object of "the ridicule of the world," and the influence of the wicked mother can only scar his wronged children even further. Leave well enough alone, advises the good doctor, and let the miserable woman starve in the gutter as she deserves.

Anne Royall, a journalist, "was kicked around like a mangy cur" when she protested the cruel injustice of forcing erring women into either prostitution or starvation. And when in 1829 she accused the U.S. Congress of an "un-Christian" callousness toward the female sex, that august body, incredibly, sentenced her to be *ducked* in the Anacostia River as a "common scold." [12]

Anne Royall had had the unique good fortune of having married a man who believed that wives should be allowed to inherit their husbands' money; and when he died he left his wealth, as firmly as the law allowed, in his wife's control. In the few years it required the law to wrench it out of her hands and bestow it on her deceased husband's nearest male relative, Anne had made good use of it. She had traveled.

In her travels around the new, young United States, initially undertaken for pleasure, she was appalled at the conditions she found among "working" and "fallen" women. She wrote articles on her travels, burying in them, at first unnoticed by the editors who published them, facts about the shocking conditions in which the vast majority of laboring women and children were forced to work. The penny-an-hour slave-laborers in the sweat shops—all women and children—aroused her burning ire. But her reports on these abuses went unnoticed. The plight of "fallen" women who preferred starvation to prostitution was also reported in her articles, and still no one heeded.

After her money had been taken from her and she had been forced to give up her travels, she moved into a small cottage in Washington and there attempted to eke out a meager living with her pen. Despite her own poverty, she took "fallen" women into her home and shared with them what little she possessed. Then, at last, notice was taken. She was arrested for harboring disorderly persons!

"What did our Savior?" she asked in her defense; and the charges were dropped. But the experience did not silence her. She continued stubbornly to share her small home and her smaller means with the abandoned, homeless women and to write article after article in their behalf and in behalf of the slave-laborers in the sweat shops. Finally, utterly disillusioned by the stony harshness of the government and the law toward helpless women and children, she publicly abjured Christianity, citing as her reason that "the good Christians in power in Washington do not see any connection between their religion and the social conditions around them."

For these and other unfeminine words, Anne was sentenced to a public ducking, and the Washington Navy Yard was ordered to prepare a ducking stool for her punishment. But at the last moment Congress relented. The woman was aging, she was no larger than a child, and she was "light as a feather." They feared the experience of being ducked in the chilly Anacostia River would kill her, and they did not want her death on their consciences. She was freed, but the terrifying experience had broken her spirit and for the remainder of her life she observed complete silence in the public press. The nation and the Congress soon forgot her, and for the rest of the nineteenth century she was unheard of. She has had a revival in the 1960's, however, and some of her books are back in print today.

Anne Royall had not been able to help her "fallen" sisters, and the harsh and merciless attitude toward them continued well into the present century. The Reverend Dr. R. J. Campbell, writing in 1907, asked: "Why do we persecute a woman for surrendering her virginity? Why do we discriminate against the unfaithful *wife* only?" Woman's unchastity, he concludes, is an infringement on male property rights, and for this reason "we hedge our wives around with so many penalties and pains that if one offends we thrust her into the ranks of prostitutes, and persuade ourselves that this is *moral* and Christian. . . . As a matter of fact, it is the meanest, shabbiest, most selfish plan ever devised by selfish man for keeping his hold on his private property, woman. It leaves the ordinary woman," concludes Campbell, "a kind of Hobson's choice: reputable or disreputable dependence on the male sex." [13]

With all avenues of reputable subsistence effectively closed against her by "the malice of patriarchal society," nineteenth- and twentieth-century woman had no choice and was forced by the pressure of society into either remaining as an unpaid servant in the home of some male relative or into marriage with the first man who was willing to support her. Yet spinsterhood offered even less inducement than "work." Like the prostitute and the working woman, the old maid was the whipping boy of society.

"The contempt with which the single woman has been regarded is different from that bestowed on her fallen sister, but it is no less real," remarks Campbell.[14] While the prostitute was filthily odious, the old maid was odiously ridiculous.

Jane Austen had written in *Emma*, early in the century: "A single woman with a narrow income, must be a ridiculous, disagreeable old maid, the proper sport of boys and girls, but a single woman of fortune is always respectable, and may be as sensible and pleasant as anybody else." [15] But how many "single women of fortune" were there in the nineteenth and twentieth centuries?

These unfortunate human beings were spoken of publicly as "surplus women," and they became more and more of a problem as time wore on. There were movements in the masculine establishment to "sequester them in institutions . . . where they would have their activities, their *opinions,* and their wealth, if they were possessed of any, wisely *controlled* [author's italics] by a policy beneficient to the nation as a whole." [16] In short, they were to be looked upon as criminals for the crime of being that frightful anomaly, an unowned, non-male-oriented female, a satellite out of orbit.

The one and only reputable calling available to woman was marriage, and to this blessed and honorable estate she was taught from infancy to aspire. Her youth was an unbroken frenzy of desperate and agonizing fear that she would be "passed over," forced to live out her life in the shame of celibacy, a surplus woman. And when she was lucky enough to find her man she was expected to be eternally grateful, no matter how miserable her marriage proved to be. "Love in the heart of a wife," advises a popular book written for the instruction of young ladies in 1847, "should partake largely of the nature of *Gratitude.* She should fill her soul with gratitude to God and to the Man who has chosen *her* to be his helpmate for time and for Eternity." [17]

And for what was she expected to be grateful?

Late in the nineteenth century, Judge Lucillius Alonzo Emery of the Maine Supreme Court, wrote: "The whole theory of the law where it concerns women, is a slavish one. The merging of the wife's name with that of her husband is emblematic of all her legal rights. The Torch of Hymen serves but to light the Pyre on which these rights are offered up." [18]

The Pyre of Hymen

Until quite recently, and still in a few of the United States of America, a married woman had no rights at all. Single women and widows were not considered citizens, it is true, but at least they had rights over their own bodies, as married women did not. A married woman "belonged" completely to her husband, in the same way that his clothes, his horse, and his dog belonged to him. He could assault her, keep her locked up, even *sell* her, with the full sanction of the law. In 1815 a man named John Osborne sold his wife and child at Maidstone, England, for the sum of one pound, to a man named William Serjeant. "The business was conducted in a very regular manner, a deed and covenant being given by the seller, of which the following is a literal copy: 'I, John Osborne, doth agree to part with my wife, Mary Osborne, and child, to William Serjeant, for the sum of one pound, in consideration of giving up all claims whatever, whereunto I have made my mark as an acknowledgement. Maidstone, Jan. 3, 1815.' " [19]

Later, reports John Ashton, a young lady was sold at auction at Smithfield. She was exposed in a halter and the price demanded for her was eighty guineas. She was finally sold to a celebrated horse dealer for fifty plus the horse on which he, the buyer, was mounted. The woman's husband was a well-to-do cattleman from near London.

"The custom of wife selling," writes Nina Epton, "appears to have been fairly common" in the nineteenth century.[20]

Up until the year 1885, less than a hundred years ago, in England a man could still sell his wife or daughter into prostitution. In that year it was made illegal to sell or kidnap a girl for the purposes of prostitution *until she was sixteen years old.* After that "age of consent" it was still legal. It was only in the 1880's, too, that the law allowed a wife who had been habitually beaten by her husband to the point of "endangering her life" to separate from (not divorce) him. In 1891 the law for the first time forbade a man to keep his wife imprisoned under lock and key, as a Governor Yeo, for one, had done to his wife each time he went to sea.[21]

Even after all these "improvements" in the condition of women, a wife could still not own her house, her inheritance, or even the paltry sums she earned at home by sewing, preserving fruits, or taking in wash. Even the children of her own body were not legally hers. No matter how wicked and unworthy the husband, he had complete rights under the law over the children. He was allowed to banish his wife and live openly with another woman, yet the children remained his, and their mother could see them or correspond with them only at his pleasure and with his permission. A woman might inherit a fortune, yet she had no say in its management or its disposal. Her husband could, and often did, squander his wife's fortune on his own pleasure, leaving his wife and children in actual want. Yet no law compelled him to account for a penny of it.

This very outrage was committed against his wife and children in the latter nineteenth century by the Duke of Queensberry, who was the father of Lord Alfred Douglas, friend of Oscar Wilde. The duke banished his wife from the ducal mansion, took unto himself a series of paramours, lived like a sultan on his wife's money, and refused to contribute a shilling to the support of his family. The duchess and her children lived in actual poverty while the duke squandered the fortune his wife had brought him at their marriage, and no voice was heard to rise in protest in all of official or legal England. The result was that young Lord Alfred grew up with a consuming hatred for his father and a passionate love for and protectiveness toward his mother.

At least in the case of the duke his children had been allowed to live with their mother, a blessing denied Prince Albert of Saxe-Coburg, the consort of Queen Victoria. His mother had been repudiated and banished by her husband, and young Albert, to his lasting grief, had grown up in ignorance even of her whereabouts; and by the time he reached manhood she had died of want. Prince Albert, like Lord Alfred, had been deeply affected by this traumatic experience of his childhood and, again like Lord Alfred, he hated his father all his life and could never speak of his beautiful and tragic young mother without tears in his eyes.

Yet if two such great and influential "gentlemen" as a Saxon kinglet and an English duke could get away with so much open cruelty to their wives, for how much worse crimes must the ordinary husband have gone uncensured. As Mill writes:

The power [of men over women] is a power given not to good men, or to decently respectable men, but to all men: the most brutal, the most criminal. . . . Marriage is not an institution designed for a select few men. Men are not required as a preliminary to marriage to prove that they are fit to be trusted with absolute power over another human being. . . . The vilest malefactor has some wretched woman tied to him, against whom he can commit any atrocity except killing her—and even that he can do without too much danger of the legal penalty. How many men are there who . . . indulge the most violent aggressions of bodily torment towards the unhappy wife who alone of all persons cannot escape from their brutality; towards whom her very dependence inspires their mean and savage natures, with a notion that the law has delivered her to them as their *thing*, to be

used at their pleasure. . . . The law compels her to bear everything from him. . . . Even though it be his daily pleasure to
torture her, even though she feels it impossible not to loathe him,
he can claim from her and enforce the lowest degradation of a
human being: that of being the instrument of an animal function
against her wishes.[22]

Mill's accurate assessment, in his essay *On the Subjection of
Women,* of the wrongs of women in the late nineteenth century
met with violent abuse from the masculine establishment, who,
with one voice, excoriated Mill as a traitor to his sex and his society.
One of the most furious reactions came from Anthony Ludovici, an
Englishman who indicted the entire essay as "one of the most
astonishing utterances that ever issued from the lips of an alleged
philosopher." [23] "The essay remains as the most unhappy record
of Mill's character as a thinker." [24]

"It is my conviction," announces Ludovici, "that those who, like
Mill, flatter women into the belief that their inferiority is not
natural but 'artificial,' are the true enemies of womankind. . . .
We must rid England of all traces of feminism and purge her of
these antimale influences. . . . Feminism, by striking nearer the
roots of life, is perhaps even more dangerous to civilization and
to the Race, than Democracy itself." [25] Democracy, presumably,
was undesirable because it robbed the elite male of his power over
his fellowmen, while feminism threatened to rob all men of their
power over women. And, says Campbell, it is nothing else but this
fear of losing their last "minority" to lord it over that causes men
to resist "the just demands of women for even the slightest relaxa-
tion of the restrictions imposed upon them." And for this reason
only, men have purposely, and with malice aforethought, says
Campbell, "openly or insidiously repelled every attempt by women
to be free of them, and to live their own lives." [26]

Strangely enough, no one ever considers what this absolute power
given to men over women throughout the past few centuries might
have done to the characters of the men themselves. If Southern
slavery was deleterious to the slave owners, as modern sociologists
say it was, and the absolute power given to the slavers over their
slaves led to a decay in their moral fiber, why has not the same

power over women had the same harmful effect on the males of the species? Why has not absolute power corrupted them absolutely? Or has it?

"The effects of patriarchal marriage," wrote August Forel at the end of the nineteenth century, "are deplorable and very *immoral*. The patriarch abuses his power, and patriarchism degenerates into atrocious tyranny on the part of the head of the family, who must be looked upon as a god." [27]

If a mere two hundred odd years of slavery had so deleterious an effect on the character of black men as sociologists say it did, why haven't fifteen hundred years of slavery had the same effect on women? Perhaps woman has avoided complete inner degradation because she has an instinctive knowledge, an intuitive memory, of her original and still basic superiority; for even among blacks, it is the *women*, the stronger sex, who have managed more readily to retain their dignity, their integrity, and their self-respect.

21

The Prejudice Lingers On

Men, in general, employ their reason
to justify their inherited prejudices against
women, rather than to understand them and to
root them out.

—MARY WOLLSTONECRAFT

Some Masculine Myths About Women

The traditional belief in the inferiority of women is a doctrine that has been so thoroughly imposed in the past few centuries by the combined weight of law, religion, government, and education that its refutation by history, archeology, anthropology, and psychology will have little effect without extreme measures on the part of established authority.

In 1965, President John F. Kennedy's Commission on the Status of Women reported: "The extent of the negative attitudes among men as to the ability of women emphasizes the need for research on the sources of such attitudes and views, and the *adoption of positive policies to diminish prejudice where it exists* [author's italics]." [1]

This work has been intended as a contribution to the research on the sources of masculine prejudices against women. Diminishing these prejudices is another matter and will call for positive policies on the part of government and strict enforcement of these policies, as the Report stated. But first we must attempt to expose the accumulated myths and untruths concocted by men to justify their oppression of women.

"Men have certain fixed ideologies concerning the nature of woman," writes Horney, "that woman is innately weak, emotional, enjoys dependence, is limited in capacities for work—even that woman is masochistic by nature." [2]

Men justify their mistreatment of women with the delusion that women on the whole are satisfied with their status, that only a few unnatural women feel "deprived and imprisoned in modern society." "We hear, therefore, on this subject from only a very small segment of women who are truly not typical," opines Odenwald.[3] But it is hard to say how the good doctor knows what is typical and what is atypical among women. It is well known that, as Bertrand Russell observes, "so long as women are in subjection they do not dare to be honest about their feelings, but profess those which are pleasing to the male." [4] Especially is this so when the questioner is a male; and it is hard to imagine any woman giving an honest answer to a masculist of Dr. Odenwald's ilk.

The Myth of Masochism

Men want women to be quiet in their subjection, and whether they are happy in it or not is of small concern. Yet men really believe that women *enjoy* being abused, that they are by nature masochistic. Freud perpetuated the myth of female masochism to justify his own sadistic treatment of his long-suffering wife; and the myth has been gratefully accepted and propagated by men of gentler stuff who are unconsciously disturbed by man's cruelty to women. To believe that women "like it" eases the burden of their guilt.

We thus have such fatuous remarks as "women delight in experiencing physical pain when inflicted by a lover," from Havelock Ellis;[5] and "Most women enjoy the display of manly force even when it is directed against themselves," from Edward Westermarck;[6] and the current disgusting television commercial for a male cosmetic: "I love *men* even when they are *unkind* to me!"

It is men, not women, who have promoted the cult of brutal masculinity; and because men admire muscle and physical force, they assume that women do too. Yet this is obviously a misconception. Poll after poll among girls and women shows that they prefer gentle and intellectual men to brawny masculine types.

Women seem to know, as H. L. Mencken observed, that "complete masculinity is hardly distinguishable from stupidity." [7]

The worship of muscular male forms is a weakness of men and not of women. Likenesses of "Mr. Atlas" and "Mr. Universe" adorn almost exclusively the walls of men's and boys' quarters. They repel the normal woman. The tough movie hero, supposed to be dear to the hearts of women, is supported by primarily male audiences. The idea that women are attracted to aggressive and overblown masculinity is only one of the myths about women that have become ineradicably imprinted in the masculine mind—and hence in social attitudes.

Men admire male muscularity not only for itself but for its role in giving them mastery over physically weaker women. The majority of male physicians invariably recommend the Christian, or "missionary," position in sexual intercourse—with the man on top —in the belief that, because in this position "the woman is hemmed in, is his prisoner, and cannot escape," not only will the man's innate sadism be satisfied, but the innate masochism of the woman as well.[8]

"Wives' subjection to their husbands," writes Westermarck, "was of course the result of man's instinctive desire to exert power."[9] This remark, made nearly forty years ago, only serves to illustrate how much we have learned of prehistory and early society in the past half century. For man's desire to exert power was a very late thing in human development, and neither man's abuse of his power nor woman's submission to it was instinctive in either sex. It was the result in both cases of conscious teaching in the Western world; and the teacher, with rod and stake to enforce obedience, was the Christian Church.

The Sex Myth

The nineteenth-century fallacy that women were devoid of sexual feelings has been replaced in the late twentieth century by the older but equally false belief in the rampant sexuality of women— the view that all women "are rakes at heart." "Girls," writes Aubrey Beardsley, quoting one Dubonnet, "are for the most part confirmed in all the hateful arts of coquetry, and attend with *gusto* rather than with distaste, the hideous desires and terrible satisfactions of men."[10] This is a good example of wishful thinking on the part of men, because the idea that women are as sexy as themselves tends to excuse their own hypersexuality and to justify their incontinent sexual demands on women.

One of the many paradoxes of masculine reasoning is that, while most men believe women are diametrically different from them in all other respects, they are convinced that women resemble them in their sexual nature—the only respect in which they really *do* differ. Men imagine that women respond to the same sexual stimuli to which they respond; yet nothing could be further from the truth. Woman's sexuality is very closely bound up with love and tenderness, and soft words are far more effective in arousing her desire than is a hard phallus. Man's nude body, in fact, is more of a handicap than a help in his conquest of his sexual prey, for "women are not sexually curious about men," as Reik says. "The language has no feminine form for the word *voyeur*, and there are no female 'Peeping Toms'!" [11]

Simone de Beauvoir writes that normal women derive more sensual pleasure from caressing the soft smooth body of a child or of another woman than from stroking the rough and angular body of a man; for "crude man, with his hard muscles, and his rough and hairy skin . . . does not appear to her desirable; he even seems repulsive. . . . Worse, the man rides her as he would an animal subject to bit and reins. . . . She feels that she is an instrument: liberty rests wholly with the other." [12] Woman's love always holds more or less of the maternal, and contrary to man's love, is never exclusively sexual.

Nor can she achieve complete sexual gratification without at least the illusion of reciprocated love in her partner, a condition that certainly does not apply in the case of men, or there would be no such thing as rape.

"Hysteria" and Related Myths

The myth of woman's intellectual inferiority has been successfully refuted by statistical evidence; but the myths of her weakness, dependency, emotionalism, and timorousness still find currency among the vast majority of Americans of both sexes.

Men have always, in patriarchal ages, preferred women with these characteristics, and when such women proved to be scarce, if not actually nonexistent, men applied the words indiscriminately to all women. *All* women were thenceforth to be innately weak, emotional, timorous, and dependent. Yet, contradictorily enough, men, who want women to be clinging vines in fair weather, expect them in times of stress to become sturdy oaks—to carry the burdens, maintain their men's morale, and (to mix our metaphors) man the battlements that the men have abandoned. Man is a fair weather lord and a sunshine master.

Yet emotionalism—hysteria—is believed by men to be an exclusively feminine trait. "Today," however, "it is well known that males suffer from hysteria and hysteria-born mental diseases by a ratio of *seven to one* over females." [13] Moreover, mental deficiencies of all types are twice as frequent in men, schizophrenia three times as frequent, and miscellaneous disorders of character, behavior, and intelligence are four times as frequent in men as in women.[14]

Still, women are always being reported in newspapers as "screaming" in emergencies. Leonard Woolf observes that, with or without screaming, women in dangerous situations are more apt to turn to and do something, while men seem to relapse into a catatonic state.[15] "When all the men lose their heads," writes Stendhal, "is the moment when women display an incontestable superiority." [16] Woman's civilian involvement in the wars of the past sixty years has demolished once and for all the myth of woman's inadequacy in emergencies: "The old chestnut about women being more emotional than men has been forever destroyed by the evidence of the two world wars. Women under blockade, bombardment, concentration-camp conditions survive them vastly more successfully than men. The psychiatric casualties of populations under such conditions are *mostly* masculine . . . [at a ratio of *seventy* to one]. Women are both biologically and *emotionally* stronger than men." [17]

Hand in hand with the superior emotional strength of women goes a greater natural capacity for heroism than is found in all but the most exceptional of men. The word "hero" was, after all, originally feminine—*hera*, as philology proves;[18] and the original heroes of the human race were "heras," as the nomenclature of ancient places, even of continents, bears out. Herodotus asserts that Asia, Europe, and Libya (Africa) all received their names in ancient times from great women: Libya from "a native woman of that place"; Europe from Europa, the ancestress of the Cretans; and Asia from the wife of the aboriginal Prometheus.[19] All of these women were probably great warrior-queens—heras—of the time when women were engaged in leading the human race toward true civilization.

Today's newspapers are full of the heroic deeds of women—the earliest editions, that is to say. By the second edition the woman's name has been replaced by that of a male. In the evolution of news as of myth, as Bachofen points out, the hera is rechristened with a masculine name, while the male villain is given a feminine name.[20] Or, if the name remains, the heroine's deed has been diminished to the status of a lucky, but freakish, accident.

Recently a "skyjacker" was disarmed by an airline stewardess over Florida. The first edition of the press gave the stewardess full credit for her act of courage. By the second edition, however, the male pilot was sharing honors with her, and by the time the news *weeklies* appeared, the pilot was the *hero* of the incident.

"The heroic deeds of women are seldom recorded in books or periodicals," observes Dr. Georgio Lolli.[21] Male editors, with their preconceived notions of female timidity, brush these stories aside as having some explanation other than courage. And male judges in granting heroism awards automatically eliminate the names of girls and consider only the boys. The Carnegie Foundation awards annual medals for bravery to civilians who display selfless courage. In looking over their annual lists one is impressed by the vast majority of men's and boys' names. The preponderance of male recipients does not jibe with the preponderance of women heroes whose names appear in the early editions of local newspapers.

It all boils down to the fact that in the eyes and minds of the masculine judges, boys are heroes and girls are not. If a girl performs a heroic act it is an anomaly, a freak episode. One can only ask: how many times must an anomaly occur and recur before it ceases to be an anomaly? Odenwald, in his curiously antifeminist book, admits that "women in the past have taken their stand at the barricades and have carried, literally and figuratively, their men on their backs. But when they have done so, *everyone agreed they were exceptions* [author's italics]." [22] How long must exceptions be repeated before they become the rule? The doctor goes on: "When they do so as a *regular* thing today, however, more and more people ask, 'Well, why not?' These people are saying *there should be no clear distinctions.*" In other words, says Odenwald, women have no right to be brave. Bravery is man's province. And of course it is the acme, or nadir, of that most despicable thing, unfemininity, for women to invade man's province. Women must pretend to be cowards in order that men may appear more courageous by contrast.

Thus the masculists of Odenwald's ilk. But perhaps they are paying, all unconsciously and unintentionally, a tribute to women by implying that it takes more courage for a man to be courageous than for a woman to be. The fact must be faced that women, on the whole, are more courageous, both morally and physically, than men—"*ten times* more courageous than he is," says John Cowper Powys.[23] And Stendhal writes: "I have seen women, on occasions, *superior* to the bravest men." [24]

Men behave bravely when the eye of the camera or of the commanding officer is upon them, or when their future is at stake, or when the odds are greatly in favor of their ultimate survival. Women are *instinctively* courageous. For courage involves a forgetfulness of self, a broad compassion, and a high evaluation of another's life—all of which are feminine attitudes, rare in men.

It is not generally known that the Congressional Medal of Honor, when it was first instituted after the Civil War, was in the reach of women, and that one woman, Dr. Mary Walker, was awarded it for heroism during that conflict. This fact is completely omitted even in the biography of Mary Walker included in *Our Times,* the only twentieth-century encyclopedia in which her name can be found.[25]

Mary Walker was a medical officer in the Union Army, and her citation for bravery read in part: "She often went where shot and shell were flying, to save the wounded, when no male surgeon was willing to go for fear of being captured." [26] Her medal was reconfirmed in 1907, in a general review by Congress of the past recipients. Yet in 1917, a new Congress voted to rescind her medal and strike her name from the rolls of heroes! Their excuse was that Dr. Walker had been a noncombatant and that hereafter only actual fighting men could be considered for the medal. Yet many other noncombatant medalists—male medics, doctors, surgeons, and chaplains—of the Civil, Spanish-American, and Mexican-border wars were allowed to retain their medals. When this discrepancy was pointed out to Congress, they explained that Dr. Walker had been a *contract* surgeon, and contract surgeons were not eligible. Yet, writes Joseph Schott, in 1915 Congress had conferred the medal on John O. Skinner, a *contract surgeon,* and had *not* recalled it.[27]

The true reason for this discrimination against Dr. Walker was, of course, her sex, compounded, no doubt, by her crime in joining the suffragette movement in demanding voting rights for women—an outrage that the U.S. Congress of 1917 could not tolerate. However, and for whatever reason, this decision by Congress established the precedent once and for all that the Congressional Medal of Honor was intended for men only, and no woman need apply. To this day, no woman has. Not one, even of the superbly brave nurses at Corregidor, for instance, has ever been so much as mentioned for the medal. Yet male doctors, medics, and chaplains continue to be honored with it. Only recently two chaplains in Vietnam received the medal; yet they are surely no more "combatants" than was Mary Walker.

Dr. Walker, like Hypatia and Pope Joan before her, was reviled, ridiculed, and scorned by officialdom for her courage; and she, like them, was actually *stoned* in the streets of Washington, D.C., for her "presumption" in protesting the unfair recall of her Medal of Honor. She died in 1917, a victim of the masculine myth of the incapacity of women to perform heroic deeds.

Woman's Image

Men and women stand on opposite sides of a one-way window (if we may borrow an image from Ernest Bornemann). On the mirror side stands the man, seeing only his own strutting and gesticulating self reflected back at him, unaware that there is anything on the other side. On the transparent side, however, stands the woman, observing clearly the man in all his posturing but unable to see or realize herself.

It is thus not too remarkable, perhaps, with what patience and lack of bitterness women look upon their own image as it is paraded and parodied daily and hourly in all the communications media, from newspapers to television. What *is* remarkable is the insensitivity of the men who create and publicize this image of woman, "an image that perpetuates contempt for women by society and by women for themselves." [28] The callous lack of consideration for the feelings and dignity of one half the Amercian public on the part of the broadcasters, writers, entertainers, and newsmen is approached only by the incomprehensible insensitivity of adults who openly, and in the presence of little girls, commiserate with the parents of a baby girl, while congratulating the parents of a boy.

"The false image of women prevalent today in the mass media" [29] is insulting and degrading to women, whether or not such is its conscious intention. Mrs. Virginia Knauer, the President's Adviser on Consumer Affairs, was recently introduced in a television interview as "a fifty-five-year-old grandmother" and was then asked by the male interviewer if "anybody at the White House listened to her!" Just imagine that the interviewee had been Henry A. Kissinger or Robert H. Finch, or any other of the President's male advisers. Would he have been identified as a fifty-five-year-old grandfather and then rudely asked if anybody at the White House listened to him? Why is a woman's grandparenthood newsworthy and interesting while a man's is not? And why do male interviewers feel free to insult women officials and treat them with less respect than men officials? When Betty Furness became the first Adviser on Consumer Affairs, the news commentators branded the appointment as "window-dressing." Why?

It appears that any woman who exposes herself to an interview with a male newsman takes a great risk of having her dignity affronted, if not her very motives questioned. Even Senator Margaret Chase Smith is not immune from the patronizing jibes, veiled insults, and implied contempt of some male interviewers. And why do they nearly always call her "Mrs." Smith, while all *male* Senators are correctly addressed as "Senator"?

The news broadcasts rarely miss a chance to humble and belittle women, from female jockeys to visiting foreign officials. Yet television commercials and entertainment programs are even more offensive. Women in commercials are invariably either sex objects themselves or are engaged in sex-worshiping some condescending male. The TV-commercial wife, like the "good little Maxwell housewife," is invariably a cringing, husband-dominated, brainless sap. The most revolting example of this is embodied in the commercial for some deodorant, in which the depraved little wife, who wishes only to tell her husband that he has body odor, simpers and squirms, and giggles timorously, assuring him whimperingly, "I'm your *wife*. I *love* you. I'm on your *side!*" Is she afraid he'll haul off and belt her one? It would seem so; but perhaps submissiveness, debasement, and abject humility on her part will soften the blow?

In entertainment programs and in television drama "the woman is always subservient to the male. She is never portrayed as a serious partner or a breadwinner. TV tends to *demote* women." [30] Cretins, albinos, and mongoloids must be treated with respect by the television scriptwriter—but not so the American woman. She may be portrayed with impunity as stupid, grasping, selfish, fiendish, scatterbrained, unreliable, ignorant, irritating, and ridiculous—and no one says a word. Women are supposed to take it all like good sports —or like outsiders whose feelings are of no account.

On those serials purportedly dealing with the future, women, if they have any place at all, are invariably menials, performing slavish services for the all-important males. In *Lost in Space*, still being run and rerun and reviewed by ever renewed generations of children, the mythical difference between boys and girls is exaggerated to laughable proportions.

The office secretary, in motion pictures as well as on television, is portrayed as the servant of her boss—required to make and serve his coffee, administer his pills, attend to his personal shopping, brush his clothes, and even to straighten his tie and put his hat on his head. And through it all she is depicted as abjectly worshiping him and gratefully accepting the most condescending and inconsiderate treatment from him. That this is a faithful representation of the role and duties of the modern American female secretary and is even part of her training in business school is attested by the group of disillusioned British secretaries who recently left our shores, indignant at the expectation that they would double as valet, nursemaid, and butler to the American executive.

Even more devastating to feminine pride and dignity than the image of herself as an idiot and a menial is the stereotype of young women as "sex kittens" or "playboy bunnies," a demotion even from the nineteenth-century image of young women as household pets and playthings. Men seem to believe that women like to be thought of as sex objects, that they like to be ogled, mauled, patted, grabbed, pinched, and whistled at. Too many women pretend that this is true, that they are flattered to be whistled at by truck drivers. But this, like so many pretenses of women, is a lie deliberately designed to draw approving glances from the almighty male and is not the genuine sentiment of ninety percent of girls or women.

"TV commercials glorify women as sex objects and very little else. . . . Bunny psychology, however, is very degrading to women." [31] Two hundred years ago, Mary Wollstonecraft expressed the same revulsion at the portrayal of women as sex objects. "The pernicious tendency," she wrote in 1791, "of those books in which the writers insidiously degrade the sex while lauding their personal charms cannot be too severely exposed." [32]

As far back as 1965 the President's Commission on the Status of Women took note of the deleterious effect of such antifeminist propaganda and recommended that the broadcasting industry "modify existing stereotypes" and present a more realistic portrayal of women. Six years later, the offense is not only still being committed, it is being committed to an ever greater degree.

It is small wonder that the average American woman, unacquainted with past history and incapable of plumbing the depths of man's ancient psychopathic compulsion to punish her, accepts this image of herself and concludes that there must be some truth in it and that therefore she must deserve her place on the bottom rung of the latter. "It is obvious that these male ideologies function not only to reconcile women to their subordinate role by presenting it as an unalterable one, but also to plant the belief that it represents . . . an ideal for which it is commendable to strive." [33]

Men have succeeded so well in brainwashing women to a belief in their own incapacities that a recent poll of college girls revealed that the majority of the girls downgraded the work of professionals of their own sex and believed that men were better at *everything*— even teaching and dietetics—than women were.[34] An Institute of Public Opinion poll in 1963 showed that while fifty-eight percent of men would vote for a woman President, only fifty-one percent of women would do so. And Theodore Sorensen, writing in *Redbook* in April, 1968, said: "Not only do women fail to show any preference for female candidates; there appears to be some evidence that they often even oppose women for public office." [35]

This apparent lack of confidence in their own sex is the result of their overexposure to the current television image of them and the contempt and lack of respect shown to prominent women by male commentators and newsmen. Their antifeminist attitude is not the result of conviction but of indoctrination: they are still being taught, at home, at school, in church, and by all communications media, that they are the inferior sex.

Thus, as Lolli writes, "some women, because of real beliefs fostered by male society, or because of *opportunism,* are willing to endorse the very dubious superiority of men." [36] And Montagu says: "I'm not sure that all women know the truth [of man's inferiority to them]. It is time that they learned. . . . There appears to be a conspiracy of silence on the subject of male inferiority," and women are usually the first to rise to the defense of male supremacy, feeling, perhaps, "that men should be maintained in the illusion of their superiority because it might not be good for men to learn the truth." [37]

But it is not men that most women worry about when they rise to the defense of the status quo. Their apparent endorsement of male supremacy is, rather, a pathetic striving for self-respect, self-justification, and self-pardon. After fifteen hundred years of subjection to men, Western woman finds it almost unbearable to face the fact that she has been hoodwinked and enslaved by her *inferiors*— that the master is lesser than the slave. It would be unbearable to know with certainty, and to admit openly, that the long centuries of abuse and cruelty and disdain she has suffered at the hands of her masters were the result of an unnecessary miscarriage of justice, to know that she has been far more wronged than she had thought in the days when she had comforted herself with the church-generated belief that she was indeed inferior, that God had created her from man's rib to be man's slave, that her condition of servitude had been preordained, was right and just, was God's will, and was, above all, unalterable.

The innately logical mind of woman, her unique sense of balance, orderliness, and reason, rebels at the terrible realization that justice has been an empty word, that she has been forced for nearly two millennia to worship false gods and to prostrate herself at their empty shrines.

22

Woman in the Aquarian Age

*In sad plight would we be if we
might not already, lighting up the horizon
from East and West and North and South,
discern the new young women of today who, as the
period of feminine enslavement passes away,
send glances of recognition across the ages
to their elder sisters.*

—EDWARD CARPENTER

⏵§ In the eyes of man there are two kinds of women: the sex object, and "the other." The class of the sex object includes wife, mother, mistress, and the mass of nubile young women who may become wife, mother, or mistress. For this class of women men have a tolerance that conceals even from themselves the underlying fear and hatred that all men feel for all women.

"The other," the class of the non-sex-object, includes all unmarried women over forty, nearly all intellectual women, and above all, all women who are not primarily male-oriented. To the masculist these women have no human rights, no reason for existence. They are expendable. They are allowed to exist only if they accept their inferiority in a "womanly" way, asking nothing of life, expecting neither justice nor consideration, and proclaiming the shame in their sex that Saint Clement of Alexandria said all women should feel. "Every woman," said this pillar of the early church, "should be overwhelmed with shame at the thought that she is a woman."

And this Clementine philosophy has dominated the thought of Western society for nearly two thousand years. The belief is inherent in every phase of modern culture, in our customs, our attitudes, our educational values, in our very laws. In spite of the social advances of the past hundred years, the doctrine of female inferiority is still tacitly accepted by the vast majority of the population of the United States, female as well as male. "In actual fact," writes Horney, "a girl is exposed from birth onward to the suggestion—inevitable whether conveyed brutally or delicately—of her lack of worth, of her inferiority." [1] And conversely, a boy is taught from birth onward that he is the most valuable of God's creations. That this doctrine of male superiority is an artificial imposition, a purely Judeo-Christian misconception, is illustrated by a class viewed in January, 1969, on a Public Broadcast Laboratory program, in which black American women were being indoctrinated in the white man's attitude toward the sexes. The lesson of the class was that "men are the natural leaders, and black women must therefore support and respect them." "Male supremacy," said the instructor, "is based on three things: tradition, acceptance, and reason."

The instructor of the class was only repeating what she had been told to expound as the ideal relation between the sexes in a masculist society. But what "tradition"?—Judeo-Christian? What "acceptance"?—man's? And what "reason"?—none, but that of the baseless egoism of the male. Still, these black women who for untold millennia had been the brains, backbones, and breadwinners of their families, had to sit still and pretend to swallow this white masculist propaganada. It is interesting to speculate what the reaction would have been had the word *white* been substituted for *male*. "*White* supremacy is based on three things . . . !" Yet the canard of *male* supremacy can be no less insulting to women than that of *white* supremacy is to the black.

The black woman's lack of participation in the women's liberation movement was recently commented upon by a public figure who obviously did not understand that in her own world the black woman has no "identity" problem like the white woman's. It is only in the white world that sex is a handicap. Representative Shirley Chisholm of New York, the only black woman in the U.S. Congress, recently admitted in a television interview that in the white world her *sex* was a greater handicap than her *color*. In the civil rights movement black men and women have shared equally in the administrative and policy-making echelons; while in the various student movements, white girls complain that they are as-signed by the white boys to subordinate jobs such as addressing envelopes, making coffee, and serving as sex conveniences.

It is thus obvious that in Western society, at least, the cult of the inferiority of women is a product of our Judeo-Christian teaching and is neither natural nor innate in the human species. As a mat-ter of fact, it is the very reverse of nature's usual arrangement. In nature, the female is the all-important pillar that supports life, the male merely the ornament, the "afterthought," the expendable sexual adjunct. Observe with what care the female of all species is protected and sheltered and preserved by nature. It is the female, according to naturalists, biologists, and human geneticists, who is given the protective covering, the camouflaged plumage, the reserve food supply, the more efficient metabolism, the more spe-cialized organs, the greater resistance to disease, the built-in im-munity to certain specific ailments, the extra X chromosome, the more convoluted brain, the stronger heart, the longer life.[2] In nature's plan the male is but a "glorified gonad." [3] The female is the species.

If the human race is unhappy today, as all modern philosophers agree that it is, it is only because it is uncomfortable in the mirror-image society man has made—the topsy-turvy world in which na-ture's supporting pillar is forced to serve as the cornice of the architrave, while the cornice struggles to support the building. The fact is that men need women more than women need men; and so, aware of this fact, man has sought to keep woman depend-ent upon him economically as the only method open to him of mak-ing himself necessary to her. Since in the beginning woman would not become his willing slave, he has wrought through the centuries a society in which woman must serve him if she is to survive. For fifteen hundred years Western man has rationalized his enslave-ment of woman on the grounds of her "sexual role," the fact that, as Roy Wilkins said recently, "God made her that way," that God himself handicapped her by assigning to her the childbearing func-tion. This widespread belief, shared by modern masculists of both sexes, is based on two false premises: first, that all women must be and will be mothers; and second, that feminine functions are neces-sarily handicapping and crippling.

As a matter of cold statistics, however, the first assumption is palpably false. The U.S. Bureau of the Census reports that in 1967 of seventy-three million adult women in the United States only forty-three million, or forty-one percent, had "viable husbands"; and of these, only fifty-six percent, or twenty-four million, had minor children.[4] Thus, of all the adult women in the United States only thirty-two percent, less than one-third, fall into the category in which masculine ideology places *all* women.

Yet society persists in using the argument of woman's reproductive role as justification for keeping her in servitude. Because she has a womb she is not quite human; because she is blessed with life-giving equipment she is inferior. Because of the off-chance that she may become pregnant she must resign herself to accepting the second-best jobs, the second-best pay, the second-best education, the second-best medical care, the second-best justice—and even the second-best cut off the joint. She must expect to wait longer at the doors and windows of officialdom, to pay more for all services, and to be fair game for every bilking repairman, doctor, lawyer, merchant, chief, tinker, tailor, wiseman, thief. She must even be resigned to suffer needlessly, because the doctors of our country, ninety-five percent male, have been bred in the "curse of Eve" tradition that it is normal and natural for women to suffer. "God made them that way."

That woman is handicapped by her womanhood is the fault of society and not of nature. In earlier societies feminine functions were the norm, the adjunctive traits of the superior "majority" sex, and society adjusted itself to them. As we have seen, men even felt compelled to imitate these feminine functions in order to be "in" with the majority.

But patriarchal male-oriented society has turned these natural functions into peculiarities of the inferior minority, undesirable from the standpoint of male society except as they are necessary for the continuance of the race. And this is what has caused women's natural functions to become, in too many instances, real handicaps in an increasingly masculinized society. All women today live in a male world where women's human attributes are devalued and denied while their merely sexual attributes are overrated and overstressed. The awe with which man has always regarded the mysterious functions of women has ended in the male attempt to denigrate and brush under the rug the whole business and, with it, woman herself.

Such denial of personhood creates strain and tension in its victims and leads inevitably to feelings of insecurity. Primitive people, as well as apes and monkeys, reared in an atmosphere of constant tension also develop menstrual and childbearing difficulties that are unknown to them in their natural habitats. When women are once again treated and valued as persons and not as sex objects, when their selfhood and dignity are given the same consideration as are man's today, their "female handicaps" will disappear.

Certainly Tomyris, Hiera, Artimisia, Camilla, Veleda, Boadicea, Cartismandua, and Joan of Arc were not handicapped by their femininity in the most masculine of pursuits, that of war. To the ancients, feminine valor and heroism were not considered anomalous or freakish. Nor did they look upon creative and intellectual women of the breed of Aspasia, Sappho,[5] Corinna, and Nausicaa as anomalies. It is only in modern times that Western man has placed the "biological barrier" in woman's way. It was only after "the Church had gained a stranglehold . . . that woman, debarred from the priesthood and despised as the intellectual inferiors of their fathers and brothers, could nurse no aspirations beyond a husband, many children, and a Christian death." [6] Woman *must be a sex object*, a breeder, a mother, and no more because, in the dogma of the Christian Church, God made her that way.

The pagan philosopher Plato, over two thousand years ago, wrote: "The difference in the sexes consists only in women bearing children and men begetting them, and this does not prove that a woman differs from man in other respects." [7] In Plato's time and for long before in enlightened Greece, boys and girls received identical educations and prepared for identical lives of the mind.

In denial of all the aspersions on women's intelligence, it has long been observed that girl children are mentally quicker than boys, that they walk and talk earlier in life, learn to read and write sooner, and mature earlier. So obvious is this that today there is serious discussion in education circles of starting boys a year or two later in school so that they will not be outstripped by the girls. In the nineteenth century this very precocity of girls was held against them as constituting proof of their inferiority: ape babies and the offspring of African savages, went the argument, matured earlier than white children; and white human beings were certainly more intelligent than apes and African savages; *ergo,* male human beings were more intelligent than their feminine opposites.

When it was later found, after girls were again allowed to go to school with their brothers, that this female precocity persisted through all the school years, it was explained that girl students only *seemed* smarter than boys because, being smaller and manually more dexterous, they were better at reading and writing, and being more "docile" and submissive, they were better students. But this early superiority, parents and educators were assured, would vanish in college, where the "deeper" intellect of the boys would reveal itself. This worked fine through all the years when only the boys went to college. Everybody was convinced that even though sonny was a blockhead at sixteen compared to sister at fourteen, as soon as sonny got to college and sister dropped out of competition, sonny would come into his own.

Then, after the First World War, when sister also was allowed to go to college, *mirabile dictu,* sister was still smarter than sonny even in college. So now, how to explain that? After a few trial balloons, psychologists and educators came up with an answer: girls were better students in college because, having no *ambition* (!), they were willing to apply themselves to all their subjects equally. But just wait, they said, until graduate school. *Then* male intelligence and male aptitude for *abstract thought* would manifest themselves. We now bolster this belief by making it as difficult as possible for girls to go on to graduate school and advanced degrees —except in home economics and social work, where there is little male competition.

Yet a study published by the National Manpower Council of Columbia University in 1967 says, "Women . . . account for three out of five [college students] with ability to graduate, but do not." Of the high ability group, of whom women constitute nearly sixty percent, only one woman out of three hundred, or three-tenths of one percent, goes on to acquire, an advanced degree. Even before this point, however, seventy-five percent of the brainy women have been left behind at the high school gate. The same study revealed that a higher percentage of girls than of boys capable of college work graduate from high school each year. "But of this [gifted] group, one-half of the boys and only one-quarter of the girls enter and graduate from college." [8] Needless to say, a large number of boys who are not in this gifted group also go on to college, proving that we are not educating our best brains even at the college level, let alone at the graduate level.

The most wasteful "brain drain" in America today is the drain in the kitchen sink, down which flow daily with the dishwater the aspirations and the talents of the brainiest fifty-nine and ninety-seven-hundredths percent of our citizenry—housewives whose IQ's dwarf those of the husbands whose soiled dishes they are required to wash. Stendhal very truly said that "all geniuses who happen to be born women are lost to the world."

As for abstract thought, the last refuge of the masculine mental supremacists, Father Stanley de Zuska, head of the Mathematics Department of Boston College, said in an interview on May 30, 1968, that in his teaching of the new math to girls and boys of all ages, he had found that girls were more interested in and took more readily to abstract ideas than boys.[9] So much, then, for the old bromide of abstract thought for boys, rote memory for girls and idiots.

Only recently have we learned, from the study of nationwide tests, that girls, from kindergarten through college, actually are possessed of higher average IQ's than boys.

Still the belief persists, like the proverbial bloodstain in the stone, that women and girls are not as intelligent as men and boys! How much more proof to the contrary is required? Women are in the unfair position of having to prove over and over again, generation after generation, individual after individual, that they are at least as capable in all fields as are men. Their ability is never taken for granted. They must always demonstrate that they are in fact *superior* to the average male in order to receive any recognition at all. And in too many fields they are still denied even the opportunity to prove themselves.

Men insist that they don't mind women succeeding so long as they retain their "feminity." Yet the qualities that men consider "feminine"—timidity, submissiveness, obedience, silliness, and self-debasement—are the very qualities best guaranteed to assure the defeat of even the most gifted aspirant. And what *is* this vaunted "femininity"? To the masculists of both sexes, "femininity" implies all that *men* have built into the female image in the past few centuries: weakness, imbecility, dependence, masochism, unreliability, and a certain "babydoll" sexuality that is actually only a projection of male dreams. To the "feminist" of both sexes, femininity is synonymous with the eternal female principle, connoting strength, integrity, wisdom, justice, dependability, and a psychic power foreign and therefore dangerous to the plodding masculists of both sexes.

The misnamed "feminine" woman, so admired by her creator, man—the woman who is acquiescent in her inferiority and who has swallowed man's image of her as his ordained "helpmate" and no more—is in reality the "masculine" woman. The truly feminine woman "cannot help burning with that inner rage that comes from having to identify with her exploiter's negative image of her," and having to conform to her persecutor's idea of femininity and its man-decreed limitations.[10]

These latter are the women who "are determined that they will no longer endure the arrogant egoism of men, nor countenance in themselves or other women the craft and servility which are the necessary complements of the male-female relation." [11] They are the young women of today who, weary of their role as the vassals of man and the vessels of his lust, have set out to restore their own sex to its ancient dignity.

For all these reasons, social psychologists, both amateur and professional, insist that the modern American woman is "confused about her role." It is not woman, however, but man who is confused about woman's role. Man, not woman, clings to the outmoded patriarchal concept of woman as merely a helpmate to man. Woman looks further back, over the heads of the patriarchs, and she sees herself as nature intended her to be—the primary force in human advancement.

Ever since man first abrogated to himself the role of god on earth and proclaimed himself the master of woman, he has sought to mold her to his desires; and, as Mill says, by clipping here and watering there, by first freezing and then burning off unwanted growth, "he has cultivated woman for the benefit and pleasure of her master; and now he indolently believes that the tree grows of itself in the way that he has made it grow." [12] And so, like the majestic mountain pine, potted and pruned to grotesque dwarfism by a ruthless gardener, the stunted roots and branches of woman's essential being struggle to be free again, to know once more the boundless sky and unrestricting earth of ther native peak.

During most of man's history on earth, woman was the leader. Even in the brief period of historical times, before the invention of property and its complement of war and plunder, brains, insight, and understanding were far more important for survival than was brute strength. If brute strength had been the secret of survival, man would long ago have succumbed to the larger animals that coexisted with him. But force was not a necessity for survival. Perception, foresight, intuition, and intelligence were; and in these more important qualities women excelled. It was to the women that men looked for guidance, for the interpretation of natural phenomena, and for communication with nature and with divinity. Woman was prophet, priest, arbiter, medicine man, queen, and goddess.

Man's eventual discovery that force—physical coercion and brutality—could cow not only the smaller animals but even his own mental and spiritual superior, woman, was no doubt the "knowledge of evil" that constituted man's "original sin," his "fall from grace."

With the new consciousness of his physical superiority, man little by little appropriated to himself all of woman's traditional prerogatives, ousting her finally from the very throne from which she had educated and guided her people, and thrusting her further and further into the role of courtesan. Only in the past thousand years, a mere moment in time, has Western man succeeded in relegating her to an exclusively supporting role as an object of his sexual needs and a slave to his convenience. The result has been that which we see today—violence, misery, confusion, and the most pronounced *ideological* stratification of society ever experienced in history.

Man is by nature a pragmatic materialist, a mechanic, a lover of gadgets and gadgetry; and these are the qualities that characterize the "establishment" which regulates modern society: pragmatism, materialism, mechanization, and gadgetry. Woman, on the other hand, is a practical idealist, a humanitarian with a strong sense of *noblesse oblige,* an altruist rather than a capitalist.

Man is the enemy of nature: to kill, to root up, to level off, to pollute, to destroy are his instinctive reactions to the unmanufactured phenomena of nature, which he basically fears and distrusts.

Woman, on the other hand, is the ally of nature, and her instinct is to tend, to nurture, to encourage healthy growth, and to preserve ecological balance. She is the natural leader of society and of civilization, and the usurpation of her primeval authority by man has resulted in the uncoordinated chaos that is leading the human race inexorably back to barbarism.

Buckminster Fuller, on a television broadcast in 1968, shocked his studio audience into nervous giggles when he suggested that society might be saved by restoring women to their age-old leadership in government while men confine themselves to their gadgetry and games. This is excellent advice, and its heeding may constitute the last hope for mankind. Only masculine ego, an acquired characteristic and not an innate one, stands in the way of a decent society, dedicated to humanitarianism and characterized by the feminine virtues of selflessness, compassion, and empathy.

When man became enamored of his own image, the masculine defects of arrogance, conceit, pugnacity, and selfishness were transmuted into virtues by the alchemy of his own self-love; while their opposites, humility, gentleness, patience, concern, were debased into faults characteristic of the "weaker" sex.

When man first resolved to exalt the peculiarities of his own sex, muscularity and spiritual immaturity, he adopted the policy that reality meant tangibility and that what could not be seen or touched did not exist. "Anything that was imperceptible . . . to his senses was declared a doubtful or fictitious pseudo-value," as Pitirim Sorokin says.[18] By discrediting the mystic power of woman, man cut himself off from the higher things, the "eternal verities" the sense of which had distinguished him from the lower animals. By crushing every manifestation of supersensory or extrasensory truth and worshiping only sensate matter, man made of himself a mere biological organism and denied to himself the divine ray that once upon a time woman had revealed to him. Woman as magician, she who had allowed him to see himself with a rudimentary halo and a faint aura of immortality, now had to be declared of no value.

Her animal body, however, remained a necessary adjunct to the new physical man, and he set about to remold her from his own base material into a mere biological organism like himself—a fit mate, a help "meet" for him—his biological complement. Through the long centuries he succeeded in brainwashing her to the belief that she was indeed made from his rib, that she was formed to be a comfort to him, the receptacle of his seed, and the incubator of *his* heirs, who were the perpetuators of *his* name.

Thus the sacred flame of her primordial and divine authority was banked and dampened and finally smothered almost to extinction. Throughout the Arian and Piscean ages of strife and materialism, man's denser nature held sway while woman's etheric light lay hidden under the bushel of masculine domination.

We are on the threshold of the new Age of Aquarius, whom the Greeks called Hydrochoos, the water-bearer, the renewer, the reviver, the quencher of raging fire and of thirst. It was at the dawn of another aquarian age, fifty-two thousand years ago, that Basilea, the great queen, brought order and justice to a chaotic world aflame with lawlessness and strife, a world similar to our own of the twentieth century. Today, as then, women are in the vanguard of the aborning civilization; and it is to the women that we look for salvation in the healing and restorative waters of Aquarius.

It is to such a new age that we look now with hope as the present age of masculism succeeds in destroying itself, as have all its predecessors in the incredibly long history of civilizations on our globe. The oldest written history we have today tells of the Sumerian goddess Tiamat, who many thousands of years ago *restored* civilization to a dying race of men. In Egypt the great queen-goddess Isis brought a new and revived civilization after Typhon and Osiris in their wars had destroyed an earlier civilization. Plato writes that the goddess Athene created a new race of Greeks after the Titans had brought the old order crashing to a fiery end. And in Polynesian myth the goddess Atea re-created the world after the sky had fallen in flames, lit by a terrible war of the old gods.

In the 1930's and '40's, Pitirim Sorokin, the Harvard sociologist, foresaw the present sociocultural revolution of the '60's and '70's and predicted that it would mark the end of civilization as we have known it in historical times, that it would herald "one of the great transitions in human history from one of its main forms of culture to another." [14] Sorokin describes this new culture in terms that agree to an amazing extent with other men's descriptions of matriarchy—a utopia founded on love and trust, mutual respect and concern, in which all men and women are truly brothers and sisters

under the just guidance of a beneficent deity and where laws are
enforced by persuasion and goodwill rather than by force and coercion.

In *Critias,* Plato says that the goddess Athene "tended us human
beings as a shepherd tends her sheep—not with blows or bodily
force but by the rudder of *persuasion.* Thus did she guide her mortal creation." [15] During the golden and silver ages of goddess-rule,
writes Hesiod, "men lived without cares, never growing old or
weary, dancing and laughing much; death to them was no more terrible than sleep." Contrarily, after the demise of the goddess, "the
optimistic conception of the next world, in which [mankind] had
believed in resurrection in the bosom of the Great Goddess, gave
way to a gloomy pessimism. . . . With the retreat of the primitive
maternal world and the appearance of new male gods, the world
grew ugly. . . ." [16]

The rot of masculist materialism has indeed permeated all spheres
of twentieth-century life and now attacks its very core. The only
remedy for the invading and consuming rot is a return to the values
of the matriarchates, and the rediscovery of the nonmaterial universe that had so humanizing an influence on the awakening minds
of our ancestors. Physicists of many nations are today gaining a
new understanding of this invisible world as they discover almost
daily some new phenomenon of nature that cannot be explained by
our accepted laws of physics. There is, apparently, a physics of the
supernatural whose laws modern man has been totally unaware of
and to which he is only now becoming attuned.

It was the knowledge of this other world, possessed by the women
of old and utterly discredited by later materialistic man, that gave
early woman her power over man.

The elevation of woman over man arouses our amazement most
especially by its contradiction to the relation of physical strength.
Nature seems to confer the sceptre of power on the stronger. If
it is torn from him by a weaker hand, *other aspects of Nature*
must have been at work, deeper powers must have made their
influence felt. We scarcely need the help of ancient witnesses to
realize what power had most to do with woman's victory. At all
times woman has exerted a great influence on men and on the
education and culture of nations through her inclination towards
the supernatural and divine. In innumerable cases woman was the

recipient and the repository of the first revelation. This observation is confirmed by the historical facts of all times and all peoples. Prophecy began with women. Though physically weaker, woman is capable of rising far above man. To man's superior physical strength woman opposes the mighty influence of her consecration: she counters violence with peace, enmity with conciliation, hate with love. And thus she guides wild and lawless man towards a milder, gentler culture, in whose center she sits enthroned as the embodiment of the higher principle, the manifestation of divine commandment. Herein lies the magic power of the woman, which makes her the sacrosanct prophetess and judge, and in all things gives her will the prestige of supreme law. Endowed with such powers *the weaker sex can take up the struggle with the stronger and emerge triumphant* [author's italics].[17]

The ages of masculism are now drawing to a close. Their dying days are lit up by a final flare of universal violence and despair such as the world has seldom before seen. Men of goodwill turn in every direction seeking cures for their perishing society, but to no avail. Any and all social reforms superimposed upon our sick civilization can be no more effective than a bandage on a gaping and putrefying wound. Only the complete and total demolition of the social body will cure the fatal sickness. Only the overthrow of the three-thousand-year-old beast of masculist materialism will save the race.

In the new science of the twenty-first century, not physical force but spiritual force will lead the way. Mental and spiritual gifts will be more in demand than gifts of a physical nature. Extrasensory perception will take precedence over sensory perception. And in this sphere woman will again predominate. She who was revered and worshiped by early man because of her power to see the unseen will once again be the pivot—not as sex but as divine woman—about whom the next civilization will, as of old, revolve.

Notes

INTRODUCTION

1. The cognitive minority is a group of people whose view of the world differs significantly from the one generally taken for granted in its society. It is this minority, considered offbeat by its contemporaries, that nearly always foresees the true knowledge of the future. The term "knowledge" always refers to what is *taken* to be or is *believed* to be "knowledge." The use of the term is strictly neutral on the question of whether socially held knowledge is true or false. It represents only that which has always been believed or that which it is socially acceptable to believe. True knowledge is derived from a body of facts that will not go away, no matter how these facts may be interpreted or misinterpreted by the establishment. True knowledge is always a generation or two ahead of the disseminators of what is known as knowledge—that is, socially accepted knowledge.—With acknowledgment to Peter L. Berger, *A Rumor of Angels* (New York, Doubleday, 1969).
2. Sylvain Bailly, *A History of Ancient and Modern Astronomy* (1776), as quoted in Vol. II Alexander Tytler, Lord Woodhouselee, *Universal History,* (Boston, Jordan & Wiley, 1846), p. 356.
3. Geoffrey Ashe, *The Quest for Arthur's Britain* (New York, Praeger, 1969), pp. 235, 238.
4. R. J. Cruikshank, *Charles Dickens and Early Victorian England* (London, Pitman, 1949), p. 150.
5. Karen Horney, *Feminine Psychology* (New York, Norton, 1967), p. 136.
6. Edward Carpenter, *Love's Coming of Age* (Manchester, England, Labour Press, 1896), p. 28.
7. Margaret Sanger, *Woman and the New Race* (New York, Brentano's, 1930), pp. 168–69.
8. Anne Biezanek, *All Things New* (New York, Harper and Row, 1964), p. 98.

PROLOGUE—The Lost Civilization

1. A tradition preserved among the Chaldeans, and chronicled by Berosus, Polyhistor, Abydenus, and Apollodorus, dated the beginning of civilization on earth at 120 sari, or 432,000 years, before the Biblical Flood. See I. S. Shklovskii and Carl Sagan, *Intelligent Life in the Universe* (San Francisco, Holden Day, 1966), p. 458; and Immanuel Velikovsky, *Worlds in Collision* (New York, Macmillan, 1950), p. 334.
2. G. Ernest Wright, *Schechem* (London, Duckworth, 1965), p. 17.
3. Jean Jacques Rousseau, "Essay on Inequality," in *Beaconlights of Western Culture,* Vol. I (Boston, Beacon Press, 1952), p. 334.
4. Georg Wilhelm Hegel, *Reason in History,* trans. by Robert Hartman (New York, Liberal Arts Press, 1953), pp. 76–77.

5. Theodor Mommsen, *The History of Rome,* Vol. I, trans. by William P. Dickson (New York, Scribner's, 1903), p. 18.

6. In Hindu myth, civilization was first introduced by "red men of the southern continent" 50,000 years before Christ (our reckoning). See Edouard Schuré, *The Great Initiates,* Vol. I (New York, McKay, 1913), p. 6. The redness or red-hairedness of these original civilizers may be reflected in the name Adam (red man); in the convention of the Egyptian artists of painting their own countrymen's likenesses red; in the red topknot (hair) of the Easter Island megaliths; in the astonished reaction to the red-haired Celts by the Mediterranean peoples, reported by Terence Powell, and of the early people of India at the appearance of Celtic Rama and his red-blond followers; also in the names of the Erythrean (Red) Sea for the Persian Gulf, and the Red Sea between Arabia and Egypt.

7. Flavius Josephus, *Antiquities of the Jews,* Vol. I (Philadelphia, Woodward, 1825), p. 9.

8. Louis Ginzberg, *The Legends of the Jews,* 6th ed., Vol. I (Philadelphia, Jewish Publications Society, 1909), p. 5.

9. Shklovskii and C. Sagan, *op. cit.,* p. 456 ff.

10. S. R. K. Glanville, *The Legacy of Egypt,* as quoted in Charles Hapgood, *Maps of the Ancient Sea Kings* (Philadelphia, Chilton, 1966), p. 197.

11. H. J. Massingham, *Downland Man* (New York, Doran, 1936), pp. 83–102.

12. Hugh Auchincloss Brown, *Cataclysms of the Earth* (New York, Twayne, 1967), p. 69; also Hapgood, *op. cit.,* p. 107.

13. Mommsen, *op. cit.,* pp. 20, 39. Further proof of the vast antiquity of sea travel is offered by the evidence that the words for "ship" and for "sea" occurred in the original Indo-European language.

14. Herodotus tells the tale of the Egyptian captain who was impaled by the pharaoh because he refused to sail as ordered beyond Gibraltar into the ocean. He preferred certain death to sea travel.

15. Terence G. E. Powell, *The Celts* (New York, Praeger, 1958), p. 66.

16. Edmund Curtis, *A History of Ireland,* 6th ed. (London, Methuen, 1950), p. 1.

17. Herodotus, *The Histories,* Bk. IV, trans. by George Rawlinson (New York, Tudor, 1944), p. 206.

18. *Ibid.,* Bk. V, pp. 294–95; Plutarch, *De Defectu Oraculorum,* as quoted in Louis H. Gray, ed., *Mythology of All Races,* Vol. III (New York, Cooper Square, 1964), p. 15.

19. Richard Payne Knight, *A Discourse on the Worship of Priapus* (1786) (London, The Dilettanti Society, n.d.), p. 34.

20. Mommsen, *op. cit.,* p. 21.

21. Herodotus, *op. cit.,* Bk. IV, p. 207.

22. Charles Fort, *The Book of the Damned* (New York, The Fortean Society, 1944), p. 32 ff.

23. Lewis Spence, *History of Atlantis* (New Hyde Park, New York, University Books, 1968), p. 94.

24. Plato, *Critias,* in *The Works of Plato,* trans. by Benjamin Jowett (New York, Tudor, n.d.), p. 383.

25. Plato, *Republic,* in *The Works of Plato,* trans. by Benjamin Jowett (New York, Tudor, n.d.), p. 191.

26. Spence, *op. cit.,* pp. 94–5.

27. Plato, *Timaeus,* in *The Works of Plato,* trans. by Benjamin Jowett (New York, Tudor, n.d.), p. 367.

28. Plato, *Critias, op. cit.,* p. 382.

29. Peter H. Buck, *Vikings of the Pacific* (Chicago, University of Chicago Press, 1959), p. 48.

30. J. J. Bachofen, *Myth, Religion and Mother Right: Selected Writings of Johann Jakob Bachofen,* trans. by Ralph Manheim (Princeton, Princeton University Press, 1967), p. 150.

31. Spence, *op. cit.*, p. 100.
32. As quoted in Alexander Tytler, Lord Woodhouselee, *Universal History*, Vol. II (Boston, Jordan & Wiley, 1846), p. 358.

CHAPTER 1—Woman and the Second Sex

1. *The Enuma Elish*, trans. by William Muss-Arnolt, in *Assyrian and Babylonian Literature, Selected Translations* (New York, Appleton, 1901), p. 382 ff.
2. Plato, *The Symposium*, in *The Works of Plato*, trans. by Benjamin Jowett (New York, Tudor, n.d.), p. 315 ff.
3. J. J. Bachofen, *Myth, Religion and Mother Right*, trans. by Ralph Manheim (Princeton, Princeton University Press, 1967), p. 112.
4. Raymond de Becker, *The Other Face of Love*, trans. by M. Crosland and A. Daventry (New York, Grove, 1969), p. 187.
5. Susan Michelmore, *Sexual Reproduction* (New York, Natural History Press, 1964), p. 130.
6. Frank Lester Ward, as quoted in Helen Beale Woodward, *The Bold Women* (New York, Farrar, 1953), p. 339.
7. Robert Graves, *The Greek Myths*, Vol. I (New York, Braziller, 1957), p. 37.
8. James Mellaart, *Catal Huyuk* (New York, McGraw-Hill, 1967), pl. 84 (caption).
9. Graves, *op. cit.*, Vol. I, p. 13.
10. *Ibid.*, p. 28.
11. Bachofen, *op. cit.*, pp. 174-75.
12. Charles Seltman, *The Twelve Olympians* (New York, Apollo, 1962), p. 27.
13. Robert Eisler, *Man into Wolf* (London, Spring Books, 1949), p. 177.
14. Graves, *op. cit.*, Vol. II, p. 163.
15. Margaret Mead, *Male and Female* (New York, Morrow, 1949), p. 98.
16. Robert Briffault, *The Mothers* (New York, Grosset & Dunlop, 1963), p. 398.
17. *Journal of Expedition and Discovery into Central America*, 1:212 (1845).
18. *Ibid.*, p. 273.
19. Paolo Mantegazza, *The Sexual Relations of Mankind* (Baltimore, Maryland, Eugenics Publishing Co., 1935), p. 113.
20. *Ibid.*
21. John Davenport, *Curiositates Eroticae Physiologiae* (London, privately printed, 1875), p. 85.
22. Theodor Reik, *The Creation of Woman* (New York, Braziller, 1960), pp. 115-16.
23. Euripides, *The Bacchae*, trans. by Gilbert Murray, as quoted in Jane Ellen Harrison, *Epilegomena to the Study of Greek Religion* (New York, University Books, 1962), p. 33.
24. Mead, *op. cit.*, p. 104.
25. *Ibid.*, p. 103.
26. Bachofen, *op. cit.*, pp. 79, 144.
27. Buckminster Fuller, "The Goddesses," *Saturday Review* 51(9):14,45 (March 2, 1968).
28. Graves, *op. cit.*, Vol. I, p. 13.
29. Kenneth MacGowan and Joseph A. Hester, Jr., *Early Man in the New World*, rev. ed. (New York, Doubleday, 1962), pp. 37-38.
30. *Ibid.*, pp. 38-39.
31. *Ibid.*, p. 39.
32. *Ibid.*, pp. 38, 41.
33. *Ibid.*, p. 41.
34. *Ibid.*, p. 39.
35. Irven DeVore, as quoted in *The Christian Science Monitor* (June 3, 1969).
36. Joseph Goetz, *Prehistoric Religions*, in Frederic-Marie Bergounioux, *Primitive and Prehistoric Religions*, trans. by C. R. Busby (New York, Hawthorn, 1966), pp. 65-66.

37. Briffault, *op. cit.*, p. 208.
38. Theodor Mommsen, *The History of Rome*, Vol. I, trans. by William P. Dickson (New York, Scribner's, 1903), pp. 20–21.
39. Bachofen, *op. cit.*, p. 91.
40. *Ibid.*
41. *Ibid.*, p. 92.
42. *Ibid.*, p. 106.
43. Graves, *op. cit.*, Vol. I, p. 257.
44. Herodotus, *The Histories*, Bk. I, trans. by George Rawlinson (New York, Tudor, 1944), pp. 37, 68–69.
45. See Chapter 8.
46. *The Interpreter's Dictionary of the Bible* (Nashville, Abingdon Press, 1962).
47. Louis H. Gray, ed., *The Mythology of All Races*, Vol. V (New York, Cooper Square, 1964), p. 403.
48. Robert Eisler, *Man Into Wolf*, (London, Spring Books, 1949), p. 183, n. 157: "Tag-Tug is an alternative transliteration of identical cuneiform characters as those for Tibir."
49. Herodotus, *op. cit.*, p. 222.
50. Graves, *op. cit.*, Vol. I, p. 96.
51. Jacques Heurgeon, *Daily Life of the Etruscans* (New York, Macmillan, 1964), p. 96.
52. B. Z. Goldberg, *The Sacred Fire* (New York, Liveright, 1930), p. 123.
53. Bachofen, *op. cit.*, p. 144.
54. Edouard Schuré, *The Great Initiates*, Vol. I (New York, McKay, 1913), p. 15.
55. H. L. Mencken, *In Defense of Women* (New York, Knopf, 1922), pp. 17–18.
56. Bachofen, *op. cit.*, p. 144.
57. Schuré, *op. cit.*, p. 11 ff.
58. Leonard Cottrell, ed., *Concise Encyclopedia of Archaeology* (New York, Hawthorn, 1960), p. 400.
59. Violeta Miqueli, *Woman in Myth and History* (New York, Vantage, 1962), p. 143.
60. Henry Fairfield Osborn, *Men of the Old Stone Age* (New York, Scribner's, 1915), pp. 315–16. Also *cf.* Mellaart, *op. cit.*, p. 23.
61. Leonard Cottrell, *Realms of Gold* (New York, New York Graphic Society, 1963), p. 104.
62. Seltman, *op. cit.*, p. 27.

CHAPTER 2—Mythology Speaks

1. A. C. Haddon, "Introduction," in E. B. Tylor, *Anthropology*, Vol. I (London, Watts, 1930), p. vii.
2. *Ibid.*, p. viii.
3. H. J. Massingham, *Downland Man* (New York, Doran, 1936), p. 291.
4. *Ibid.*, p. 297.
5. As quoted in *Ibid.*
6. Tacitus, *Germania*, in *Complete Works of Tacitus*, trans. by A. J. Church and W. J. Brodribb, (New York, Modern Library, 1942), p. 728.
7. Massingham, *op. cit.*, p. 297.
8. Richard Payne Knight, *A Discourse on the Worship of Priapus* (London, The Dilettanti Society, n.d.), p. 34.
9. John A. McCulloch, "Celtic Mythology," in Louis H. Gray, ed., *The Mythology of All Races*, Vol. III (New York, Cooper Square, 1964), p. 117.
10. As quoted in I. S. Shklovskii and Carl Sagan, *Intelligent Life in the Universe* (San Francisco, Holden Day, 1966), p. 457. Berosus is quoted by Polyhistor.
1. Sabine Baring-Gould, *Curious Myths of the Middle Ages* (New York, University Books, 1967), p. 500.

12. As quoted in Theodor Reik, *Pagan Rites in Judaism* (New York, Farrar, 1964), p. 70.

13. Peter N. Buck, *Vikings of the Pacific* (Chicago, University of Chicago Press, 1959), p. 73.

14. Robert Briffault, *The Mothers* (New York, Grosset & Dunlop, 1963), p. 342. The genetic symbol for the female— ♀ —is the ancient symbol for the moon-goddess— her cross surmounted by the full moon.

15. Hesiod, *Works and Days*, as quoted in Plato, *Republic*, in *The Works of Plato*, trans. by Benjamin Jowett, Bk. V (New York, Tudor, n.d.), p. 205.

16. Edward Gibbon, *The Decline and Fall of the Roman Empire*, Vol. II (New York, Hurst, n.d.), p. 297; Harold Mattingly, *Christianity in the Roman Empire* (New York, Norton, 1967), p. 72.

17. Shklovskii and Sagan, *op. cit.*, pp. 459–60.

18. *Ibid.*, p. 461. Since Venus is a new planet, as Immanuel Velikovsky theorized (*Worlds in Collision*) and as recent Venus probes seem to indicate, and had not yet appeared in the sky in Sumerian times, it is possible that the ninth planet was Hypotheticus, the lost planet that once orbited our sun just beyond the orbit of Mars and which is now represented by the thousands of planetoids, or asteroids, that pursue the same orbit today. (See Dandridge Cole, *Islands in Space*. Philadelphia, Chilton Books, 1964.) It is possible, as Velikovsky writes, that this hypothetical planet was destroyed by the *comet* Venus on its way to its present position and its metamorphosis into planethood. This comet may have struck earth, also, in its passage through space, thus causing the shifting of earth's axis that resulted in the world catastrophe of historical times. It could well have caused, too, the slowing down of the earth's rotation on its axis as well as of its revolution around the sun, thus accounting for the shorter day and shorter year of Sumerian, ancient Egyptian, and ancient Mexican (Toltec and Mayan) calendars. It is impossible that the Sumerians and Egyptians, at any rate, could have been wrong in their measurement of diurnal and solar time, knowledgeable as they were in astronomy and other sciences that modern man is just beginning to learn.

19. Herodotus, *The Histories*, Bk. VII, trans. by George Rawlinson (New York, Tudor, 1944), p. 389.

20. *Ibid.*, p. 214.

21. Geoffrey of Monmouth, *History of the Kings of Britain* (London, Penguin, 1965), p. 65.

22. *Ibid.*

23. Thomas Fuller, *The Worthies of England* (London, Allen and Unwin, 1952), p. 344.

24. Knight, *op. cit.*, p. 34.

25. *Ibid.* Similar mines were discovered in the eighteenth century in Krasnoyarsk, Siberia, by a team of "antiquarians" commissioned by the Empress Catherine the Great of Russia. "There were ancient mines discovered which had been wrought in some former period, of which there is no account or tradition. Near Krasnoyarsk they found ornaments of copper and gold; some of them adorned and embossed with figures of exquisite workmanship. There is a curious circumstance which evidences the prodigious antiquity of these mines. The props are now petrified, and this petrifaction contains gold. So much time has therefore elapsed since these props were erected that nature has gone through the tedious process of forming metals; and the same course of time has entirely annihilated every vestige of the towns and houses in which these miners must have dwelt, for we must suppose they dwelt in towns. *But of such towns and edifices not a trace remains.*" (Author's italics.)—Alexander Tytler, Lord Woodhouselee, *Universal History*, Vol. II (Boston, Jordan & Wiley, 1846), p. 360.

This puzzling lack of dwelling places is reminiscent of the ancient mines and megalithic fortlike structure at Zimbabwe in Rhodesia, where the lack of dwellings has led archeologists to conclude that the mysterious gold miners and builders of ancient Zimbabwe were visitors and not inhabitants of the country in which they mined for gold. Where they came from, or when, and whither they carried the gold they mined, remains a mystery, as does the identity of the ancient miners of Krasnoyarsk and of Thrace.

26. Gibbon, *op. cit.*, p. 312.
27. Philostratus, *Apollonius of Tyana*, trans. by J. S. Phillimore, Vol. II, Bk. 8 (London, Oxford University Press, 1912), p. 233.
28. W. K. C. Guthrie, *Orpheus and Greek Religion*, rev. ed. (New York, Norton, 1966), p. 224.
29. Robert Graves, *The Greek Myths*, Vol. I (New York, Braziller, 1957), p. 113.
30. "Druidism," *Encyclopaedia Britannica*, 11th ed.
31. Porphyry, "The Life of Pythagoras," in Moses Hadas, ed., *Heroes and Gods* (London, Routledge, 1965), pp. 105–28.
32. *Ibid.*, p. 112.
33. Geoffrey of Monmouth, *op. cit.*, p. 65.
34. Robert Graves, *On Poetry* (New York, Doubleday, 1969), p. 13.
35. E. R. Dodds, *The Greeks and the Irrational*, as quoted in Hadas, *op. cit.*, p. 39.
36. Not only were Morgan le Fay, Morrigan, and Morgana Celtic fairy queens, but Queen Medb or Mav, "the greatest personality of the Irish Heroic Age," as Dillon and Chadwick dub her, after her quite natural death became a fairy queen of the underworld—*the* fairy queen, Queen Mab, in fact. Celtic heroes from Cuchulain to Arthur had affairs with fairy women, most of them to their sorrow but some to their great benefit. As an example of the latter, Marie of France tells a beautiful lay of a fairy queen who greatly assists her mortal lover, Sir Graelent of Brittany. (See *The Lays of Marie de France*, trans. by Eugene Mason. London, Dent, 1911, pp. 148–62.)
37. Robert Graves, *The White Goddess* (New York, Farrar, 1948), p. 115. Apollonius Rhodius said that these were the oaks that Orpheus' music had caused to dance down from the Pierian Mount.
38. Lewis Spence, *The History of Atlantis* (New York, University Books, 1968), p. 112.
39. André Parrot, *Nineveh and the Old Testament* (New York, Philosophical Library, 1955), p. 24.
40. Spence, *op. cit.*, p. 185.
41. A. B. Cook, *Zeus*, as quoted in Guthrie, *op. cit.*, p. 147, n. 38.
42. Guthrie, *op. cit.*, p. 115.
43. Leonard Cottrell, *Realms of Gold* (New York, New York Graphic Society, 1963), p. 163.
44. Guthrie, *op. cit.*, p. 115.
45. Spence, *op. cit.*, p. 42.
46. *Ibid.*, p. 182.
47. *Ibid.*, p. 183.
48. U. Bahadir Alkim, *Anatolia I*, trans. by James Hogarth (New York, World, 1968), p. 65.
49. Spence, *op. cit.*, p. 183.

CHAPTER 3—The Golden Age and the Blessed Lady

1. Norman O. Brown, *Hermes the Thief: the Evolution of a Myth* (Madison, University of Wisconsin Press, 1947), p. 60.
2. Hesiod, *Works and Days*, as quoted in Robert Graves, *The Greek Myths*, Vol. I (New York, Braziller, 1957), p. 36.
3. *Ibid.*
4. *Ibid.*

5. Erich Fromm, *The Art of Loving* (New York, Harper, 1956), p. 55.
6. Graves, *op. cit.*, p. 36.
7. Terence G. E. Powell, *The Celts* (New York, Praeger, 1958), pp. 162, 177–78. This fact renders the etymology of "pixie," the little dark men of faerie, from "Picts" ludicrous and impossible. The Celts were large and blond.
8. Stuart Piggott, ed., *The Dawn of Civilization* (New York, McGraw-Hill, 1961), p. 224.
9. Graves, *op. cit.*, p. 36.
10. The people of the Golden Age at the time of the patriarchal Zeus revolution in Thrace had ascended to the upper world and had become minor gods and goddesses; whereas the people of the Silver and Bronze ages were consigned by the Iron Age Dorians to Hades—all on account of "their refusal to pay due honor to Zeus and his Olympians."—Erwin Rohde, *Psyche*, Vol. I, trans. by W. B. Hillis (New York, Harper, 1966), p. 73.
11. Jane Ellen Harrison, "Themis," in her *Epilegomena to the Study of Greek Religion and Themis* (New Hyde Park, New York, University Books, 1962), p. 498.
12. Robert Briffault, *The Mothers* (New York, Grosset & Dunlop, 1963), p. 95. In the third century A.D. another woman, Julia Soemias, was to sit in the Roman Senate and "was placed by the side of the consuls, and subscribed as a regular member the decrees of the legislative assembly."—Edward Gibbon, *The Decline and Fall of the Roman Empire*, Vol. I (New York, Hurst, n.d.), p. 148.
13. Virgil, "Eclogue IV," in *Poems of Virgil*, trans. by James Rhoades (Oxford, England, Oxford University Press, 1921), pp. 401–2.
14. Lucretius, *De Rerum Natura*, trans. by H. A. J. Munro (London, Bell, 1929), pp. 1–2.
15. H. J. Massingham, *Downland Man* (New York, Doran, 1936), p. 351.
16. James Breasted, *The History of Egypt* (New York, Scribner's, 1912), pp. 135, 17.
17. Arthur Evans, as quoted in Massingham, *op. cit.*, p. 101.
18. Leonard Cottrell, *The Land of Shinar* (London, Souvenir Press, 1965), pp. 123, 126.
19. Leonard Woolley, *A Forgotten Kingdom* (London, Penguin, 1953), p. 116.
20. G. Ernest Wright, *Shechem* (London, Duckworth, 1965), p. 17.
21. Massingham, *op. cit.*, p. 217 ff.
22. August Thebaud, *Ireland Past and Present* (New York, Collier, 1878), p. 71.
23. *Ibid.*, p. 68.
24. G. Eliot Smith, as quoted in Massingham, *op. cit.*, p. 352.
25. E. O. James, *The Cult of the Mother Goddess* (New York, Praeger, 1959), p. 250.
26. Theodor Reik, *Pagan Rites in Judaism* (New York, Farrar, 1964), p. 76.
27. Robert Aron, *The God of the Beginnings* (New York, Morrow, 1966), pp. 10–11.
28. Raphael Patai, *The Hebrew Goddess* (New York, Ktav, 1968).
29. E. O. James, *The Ancient Gods* (New York, Putnam's, 1960), p. 91.
30. Reik, *op. cit.*, pp. 69–70.
31. James, *The Ancient Gods, op. cit.*, pp. 91–92.
32. *Ibid.*, p. 40. Such was the case in Greece, Egypt, Phrygia, Syria, Iraq, Palestine, and Canaan.
33. Oswald Spengler, *The Decline of the West* (New York, Knopf, 1926).
34. Ruth Benedict, *Patterns of Culture* (Boston, Houghton-Mifflin, 1935), p. 59.
35. Edward Carpenter, *Love's Coming of Age* (Manchester, England, Labour Press, 1896), p. 28
36. James, *The Cult of the Mother Goddess, op. cit.*, p. 260.
37. Robert Graves, *The White Goddess* (New York, Farrar, 1948), p. 391.
38. Paul Misraki, *Les Extraterrestress* (Paris, Plon, 1962).
39. Barry H. Downing, *The Bible and Flying Saucers* (Philadelphia, Lippincott, 1968).
40. Apuleius, *The Golden Ass*, trans. by W. Adlington (London, Heinemann, 1915), pp. 545–47.
41. *Ibid*, p. 551.

42. Carpenter, *op. cit.*, p. 133.
43. Apuleius, *op. cit.*, p. 543.

CHAPTER 4—Archeology Speaks

1. James Mellaart, *Earliest Civilizations in the Near East* (New York McGraw-Hill, 1965), p. 18.
2. Ivar Lissner, *Man, God, and Magic* (New York, Putnam's, 1961), p. 192.
3. *Ibid.*, p. 209.
4. E. O. James, *The Cult of the Mother Goddess* (New York, Praeger, 1959), pp. 45, 11, 180.
5. Wolfhart Westendorf, *Painting, Sculpture, and Architecture of Ancient Egypt* (New York, Abrams, 1968), p. 13.
6. Glyn Daniel, ed., *Ancient Peoples and Places* (New York, Praeger, 1956–).
7. J. J. Bachofen, *Myth, Religion and Mother Right*, trans. by Ralph Manheim (Princeton, Princeton University Press, 1967), p. 71.
8. *Ibid.*, p. 70.
9. Sabine Baring-Gould, *Curious Myths of the Middle Ages* (New Hyde Park, New York, University Books, 1967), p. 126.
10. *Ibid.*, p. 127.
11. Bachofen, *op. cit.*, pp. 150–51.
12. Alexander Pope, "Preface," in Homer, *Iliad*, trans. by Alexander Pope (London, Oxford University Press, n.d.), p. vii.
13. Erwin Rohde, *Psyche*, Vol. I, trans. by W. B. Hillis (New York, Harper, 1966), p. 69.
14. As quoted in Joseph Campbell, "Introduction," in Bachofen, *op. cit.*, p. xxxi.
15. Erich Fromm, *The Forgotten Language* (New York, Holt, 1951), p. 210.
16. Campbell, *op. cit.*, p. lv.
17. U. Bahadir Alkim, *Anatolia I*, trans. by James Hogarth (New York, World, 1968), p. 65.
18. Jean Marcadé, "Preface," in Alkim, *op. cit.*, p. 11.
19. Alkim, *op. cit.*, p. 68.
20. *Ibid.*, p. 47.
21. *Ibid.*, p. 78.
22. *Ibid.*, p. 68.
23. *Ibid.*, p. 70.
24. James Mellaart, *Catal Huyuk* (New York, McGraw-Hill, 1967), pp. 60, 202, 207, 225, chaps. VI, IX–XI.
25. Bachofen, *op. cit.*, pp. 80–81.
26. *Ibid.*, p. 139.
27. A. M. Hocart, *Social Origins* (London, Watts, 1954), p. 3.
28. Alkim, *op. cit.*, p. 68.
29. *Ibid.*
30. *Ibid.*, p. 62.
31. Bachofen, *op. cit.*, p. 141.
32. Frederic-Marie Bergounioux, *Primitive and Prehistoric Religions*, trans. by C. R. Busby (New York, Hawthorn, 1966), p. 50.
33. J. F. S. Stone, *Wessex before the Celts* (New York, Praeger, 1958), p. 98.
34. Alkim, *op. cit.*, p. 68.
35. Mellaart, *Catal Huyuk, op. cit.*, pl. 84 (caption).
36. Kenneth MacGowan, *Early Man in the New World*, rev. ed. (New York, Doubleday, 1962), pp. 40–41.
37. Axel Persson, as quoted in Leonard Cottrell, *Realms of Gold* (New York, New York Graphic Society, 1963), p. 96.
38. Mellaart, *Catal Huyuk, op. cit.*, pp. 207, 225.

39. As quoted in Leonard Cottrell, *The Land of Shinar* (London, Souvenir Press, 1965), p. 116.
40. *Ibid.*, p. 113.
41. Jacques Heurgeon, *Daily Life of the Etruscans*, trans. by James Kirkup (New York, Macmillan, 1964), pp. 94, 95.
42. Mellaart, *Catal Huyuk, op. cit.*, p. 207.
43. Stone, *op. cit.*, p. 108.
44. Bergounioux, *op. cit.*, p. 57.
45. G. E. Mylonas, *Ancient Mycenae* (Princeton, Princeton University Press, 1957), pp. 147-48.
46. Heurgeon, *op. cit.*, p. 95.
47. Terence G. F. Powell, *The Celts* (New York, Praeger, 1958), p. 72.
48. *Ibid.*, pp. 72-73.
49. *Ibid.*
50. "Plutarch, in his *Defectu Oraculorum*, mentions golden cups as part of the ritual furniture of the second-century (A.D.) druids of Ireland."—John A. MacCulloch, "Celtic Mythology," in Louis H. Gray, ed., *Mythology of All Races*, Vol. III (New York, Cooper Square, 1964), p. 15.
51. Bergounioux, *op. cit.*, p. 50.
52. *Ibid.*
53. Alkim, *op. cit.*, p. 68.
54. As quoted in H. J. Massingham, *Downland Man* (New York, Doran, 1936), p. 313.

CHAPTER 5—Anthropology Speaks

1. Lewis Henry Morgan, *Ancient Society* (Cambridge, Harvard University Press, 1965), p. 397.
2. Roland Kent, *Language and Philology* (New York, Cooper Square, 1963), p. 11.
3. *Ibid.*, p. 9.
4. Bronislaw Malinowski, "Baloma; the Spirits of the Dead in the Tobriand Islands," in his *Magic, Science, and Religion* (New York, Doubleday, 1965), p. 226.
5. *Ibid.*
6. Robert Briffault, *The Mothers* (New York, Grosset & Dunlap, 1963), p. 433.
7. Morgan, *op. cit.*, p. 397.
8. B. Y. Somerville, "Notes on Some Islands of the New Hebrides," in *Journal of the Anthropological Institute*, 24:4 (1894).
9. Peter H. Buck, *Vikings of the Pacific* (Chicago, University of Chicago Press, 1959), p. 265.
10. H. R. Codrington, as quoted in Ernest Crawley, *The Mystic Rose*, Vol. I (New York, Meridian Books, 1960), p. 262.
11. Ernest Crawley, *The Mystic Rose*, Vol. I (New York, Meridian Books, 1960), pp. 262-63.
12. W. Mariner, as quoted in Crawley, *op. cit.*, p. 263.
13. Buck, *op. cit.*, p. 309.
14. Tacitus, *Germania*, in *Complete Works of Tacitus*, trans. by A. J. Church and W. J. Brodribb (New York, Modern Library, 1942), p. 719.
15. Crawley, *op. cit.*, p. 263.
16. *Ibid.*, p. 264.
17. W. E. Griffis, as quoted in Crawley, *op. cit.*, p. 263.
18. L. L. Bird, as quoted in Crawley, *op. cit.*, p. 264.
19. Susan Michelmore, *Sexual Reproduction* (New York, Natural History Press, 1964), p. 15.
20. G. Ernest Wright, *Shechem* (London, Duckworth, 1965), p. 17.
21. E. B. Tylor, *Anthropology*, Vol. II (London, Watts, 1930), p. 132.
22. *Ibid.*

23. Paolo Mantegazza, *The Sexual Relations of Mankind* (Baltimore, Maryland, Eugenics Publishing Co., 1935), p. 61.
24. J. MacDonald, "Manners, Customs, Superstitions, and Religions of South African Tribes," *Journal of the Anthropological Institute*, 20:119 (1891).
25. M. H. Kingsley, as quoted in Crawley, *op. cit.*, p. 254.
26. Crawley, *op. cit.*, p. 254.
27. Mantegazza, *op. cit.*, p. 61.
28. Erich Fromm, *The Forgotten Language* (New York, Holt, 1951), p. 213.
29. Michelmore, *op. cit.*, p. 145.
30. W. Jochelson, "The Koryak," in *Publications of the North Pacific Expedition* VI: 741 (1908). Also cf. Eisler, *op. cit.*, p. 212.
31. James Bowring, as quoted in Crawley, *op. cit.*, Vol. II, p. 87.
32. Aelian, as quoted in Crawley, *op. cit.*, Vol. II, p. 81.
33. Crawley, *op. cit.*, Vol. II, p. 79.
34. G. A. Erman, as quoted in Crawley, *op. cit.*, p. 82.
35. Crawley, *op. cit.*, Vol. II, p. 78.
36. Lester Frank Ward, as quoted in Helen Beale Woodward, *The Bold Women* (New York, Farrar, 1953), pp. 339–40.
37. Karen Horney, *Feminine Psychology* (New York, Norton, 1967), p. 232.
38. Tacitus, *op. cit.*, p. 719.
39. Edward Carpenter, *Love's Coming of Age* (Manchester, England, Labour Press, 1896), pp. 65–66.
40. Mary Wollstonecraft, *Vindication of the Rights of Women* (New York, Norton, 1967), p. 86.
41. Horney, *op. cit.*, p. 231.
42. Carpenter, *op. cit.*, p. 66.
43. Edmond Perrier, as quoted in André Gide, *Corydon* (New York, Farrar, 1950), p. 60.
44. Leslie Frank Ward, as quoted in Gide, *op. cit.*, p. 60.
45. Robert Eisler, *Man into Wolf* (London, Spring Books, 1949), p. 33.
46. Louis Berman, *Food and Character* (London, Methuen, 1933), p. 158.

CHAPTER 6—Fetishes and Their Origins

1. Jacquetta Hawkes, *The Dawn of the Gods* (New York, Random, 1968), p. 131.
2. Law and medicine may be cited as cases in earlier times; and in recent years, public school teaching, librarianship, child psychology, and social work offer horrible examples of the deterioration that sets in when males "organize" feminine professions.
3. B. Z. Goldberg, *The Sacred Fire* (New York, Liveright, 1930), p. 70.
4. *Ibid.*, pp. 93–95.
5. *Ibid.*, p. 125.
6. Thomas Wright, *The Worship of the Generative Powers* (London, Dilettante Society, n.d.), p. 50.
7. *Ibid.*, p. 52.
8. Ernest Crawley, *The Mystic Rose*, Vol. II (New York, Meridian Books, 1960), p. 107.
9. *Ibid.*
10. Robert Lowrie, *Primitive Religion* (New York, Grosset & Dunlap, 1952), p. 245.
11. Crawley, *op. cit.*, p. 109 ff.
12. Herodotus, *The Histories*, Bk. I, trans. by George Rawlinson (New York, Tudor, 1944), p. 41.
13. Crawley, *op. cit.*, p. 107.
14. Lowie, *op. cit.*, p. 243.
15. Edward Westermarck, *The Origin and Development of the Moral Ideas*, Vol. II, 2d ed. (London, Macmillan, 1917), p. 456.

16. James G. Fraser, *The Golden Bough* (New York, Macmillan, 1958).
17. Herodotus, *op. cit.*, Bk. II, p. 115.
18. *Ibid.*
19. John Davenport, *Curiositates Eroticae Physiologiae* (London, privately printed, 1875), p. 80.
20. Goldberg, *op. cit.*, p. 69.
21. Theodor Reik, *The Creation of Woman* (New York, Braziller, 1960), p. 152 n.
22. *Newsweek*, 72 (17), 72 (Oct. 21, 1968).
23. As quoted in Davenport, *op. cit.*, p. 82.
24. Davenport, *op. cit.*, p. 85.
25. *Ibid.*
26. *Ibid.*, p. 84.
27. Pierre Grimal, *In Search of Ancient Italy*, trans. by P. D. Cummins (London, Evans, 1964), p. 236.
28. *Ibid.*, p. 237.
29. T. Bell, *Kalogynomia* (London, Stockdale, 1821), p. 71.
30. *Ibid.*
31. *Ibid.*
32. J. J. Bachofen, *Myth, Religion, and Mother Right*, trans. by Ralph Manheim (Princeton, Princeton University Press, 1967), p. 89.
33. Theodor Mommsen, *The History of Rome*, trans. by William P. Dickson, rev. ed., Vol. I (New York, Scribner's, 1903), p. 21.
34. *Ibid.*, p. 122.
35. Robert Graves, *The Greek Myths*, Vol. I (New York, Braziller, 1957), p. 16.
36. Wright, *op. cit.*, p. 35.
37. Herodotus, *op. cit.*, Bk. II, p. 114.
38. Wright, *op. cit.*, p. 38.
39. Herodotus, *op. cit.*, Bk. II, p. 93.
40. Goldberg, *op. cit.*, p. 123.
41. *Ibid.*
42. Theodor Reik, *Pagan Rites in Judaism* (New York, Farrar, 1964), p. 76.
43. Bachofen, *op. cit.*, p. 89.
44. George Rawlinson, *Ancient Egypt* (New York, Putnam's, 1887), p. 92.
45. Bachofen, *op. cit.*, p. 94.
46. *Ibid.*, pp. 104–5.
47. *Ibid.*
48. *Ibid.*
49. The *pre*-Victorians, however, knew that the Sphinx was female, for the first edition of the *Encyclopaedia Britannica*, published in 1771, describes the great Sphinx as "a monfter . . . with the head and breaft of a woman, the claws of a lion, and the reft of the body like a dog."

CHAPTER 7—Mother-Right

1. Jane Ellen Harrison, *Epilegomena to the Study of Greek Religion and Themis* (New Hyde Park, New York, 1962), p. 495. Mary Daly, *The Church and the Second Sex* (New York, Harper, 1968), p. 139.
2. Erich Fromm, *The Art of Loving* (New York, Bantam, 1963), pp. 35–36.
3. "Constantine," in Charles G. Herberman, ed., *Catholic Encyclopedia*, 1910 ed. So sacred had fetal life become among the Christians by the tenth century, that in the reign of the Holy Roman Emperor Henry II (973–1024) a woman who miscarried, whether by design or by *accident*, was condemned to death at the stake. (Montesquieu, *The Spirit of the Laws*, trans. by Thomas Nugent, Vol. II, New York, Hafner, 1949, p. 60.) The justification for this atrocity was that the

sex of the fetus could not be determined before birth, whereas the sex of the mother was indubitably inferiorly female. And an unformed male fetus was, of course, more valuable than a living woman. A recent article in *Look* magazine (November 4, 1969) quotes a woman whose life was risked by the medical profession in order that her fetus might live as asking why the doctors considered the fetus' life "more important than mine." Why, indeed.

4. *Cf.* Henry Hallam, *A View of the State of Europe During the Middle Ages*, Vol. I (New York, Appleton, 1901), pp. 84–85.

5. Robert Graves, *The White Goddess* (New York, Farrar, 1948), p. xii.

6. Doris Faber, *The Mothers of the American Presidents* (New York, New American Library, 1968), p. xiii. Sigmund Freud ("A man who has been the favorite of his mother retains for life a confidence of success that often leads to real success") *Collected Works*, Vol. IV. London, Hogarth Press, 1952, p. 367.

7. *Ibid.*, p. xv.

8. Jane Ellen Harrison, *Epilegomena to the Study of Greek Religion and Themis* (New Hyde Park, New York, University Books, 1962), p. 495.

9. *Ibid.*, p. 497.

10. J. J. Bachofen, *Myth, Religion and Mother Right,* trans. by Ralph Manheim (Princeton, Princeton University Press, 1967), p. 80.

11. *Ibid.*, p. 81.

12. Sybille von Cles-Redin, *The Realm of the Great Goddess* (Englewood Cliffs, New Jersey, Prentice-Hall, 1962), p. 53.

13. Bachofen, *op. cit.*, p. 79.

14. Theodor Reik, *The Need To Be Loved* (New York, Farrar, 1936), p. 149.

15. Robert Eisler, *Man into Wolf* (London, Spring Books, 1949?), n.200, pp. 218, 220.

16. Georg Simmel, as quoted in Karen Horney, *Feminine Psychology* (New York, Norton, 1967), p. 55.

17. Harrison, *op. cit.*, p. 494.

18. John Stuart Mill, *On the Subjection of Women* (Oxford, Oxford University Press, 1912), p. 490.

19. Montesquieu, *The Spirit of the Laws,* trans. by Thomas Nugent, Vol. I (New York, Hafner, 1949), p. 108.

20. Ashley Montagu, "The Natural Superiority of Women," in *The Saturday Review Treasury* (New York, Simon & Schuster, 1957), p. 473.

21. Montesquieu, *op. cit.*

22. Robert Graves, *The Greek Myths*, Vol. I (New York, Braziller, 1957), p. 12.

23. *Ibid.*, p. 13.

24. *Ibid.*

25. Bachofen, *op. cit.*, p. 141.

26. A. M. Hocart, *Social Origins* (London, Watts, 1954), p. 76.

27. That sister-brother marriages were an exclusively royal or upperclass prerogative in the ancient civilization is indicated by the fact that in Polynesia today "sister-brother marriages are permitted only among the few aristocratic families."— Peter H. Buck, *Vikings of the Pacific* (Chicago, University of Chicago Press, 1959), p. 264.

28. E. B. Tylor, *Anthropology*, Vol. II (London, Watts, 1930), p. 132.

29. Lewis Henry Morgan, *Ancient Society* (Cambridge, Harvard University Press, 1964), p. 292.

30. Ernst Curtius, *The History of Greece,* trans. by A. W. Ward, Vol. I (Oxford, Clarendon Press, 1871), p. 94.

31. Polybius, as quoted in Morgan, *op. cit.*, p. 298.

32. Bronislaw Malinowski, *Magic, Science, and Religion* (New York, Doubleday, 1955), p. 115.

33. Paolo Mantegazza, *The Sexual Relations of Mankind*, trans. by Samuel Putnam (Baltimore, Maryland, Eugenics Publishing Co., 1935), p. 215.

34. Buck, *op. cit.*, p. 309.

35. Ruth Benedict, *Patterns of Culture* (New York, New American Library, 1964), pp. 76–77.
36. As quoted in Bachofen, *op. cit.*, p. 71.
37. *Ibid.*
38. Herodotus, *The Histories*, trans. by George Rawlinson, Bk. I (New York, Tudor, 1944), p. 36.
39. As quoted in P. L. Shinnie, *Meroë* (New York, Praeger, 1967), p. 46.
40. Montesquieu, *op. cit.*, Vol. II, p. 85.
41. Basil Davidson, *Old Africa Rediscovered* (London, Gollancz, 1959), p. 69.
42. Leonard Cottrell, *The Land of Shinar* (London, Souvenir Press, 1965), p. 113.
43. Immanuel Velikovsky, *Ages in Chaos* (New York, Doubleday, 1952), chap. III.
44. James Henry Breasted, *History of Egypt* (New York, Scribner's, 1912), pp. 270, 269. Yet Breasted acknowledges (p. 266) that "the one valid title to the crown" that Hatshepsut's father, Thutmose I, had was through his marriage to Queen Ahmose, who was Hatshepsut's mother. Also, that later Thutmose III claimed the throne solely by virtue of his marriage to his sister, Queen Hatshepsut, daughter of Queen Ahmose. These facts certainly prove the fact of legal matriliny in Egypt, yet Breasted still calls Hatshepsut's wresting of power from her brother-consort an "enormity."
45. George Rawlinson, *Ancient Egypt* (New York, Putnam's, 1887), p. 173. He also calls her "one of the greatest of sovereigns" (p. 187).
46. Margaret Mead, *Male and Female* (New York, Morrow, 1949), p. 103.
47. Livy, *Roman History*, trans. by J. H. Freese *et al.* (New York, Appleton, 1901), p. 16.
48. Tacitus, *Annals*, trans. by A. J. Church and W. J. Brodribb. (New York, Modern Library, 1942), p. 186.
49. Pierre de Bourdeille, Abbé de Brantôme, *The Lives of Gallant Ladies* (London, Elek Books, 1961), p. 76.
50. Cottrell, *op. cit.*, p. 162.
51. Hallam, *op. cit.*, Vol. I, pp. 37, 73, 108, 200.
52. Montesquieu, *op. cit.*, Vol. I, p. 285.
53. *Ibid.*, p. 284.
54. *Ibid.*, p. 285.
55. Tacitus, *Agricola*, trans. by A. J. Church (New York, Modern Library, 1942), p. 686.
56. Louis Ginzberg, *The Legends of the Jews*, Vol. I (Philadelphia, Jewish Publications Society, 1909), p. 203.
57. *Ibid.*, p. 287.
58. *Ibid.*, p. 288.
59. Robert Briffault, *The Mothers* (New York, Grosset and Dunlap, 1963), p. 80.
60. Sigmund Freud, *Moses and Monotheism* (New York, Random, 1939), p. 78.
61. Demosthenes, as quoted in Morgan, *op. cit.*, p. 296.
62. Joseph Gaer, *The Lore of the New Testament* (Boston, Little, Brown, 1952), p. 13.
63. *Ibid.*

CHAPTER 8—Ram Versus Bull

1. Richard Payne Knight, *A Discourse on the Worship of Priapus* (London, Dilettanti Society, n.d.), pp. 65–66.
2. Bronislaw Malinowski, *Magic, Science, and Religion,* (New York, Doubleday, 1955), p. 220 ff. See also A. M. Hocart, *Social Origins* (London, Watts, 1954), p. 99.
3. Fabre d'Olivet, *Histoire Philosophique du Genre Humain,* in Edouard Schuré, *The Great Initiates*, Vol. I (New York, McKay, 1913), pp. 26–52.

4. The Aquarian Age, upon whose threshold we now stand, will be "inimical to man," as Macrobius prophesied in the early days of the Piscean Age. The "new morality" of the Aquarian youth of our day perhaps bespeaks a return to matriarchal mores too long suppressed by the materialistic patriarchal values that have prevailed for the past two thousaid years in the Occidental world. The Aquarian Age of the next two thousand years will seen an end to patriarchal Christianity and a return to goddess worship and to the peaceful social progress that distinguished the Taurian Age of four millennia ago.

5. The Grand Precession of the Equinox requires 26,000 years, slightly more than 2,000 years for each Zodiacal Age.

6. J. J. Bachofen, *Myth, Religion, and Mother Right*, trans. by Ralph Manheim (Princeton, Princeton University Press, 1967), pp. 80–81.

7. Flavius Josephus, *The Antiquities of the Jews* (Philadelphia, Woodward, 1825), p. 11.

8. Louis Ginzberg, *The Legends of the Jews*, Vol. I (Philadelphia, Jewish Publications Society, 1909), p. 112.

9. Robert Eisler, *Man into Wolf* (London, Spring Books, 1949), p. 34.

10. Immanuel Velikovsky, *Earth in Upheaval* (New York, Doubleday, 1955).

11. Eisler, *op. cit.*, p. 33.

12. Ginzberg, *op. cit.*, Vol. I, p. 166.

13. Eisler, *op. cit.*, p. 29.

14. Montesquieu, *The Spirit of the Laws*, trans. by Thomas Nugent, Vol. II (New York, Hafner, 1949), p. 47. The concept that man was the rightful exploiter and murderer of his fellow beasts was so new and revolutionary that the patriarchal writers of the Old Testament felt it necessary to inject it as propaganda into the first book of the Bible. This cruel canard is rivaled only by the myth of Eve's disobedience in the lasting damage it has wrought, in the price it has exacted in man's rape of nature, and in the inhumanity toward and exploitation of the weak that has resulted from it.

15. Leonard Cottrell, *The Land of Shinar* (London, Souvenir Press, 1965), p. 101.

16. *Ibid.*

17. Leonard Woolley, *A Forgotten Kingdom* (London, Penguin, 1954), pp. 167, 112.

18. *Ibid.*, p. 85.

19. Herodotus, *The Histories* Bk I; trans. by George Rawlinson (Tudor, 1949), p. 93.

20. *The Ramayana*, trans. by Romesh Dutt (London, Dent, 1899).

21. As quoted in Mary Wollstonecraft, *A Vindication of the Rights of Women* (New York, Norton, 1967).

22. Jean Jacques Rousseau, *The Social Contract* (Hafner, 1947), pp. 7–9.

23. P. Donaldson, as quoted in Margaret Sanger, *Woman and the New Race* (New York, Brentano's, 1920), p. 176.

24. Edouard Schuré, *The Great Initiates*, Vol. I (New York, McKay, 1913), p. 117.

25. H. J. Massingham, *Downland Man* (New York, Doran, 1936), p. 109.

26. C. F. Keary, *The Dawn of History* (New York, Scribner's, n.d.), p. 22.

27. Theodor Reik, *Pagan Rites in Judaism* (New York, Farrar, 1964), p. 100.

28. Contrary to the impression gleaned from the Old Testament, the Canaanites were a highly cultured people, from whom the less civilized Hebrews learned much. "Their poetry had a high standard; their language, alphabet, style, and rhythm were inherited by the Jews," as were their "ethos of social justice" and their predilection for religious prophecy.—Immanuel Velikovsky, *Ages in Chaos* (New York, Doubleday, 1952), p. 196.

"The traditions, culture, and religion of the Israelites are bound up inextricably with the early Canaanites. The compilers of the Old Testament were fully aware of this, hence their obsession to conceal their indebtedness.—Claude F. A. Schaeffer, as quoted in Velikovsky, *op. cit.*, p. 192.

The myth of the passage through the Red Sea, when the waters were rolled back to allow the refugees to cross, is found in a Canaanite text of the fifteenth century B.C., at a time before the Exodus when the children of Israel were still in bondage in Egypt.—R. Dussaud, as quoted in Velikovsky, *op. cit.*, p. 190. The foregoing extracts give some idea of the reliability of the Bible as history. Yet historians until quite recently based historical world chronology on the Old Testament!

29. Reik, *op. cit.*, p. 101.
30. "The Enuma Elish," trans. by William Muss-Arnolt, in *Assyrian and Babylonian Literature* (New York, Appleton, 1900), pp. 282–83.
31. Robert Graves, *Adam's Rib* (New York, Yoseloff, 1958), p. 12.
32. Theodor Reik, *The Creation of Woman* (New York, Braziller, 1960), p. 59.
33. Reik, *Pagan Rites in Judaism*, *op. cit.*, p. 69.
34. Graves, *op. cit.*, p. 8.
35. *Ibid.*
36. According to an ancient Celtic poem, Eve was of the primeval race of Hermaphrodites, the self-perpetuating, bisexual females to whom Plato alludes in the *Symposium*:

> She was self-bearing,
> The mixed burden of man-woman.
> She brought forth Abel
> And Cain, the solitary homicide.

—As quoted in Robert Graves, *The White Goddess* (New York, Farrar, 1948), p. 134.
37. Robert Graves, *The White Goddess* (New York, Farrar, 1948), p. 215.
38. Edouard Schuré, *The Great Initiates*, Vol. I (New York, McKay, 1913), p. 251.
39. Graves, *Adam's Rib*, *op. cit.*, p. 13.
40. *Ibid.*
41. Erich Fromm, *The Forgotten Language* (New York, Holt, 1951), p. 234.
42. *Ibid.*
43. Louis Ginzberg, *The Legends of the Jews*, Vol. I (Philadelphia, Jewish Publications Society, 1909), p. 97.
44. Karen Horney, *Feminine Psychology* (New York, Norton, 1967), p. 112.
45. Jane Ellen Harrison, *Epilegomena to the Study of Greek Religion, and Themis* (New Hyde Park, New York, University Books, 1961), p. 500.
46. Norman O. Brown, *Hermes the Thief, the Evolution of a Myth* (Madison, University of Wisconsin Press, 1947), p. 62.
47. Harrison, *op. cit.*, p. 500.
48. Jacquetta Hawkes, *The Dawn of the Gods* (New York, Random, 1968), p. 285.
49. W. K. C. Guthrie, *Orpheus and Greek Religion* (New York, Norton, 1966), p. 81.
50. *Ibid.*, p. 80.
51. *Ibid.*, p. 62.
52. *Ibid.*
53. A. J. Symonds, *A Problem in Greek Ethics* (London, privately printed, 1901).
54. *Ibid.*, p. 16, 30.
55. Robert Graves, *The Greek Myths*, Vol. I (New York, Braziller, 1957), p. 117.
56. Suetonius, *The Lives of the Twelve Caesars*, trans. by Joseph Gavorse (New York, Modern Library, 1931).
57. Robert Burton, *The Anatomy of Melancholy* (New York, Tudor, n.d.), p. 652.

CHAPTER 9—The Sexual Revolution

1. J. J. Bachofen, *Myth, Religion, and Mother Right*, trans. by Ralph Manheim (Princeton, Princeton University Press, 1967), p. 75.
2. Edward Westermarck, *The Future of Marriage in Western Civilization* (New York, Macmillan, 1963), p. 241.
3. *Ibid.*, pp. 250–51.
4. *Ibid.*, p. 241.

5. Anthony M. Ludovici, *Woman, a Vindication* (New York, Knopf, 1923), p. 258.
6. Georg Simmel, as quoted in Karen Horney, *Feminine Psychology* (New York, Norton, 1967), p. 55.
7. Margaret Sanger, *Woman and the New Race* (New York, Brentano's, 1920), p. 179.
8. Mary Wollstonecraft, *A Vindication of the Rights of Woman* (New York, Norton, 1967), pp. 126, 121.
9. Richard L. Evans, ed., *Dialogue with Erik Erikson* (New York, Harper, 1967), p. 44.
10. Karen Horney, *Feminine Psychology* (New York, Norton, 1967), p. 62.
11. *Ibid.*, p. 136.
12. Erich Fromm, *The Forgotten Language* (New York, Holt, 1951), p. 233.
13. Erich Fromm, *Sigmund Freud's Mission* (New York, Harper, 1959), pp. 31, 22.
14. Evans, ed., *op. cit.*, p. 43. Yet in his old age, Freud concedes that "at one period great mother deities appeared, probably before the male gods, and they were worshipped for a long time to come."—Sigmund Freud, *Moses and Monotheism* (New York, Knopf, 1939), p. 105.
15. Harold Kelman, "Introduction," in Karen Horney, *Feminine Psychology* (New York, Norton, 1967), pp. 8–9.
16. Theodor Reik, *The Need To Be Loved* (New York, Farrar, 1963), p. 147.
17. Horney, *op. cit.*, p. 61.
18. Gregory Zilboorg, "Male and Female," in Kelman, *op. cit.*, p. 21.
19. Horney, *op. cit.*, p. 60.
20. *Ibid.*, p. 136.
21. *Ibid.*, pp. 116–17.
22. Margaret Mead, *Male and Female* (New York, Morrow, 1949), pp. 102–3.
23. Edward Carpenter, *Love's Coming of Age* (Manchester, England, Labour Press, 1896), p. 27.
24. Richard Burton, *Love, War, and Fancy; Notes to the Arabian Nights* (London, Kimber, 1954), p. 108.
25. John Davenport, *Curiositates Eroticae Physiologiae* (London, privately printed, 1875), p. 100. Dr. T. Bell, on the other hand, says that a woman could not conceive *without* orgasm.
26. *Ibid.*, p. 95.
27. *Ibid.*, p. 96.
28. *Ibid.*
29. *Ibid.*, pp. 102–3.
30. *Ibid.*, p. 94.
31. T. Bell, *Kalogynomia* (London, Stockdale, 1821), p. 177.
32. Richard Burton, *op. cit.*, p. 107.
33. *Ibid.*, p. 108.
34. *Ibid.*, p. 107.
35. Even in the nineteenth and early twentieth centuries in the United States, male sexual envy took its toll of clitorides, for medical men were "quick to remove by knife or by cauterization, the ovaries or the *clitoris* [author's italics]" of any female patient whose husband considered her dangerously responsive or who showed the effects of sexual frustration. "Nineteenth-century ladies were not supposed to be sexual at all, and men avenged themselves [by means of medical circumcision] upon women for having a womb."—Ashley Montagu, *The Natural Superiority of Women* (New York, Macmillan, 1952), pp. 95–96.
36. Paolo Mantegazza, *The Sexual Relations of Mankind* (Baltimore, Maryland, Eugenics Publishing Co., 1935), pp. 121–22.

CHAPTER 10—Patriarchy and Hymenolatry

1. Ernest Crawley, *The Mystic Rose*, Vol. II (New York, Meridian Books, 1962), p. 69.

2. *Ibid.*
3. *Ibid.*
4. Robert Eisler, *Man into Wolf* (London, Spring Books, 1949), p. 200, n. 85.
5. Herodotus, *The Histories*, trans. by George Rawlinson, Bk. I (New York, Tudor, 1944), p. 74.
6. John Davenport, *Curiositates Eroticae Physiologiae* (London, privately printed, 1875), p. 36.
7. Crawley, *op. cit.*, Vol. II, p. 69.
8. *Ibid.*, p. 67.
9. As quoted in Crawley, *op. cit.*, Vol. II, pp. 74–75.
10. Crawley, *op. cit.*, Vol. II, p. 72.
11. Louis Ginzberg, *The Legends of the Jews* (Philadelphia, Jewish Publications Society, 1909), p. 166.
12. Montesquieu, *The Spirit of the Laws*, trans. by Thomas Nugent, Vol. II (New York, Hafner, 1949), p. 47, quoting Porphyry.
13. Eisler, *op. cit.*, pp. 36–41.
14. As quoted in Franz Hartman, *The Life of Paracelsus*, 2d ed. (London, Kegan Paul, Trench and Trubner, 1841?), p. 78.
15. Eisler, *op. cit.*, p. 200, n. 185.
16. As quoted in Davenport, *op. cit.*, p. 35.
17. Eric John Dingwall, *The Girdle of Chastity* (London, Routledge, 1931), p. 3.
18. Paolo Mantegazza, *The Sexual Relations of Mankind* (Baltimore, Maryland, Eugenics Publishing Co., 1935), p. 117.
19. Dingwall, *op. cit.*, pp. 108–10.
20. *Ibid.*, pp. 109 n., 110 n.
21. *Ibid.*, p. 4.
22. Mantegazza, *op. cit.*, pp. 118–19.
23. Dingwall, *op. cit.*, p. 13.
24. As quoted in Dingwall, *op. cit.*, p. 43.
25. Pierre de Bourdeille, Abbé de Brantôme, *Les Vies des Dames Galantes* (London, Elek Books, 1961), p. 86.
26. *Ibid.*, p. 87.
27. *Ibid.*
28. Dingwall, *op. cit.*, pp. 118–19.
29. *Ibid.*, p. 120.
30. "The belief that young pigeon's blood resembles the vaginal discharge is universal."—Richard Burton, *Love, War, and Fancy* (London, Kimber, 1964), p. 149.
31. Brantôme, *op. cit.*, p. 244.
32. T. Bell, *Kalogynomia* (London, Stockdale, 1821), p. 196.
33. As quoted in Davenport, *op. cit.*, p. 36, and translated by Davis.
34. Bell, *op. cit.*, p. 197.
35. *Ibid.*, p. 198.
36. *Ibid.*, pp. 194–96.
37. *Ibid.*, p. 230.
38. *Ibid.*
39. Davenport, *op. cit.*, p. 34.
40. *Ibid.*, p. 35.
41. As quoted in *Ibid.*, p. 37.
42. *Ibid.*, p. 32.
43. *Ibid.*, pp. 33–34.
44. *Ibid.*

CHAPTER 11—The Pre-Hellenes

1. Charles Seltman, *The Twelve Olympians* (New York, Apollo Editions, 1962), p. 27.
2. Stuart Piggott, ed., *The Dawn of Civilization* (New York, McGraw-Hill, 1961), p. 224.

3. Herodotus, *The Histories,* trans. by George Rawlinson, Bk. I (New York, Tudor, n.d.), pp. 36–37.
4. *Ibid.,* p. 37. It is interesting that the great stone works and engineering marvels of historical Babylon, which were numbered among the seven wonders of the ancient world, are credited to the genius of two women, the queens Nitocris and Semiramis.
5. John M. Cook, *The Greek in Ionia and the East* (New York, Praeger, 1963), p. 62.
6. Herodotus, *op. cit.,* p. 65.
7. Herodotus, *op. cit.,* p. 64.
8. *Ibid.,* Bk. VII, p. 385.
9. Philostratus, *Apollonius of Tyana,* trans. by J. S. Phillimore, Vol. II (Oxford, Clarendon Press, 1912), p. 20.
10. J. J. Bachofen, *Myth, Religion and Mother Right,* trans. by Ralph Manheim (Princeton, Princeton University Press, 1967), p. 107 and 107 n.
11. As quoted in Immanuel Velikovsky, *Ages in Chaos* (New York, Doubleday, 1952), p. 200.
12. Herodotus, *op. cit.,* Bk. I, p. 61.
13. Virgil, *Aeneid,* trans. by James Rhoades, Bk. VII (London, Oxford University Press, 1921), lines 801–17, p. 178.
14. Theodor Mommsen, *The History of Rome,* trans. by William P. Dickson, Vol. I (New York, Scribner's, 1903), p. 422n.
15. Pierre Grimal, *In Search of Ancient Italy,* trans. by P. D. Cummins (London, Evans, 1964), pp. 195–96.
16. *Ibid.,* p. 164.
17. *Ibid.,* p. 163.
18. Livy, *Roman History,* trans. by J. H. Freese, A. J. Church and W. J. Brodribb (New York, Appleton, 1901), p. 16.
19. Tacitus, *Annals* 64, in *Complete Works of Tacitus,* trans. by A. J. Church and W. J. Brodribb (New York, Modern Library, 1942), p. 182. Cf. Virgil, *op cit.,* Bk. VII, lines 712–13, p. 175.

CHAPTER 12—Women of Greece and Italy

1. J. J. Bachofen, *Myth, Religion and Mother Right,* trans. by Ralph Manheim (Princeton, Princeton University Press, 1967), pp. 157–58.
2. Aeschylus, *The Eumenides,* trans. by Richmond Lattimore (Chicago, University of Chicago Press, 1959), pp. 158, 161.
3. Montesquieu, *The Spirit of the Laws,* trans. by Thomas Nugent, Vol. I (New York, Hafner, 1949), pp. 261–62.
4. E. F. Benson, *The Life of Alcibiades* (London, Benn, 1928), p. 107.
5. Robert Flacelière, *Daily Life in Greece at the Time of Pericles,* trans. by Peter Green (New York, Macmillan, 1965).
6. *Ibid.,* p. 68.
7. *Ibid.,* p. 69.
8. Paul Harvey, ed., *The Oxford Companion to Classical Literature* (London, Oxford University Press, 1959), pp. 450–51.
9. Flacelière, *op. cit.,* p. 59.
10. Charles Anthon, ed., *Dictionary of Greek and Roman Antiquities* (New York, American Book Co., 1843), p. 277.
11. Raymond Bloch, *The Etruscans,* trans. by Stuart Hood (New York, Praeger, 1958), p. 58.
12. Jacquetta Hawkes, *The Dawn of the Gods* (New York, Random, 1968), p. 286.
13. *Ibid.,* p. 285.
14. A. J. Symonds, *A Problem in Greek Ethics* (London, privately printed, 1901), p. 64.
15. Hawkes, *op. cit.,* p. 289.
16. *Ibid.,* p. 285.

17. Plato, *Republic*, trans. by W. H. D. Rouse (New York, New American Library, 1956), p. 253.
18. Plato, *Republic*, in *The Works of Plato*, trans. by Benjamin Jowett (New York, Tudor, n.d.), p. 182.
19. Plutarch, *The Life of Pericles*, trans. by John Dryden (New York, Modern Library, n.d.), pp. 200–1.
20. Benson, *op. cit.*, pp. 57–58, quoting Athenaeus, who quotes Herodicus the Cratetian.
21. Plutarch, *The Life of Alcibiades*, trans. by John Dryden (New York, Modern Library, n.d.), p. 238. "Even as she, Hipparete, stood there before the court, her husband Alcibiades picked her up in his arms and carried her away. He just picked her up, with a kiss to stop the mouth that was about to recount his naughty ways, and ran off with her. She loved him, and knew he loved her, and her freedom was dust and ashes in her mouth compared to his real presence. So she lived with him the rest of her life."—Benson, *op. cit.*, p. 108.
22. As quoted in Edouard Schuré, *The Great Initiates*, trans. by Fred Rothwell, Vol. II (New York, McKay, 1913), p. 92.
23. Plutarch, *The Life of Lycurgus*, trans. by John Dryden (New York, Modern Library, n.d.), p. 60.
24. Schuré, *op. cit.*, Vol. II, p. 156.
25. Hawkes, *op. cit.*, p. 285.
26. Livy, *Roman History*, trans. by J. H. Freese, A. J. Church, and W. J. Brodribb (New York, Appleton, 1901), p. 67.
27. Jacques Heurgeon, *Daily Life of the Etruscans*, trans. by James Kirkup (New York, Macmillan, 1964), p. 96.
28. J. A. Cramer, *A Geographical and Historical Description of Ancient Italy*, Vol. I (Oxford, Clarendon Press, 1825), p. 153.
29. Heurgeon, *op. cit.*, p. 86.
30. Livy, *op. cit.*, p. 57.
31. Heurgeon, *op. cit.*, p. 87.
32. Bloch, *op. cit.*, p. 58.
33. Heurgeon, *op. cit.*, pp. 95, 96.
34. Tacitus, *Annals* 2:22, in *Complete Works of Tacitus*, trans. by A. J. Church and W. J. Brodribb (New York, Modern Library, 1942), p. 157.
35. Livy, *op. cit.*, p. 16.
36. Bronislaw Malinowski, *Magic, Science, and Religion* (New York, Doubleday, 1955), p. 225.
37. Tacitus, *Annals* 4:64, *op. cit.*, p. 182.
38. Myles Dillon and Nora Chadwick, *The Celtic Realms* (New York, New American Library, 1967), p. 153.
39. Juvenal, *Satires* VI: 246, as quoted in Jerome Carcopino, *Daily Life in Ancient Rome*, trans. by E. O. Lorimer (New Haven, Yale University Press, 1940), p. 92.
40. Martial, *Epigrams* XI:53, as quoted in Carcopino, *op. cit.*, p. 91.
41. Montesquieu, *op. cit.*, Vol. II, p. 22.
42. *Ibid.*, p. 21.
43. *Ibid.*
44. Montesquieu, *op. cit.*, Vol. II, p. 60.
45. Plutarch, *The Life of Alcibiades*, *op. cit.*, p. 238.
46. Juvenal, *Satires* VI: 224, as quoted in Carcopino, *op. cit.*, p. 99.
47. P. Donaldson, as quoted in Margaret Sanger, *Woman and the New Race* (New York, Brantano, 1920), pp. 175–76.
48. Edward Gibbon, *The Decline and Fall of the Roman Empire*, Vol. II (New York, Hurst, n.d.), p. 298. See also Harold Mattingly, *Christianity in the Roman Empire* (New York, Norton, 1967), p. 75.
49. James Cleugh, *Love Locked Out* (New York, Crown, 1963), p. 9.
50. Paul was not only an epileptic all his life but, worse, he was a leper, according

to the Viennese scholar Hanz Leitzmann. As a result of leprosy, wrote Wendland and Preuschen, he was deformed, disfigured, and semiblind.—Frederick Cony-beare, *The Origins of Christianity* (New York, University Books, 1958), "Notes," p. 363.

51. Jerome Carcopino, *Daily Life in Ancient Rome*, trans. by E. O. Lorimer (New Haven, Yale University Press, 1940), p. 87.
52. Juvenal, *Satires* VI:284, as quoted in Carcopino, *op. cit.*, p. 93.
53. Carcopino, *op. cit.*, p. 85.
54. Edward Gibbon, *The Decline and Fall of the Roman Empire*, Vol. I (New York, Hurst, n.d.), p. 130.
55. J. S. Phillimore, "The Author and His Times," in Philostratus, *Apollonius of Tyana*, trans. by J. S. Phillimore, Vol. I (Oxford, Clarendon Press, 1912), pp. lxi, lxxi, lxxxiii.
56. H. M. D. Parker, *A History of the Roman World, A.D. 138–337*, 2d ed. (London, Methuen, 1958), p. 99.
57. Gibbon, *op. cit.*, p. 142.
58. *Ibid.*, p. 148.
59. *Ibid.* The respective husbands of the two younger Julias, daughters of Julia Maesa, were virtual nobodys.
60. *Ibid.*, p. 149.
61. *Ibid.*, p. 155.

CHAPTER 13—The Celts

1. Terence G. E. Powell, *The Celts* (New York, Praeger, 1958), p. 52.
2. Myles Dillon and Nora Chadwick, *The Celtic Realms* (New York, New American Library, 1967), p. 17.
3. Hugh Hencken, *Tarquinia and Etruscan Origins* (New York, Praeger, 1968), p. 157.
4. Stuart Piggott, *The Druids* (New York, Praeger, 1968), p. 45.
5. *Ibid.*
6. *Ibid.*, p. 42.
7. *Ibid.*, p. 43.
8. W. Wistar Comfort, ed., *Arthurian Romances of Chretien de Troyes* (London, Dent, 1914), p. ix.
9. Lady Charlotte Guest, "Original Introduction," in *Mabinogion* (London, Dent, 1906), pp. 6, 12.
10. Piggott, *op. cit.*, p. 54.
11. Robert Graves, "The Divine Rite of Mushrooms," in *Atlantic*, 225(2): 110 (February, 1970).
12. Henry Hallam, *A View of the State of Europe during the Middle Ages*, Vol. I (New York, Appleton, 1901), p. 84.
13. Jules Michelet, *Satanism and Witchcraft* (New York, Citadel, 1939), chap. I.
14. As quoted in Dillon and Chadwick, *op. cit.*, p. 154.
15. Julius Caesar, *The Gallic Wars*, trans. by John Warrington, Bk. I (New York, Dutton, 1958), p. 27.
16. Tacitus, *Histories* 5:22, in *Complete Works of Tacitus*, trans. by A. J. Church and W. J. Brodribb (New York, Modern Library, 1942), p. 671.
17. *Ibid.*, 5:25, p. 672.
18. G. F. Browne, as quoted in Anthony Ludovici, *Woman: A Vindication* (New York, Knopf, 1923), p. 255.
19. Edward Gibbon, *The Decline and Fall of the Roman Empire*, Vol. I (New York, Hurst, n.d.), pp. 212–13.
20. Edward Carpenter, *Love's Coming of Age* (Manchester, England, Labour Press, 1896), p. 64.
21. Tacitus, *Germania* 18, in *Complete Works of Tacitus*, *op. cit.*, p. 718.

22. *Ibid.*, p. 717.
23. *Ibid.*, p. 718.
24. *Ibid.* 20, p. 718.
25. *Ibid.* 7, p. 712.
26. *Ibid.* 40, pp. 728–31.
27. *Ibid.* 20, p. 719.
28. J. J. Bachofen, *Myth, Religion and Mother Right*, trans. by Ralph Manheim (Princeton, Princeton University Press, 1967), p. 73.
29. *Ibid.*, p. 74.
30. *Ibid.*
31. Herodotus, *The Histories*, trans. by George Rawlinson, Bk. I (New York, Tudor, n.d.), pp. 76–79.
32. Tacitus, *Annals* 14:35, in *Complete Works of Tacitus, op. cit.*, p. 340.
33. Dio Cassius, *Roman Histories* (Epitome) Bk. 62:3–4, as quoted in Agnes Strickland, *Lives of the Queens of England*, Vol. I (Philadelphia, Lea & Blanchard, 1850), p. xiv.
34. G. R. Dudley, as quoted in Dillon and Chadwick, *op. cit.*, p. 27.
35. Tacitus, *Annals* 12:37, in *Complete Works of Tacitus, op. cit.*, p. 267.
36. *Ibid.*
37. Dillon and Chadwick, *op. cit.*, p. 25.
38. Tacitus, *History* 3:45, in *Complete Works of Tacitus, op. cit.*, p. 564.
39. Tacitus, *Agricola* 16, in *Complete Works of Tacitus, op. cit.*, p. 686.
40. *Ibid.* 31, p. 695.
41. Dillon and Chadwick, *op. cit.*, p. 27.
42. Tacitus, *Annals* 14:30, in *Complete Works of Tacitus, op. cit.*, p. 337.
43. *Ibid.*, 14:36, p. 340.
44. Tacitus, *Agricola* 11, in *Complete Works of Tacitus, op. cit.*, p. 683.
45. Robert Graves, *The White Goddess* (New York, Farrar, 1948), p. 261.
46. Powell, *op. cit.*, p. 166. *Cf.* Dillon and Chadwick, *op. cit.*, p. 3 n.
47. Dillon and Chadwick, *op. cit.*, p. 158.
48. Bachofen, *op. cit.*, p. 74.
49. Graves, *op. cit.*, p. 50.
50. John Stow, *The Survey of London*, rev. ed. (London, Dent, 1956), p. 3.
51. Thomas Fuller, *The Worthies of England* (London, Allen & Unwin, 1952), p. 344. For the similarities between the ancient British and Thracian worship of Dana-Diana, see Chapter 2, "Sumer and the Celtic Cross."
52. Sheumas MacManus, *The Story of the Irish Race*, 4th ed. (New York, Devin-Adair, 1944), p. 2.
53. *Ibid.*, p. 7.
54. Edmund Curtis, *A History of Ireland*, 6th ed. (London, Methuen, 1950), p. 1.
55. *Funk & Wagnalls New Standard Encyclopedia*, Frank Vizetelly, ed., Vol. IV (New York, Funk & Wagnalls, 1934), p. 183.
56. Powell, *op. cit.*, p. 52.
57. Hallam, *op. cit.*, pp. 37, 73, 108.
58. *Ibid.*, p. 200.
59. *Cambridge Mediaeval History*, 1925 ed., Vol. V, p. 717.
60. *Ibid.*
61. *Funk & Wagnalls New Standard Encyclopedia, op. cit.*, Vol. IV, p. 183. *Cf.* Mac-Manus, *op. cit.*, pp. 153–55.
62. Raphael Holinshed, *A Description of England* (1577), as quoted in Strickland, *op. cit.*, p. xiv. Also *cf.* Geoffrey of Monmouth, *History of the Kings of Britain* (London, Penguin, 1965), p. 101.
63. *Funk & Wagnalls New Standard Encyclopedia, op. cit.*, Vol. IV, p. 183.
64. *Ibid.*
65. Dillon and Chadwick, *op. cit.*, p. 153.
66. *Ibid.* See also Robert Graves, *On Poetry* (New York, Doubleday, 1969).
67. Nora Chadwick, *Celtic Britain* (New York, Praeger, 1963), p. 154.

68. As quoted in Lionel Smithett Lewis, *Glastonbury, the Mother of Saints*, A.D. *37–1539*, 2d ed. (London, Mowbray, 1927), p. xv.
69. As quoted in *Ibid.*, p. 77.
70. John Edward Lloyd, "The English Settlement," in Walter Hutchinson, ed., *Hutchinson's Early History of the British Nations* (London, Hutchinson, 1940), pp. 97–124.
71. Herodotus, *op. cit.*, p. 222.
72. Graves, *The White Goddess, op. cit.*, p. 249.
73. Powell, *op. cit.*, p. 120.
74. Graves, *The White Goddess, op. cit.*, p. 249.
75. Herodotus, *op. cit.*, p. 37.
76. Graves, *The White Goddess, op. cit.*, pp. 249–50.
77. See Louis H. Gray, ed., *Mythology of All Races*, Vol. III (New York, Cooper Square, 1964), p. 15.
78. See James Mellaart, *Earliest Civilizations of the Near East* (New York, McGraw-Hill, 1965), p. 93, illustration.
79. "The Grail was a genuine Celtic myth, with its roots in the mysteries of Druidism."—Sabine Baring-Gould, *Curious Myths of the Middle Ages* (New Hyde Park, New York, University Books, 1967), p. 603.
80. *The Mabinogion*, trans. by Charlotte Guest (London, Dent, 1906), p. 37.
81. See Chapter 4, "Archeology Speaks."
82. James Mellaart, *Earliest Civilizations of the Near East* (New York, McGraw-Hill, 1965), p. 77.

CHAPTER 14—The Advent of Christianity

1. Terence G. F. Powell, *The Celts* (New York, Praeger, 1968), p. 84.
2. I Timothy 2:12.
3. As quoted in James Cleugh, *Love Locked Out* (New York, Crown, 1963), p. 265.
4. Edward Gibbon, *The Decline and Fall of the Roman Empire*, Vol. I (New York, Hurst, n.d.), p. 433.
5. *Ibid.*, p. 456.
6. G. G. Coulton, ed., *Life in the Middle Ages*, Vol. I (New York, Macmillan, 1910), p. 32 n.
7. Bede, *The Ecclesiastical History of the English People* (London, Dent, 1910), p. 15.
8. Geoffrey of Monmouth, *History of the Kings of Britain* (London, Penguin, 1965), p. 132.
9. William of Malmesbury, *Antiquities of Glastonbury*, as quoted in Lionel Smithett Lewis, *Glastonbury, the Mother of Saints*, A.D. *37–1539*, 2d ed. (London, Mowbray, 1927), p. 4.
10. Geoffrey of Monmouth, *op. cit.*, p. 138. "Sophisticated" historians of the past few centuries have been wont to relegate Geoffrey's history to the realm of fairy tale, together with Homer and Herodotus. But as in the cases of those two maligned historians, recent archeological research has caused a cognitive few to reconsider this devaluation of Geoffrey's history.
11. *Ibid.*, p. 132.
12. John Stow, *The Survey of London*, rev. ed. (London, Dent, 1956), p. 7.
13. "Constantine," in Charles G. Herberman, ed., *Catholic Encyclopedia*, Vol. IV (New York, Appleton, 1912), pp. 295–301.
14. H. M. D. Parker, *A History of the Roman World*, A.D. *138–337*, 2d, ed., rev. by B. H. Warmington (London, Methuen, 1958), p. 251.
15. Harold Mattingly, *Christianity in the Roman Empire* (New York, Norton, 1967), p. 89.
16. Pierre de Bourdeille, Abbe dé Brantôme, *The Lives of Gallant Ladies* (London, Elek Books, 1961), p. 21.

17. *Cambridge Mediaeval History*, Vol. II (London, Cambridge University Press, 1926), p. 106.
18. Will and Mary Durant, *The History of Civilization*, Vol. IV, *The Age of Faith* (New York, Simon and Schuster, 1950), p. 843.
19. "Constantine," in *Catholic Encyclopedia*, *op. cit.*, Vol. IV, p. 298.
20. Charles G. Herberman, ed., *Catholic Encyclopedia*, Vol. VII (New York, Appleton, 1912), p. 202.
21. *Ibid.*
22. *Ibid.*, Vol. IV, p. 299.
23. *Ibid.*, p. 300.
24. As quoted in Durant, *op. cit.*, p. 825.
25. As quoted in *Ibid.*, p. 826.
26. Gibbon, *op. cit.*, Vol. II, p. 301.
27. Henry Thomas, *The Story of the Human Race* (Boston, Winchell and Thomas, 1935), p. 219.
28. As quoted in Arthur Findlay, *The Curse of Ignorance*, Vol. I (London, Psychic Press, 1947), pp. 678–79.
29. Durant, *op. cit.*, p. 829.
30. *Cambridge Mediaeval History*, *op. cit.*, Vol. V, p. 724.
31. Jean Jacques Rousseau, *The Social Contract: an Eighteenth Century Translation*, rev. by Charles Frankel (New York, Hafner, 1947), pp. 119, 121, 124.
32. "The last voice in Dark-Age Europe to speak of the sphericity of the earth and the plurality of worlds was that of a Celtic monk of pre-Augustinian Britain—Ferghild—in the sixth century of our era."—Geoffrey Ashe, *The Quest for Arthur's Britain* (New York, Praeger, 1969), p. 239.
33. Findlay, *op. cit.*, pp. 658–59.
34. "Neoplatonism," in Paul Harvey, ed., *The Oxford Companion to Classical Literature* (London, Oxford University Press, 1959), p. 286.
35. Montesquieu, *The Spirit of the Laws*, trans. by Thomas Nugent, Vol. II (New York, Hafner, 1949), p. 24.
36. That Europe did not relapse into total barbarism was due entirely to Celtic influence. Right while they were being annihilated by the barbarians, the Celts were educating them. "The civilizing of the Teutons was a Celtic achievement. . . . Civilization in Europe never entirely perished; for the Celts held out against the Teutonic savages until they had ceased to be savages."—Geoffrey Ashe, *The Quest for Arthur's Britain* (New York, Praeger, 1969), pp. 235, 238.
37. James Cleugh, *Love Locked Out* (New York, Crown, 1963), p. 9.
38. Jules Michelet, *Satanism and Witchcraft* (New York Citadel, 1939), p. 87.
39. Gibbon, *op. cit.*, Vol. I, p. 380.
40. John Stuart Mill, *On Liberty* (New York, Liberal Arts Press, 1956), p. 59.

CHAPTER 15—Mary and the Great Goddess

1. Jean Jacques Rousseau, *The Social Contract: an Eighteenth-Century Translation*, rev. and ed. by Charles Frankel (New York, Hafner, 1947), p. 117.
2. Edward Gibbon, *Decline and Fall of the Roman Empire*, Vol. II (New York, Hurst, n.d.), pp. 306–7.
3. Robert Graves, *On Poetry* (New York, Doubleday, 1969), p. 14.
4. Henry Treece, *The Crusades* (New York, Random, 1962), p. 11.
5. E. O. James, *The Cult of the Mother Goddess* (New York, Praeger, 1959), p. 181.
6. Jane Ellen Harrison, *Epilegomena to the Study of Greek Religion and Themis* (New York, University Books, 1962), p. 541, 539.
   . Robert Graves, *The White Goddess* (New York, Farrar, 1948), p. 44.
8. *Ibid.*
9. James, *op. cit.*, p. 258.

10. Montesquieu, *The Spirit of the Laws*, trans. by Thomas Nugent, Vol. II (New York, Hafner, 1949), p. 45.

11. André Gide, *Theseus*, trans. by John Russell (New York, Vintage Books, 1958), p. 79.

12. Graves, *On Poetry, op. cit.*, p. 431.

13. G. G. Coulton, ed., *Life in the Middle Ages*, Vol. I (New York, Macmillan, 1910), p. 232 n.

14. Rousseau, *op. cit.*, p. 117.

15. As quoted in Harold Mattingly, *Christianity in the Roman Empire* (New York, Norton, 1967), p. 72.

16. As quoted in Mattingly, *Ibid.*, p. 74.

17. Robert Briffault, *The Mothers* (New York, Grosset, 1963), p. 429.

18. Henry Adams, *The Education of Henry Adams* (New York, Random, 1931), pp. 387–88.

19. Philippa of Hainaut, the much-beloved consort of King Edward III of England, with her infant son Edward, the Black Prince, at her breast, is said to have been the model for most of the sculptures and paintings of the Madonna and Child after the twelfth century throughout Europe.

20. Joseph Gaer, *The Lore of the New Testament* (Boston, Little, Brown, 1952), pp. 260–61.

21. Lionel Smithett Lewis, *Glastonbury the Mother of Saints*, A.D. *37–1539*, 2d ed. (London, Mowbray, 1927), p. 74. In support of this tradition, Cardinal Baronius found an ancient manuscript in the Vatican Library which tells of Joseph, Lazarus, Mary, Martha, and others unnamed sailing in an open boat to Marseilles and landing there in 35 A.D.—*Ibid.*, p. 2.

22. William of Malmesbury quotes Freculphus, bishop of Lisieux in the ninth century, as having recorded that Philip the Apostle came to France and then went on to Britain to preach, later sending twelve persons under Joseph of Arimathea, "his dearest friend," to convert Britain.—Smithett Lewis, *op. cit.*, p. 3.

23. Smithett Lewis, *op. cit.*, p. 74.

24. *Ibid.*, p. 75.

25. John of Glastonbury, quoted in *Ibid.*, p. 74 n. In Mallory it is Sir Galahad, not Arthur, who is descended from Joseph.

26. Geoffrey Ashe, *The Quest for Arthur's Britain* (New York, Praeger, 1969), p. 56. Also *cf.* "Arthur put on a leather jerkin worthy of so great a king. On his head he placed a golden helmet with a crest carved in the shape of a dragon; and across his shoulders a circular shield called Pridwen, on which there was painted a likeness of Blessed Mary, Mother of God, which forced him to be thinking perpetually of her."— Geoffrey of Monmouth, *History of the Kings of Britain* (London, Penguin, 1965), p. 217.

CHAPTER 16—Women in the Middle Ages

1. Harold Mattingly, *Christianity in the Roman Empire* (New York, Norton, 1967), p. 71, 72.

2. G. G. Coulton, ed., *Life in the Middle Ages*, Vol. III (New York, Macmillan, 1910), p. 119.

3. Eugene Mason, "Introduction," in Marie de France, *The Lays of Marie de France* (London, Dent, 1911), pp. x, xv.

4. Bernardino of Siena, *Sermons*, in Coulton, ed., *op. cit.*, Vol. I, p. 224.

5. Jules Michelet, *Satanism and Witchcraft* (New York, Citadel, 1939), p. 53 n.

6. *Ibid.*, p. 35.

7. *Ibid.*, pp. 52–53.

8. Geoffrey de la Tour de Landry, *Book of the Knight of the Tower* (1371), in Coulton, ed., *op. cit.*, Vol. III, pp. 114–15.

9. *Custumal* of Lanfranc's and Anselm's Abbey of Bec, in Coulton, ed., *op. cit.*, Vol. IV, p. 100.
10. Berthold of Regensburg (Ratisbon), *Sermons* (1250), in Coulton, ed., *op. cit.*, Vol. III, p. 65.
11. Thomas More, *Dialogues*, in Coulton, ed., *op. cit.*, Vol. III, pp. 166–67.
12. Giovanni Boccaccio, *The Decameron*, trans. by John Payne, Vol. III (London, privately printed, 1886), p. 61.
13. Petrus Cantor, *Verbum Abbreviatum*, in Coulton, ed., *op. cit.*, Vol. I, p. 32 n.
14. Raymond de Becker, *The Other Face of Love* (New York, Grove, 1969), p. 104.
15. *Ibid.*, p. 106.
16. Montesquieu, *The Spirit of the Laws*, trans. by Thomas Nugent, Vol. II (New York, Hafner, 1949), p. 60.
17. Robert Burton, *The Anatomy of Melancholy* (New York, Tudor, n.d.), p. 717.
18. James Cleugh, *Love Locked Out* (New York, Crown, 1963), p. 91.
19. *Ibid.*, pp. 91–92.
20. Bernardino of Siena, *Sermons* (1427), in Coulton, ed., *op. cit.*, Vol. I, p. 229.
21. Cleugh, *op. cit.*, p. 288.
22. Flavius Josephus, *The Antiquities of the Jews*, Vol. II (Philadelphia, Woodward, 1826), p. 79.
23. The Christian fathers, says Robert Graves, were "grateful even to [the Feminist] Hesiod for describing Pandora as 'a beautiful evil.' "—Robert Graves, *Five Pens in Hand* (Freeport, New York, Books for Libraries, 1970), p. 94.
24. Ralph of Coggeshall, *Chronicle of Ralph, Abbot of Coggeshall*, in Coulton, ed., *op. cit.*, Vol. I, pp. 29–32.
25. Cleugh, *op. cit.*, p. 97.
26. Francis Maziere, *Mysteries of Easter Island* (New York, Norton, 1967), p. 30.
27. Pierre de Bourdeille, Abbé de Brantôme, *The lives of Gallant Ladies* (London, Elek Books, 1961), pp. 9, 13.
28. *Ibid.*, p. 24.
29. Giovanni Boccaccio, as retold by Brantôme, *op. cit.*, p. 429.
30. Karen Horney, *Feminine Psychology* (New York, Norton, 1967), p. 113.
31. Michelet, *op. cit.*, p. x.
32. Margaret Sanger, *Woman and the New Race* (New York, Brentano's, 1920), p. 179.
33. Roger Sherman Loomis, "Introduction," in Thomas of Britain, *Tristram and Isolt* (New York, Dutton, 1967), p. xvi.
34. Johann Nider, *Formicarius* (1438), in Coulton, ed., *op. cit.*, Vol. I, pp. 213–15.
35. Michelet, *op. cit.*, p. ix.

CHAPTER 17—Some Medieval Women

1. Johann Nider, *Formicarius* (1438), in G. G. Coulton, ed., *Life in the Middle Ages*, Vol. I (New York, Macmillan, 1910), pp. 212–13.
2. R. E. L. Masters and Eduard Lea, *Perverse Crimes in History* (New York, Julian Press, 1963), p. 30.
3. "Joan, Pope," in Charles G. Herberman, ed., *Catholic Encyclopedia*, Vol. VIII (New York, Appleton, 1910), p. 407.
4. *Ibid.*
5. Raymond de Becker, *The Other Face of Love* (New York, Grove, 1969), p. 95.
6. As quoted in Sabine Baring-Gould, *Curious Myths of the Middle Ages* (New Hyde Park, New York, University Books, 1967), pp. 177–78.
7. *Ibid.*, p. 187.
8. See Chapter 19, "The Age of Reason."
9. Eric John Dingwall, *The American Woman* (New York, New America Library, 1958), p. 9.

10. Arnold J. Toynbee, *A Study of History*, abridgement by D. C. Somervell, Vol. II (London, Oxford University Press, 1946), pp. 142–43.
11. *Ibid.*
12. Emily James Putnam, *The Lady* (Chicago, University of Chicago Press, 1970), p. 46.
13. James Boswell, *Journal of a Tour to the Hebrides* (New York, Literary Guild, 1936), p. 188.
14. Robert Graves, *Five Pens in Hand* (Freeport, New York, Books for Libraries, 1970), p. 140.
15. Agnes Strickland, *Lives of the Queens of England*, Vol. II (Philadelphia, Lea & Blanchard, 1850), p. 196.
16. As quoted in Strickland, *op. cit.*, Vol. II, p. 197.
17. *Ibid.*, p. 178.
18. *Ibid.*, pp. 178–79.
19. John Froissart's *Chronicles*, as quoted in Strickland, *op. cit.*, Vol. II, p. 188. Strickland had access to an early, unexpurgated edition of Froissart, for the copy available to this writer, "revised" by Thomas Johnes and published by Collier in 1901, has obviously been masculized in accordance with nineteenth-century rules of scholarship to eliminate as much feminine history as possible. The eulogistic references to Philippa quoted by Strickland, save the one in footnote 26 below, have been expurgated in this edition.
20. Strickland, *op. cit.*, Vol. II, p. 193.
21. *Ibid.*, p. 201.
22. Froissart, as quoted in Strickland, *op. cit.*, Vol. II, p. 201.
23. *Ibid.*, p. 201 n.
24. Strickland, *op. cit.*, Vol. II, p. 177.
25. *Ibid.*
26. John Froissart, *Chronicles of England, France, Spain, and Adjoining Countries*, trans. and ed. by Thomas Johnes, rev. ed., Vol. I (New York, Collier, 1901), p. 126.
27. *Foedera, Conventiones, et Cujuscunque Generis Acta Publica*, as quoted in Strickland, op. cit., Vol. II, p. 204.
28. Strickland, *op. cit.*, Vol. II, p. 205.
29. Raphael Holinshed, as quoted in Strickland, *op. cit.*, Vol. I, p. xv.
30. Geoffrey of Monmouth, *History of the Kings of Britain* (London, Penguin, 1965), p. 101.
31. As quoted in Will and Mary Durant, *The History of Civilization*, Vol. IV, *The Age of Faith* (New York, Simon and Schuster, 1950), p. 488.
32. *Anglo-Saxon Chronicle*, trans. and ed. by Dorothy Whitelock (New Brunswick, New Jersey, Rutgers University Press, 1961), p. 67.
33. *Ibid.*
34. William of Malmesbury, *Chronicle of the Kings of England*, Vol. II (Oxford, Clarendon Press, 1884), p. 5.
35. *Anglo-Saxon Chronicle*, *op. cit.*, p. 176.
36. *Saxon Chronicle*, as quoted in Strickland, *op. cit.*, Vol. I, p. 95.
37. *Ibid.*
38. Strickland, *op. cit.*, Vol. I, p. 97.
39. *Ibid.*
40. *Ibid.*, p. 96.
41. *Ibid.*, p. 97.

CHAPTER 18—Women in the Reformation

1. John Augustus Zahm, *Women in Science* (New York, Appleton, 1913), p. 63.
2. Myra Reynolds, *The Learned Lady in England, 1650–1760* (Gloucester, Massachusetts, Peter Smith, 1964), p. 4.

3. George Ballard, *Memoirs of Several Ladies of Great Britain*, as quoted in Reynolds, *op. cit.*, p. 15.

4. Cresacre More, *The Life of Sir Thomas More* (1726), as quoted in Reynolds, *op. cit.*, p. 10.

5. Ballard, as quoted in Reynolds, *op. cit.*, p. 10.

6. Thomas Fuller, *The Worthies of England* (London, Allen & Unwin, 1952), p. 358.

7. *Ibid.*

8. Foster Watson, *Vives and the Renascence Education of Women* (London, Longmans Green, 1912), p. 43.

9. Desiderius Erasmus, *Select Colloquies*, Merrick Whitcomb, ed. (Philadelphia, University of Pennsylvania Press, 1902), p. 179.

10. Reynolds, *op. cit.*, p. 19.

11. John Aubrey, *Brief Lives*, Oliver Lawson Dick, ed. (London, Secker & Warburg, 1950), pp. 138-39.

12. Arthur Quiller-Couch, ed., *The Oxford Book of English Verse* (Oxford, Clarendon Press, 1926), p. 264.

13. William Wotton, *Reflections on Ancient and Modern Learning*, as quoted in Reynolds, *op. cit.*, p. 22.

14. "Calvinism," in Charles G. Herberman, ed., *Catholic Encyclopedia*, Vol. III (New York, Appleton, 1912), p. 203.

15. This practice seems to be endemic in men who are given authority over young women in groups. During World War II the military doctors of the U.S. Army and Navy were so given to it that it became a rueful joke among the WAC's and the WAVE's that if they reported to sick bay with a cold in the head they were more than likely to be "raped," the slang expression for the frequent vaginal probe. The proof of this allegation lies in the fact that toward the end of the war, orders came down from "BuMed" in Washington to all Navy doctors that the pelvic examination would thereafter be made only when medically indicated.

16. Recent studies by Curt Stern and Arthur Jensen show that the female X chromosome carries more gene loci than does the male Y chromosome; and it is the mother who contributes the X chromosomes to the offspring—two to a daughter and one to a son. It is this extra X chromosome in girls, they find, that accounts for the superior physiological makeup in women as well as for their greater intelligence. Females, from kindergarten through college, "are on the average two to five IQ points smarter than men." See syndicated article by Marcia Hayes of Women's News Service in St. Petersburg (Florida) *Times* and other newspapers for November 15, 1970.

17. Franz Hartman, *The Life and Teachings of Philippus Theophrastus Bombast of Hohenheim (Paracelsus) 1493-1541* (London, Kegan Paul, Trench & Trubner, 1841), p. 73.

18. *Ibid.*, pp. 257-58.

19. Reynolds, *op. cit.*, p. 46.

20. John Milton, *Paradise Lost*, in Frank Patterson, ed., *Poems of John Milton* (New York, Macmillan, 1930), p. 301.

21. Reynolds, *op. cit.*, p. 23-5.

22. Doris Mary Stenton, *The English Woman in History*, as quoted in Maurice Ashley, *The Stuarts in Love* (New York, Macmillan, 1964), p. 29.

23. Elizabeth Jocelyn, as quoted in Reynolds, *op. cit.*, p. 30.

24. As quoted in Ashley, *op. cit.*, p. 69.

25. As quoted in Reynolds, *op. cit.*, p. 317.

26. As quoted in Raymond de Becker, *The Other Face of Love* (New York, Grove, 1969).

CHAPTER 19—The Age of Reason—The Eighteenth Century

1. Mary Astell, as quoted in Myra Reynolds, *The Learned Lady in England, 1650–1760* (Gloucester, Massachusetts, Peter Smith, 1964), p. 300.
2. *Ibid.*
3. Maurice Ashley, *The Stuarts in Love* (New York, Macmillan, 1964), pp. 7–8.
4. James Boswell, *Journal of a Tour to the Hebrides* (New York, Literary Guild, 1936), p. 188.
5. Myra Reynolds, *The Learned Lady in England, 1650–1760* (Gloucester, Massachusetts, Peter Smith, 1964), p. 351.
6. George Ballard, as quoted in Reynolds, *op. cit.*, p. 362.
7. Mary Wollstonecraft, *A Vindication of the Rights of Women* (New York, Norton, 1967), p. 91.
8. *Ibid.*, p. 84.
9. As quoted in Wollstonecraft, *op. cit.*, p. 131.
10. Wollstonecraft, *op. cit.*, pp. 95, 86.
11. As quoted in *Ibid.*, p. 134.
12. *Ibid.*, p. 114.
13. As quoted in *Ibid.*, p. 135.
14. *Ibid.*, p. 135.
15. As quoted in *Ibid.*, p. 132.
16. *Ibid.*, p. 133.
17. Wollstonecraft, *op. cit.*, p. 96.
18. John Stuart Mill, *On the Subjection of Women* (London, Oxford University Press, 1912), pp. 518, 522.
19. Wollstonecraft, *op. cit.*, p. 86.
20. *Ibid.*, p. 287.
21. English novelist and close friend of Thomas Paine, author of *The Rights of Man*. Mary Wollstonecraft and William Godwin became the parents of Mary Wollstonecraft Shelley, author of *Frankenstein* and wife of the poet Percy Bysshe Shelley.
22. Wollstonecraft, *op. cit.*, p. 147.
23. Edwin Valentine Mitchell, ed., *The Newgate Calendar* (Garden City, New York, Garden City Publishing Company, 1926), pp. 84–87.
24. *Ibid.*, pp. 115–30, 63–65, 89–94.
25. M. Dorothy George, *London Life in the Eighteenth Century* (London, Kegan Paul, Trench, and Trubner, 1925), p. 231.
26. *Ibid.*, p. 232.
27. *Ibid.*

CHAPTER 20—Not Quite People—The Nineteenth Century

1. Alice Clarke, *The Working Life of Women in the Seventeenth Century*, as quoted in Anthony Ludovici, *Woman, A Vindication* (New York, Knopf, 1923), p. 259.
2. M. Dorothy George, *London Life in the Eighteenth Century* (London, Kegan Paul, Trench, and Trubner, 1925), pp. 427–29.
3. Grant Allen, as quoted in Helen Beale Woodward, *The Bold Women* (New York, Farrar, 1953), p. 339.
4. Mrs. John Farrar, *The Young Lady's Friend*, 2d ed. (New York, Samuel and William Wood, 1847), p. 287.
5. *Ibid.*, pp. 219, 212.
6. Helen Beale Woodward, *The Bold Women* (New York, Farrar, 1953), pp. 15–16.
7. Farrar, *op. cit.*, p. 215.
8. Montesquieu, *The Spirit of the Laws*, trans. by Thomas Nugent, Vol. II (New York, Hafner, 1949), p. 2.

9. T. Bell, *Kalogynomia* (London, Stockdale, 1821), pp. 245-46, quoting Montesquieu, *op. cit.*, pp. 2-3.

10. *Ibid.*, pp. 248, 284.

11. *Ibid.*, pp. 298-99.

12. Woodward, *op. cit.*, pp. 15, 22. "She was no longer young and the appearance of a woman without personal attractions in the public eye has always seemed to provoke the antifeminists to a special pitch in obscenity."—*Ibid.*, p. 16.

13. R. J. Campbell, *Christianity and the Social Order* (New York, Macmillan, 1907), p. 267.

14. *Ibid.*, p. 262.

15. Jane Austen, *Emma*, in *The Complete Novels of Jane Austen* (New York, Modern Library, n.d.), p. 814.

16. Anthony Ludovici, *Woman, a Vindication* (New York, Knopf, 1923), p. 244.

17. Farrar, *op. cit.*, p. 313.

18. As quoted in F. W. Marshall, *Common Legal Principles*, Vol. 1 (New York, Funk & Wagnalls, 1929), p. 147.

19. John Ashton, as quoted in Nina Epton, *Love and the English* (New York, Collier Books, 1963), p. 338.

20. Nina Epton, *Love and the English* (New York, Collier Books, 1963), p. 339.

21. *Ibid.* Governor Yeo was a Portsmouth, England, neighbor of Susan Sibbald, who refers with horror to the incident in her memoirs, referred to in Epton.

22. John Stuart Mill, *On the Subjection of Women* (London, Oxford University Press, 1912), pp. 521, 467, 463.

23. Ludovici, *op. cit.*, p. 248.

24. *Ibid.*, p. 253.

25. *Ibid.*, pp. 316-19.

26. Campbell, *op. cit.*, p. 268.

27. August Forel, *The Sexual Question*, 2d ed. rev., trans. by C. F. Marshall (Brooklyn, Physicians' and Surgeons' Book Co., 1922), p. 160.

CHAPTER 21—The Prejudice Lingers On

1. Margaret Mead and Frances B. Kaplan, eds., *American Women: the Report of the President's Commission on the Status of Women* (New York, Scribner's, 1965), p. 53.

2. Karen Horney, *Feminine Psychology* (New York, Norton, 1967), p. 231.

3. Robert P. Odenwald, *The Disappearing Sexes* (New York, Random, 1965), p. 75.

4. Bertrand Russell, *Marriage and Morals* (London, Allen & Unwin, 1929), p. 170.

5. Havelock Ellis, *Studies in the Psychology of Sex* (Philadelphia, F. A. Davis, 1901), p. 66 ff.

6. Edward Westermarck, *The Future of Marriage in Western Civilization* (New York, Macmillan, 1936), p. 94.

7. H. L. Mencken, *In Defense of Women* (New York, Knopf, 1922), pp. 6-7.

8. Odenwald, *op. cit.*, p. 41.

9. Westermarck, *op. cit.*, p. 93.

10. Aubrey Beardsley, *Under the Hill* (London, The Bodley Head, 1903), p. 26.

11. Theodor Reik, *The Need To Be Loved* (New York, Farrar, 1963), p. 150.

12. Simone de Beauvoir, *The Second Sex*, trans. by H. M. Parshley (New York, Bantam, 1961), pp. 353, 361.

13. Ashley Montagu, "The Natural Superiority of Women," in *The Saturday Review Treasury* (New York, Simon & Schuster, 1957), p. 474.

14. Ashley Montagu, *Human Heredity*, 2d ed. rev. (New York, World, 1959), pp. 182, 186.

15. Leonard Woolf, *Beginning Again* (New York, Harcourt, 1964), p. 107 ff.

16. Stendhal, *On Love* (New York, Brentano's, n.d.), p. 98.
17. Montagu, "The Natural Superiority of Women," *op. cit.*, p. 473. See also R. D. Gillespie, "The Physiological Effects of War on Citizen and Soldier," in Ashley Montagu, *The Natural Superiority of Women* (New York, Macmillan, 1952), pp. 92–93. The interpolation in brackets is taken from a television interview with Montagu broadcast from Tampa, Florida, on July 23, 1970.
18. Robert Eisler, *Man into Wolf* (London, Spring Books, 1949?), p. 177.
19. Herodotus, *The Histories*, trans. by George Rawlinson (New York, Tudor, 1944), p. 218.
20. J. J. Bachofen, *Myth, Religion, and Mother Right*, trans. by Ralph Manheim (Princeton, Princeton University Press, 1967), p. 74.
21. Georgia Lolli, *Social Drinking* (New York, World, 1960), p. 252.
22. Odenwald, *op. cit.*, p. 23.
23. John Cowper Powys, *The Art of Happiness* (New York, Simon & Schuster, 1935), p. 197.
24. Stendhal, *op. cit.*, p. 98.
25. Mark Sullivan, ed., *Our Times: the United States, 1900–1925*, Vol. VI (New York, Scribner's, 1935), pp. 511–13.
26. Helen Beale Woodward, *The Bold Women* (New York, Farrar, 1953), p. 292.
27. Joseph L. Schott, *Above and Beyond: the Story of the Congressional Medal of Honor* (New York, Putnam's, 1963), p. 94.
28. National Organization for Women, *Statement of Purpose* (Washington, N.O.W., 1966), p. 5.
29. *Ibid.*
30. Mead and Kaplan, eds., *op. cit.*, p. 215.
31. *Ibid.*
32. Mary Wollstonecraft, *A Vindication of the Rights of Women* (New York, Norton, 1967), p. 147.
33. Horney, *op. cit.*, p. 231.
34. St. Petersburg (Florida), *Times*, April 7, 1968.
35. Theodore Sorenson, "Special Report on the Woman Voter," *Redbook* 130:4, 61 (June 22, 1968).
36. Lolli, *op. cit.*, p. 251.
37. Montagu, "The Natural Superiority of Women," *op. cit.*, p. 476.

CHAPTER 22—Woman in the Aquarian Age

1. Karen Horney, *Feminine Psychology* (New York, Norton, 1967), p. 69.
2. See Amram Scheinfeld, *Women and Men* (New York, Harcourt, 1944); Theodosius Dobzhansky, *Heredity and the Nature of Man* (New York, World, 1964); Remy de Goncourt, *The Natural Philosophy of Love* (New York, Boni and Liveright, 1922); Ashley Montagu, *The Natural Superiority of Women* (New York, Macmillan, 1952); Havelock Ellis, *Man and Woman* (London, Heinemann, 1934); Frank Leslie Ward, *Pure Sociology* (New York, Macmillan, 1911); Louis Dublin, *The Facts of Life from Birth to Death* (New York, Macmillan, 1951); Susan Michelmore, *Sexual Reproduction* (New York, Natural History Press, 1964); Edward Carpenter, *Love's Coming of Age* (Manchester, England, Labour Press, 1896), among other books and articles.
3. Susan Michelmore, *Sexual Reproduction* (New York, Natural History Press, 1964), p. 145.
4. U.S. Bureau of the Census, *Current Population Reports: Population Characteristics*, Series P–20, no. 170. (February 23, 1968).
5. "The *very greatest* poet who ever lived," says Algernon Swinburne.—Mark Van Doren, ed., *An Anthology of World Poetry* (New York, Boni, 1928), p. 257.
6. Robert Graves, *On Poetry* (New York, Doubleday, 1969), p. 177.

7. Plato, *Republic,* in *The Works of Plato,* trans. by Benjamin Jowett (New York, Tudor, n.d.), p. 182.
8. National Manpower Council, *Womanpower* (New York, Columbia University Press, 1957), p. 208.
9. National Broadcasting Company, *Today Show* (May 30, 1968).
10. Richard L. Evans, ed., *Dialogue with Erik Erikson* (New York, Harper, 1967), p. 44.
11. Edward Carpenter, *Love's Coming of Age* (Manchester, England, Labour Press, 1896), pp. 83–84.
12. John Stuart Mill, *On the Subjection of Women* (London, Oxford University Press, 1912), p. 452.
13. Pitirim Sorokin, *The Crisis of Our Age* (New York, Dutton, 1941), p. 312.
14. *Ibid.,* p. 315.
15. Plato, *Critias,* in *The Works of Plato,* trans. by Benjamin Jowett (New York, Tudor, n.d.), pp. 381–82.
16. Sybille von Cles-Redin, *The Realm of the Great Goddess* (Englewood Cliffs, New Jersey, Prentice-Hall, 1962), p. 53.
17. J. J. Bachofen, *Myth, Religion and Mother Right,* trans. by Ralph Manheim (Princeton, Princeton University Press, 1967), pp. 85–86.

Index